Nancy James
583-5272

Nancy James
8515 Costa Verde Blvd Unit 1803
San Diego, CA 92122-1148

858-558-7331

The Popular Guide to Classical Music

OTHER BOOKS BY THE AUTHOR

The Wonderful World of San Diego, First and Second Editions
Where Have You Been All Your Life?
How to Hang On to Your Husband

The Popular Guide to

CLASSICAL MUSIC

by Dr. Anne Gray

A Birch Lane Press Book
Published by Carol Publishing Group

A Birch Lane Press Book
Published by Carol Publishing Group
Birch Lane Press is a registered trademark of Carol Communications, Inc.
Editorial Offices: 600 Madison Avenue, New York, N.Y. 10022
Sales and Distribution Offices: 120 Enterprise Avenue, Secaucus, N.J. 07094
In Canada: Canadian Manda Group, P.O. Box 920, Station U, Toronto, Ontario M8Z 5P9
Queries regarding rights and permissions should be addressed to Carol Publishing Group,
600 Madison Avenue, New York, N.Y. 10022

Carol Publishing Group books are available at special discounts for bulk purchases, for sales
promotion, fund-raising, or educational purposes. Special editions can be created to
specifications. For details, contact: Special Sales Department, Carol Publishing Group,
120 Enterprise Avenue, Secaucus, N.J. 07094

Manufactured in the United States of America
10 9 8 7 6 5 4 3 2 1

Library of Congress Cataloging-in-Publication Data

Gray, Anne.
    The popular guide to classical music / by Anne Gray.
        p.   cm.
    "A Birch Lane Press book."
    Includes bibliographical references.
    ISBN 1-55972-165-0 (cloth)
    1. Music appreciation.   I. Title.
    MT6.G74P6   1993   92-21111
    781.6'8—dc20   CIP
                                                             MN

Contents

MODERNISTS: Taylor, Grofé, Piston, Grant Still, Hanson,
Sessions, Thomson, Cowell, Harris, Antheil, Blitzstein,
Creston, Carter, Barber, Schuman, Hovhaness, Menotti,
Cage, Gould, Dello Joio, Diamond, Foss, Rorem, Schuller,
Glass, Reich, Corigliano, Harbison, Rosner, Adams, Babbitt,
Rochberg, Kraft, Powell, Rosenman, Brown, Feldman,
Crumb, Subotnick, Reynolds, Riley, Balcom
The Masters: Gershwin, Copland, Bernstein
The Land of the Silver Screen

A MAN FOR ALL COUNTRIES: Schweitzer

FIN DE SIÈCLE: Into the Twentieth Century
GERMANY: Bruckner, Wolf, Mahler, Richard Strauss, Reger,
Hindemith
ITALY: Respighi
FRANCE: Chausson, D'Indy, Dukas, Roussel, Honegger, Ibert,
Poulenc, Milhaud
RUSSIA: Rachmaninoff, Stravinsky, Prokofiev, Khatchaturian,
Kabalevsky, Shostakovich
The Second Viennese School: Schoenberg, Webern, Berg
Avant-Garde: Messiaen, Stockhausen

EARLY AND RENAISSANCE: Hildegard of Bingen, Anne Boleyn,
Elizabeth I, Caccini
BAROQUE: Strozzi, Leonarda, Bembo, Jacquet de la Guerre
CLASSICAL: Princess Anna Amalia, Duchess Anna Amalia,
Sirmen, Martinez, von Paradis, Schröter, Candeille
WOMEN AND THE ROMANTIC SPIRIT: Reichardt, Szymanowska,
Farrenc, Clara Schumann, Fanny Mendelssohn, Viardot-
Garcia
TALENT AND TRIUMPH: BLACK WOMEN COMPOSERS: Price,
Moore, Pittman, Perry, McLin, Rudd Moore, Leon
THE SECOND NEW ENGLAND SCHOOL: Rogers, Hopekirk,
Ruthven Lang, Beach
INTO THE TWENTIETH CENTURY: Daniels, Howe, Bauer,

Contents

Who Reads Acknowledgments?

Not me, if the author mentions every great aunt's cousin twice removed who might have given a pat on the back. But having (unbelievably) reached the end of this book after what seems like a lifetime of reading, research, writing, revising, re-writing, and dueling with daunting deadlines, I realize that even I couldn't have done the whole thing without a little help. So here goes, but let's try to keep the format simple:

1. Birch Lane President Hillel Black who had the superior erudition to accept the manuscript, his assistant Denise O'Sullivan who had to read it in one go—eyes crossing with all those dates(!).

2. My husband who designates himself as "computer surly", but spent a few hours at the objectionable machine to give my aching eyeballs a break from the 12-18 hour daily sieges.

3. No. 1 Son, Charles who put most of the 280 word-plus definitions of the Glossary into *his* computer.

4. The founts of knowledge at KFSD-FM, our classical music station, Barry Zacker, Will Erickson, Frank Warlick and especially Kingsley McLaren, the program director.

5. Gene Fischer, Music Specialist, and Christina Clifford of the San Diego Public Library who spent countless hours peering into murky microfiche screens for me.

6. Jeanne Singer who introduced me to 10 centuries of fellow Women Composers. Thus I "met" via telephone Joan Tower, Ellen Zwilich, Ruth Schönthal, Vivian Fine, Marga Richter, Judith Zaimont, Katherine Hoover, Barbara Kolb, Thea Musgrave, Ursula Mamlok, Miriam Gideon and Louise Talma. Helpful composer Libby Larsen acquainted me with Leonard Slatkin, Sir Neville Marriner and Iona Brown. Chicago Symphony composer in residence Shulamit Ran also came onto my phoneline, as did Pozzi Escot in Boston and Sylvia Glickman of Hildegard Publishing.

7. Contacting the Women's Philharmonic in San Francisco unleashed new floodgates: with intros to musicologist Judith Rosen and conductor-designate Sara Jobin who flew here and helped organize the ENTIRE women's section of the book!

8. Sara's phonelist opened more worlds: Friendly JoAnn Falletta, conductor

of the Long Beach Symphony and Women's Philharmonic, who gave me access to just about everyone else in her field, leading to warmly informative conversations with Kate Tamarkin in Dallas, Barbara Yahr in Pittsburgh, Madeline Schatz in Fairbanks, Alaska, Marin Alsop in Eugene, Oregon, Catherine Comet in Grand Rapids, Michigan, Eve Queler in New York, Odaline de la Martinez in London, Victoria Bond in Roanoke, Virginia, (who introduced me to 18 year old composer Dalit Hadass Warshaw), and Rachel Worby at the Governor's mansion in Charleston, West Virginia, who besides being First Lady of the state, is also conductor of the Wheeling Symphony Orchestra.

9. Not to be missed are the nicest personnel at Theodore Presser Music Company in Bryn Mawr, PA., especially vice-president Tom Broido who responded immediately to varied long-distance SOS calls.

10. Honorable mention must be made of Lance Bowling, Cambria Records, Alexandra Photography of La Jolla, and all those wonderful people from all those AGENCIES and ORCHESTRAS who sent me PHOTOS!: Jill Moccia (IMG), Amy Guertin (CAMI), Shirley Kirschbaum & Associates, Wendy Magro (Colbert), M.L. Falcone, Kim Pancich (Gurtman & Murtha), Christine Roberts (Carson), Frank Vigeant (Shaw Concerts), Lynn Ozer (C.F. Peters), and Audrey Michaels.

Inestimable thanks are owed conductor David Amos for borrowing his time and his Grove Encyclopedias; and to Rolf Hölzer, principal cello of the Halle (Germany) Philharmonic for procuring pictures of the great composers—male and female.

11. Plaudits to my ageless agent, Bertha Klausner, who at ninety-three is still all efficiency and expertise.

Finally, I come to my No. 2 son, Adrian, age nineteen, who besides being a fine violinist, is concertmaster of the University of San Diego Orchestra, a member of the San Diego Youth Symphony, spends 10 hours a week in rehearsal, gets straight A's, and still managed to find time to put my dictation into the computer, organize all the pictures, help me with the Index, and really make it possible for me to FINISH!

Thank you all, and you dear readers. Enjoy the book! Enjoy the music!

Anne Gray, Ph.D.
La Jolla, California
1993

Introduction

Unveiling the Mystique of Classical Music

W hat is the mystique of classical music? What kind of people line up for months in advance to buy tickets to an opera? Who fills concert halls all over the world? "Bluebloods?" "Longhairs?" "Stuffed shirts?"

It is time to dispel the myth that this kind of music is only for "highbrows." Concertgoers have no age limit, no college degree prerequisite, no income level requirement.

What makes some folks choose to go without some of life's necessities in order to afford the luxury of season tickets to their local symphony orchestra?

What inspires the very wealthy to donate millions of dollars to support the arts?

The answer is all-encompassing—it lies in the love for these unique sounds, in the feeling of personal excitement of hearing the exquisite talent of a particular performer, in being part of an audience sharing a sublime experience; all of which "find their way into the secret places of the soul." (Plato *c*428-347 B.C.)

The love of it does not make every concertgoer an authority on classical music. There are notes in the program to provide information about the composer and the selections to be played. Usually, not all the music on the program is familiar to everyone, which gives us exposure to something new.

Just how do these concertos and symphonies become so popular? What makes audiences keep coming back for more of the same? What is the magic of Beethoven's Fifth Symphony that there are at least twenty different recordings in the current catalogue? Its popularity is so great that Beethoven's Fifth is being played somewhere in the world even as you read these words.

The aim of this book is to demystify classical music, to prove that most of us know a lot more about it than we realize. That many well-known melodies have been borrowed from, or originated in, the classics. That everyone can find something to enjoy in the wealth of compositions which come under the heading Classical Music.

A little knowledge can be a wonderful thing. It becomes obvious that the evolving styles of music reflect the enlightenment of humanity through the ages. Interesting glimpses into the lifestyles and characters of the composers give insight to the geniuses who helped shape our culture. Understanding terms like *concerto, symphony, opera,* etc., leads to an appreciation of how these masterpieces were created and have endured. Most important, listening to recordings, attending concerts, and familiarizing yourself with the music becomes a continually enriching personal experience.

That there is very little unfamiliar classical music can be traced to several sources. Before the advent of television, radio shows used many classical excerpts. The most famous radio serial immortalized Rossini's *William Tell* Overture as the theme for "The Lone Ranger." Today, TV commercials constantly use classical music to sell anything from detergent to diapers, wine to wheels. Peer at the title credits of recent hit movies and you'll find Mozart, Chopin, and Puccini plus a parade of other composers from the last four centuries. The plot of *Moonstruck* revolved around the lovely melodies from Puccini's opera *La Bohème*. *Pretty Woman* featured colorful scenes from Verdi's *La Traviata* at the San Francisco Opera.

Music written especially for movies has also become classic, such as *The Warsaw Concerto* from the World War II film, *Dangerous Moonlight,* to selections from *Star Wars* and *Superman*. (The action in silent movies was always accompanied by classical music played live by a pianist or organist in the theater.)

Cartoons and classical tunes have been partners since Walt Disney brought out his animated blockbuster, *Fantasia*, in 1940. Re-released in

1977 with re-channeled stereophonic sound, and again in the eighties with further soundtrack updating, this movie has introduced great music to three generations. You might not remember a fancy title like "The Dance of the Hours" from *La Gioconda* by Ponchielli, but you'd hardly forget a herd of hippos wearing ballet shoes cavorting with ostriches in tutus. *The Sorcerer's Apprentice*, a tone poem by French composer Paul Dukas, is also liable to stick in your memory when it stars Mickey Mouse dressed as a mini-wizard fighting off a constantly multiplying horde of broomsticks carrying buckets of sloshing water.

Numerous popular songs evolved from classical compositions. The first movement of Tchaikovsky's Piano Concerto No. 1 became the theme song of Freddy Martin, one of the Big Band conductors. Titled "Tonight We Love," it reached Number One on the radio show "Your Hit Parade" on December 7, 1941, the day Pearl Harbor in Hawaii was bombed and World War II was declared in this country. "I'm Always Chasing Rainbows" is the middle section of Chopin's piano piece *Fantasie Impromptu*, while songs like "Fascination" and "Melody of Love" simply added words to the original melodies.

Many movies have been made portraying the lives of composers such as Chopin, Wagner, Liszt, and Mahler. One of the biggest boosts to classical music was the film *Amadeus* (1984). Even if Hollywood fuzzied some of the facts on the composer's life, at least a whole new segment of the movie-going public was exposed to the magnificent music of Mozart.

Broadway musicals crossed a new frontier into the world of classical music beginning with Jerome Kern's *Show Boat* (1927)—from the novel by Pulitzer Prize-winner Edna Ferber—the first musical production to follow a serious plot and to feature believable human characters. Almost every show written by Rodgers and Hammerstein has been made into a movie, enabling millions worldwide to enjoy the lilting songs in *Oklahoma* (1943), *Carousel* (1945), *South Pacific* (1949), *The King and I* (1941), and everyone's favorite, *The Sound of Music* (1959). In the past two decades, British composer Andrew Lloyd Webber has been creating history with *Jesus Christ, Superstar* (1971), *Evita* (1978), *Cats* (1981) and the fabulous *Phantom of the Opera* (1986).

It may be concluded that somewhere, sometime, most classics have been heard before. As you go from the familiar, and develop a liking for the style of certain composers, you will want to hear more of their music and expand your horizons. The more you listen, the more you will establish your personal taste and choices.

In our age, via television, radio, stereo equipment, video, and recordings, we are able to have the world's finest orchestras and soloists in our homes. But the greatest thrill is still the emotional impact of a live performance. There is a special universality in being a member of an audience, in sharing the feelings evoked by the music—be it serene and soothing, or wild and stirring—and with it all enjoying the growing pleasure of knowing that *you* are a part of this experience.

Armed with the knowledge imparted in this book, you will gain a deeper appreciation and understanding of the wealth of sound surrounding you. Allow your imagination to "see" the scenes and hear the message woven by exciting harmonies and delicate melodies, experience the grandeur of emotion infused into the great symphonies and concertos. Embrace this wonderful way to elevate your spirit into the glorious infinity that is the true satisfaction of classical music!

CHAPTER ONE

The Tuneful Path of Classical Music

Literature touches us intellectually. Paintings arouse our emotions visually. Music elicits a response from that intangible entity: our soul.

Classical music is the refinement of personal expression throughout the ages. It reflects how we express our innermost thoughts, how we relate to the world around us and how we feel about that equally intangible entity called God.

A myriad of aspects must come together to define the open-ended concept of classical music.:

1. The human interest in the life stories of the great composers. Bach, for instance, had two wives and twenty children. Beethoven never married, but was said to have had a secret, unattainable love. Wagner stole another man's wife, as did Liszt. Tchaikovsky was homosexual. For all his fame, Mozart's body ended up in an unmarked grave.

2. The history, shapes and sounds of the instruments—and there are some strange ones—could fill their own book. Early orchestras were

made up of servants and were mostly used to accompany singers. Today's orchestras are big business.

3. The human voice, our first instrument, and how it has been utilized—from strolling minstrels to pampered opera stars—provides the foundation of all music.

4. Opera, ballet, operetta, and musical comedy are the highly visual forms of classical music. Their plots range from fairy tales to stark tragedy and have caused riots—as at the premiere of Stravinsky's ballet, *The Rite of Spring*—induced patriotic fervor (Wagner's operas), and crossed political barriers (The Ballets Russes de Monte Carlo smuggled some of the world's finest dancers out of Communist Russia).

With such a vast canvas to cover, the best way is to explore classical music as it has evolved through the ages.

The Backbone of Our Culture

Music can be said to be the backbone of all culture and civilization. It is entwined in our history, geography, sociology, and economics.

Historically, music can be traced to the first chants of our cave ancestors. Ancient civilizations, especially in the Orient, were controlled by rulers who knew the power of music and strictly regulated what could be played and listened to. Battles have been won and revolutions begun through the inspiration of patriotic anthems. The swirl of bag-pipes was originally used to frighten the enemies of Scottish armies. Wars have forced great musicians to flee their homelands, absorb new cultures and enrich their adopted countries. Rachmaninoff, Stravinsky, and other Russians evaded the Communists. Many German, Austrian, Polish, and Czech composers and artists fled Hitler's reign of terror before World War II.

Inventions over the centuries have improved the quality of the ancient forebears of musical instruments and added new ones. Mozart and Beethoven would have loved to hear their piano works on a modern concert grand.

In the field of musical reproduction we have progressed from crystal sets and Edison's cylinders to compact disks and digital audio tapes. We take for granted the unlimited variety of instant music at the tips of our fingers as we turn on a radio.

Geographically, music has always transcended all international boundaries. As the cradle of Western culture, Europe has produced the most composers and musicians. With expansion and colonization, music and the arts spread to the Americas and other parts of the world. In the twentieth century American composers like Gershwin, Copland, and Bernstein, among others, have entered the ranks of the great masters after achieving fame through their lighter works. Scores of fine instrumental soloists and singers were born in or make their home in the United States. Current demographic changes are bringing more Asian soloists into prominence.

Economics has always been an important factor in music. Early composers were dependent on and in the service of kings, princes, and other members of the nobility for their livelihood. Not until the time of Beethoven in the late eighteenth century was a composer paid some sort of royalty for his work and able to achieve financial independence. Nowadays, economics—and unions—play a vital part in the numbers and length of a city's concert seasons, in the arrangement of the schedules of international artists, the survival of orchestral musicians, and the enormous recording industry.

The Great Eras of Music

Western Music (not Country and Western), as distinguished from Oriental Music, goes back to 300 B.C. To place it in the framework and perspective of history it is classified into six periods or eras:

ANCIENT MUSIC: From the bygone grandeur of the civilizations of China, Sumeria, Egypt, Greece, and Rome on through the Middle Ages to 1450.

THE RENAISSANCE: From 1450 to 1600, when Europe awakened out of the war-torn darkness and church domination of the Middle Ages. This was a period of revival, rebirth, discoveries, and new beginnings in all the arts and sciences as well as music.

THE BAROQUE ERA: From 1600 to 1750, when such giants of composition as Bach, Handel, and Vivaldi emerged to set the foundations of what we actually give the name *classical music.*

THE CLASSICAL PERIOD: 1750 to 1820 was dominated by Haydn, Gluck, and Mozart. This was the era of new musical forms, improved instruments, and more freedom of expression. Beethoven's birth in 1827 opened the gateway to the next epoch.

THE ROMANTIC PERIOD: 1820–1920. Most of the music written during this time continues to be the most played. This was the time of the familiar "greats": Beethoven, Schubert, Berlioz, Mendelssohn, Chopin, Liszt, Schumann, Verdi, Wagner, Bizet, Brahms, Tschaikovsky, Johann Strauss, Saint-Saëns, Rimsky-Korsakov, Dvořák, and many more, including those whose lives and music overlapped into the next period.

THE MODERN ERA: 1920– . After structured beginnings early in the century, contemporary composers tended to be independent and disregarded the rigid rules that governed the music of their predecessors. In fact, some of them make their own rules and end up with weird-sounding pieces based on twelve-tone scales and other experimental approaches to strain the ears and test our attention span. The advent of tape, synthesizer, and computer music has pushed styles and experimentation into unlimited horizons.

As in other eras, talent has arisen from all nationalities. Among the famous names of this period are Berlioz, Puccini, Grieg, Elgar, Sibelius, Richard Strauss, Prokofiev, Bruckner, Mahler, Bartók, Rachmaninoff, Fauré, Debussy, Ravel, Stravinsky, Shostakovich, Gershwin, Copland, Bernstein, Schoenberg, Cage, and an important cadre of women composers.

The next chapters will cover the characteristics of each era and the characters who played such important roles in the development of the music.

CHAPTER TWO

From Cave to Cathedral

There are pictures and writings referring to music which date back to 4000 B.C. People sang and danced long before music or anything else was written down. Rhythm and singing are built into the human psyche. When cavepersons found they had voices, they composed primitive rap songs. They sang to unseen gods to ensure their harvests, to protect them from their enemies and to ask for favorable weather. For greater effectiveness, enterprising tribe members accompanied vocals by beating on hollow logs, blowing into reeds or animal horns, and making other noises pleasing to primeval ears. Instruments were born!

Ancient Civilizations

Emperors of ancient civilizations in China and Sumeria knew the power of music and controlled their subjects by dictating the type of music

9

they were allowed to hear. Museums display instruments over 4,500 years old which have been found in archaeological digs. Egyptians danced to flutes and drums. According to the Bible, Jubal, considered the first musician, was master of the harp. David sang and played the Psalms he wrote. When he became King of the Israelites, he appointed one tribe to be his official musicians. The walls of Jericho were destroyed to the sound of trumpets. Some people thought music had magic powers and used it in ritual ceremonies, similar to the way it is used in religious services today.

It's All Greek

In the ancient world music rose to its greatest heights in Greece. The word *music* comes from the Greek *muses*—nine mythological goddesses of the arts and sciences. This ties in with the primitive belief that music reflects the laws of harmony which govern the universe. Music was regarded as "the language of the gods."

The first scientific experiments with acoustics and the mathematical relationships of tones took place around 500 B.C. in the school of Pythagoras. The Greeks established the idea of scales with whole tones and half steps and invented a system of notation, but few of their compositions still exist.

Roamin' Romans

Around 200 B.C. the Romans began conquering most of what we know as Europe. By A.D. 117 Rome ruled every country around the Mediterranean Sea, plus those on the southern shore of the Black Sea. They even overran Britain way out west across the channel from Gaul (France). Aside from a few marching songs and the invention of an army trumpet they called a tuba, the Romans did not contribute much to the evolution of music, but followed the Greek style of using choruses and instruments in their plays and religious ceremonies. They also imported the bagpipe from India, and it is rumored that *that* is what Nero really played as Rome burned.

Early Christians used Hebrew and Greek music for the sources of their hymns. From these came the chants of the Roman Catholic and Greek Orthodox Church. This is the real foundation of our western European musical style.

No Sound of Music

Around A.D. 400, wild tribes of Huns, Vandals, Goths, and Visigoths invaded Europe and conquered the Romans, smothering all culture for the next hundred years in the period in history known as the Dark Ages. There was no sound of music, only the crumbling of civilization.

The Church Almighty

A few chinks of light began to seep through the shadows around A.D. 500 which marked the beginning of the Middle Ages. As the next ten centuries rolled by, the Church, with monasteries located all around the continent, became Europe's governing body. It administered justice, instigated the "Holy" Wars (Crusades) against the Turkish "infidels," and, on the plus side, established universities where scholars collected any surviving knowledge from the Greeks, Romans, and other ancients to compile in encyclopedias.

The origin of the Church's absolute power lay in man's basic fear of the hereafter. The "nobility" consisted of whoever had fought and won land. Europe was dotted with mini-kingdoms. Their rulers and followers looked to the Church for blessing upon the continuous battles they fought to protect what they had, and prayers for future conquests.

Like the ancient emperors who controlled whole populations, now the Church dictated the destiny of music, art, and letters and employed most of the professional scribes, artists, and musicians. Compositions tended to follow the same strict forms and were mostly sung by choirs. The plots of those ancient Greek dramas were a little too spicy for the clergy, thus a whole culture was all but extinguished. A name to remember for this period is Pope Gregory I, who, in the fifth century, composed and collected music which came to be known as GREGORIAN CHANTS and are still sung today in some Catholic services.

The Renaissance (1450–1600)

> The Renaissance: "The emancipation of the human intellect."
>
> —Brewer's Dictionary of Phrase and Fable

The years 1450 to 1600 marked a period of amazing cultural awakening. The word Renaissance means rebirth. This was the era when art, architecture, literature, and music started blossoming out of the somber confines of the Church. When the genius of Leonardo da Vinci and Michelangelo forever changed the world of art and sculpture.

It was the age of discovery. The voyages of Columbus and Magellan convinced most people that the earth was round. The astronomer Copernicus proved that the earth revolved around the sun, not the other way around as had been believed since the dawn of time.

Architecture came into its prime. Under the guidance of the Italian masters, glorious churches and cathedrals soared to meet the sky.

There was music everywhere: in churches, where the Reformation had split Christianity into Catholic and Protestant; in castles, palaces and grand houses, many of which had their own resident composers and orchestras; and among the "common" folk, for whom minstrels and troubadours roamed the countryside singing ballads and strumming their lutes.

The First Names in Music

Most music was still vocal rather than instrumental. Early composers whose music influenced their successors are Josquin Des Près (c1440–1521), Orlando Lassus (1532–1594), and Palestrina (c1525–1594). The Gabrielis, Andrea (c1510–1586) and Giovanni (1557–1612), had people flocking to churches to hear the magnificent crossfire of sound from two organs, and the heavenly tones of multiple choirs.

The Press Is Mightier Than the Quill

The arrival of the printing press in 1450 revolutionized all the arts. After the inventor, Johann Gutenberg, brought out his beautifully executed

Bible, the press was immediately accepted. The art of papermaking had begun in China and spread to Europe in the thirteenth and fourteenth centuries. By the fifteenth century, paper was plentiful. The rise of a prosperous and literate middle class increased the demand for books. Martin Luther's Reformation and its subsequent religious wars depended on the printing press to supply a steady stream of pamphlets— really the first advertisements. The impact of the printing press on music was tremendous, since more could be reproduced in one month than in a year of laborious hand copying.

Instruments of the Renaissance

The instruments of the Renaissance were related to the same string, woodwind, brass, and percussion families of today, but were far from perfected. The organ had reached a high state of development, as had the clavichord and the harpsichord. Instruments were used mainly to accompany the voice. Love songs, story songs or ballads, drinking songs, and dance songs were popular. They were called *chansons* in France, *Lieder* in Germany and *frottole* in Italy.

Because of the renewed interest in Renaissance music beginning in the 1950s, viols, recorders, crumhorns and sackbutts, and other early instruments are enjoying a new renaissance via groups of Early Music *Ensembles* and *Consorts*.

The First Instrumental Music

Gradually composers began to base their work on dance forms and wrote music solely for instruments. Fast ones—*galliards* and *courantes*— would be paired with slow ones—*pavanes* and *allemandes*. The *sarabande*, which started out as a wild dance frowned on by the authorities, became stately in later years. By the seventeenth century, the musical collation of these dances had led to the development of musical forms called *suites* and *partitas*.

That's Entertainment!

Wealthy Italian families hired composers to put on elaborate productions. The first ballet was produced in 1581. The beginnings of opera appeared in attempts to recreate Greek dramas.

By 1600 Europe was ready for a new era: the Baroque.

CHAPTER THREE

The Baroque Era (1600–1750)

Named after the popular ornate architectural style, this was a time of great scientific discovery. Between 1600 and 1624, Galileo improved the telescope and the thermometer, observed spots on the sun, mountains and valleys on the moon, and discovered the four moons of Jupiter and the phases of Venus. In physics, he formulated the laws of falling bodies and moving projectiles. In history he stands as a symbol of the battle for freedom of inquiry against the authority of the Church, which had censored Copernicus' books and refused to accept his theory that the sun was the center of the universe. Following Galileo's principles, Sir Isaac Newton formulated the Law of Gravity in 1666.

By the end of the era, Ben Franklin experimented with electricity and introduced the lightning rod, the Montgolfier brothers raised the first hot air balloon in France, and James Watt had invented the steam engine.

In music the Baroque marked a period of great development in vocal and instrumental art, attaining more complex harmonies and depth of form and feeling. Kings, princes, dukes, and other nobility were trying to outdo each other in pomp and pageantry. The wealthiest had their own orchestras and a composer in residence. Often treated like servants, these men were expected to churn out compositions on command for any event—birthdays, weddings, royal visits, etc. Musicians usually *were* servants, doubling as gardeners or footmen—much to the despair of composers trying to get music out of these rustics.

Instruments of the Period

Thanks to the great violin makers of Cremona—Amati, Guarneri, and Stradivari—most stringed instruments had reached an unequaled stage of perfection.

Woodwinds and brass had yet to be enhanced by the invention of valves and other methods of easier blowing and fingering.

The clavichord and harpsichord were the main keyboard instruments. The piano was not invented until 1709.

New Musical Forms

Music had progressed a long way from chants and ballads. The main style was *contrapuntal*—that is, having two or more independent melodies that combine to make harmony. The musical forms we know today came into being:

The CANTATA, a short work for solo voices, chorus, and instruments with either a secular or religious theme was very popular. Bach wrote a *Coffee Cantata* (1732) to celebrate the growing fondness of what was then a new beverage in Europe. Mozart wrote a Masonic cantata, from which one aria (solo) became the Austrian national anthem after World War I.

The longer ORATORIO, also for soloists, chorus, and orchestra, had a strictly biblical text; it originated in 1600 in Rome, a year before the first opera was produced in Florence. The spiritual father of the oratorio was PHILIP NERI (1515–1595), who opened his services by combining sacred plays and choruses for the education and enlightenment of youth. This was the crucial time of the Reformation, when Protestantism was challenging the powerful Catholic church. For his efforts Neri was beatified and later canonized, the only musician in history to become a saint.

The most famous oratorios were written by George Frideric Handel (1685–1759), Bach's German contemporary who made his home in England and will forever be remembered for his masterpiece, *Messiah*, which is performed by countless choirs all over the world during the Christmas season.

At the end of the sixteenth century a group of enlightened men of science, literature, and music, including Vincenzo Galilei, father of the astronomer who invented the telescope, met in Florence to discuss the future of the arts. They called themselves *camerata*—literally, a small chamber. From their desire to revive the simplicity of Greek music came the beginnings of *dramma per musica*, drama by means of music, or, in other words, *opera*.

CLAUDIO MONTEVERDI (1567–1643), the first great opera composer, used the orchestra for dramatic effects rather than having musicians merely as accompanists to singers. His *La favola d'Orfeo* is one of the earliest operas still occasionally performed.

All this kind of music was of course strictly for the nobility. The middle class did not yet exist and the peasantry heard only folk songs and dances handed down from generation to generation by sons of those strolling minstrels still strumming their lutes.

With the seventeenth century came more new instrumental forms. The most important was the SONATA, which consisted of four parts, *movements*, in contrasting tempos or rhythms. Although the Italian composer, Domenico Scarlatti (1683–1757) wrote more than six hundred sonatas, Franz Joseph Haydn's (1732–1809) eighty-two sonatas established the classic form. Since the sonata is the precursor of the SYMPHONY, this earned Haydn the triple title of "Father of the Sonata, the Symphony, and the String Quartet."

Other forms emerging at this time were THEME AND VARIATIONS, which uses a simple melody upon which musicians and composers ad lib intricate improvisations.

The PASSACAGLIA, a Spanish dance form, became an important keyboard showpiece featuring a progression of bass chords that build to an exciting climax.

PRELUDES were originally short pieces played before larger piano or organ works. Johann Sebastian Bach (1685–1750) wrote forty-eight paired preludes and fugues which comprise his masterpiece, *The Well-Tempered Clavier* (1722). By the nineteenth century the prelude was no longer used as a "preamble." Chopin, Debussy, and Rachmaninoff, among others, elevated this little form into one of great beauty.

TOCCATAS, known for their rapid tempo and steady rhythm, are another type of keyboard composition to show off the technical brilliance of a performer.

FANTASIAS, or "flights of fancy," were the freest kinds of compositions, with several themes strung together with no particular set form. Walt Disney chose this as the title of his 1940 film, which memorably illustrated several great classics.

One of the most important compositions developed during the Baroque period was the SUITE, a set of four dances. It consisted at first of such courtly toe-tappers as *allemandes, courantes, sarabandes,* and *gigues,* but optional movements such as *galliards, minuets,* and *gavottes* were often added.

Bach, Handel, and other Baroque composers followed the contrapuntal style. By the nineteenth century suites had become PROGRAM MUSIC, meaning that the movements are held together by a story, a mood or an idea. This concept includes arrangements of music from operas or ballets. Tchaikovsky devised suites from his ballets, *Swan Lake, Sleeping Beauty* and *The Nutcracker.* Edvard Grieg (1843–1907) wrote two *Peer Gynt Suites* based on his incidental music to the Norwegian folklore play by Henrik Ibsen. From Russia, Nicholas Rimsky-Korsakov (1844–1908), gave us the exciting *Scheherazade* based on the *Arabian Nights.* Ferde Grofé (1892–1972) set one of our natural wonders to music with his *Grand Canyon Suite.*

The most important musical form came with the birth of the CONCERTO, a large work in three movements: *allegro* (fast), *andante* (slow), *allegro.* Written for a solo instrument accompanied by an entire orchestra, concertos show off the skill and beauty of the performer's playing. There are a few double and triple concertos: Brahms wrote a famous one for violin and cello; Beethoven, for piano, violin and cello, and Mozart composed a concerto for two pianos and one for three.

The Baroque Hall of Fame

Like that of Monteverdi, the music of HEINRICH SCHÜTZ (1585–1672) evolved from the late Renaissance into the Baroque. His importance is his adaptation of the Italian style into German music in his many choral and sacred works. His *Seven Last Words of Christ* is still performed in churches today.

The great Danish organist living in Germany, DIETRICH BUXTEHUDE (1637–1707), is now mainly remembered because Bach walked two hundred miles to hear him play!

GEORG PHILLIPP TELEMANN (1681–1767), although never attaining the greatness of Bach or Handel, wrote an enormous amount of compositions, including six hundred overtures and forty operas. His chamber music continues to be performed and recorded.

From Italy, ARCANGELO CORELLI (1653–1713) was the master of *concerti grossi* (concertos without soloists), and founder of the modern method of violin playing.

ALESSANDRO (1660–1725) and DOMENICO (1685–1757) SCARLATTI (father and son) wrote many operas, cantatas and sonatas.

Making a name for himself in England was HENRY PURCELL (1659–95). He was not only court composer to King James II, but His Majesty's harpsichordist, instrument repairer, and organist at Westminster Abbey. His most famous piece, however, the *Trumpet Voluntary*, was ironically discovered to have been written by someone named Jeremiah Clarke. For all his contemporary fame, practically the only Purcell that is played today is a theme that was used by the modern British composer, Benjamin Britten, in his *Young Person's Guide to the Orchestra* (1946), a clever composition that tells all about the instruments and how they sound.

In France, JEAN BAPTISTE LULLY (1632–87), son of a poor Italian miller, through his friendship with fifteen-year-old Louis XIV, the "Sun King" of France, became a member of the royal band of twenty-four violins, the most famous orchestra in Europe at the time. Lully also danced in royal ballets, sometimes with Louis as his partner. Working his way up to Superintendent of Music, he composed twenty operas over the years and earned the title Founder of French Grand Opera.

FRANÇOIS COUPERIN (1668–1733) came from and contributed to a long line of fine musicians. He was recognized as the leading French composer of his day through his sacred music, his chamber works, and his four elegant volumes of harpsichord pieces. In 1693 he was made court organist to Louis XIV, who discovered that music, especially Couperin's, could ease the pressure of being surrounded by enemies. Although Bach was greatly influenced by the style of this composer, Couperin's music, like that of his French contemporaries, is rarely performed.

JEAN PHILIPPE RAMEAU (1683–1764), a native-born Frenchman, established a chord harmony system that is still in use today. He is recognized as France's greatest theorist and organist. He started a new career at age fifty, composing operas and ballets with lavish settings and scenery so popular at the time.

The geniuses of this period were, of course, Antonio Vivaldi, Johann Sebastian Bach, and George Frideric Handel. Their talent overshadowed everyone else's and blazed the trail toward Haydn, Mozart, Beethoven, and the Classical period. Ironically, Bach's huge treasury of music, which was expanded by Haydn and Mozart and studied by Beethoven, lay unplayed in organ lofts until it was discovered eighty years later by Mendelssohn. Bach's death in 1750 marked the end of the Baroque Period.

It has been said Vivaldi did not write over 500 concertos, but wrote one concerto over 500 times. You will have to judge for yourself . . .

—Anne Gray

CHAPTER FOUR

The Baroque Giants

Antonio Vivaldi

Born: March 4, 1678, Venice, Italy
Died: July 28, 1741, Vienna, Austria

Vivaldi's first teacher was his father, a violinist at San Marco Cathedral in Venice. Antonio entered the Catholic priesthood, but continued his musical studies. In 1703 he became a teacher in the Venice school for foundling girls. By 1709 he was director of the school's concerts. He traveled all over Europe between 1725 and 1736, performing his own music.

THE RED PRIEST

Because of his hair, Vivaldi received the nickname, "The Red Priest." He was said to be a difficult man. Early in his priesthood he refused to say Mass, claiming that his health (chest pains from angina and asthma) would not permit it.

In 1738 he was refused entry into the town of Ferrara because of his relationship with one of his pupils with whom he travelled, the singer Anna Giraud.

In 1740 he settled in Vienna, hoping to achieve the same recognition as Mozart. This did not happen and he died there in poverty the following year.

CONCERTO KING

Vivaldi was the first composer to use the *ritornello* form, meaning the opening theme is heard again in different keys, always played by the full orchestra. His three movement formula—fast-slow-fast—has become the standard concerto form. Of his approximately 550 concertos, 350 are for a solo instrument (230 for his own instrument, the violin), there are 40 double concertos, 30 for multiple soloists and 60 for orchestra without soloists, and 20 chamber concertos for small groups of solo instruments without orchestra.

His importance is enhanced by the originality of his concertos, which were practically the foundation of this major musical form.

TREASURE REGAINED

After his death, his manuscripts, like Bach's, lay unplayed, not to be sought out until the recent Baroque revival. The number of Vivaldi recordings now rivals those of Bach.

Vivaldi is to Italy what Bach is to central Europe, their greatest Baroque composer.

His "best-sellers" are a "suite" of four short violin concertos, *The Four Seasons (Le Quatro Stagioni)*, and the Concerto for Two Violins and Orchestra in A minor, a masterpiece of contrapuntal harmonies.

COMPOSITIONS: *c*550 concertos, 40 operas, much chamber and choral music.

Johann Sebastian Bach

> *Bach opens a vista to the universe.*
> *After experiencing him. people feel*
> *there is a meaning to life after all.*
> —Helmut Walcha (1907–),
>   German organist who has recorded
>   all of Bach's organ music

Born: March 21, 1685, Eisenach, Germany
Died: July 28, 1750, Leipzig, Germany

Descendant of seven generations of musicians and organists, Bach was destined to enter their profession. His childhood was happy and secure. His father, a violinist, taught him to play the instrument. At age ten, tragedy struck; his parents died within one year of each other. In days when orphaned children were often abandoned, Johann Sebastian was adopted by his older brother, Johann Christoph, an organist and student of Johann Pachelbel, composer of the famous *Canon.* He taught J. S. keyboard and at fifteen got him his first paid position in a church choir. Throughout his life, Bach held a series of posts as church or court organist and composer.

JUST A LACKEY

It must be remembered that no matter how great the musician and composer, he was still considered a servant by his "noble" employer. In 1717, after nine years in the service of the Duke of Saxe-Weimar, Bach petitioned to be allowed to accept an offer of a higher position with another employer. He was imprisoned for a month before the Duke let him go.

WEDDING BELLS AND THE PATTER OF FORTY LITTLE FEET!

In 1707, one of Bach's uncles died, leaving him some money. This enabled him to marry the young lady who was often seen in the organ loft listening to him practice, his cousin Maria Barbara Bach. Their happiness resulted in many compositions and seven children. He was devastated when his wife died suddenly in 1720. Only thirty-five, and not up to being a single parent, he married Anna Magdalena Wilcke late in 1721. A cultured and musical young lady, she was also a good copyist—an extremely useful gift before the invention of the printing press. They had thirteen children. It was for her that he wrote or adapted all those famous minuets and other little pieces in the *Notebook for Anna Magdalena*.

Of his twenty offspring, ten died in infancy and four became composers: Wilhelm Friedmann, Carl Philipp Emanuel, Johann Christoph Friedrich, and Johann Christian.

A LIFETIME POSITION

In 1723 Bach applied for and got the prestigious post of music director and cantor of the Thomasschule in Leipzig. He was thirty-eight and at the height of his powers. He remained there for the remainder of his life.

A HIGHER POWER

Deeply religious, Bach dedicated his music to God. His organ works are considered the greatest ever written and his unaccompanied partitas are still the supreme challenge for the solo violinist. He created new technical demands and dimensions in every musical form he undertook. His style is full of grandeur and delicacy. His choral masterpieces became models for future generations of composers.

Although they lived at the same time, he never met Handel.

INTO THE DARKNESS

Blind the last few years of his life, Bach continued composing. He was operated on by the traveling English oculist, John Taylor—who botched Handel's cataracts—and it is likely that the surgery and consequent treatment may have hastened the composer's death. Bach's death in 1750 marked the end of the Baroque period.

LOST TREASURE

Ironically, Bach's huge treasury of music, which was expanded by

Haydn and Mozart and studied by Beethoven, lay unplayed in organ lofts until it was discovered eighty years later by Felix Mendelssohn.

Today most of Bach's compositions are performed regularly in churches and concert halls. In 1850 a Bach Society was formed to preserve his music.

COMPOSITIONS: 48 pieces for *The Well-Tempered Clavichord*, 198 church cantatas, 40 organ preludes and fugues, numerous toccatas and sonatas, 6 partitas for solo violin, English and French Suites, 6 *Brandenburg Concerti Grossi*, *Mass in B minor*, *St. Matthew Passion*, *Christmas Oratorio*.

Best sampling of his most popular favorites: any recording of "Bach's Greatest Hits" such as the *Air on the G String*, from Suite No. 3, *Arioso* from the Cantata No. 156, *Sheep May Safely Graze* from the *Birthday Cantata*, *The Brandenburg Concertos* (especially the second movement of No. 2 in which a flute, oboe and trumpet intertwine in a divine melody), the Concerto in D minor for Two Violins and Orchestra whose slow movement is a lovesong between the two violins, and the Toccata and Fugue in D minor, immortalized by Walt Disney in the film *Fantasia*.

George Frideric Handel

> *Handel is the greatest composer who ever lived . . . I would uncover my head and kneel down at his tomb.*
> —Ludwig van Beethoven (1770–1827)

Born: February 23, 1685, Halle, Germany
Died: April 14, 1759, London, England

Born in Germany the same year as Johann Sebastian Bach, George Frideric Handel was equal to Bach in musical stature but made his mark on the other side of the English channel. His father did not want him to waste his time with music; he wanted to be able to say, "My son, the lawyer. . ." But little George's talent was already so outstanding by age seven that friends and family pressured papa to let the boy have music lessons. By age eleven he was playing oboe, violin, organ, and harpsichord.

In 1710, after spending four years in Italy, where two of his operas were staged, he became choirmaster to the Elector of Hanover. Shortly after, he received leave to travel and went to London where he wrote a successful opera and was asked to stay, but his conscience made him return to Germany. He went back to London in 1712 and wrote *Ode to the Queen's Birthday* for which Queen Anne gave him a generous yearly income. This time his conscience couldn't talk him into leaving England—he even anglesized his name from Georg Friedrich Händel. He introduced Italian opera to England, and when the audience tired of hearing the foreign language, he switched to writing *oratorios*—Biblical dramas for soloists, chorus, and orchestra, without scenery or costumes—sung in English.

When the queen died and Handel's former employer, the Elector, became George I of England, relations were a little awkward until he wrote the *Water Music* for a festival on the River Thames. The king enjoyed this so much, he forgave the composer for having left Germany. To celebrate, Handel penned *Music for the Royal Fireworks*, which clinched his position. He received a salary from the British Court for the rest of his life.

Like Bach, Handel also became blind six years before his death, and also had the questionable Dr. John Taylor operate (unsuccessfully) on his cataracts. But he continued to perform to the end. Handel's last public appearance was directing a performance of *Messiah*, his greatest composition, which, miraculously, took only three weeks to write. When the choir started to sing the "Hallelujah Chorus" the King rose in respect. Of course, everyone else in the audience also got up. Thus it has become a tradition for everyone to stand during this anthem.

Unequaled master of the *oratorio*, Handel's music is now mainly heard in churches and chamber music recitals. His most famous pieces are the "Largo" from the opera *Xerxes*, the hymn, *Joy to the World*, and the immortal *Messiah*.

COMPOSITIONS: 40 operas, 20 oratorios, anthems, hymns, 12 concerti grossi, numerous orchestral pieces.

Nothing on earth is so well suited to
make the sad merry, the merry sad, to
give courage to the despairing, to make
proud the humble, to lessen envy and
hate, as music.
—Martin Luther (1483–1546)

CHAPTER FIVE

The Classical Era (1750–1800)

The term "classical" has come to mean art music of any era which is not popular or folk music. The *Classical* period of music refers to that written between 1750 and the early 1800s. The greatest composers of this time were Gluck, Haydn, Mozart, and the early Beethoven.

A Time of Change

At the time of Bach's death in 1750 a universal change in ideas and feelings was emerging. A few royals lost their heads in the 1789 French Revolution, while the American Revolution showed the world the meaning of democracy.

Artists and architects were finding their way out of the highly ornamental Baroque to the uncluttered style of ancient Greece. In literature writers were rejecting mystical ladies and unbelievable heros and returning to the simple beauties of nature.

Music reflected these changes. The aristocracy replaced the Church as musical patrons and wanted to hear tuneful and elegant music; thus the rigid Baroque composition rules began to give way to a freer style.

Dynamics, Contrasts, New Forms, New Instruments

Baroque music was based on unity—repeating the melody as the harmony moved from key to key, the rhythm running steadily like a motor. Classical music has many starts and stops, its movements put together by balancing phrases and sections, fitting them like parts of a jigsaw puzzle. The essence is contrast. The dynamics shifting from loud to soft, the register ranging from soprano to bass, the mood changing from major and minor keys—often within one movement. The form that best suited this style was the *sonata*. Written in two, three, or four movements, it was the perfect mold for contrasts and surprises.

New instruments and instrumental combinations of oboes, clarinets, bassoons, and horns brought *divertimenti*, *serenades* and *cassations*— the terms were used interchangeably for suites of light recreational music—to private parties and public concerts.

Bach's sons Carl Philipp Emanuel (1714–88) and Johann Christian (1735–82) and composers like Giovanni Sammartini (1701–75) and Johann Stamitz (1717–57) were forging the concept of a SYMPHONY out of the *sinfonia*—the three movement opera overture—adding a minuet between the slow second movement and the fast finale.

The piano, invented in 1709, was greatly improved by the end of the eighteenth century and replaced the harpsichord. Not only could the loudness or softness be varied from note to note, but dazzling runs were able to be heard above the other instruments. The CONCERTO for piano and orchestra became the favorite form for showing off the skills of keyboard artists. The twenty-five concerti written and performed by Mozart made him supreme in the field.

The STRING QUARTET became the most popular form of chamber music, performed in private homes or small concert halls. Haydn discovered the potential of the combination of two violins, a viola, and a cello, and earned the title "father of the string quartet." Just about every composer to the present day has written in this form.

Orchestras and Operas

Stringed instruments became the foundation for the symphony orchestra along with two horns, flutes, and timpani (kettle drums). Gradually more instruments were added. The woodwinds were especially enriched by the clarinet, which was invented in 1700, its tone much improved by the middle of the century.

Operas, which had degenerated into a string of show-off songs, again became works of art in the hands of Gluck and Mozart, whose music brought excitement and coherent meaning to the *libretto* or story.

From Entertainment to Enrichment

The Classical period drew to a close with music undergoing the same changes as society. Impersonal at the start, the era ended with great expression of personal feeling. The minuet gave way to the waltz, the charming music of 1750 was replaced with the depth and drama of Beethoven. Individualism, patriotism, and rebellion were the subjects for art. In the same fifty-year span music which had set out merely to entertain had become the enrichment of man's mind and soul.

The Classical Composers

CHRISTOPH WILLIBALD GLUCK

Born: July 2, 1714, Erasbach, Germany
Died: November 15, 1787, Vienna

The man who came to be known as the greatest opera composer of his time was born in Bavaria and received no encouragement from his father, a forester, who wanted his son to follow in his footsteps. Gluck left home at fourteen, spending several years in Prague, supporting himself by playing for dances and singing in churches. Finally, several noblemen provided the funds for him to study in Vienna and Italy. From 1745 to 1760 he traveled all over Europe, including London, where he met Handel. During these fifteen years he wrote many operas in the conventional Italian style.

THE PLOT'S THE THING!

It was not until 1761 that a book by the French balletmaster Jean-Georges Noverre made Gluck realize and agree with the author that in ballet and opera the most important elements were the story and the feelings of the characters. Until this time opera stars were calling the shots, inserting arias from other operas and showing off their talents at the expense of the plot.

In 1762 Gluck wrote *Orpheus and Eurydice* based on the tragic Greek legend. His grief-laden music and unusual range of orchestral effects carried the audience from the lashing wrath of the Furies to the serenity of the "Dance of the Blessed Spirits." For the first time, arias, choruses and dancing all fitted into the action and the plot dealt straightforwardly with human emotions instead of complicated intrigues, subplots, and disguises. The success of this work and those that followed established Gluck's fame. His operas are among the earliest still performed.

AHEAD OF HIS TIME

Another innovation was Gluck's use of instruments, which made his orchestras sound far ahead of their time, like those of Berlioz and Wagner seventy years later. He was the first to draw on clarinets, English horns, trombones, plus the cymbals, triangle, and bass drum for dramatic effect. He also did away with the twanging sound of the harpsichord. His music served as the foundation for the compositions of the next century.

COMPOSITIONS: Over 20 operas (some written in two different language versions), 4 ballets, songs, sacred works, and 8 trio sonatas.

FRANZ JOSEPH HAYDN

> *Young people can learn from my example that something can come out of nothing. What I have become is all the result of dire need.*
> —Franz Joseph Haydn,
>   when asked for advice for youth

Born: March 31, 1732, Rohrau, Austria
Died: May 31, 1809, Vienna

The son of a wagon repairer, Haydn was born into a family that loved music. At eight, his beautiful voice got him accepted into the choir of St. Stephen's Cathedral. After his voice broke, he was dismissed and found himself without money, a job, or a home. He managed to survive by singing, playing the harpsichord, and giving lessons in a merchant's shop. He got his first break when he was introduced to Count Morzin of Bohemia, who made him director of a small orchestra. In 1759, his first symphony was heard by Hungary's music-loving, richest, most powerful prince, Miklós József Esterházy. Haydn remained with the Esterházy family for the next thirty years as conductor of one of the finest private orchestras of the time. Free from financial pressure, he composed 60 symphonies, 11 operas, 5 masses, and hundreds of chamber works, especially string quartets.

UNLUCKY IN LOVE

When the girl Haydn fell in love with became a nun, he made the mistake of marrying her older sister, a woman who cared nothing for music. (She used his manuscripts to roll her hair.) She never realized her husband's greatness and when, in later years, Haydn fell in love with a young soprano, Mrs. H. was even harder to live with.

DR. HAYDN

Prince Esterházy died leaving the composer a generous annuity. His successors permitted Haydn to travel. He was widely acclaimed in England and received an honorary doctorate in music from Oxford. On hearing Handel's oratorios, he wrote his own, *The Creation*. He also composed twelve "London" symphonies. Stirred by the British national anthem, "God Save the King," Haydn wrote one for Austria. It is his most popular composition.

FAMOUS CONTACTS

Back in Vienna, for a year he took on a pupil named Ludwig van Beethoven. The hard-driving young composer studied the master's music and learned much, but found his teacher too easygoing.

In 1781 Haydn met the twenty-five-year-old Mozart, recognized his genius, and promoted his work. Mozart's music inspired new delicacy in Haydn's own compositions, while the younger man learned more of the craft of writing symphonies and quartets from the master. They often played chamber music together.

A MAN WITHOUT ENEMIES

When Haydn died at seventy-seven in 1809, it was said that the cause of death was heartbreak from the destruction Napoleon's army caused in his beloved Vienna. But he was so revered that the "enemy" put a protective guard around his house. The funeral was attended by French officers as well as the nobility of Austria. Appropriately, the music played for the occasion was Mozart's *Requiem*.

THRESHOLD OF A NEW AGE

Haydn's music, now performed mostly by chamber groups, is regaining popularity. His Symphony No. 88 is one of his most lively and listenable.

During Haydn's childhood, Bach and Handel were at their peak as the Baroque period drew to a close. At the time of his death, the world was ready to let loose its personal feelings into what would be called Romanticism.

COMPOSITIONS: 104 symphonies, 84 string quartets, 52 piano sonatas, 125 trios, 10 oratorios and cantatas, 12 Masses, 24 operas.

Mozart is just God's way of making the rest of us feel insignificant.
—David Barber (Canadian author, 1958–)

CHAPTER SIX

Wolfgang Amadeus Mozart

The Wunderkind

Born: January 27, 1756, Salzburg, Austria
Died: December 5, 1791, Vienna

A truly democratic man, Mozart was equally at ease with royalty and his working-class drinking companions. He loved Vienna, but was at home in all the capitals of Europe. Above all he is revered as a genius.

The output for his short lifetime of thirty-five years was enormous. Mozart was a gifted violinist, pianist, and conductor. Amazingly, he also managed to be a good husband and father and still found time to play billiards, bowl, and go dancing.

Almost everything he wrote was commissioned by someone, and his music reflected a personality ranging from a fairly coarse sense of humor to a noble and tragic outlook, from folk-origin simplicity to superb

33

brilliance, from elegant courtier to heroic figure full of the spirit of liberty and universal brotherhood.

Playing Favorites

Mozart's favorite musical form was opera, and his handling of the voice not only showed it off but brought it to its highest expression. Instrumentally, he favored the piano, which he loved to play and write for. His concertos and sonatas established the basic styles of pianistic composition.

The saga of this genius began in the Austrian town of Salzburg in 1756.

L'Enfant Terrifique!

One of the definitions of the word *prodigy* is "a child of extraordinary talent or genius." This applies to the boy born to Leopold Mozart, a violinist in the orchestra of the Archbishop of Salzburg. At three, Wolfgang could play little melodies on the clavichord, an early keyboard instrument. His father began giving him lessons at age four. He began composing his own music by the time he was five. During his sixth year he played before the public in Munich and Vienna, where he performed for the Emperor of Austria. While there, someone gave him a small violin which he taught himself to play. He learned to play the organ in the same way after the pedals were explained to him. When he was seven the *Wunderkind* (wonderchild), as he was called, was taken to Paris where his first compositions were published. Jolting in stagecoaches over poorly paved roads on the continent and by boat across the choppy channel to England, he visited every major city in Europe where he gave his concerts.

An Amazing Adolescent

In 1764, while visiting England, the eight-year-old composed several sonatas for violin and harpsichord, as well as his first symphonies. By age seventeen he was considered a mature composer. When the music-loving Archbishop of Salzburg, for whom Mozart had been concertmaster, died, his successor treated the great composer as harshly as his other servants. Mozart resigned in 1781. The next year he married Constanze Weber, cousin of the composer Carl Maria von Weber. Despite the amount of music Mozart turned out, including his three most successful operas, *The Marriage of Figaro* (1786), *Don Giovanni* (1787), and *The Magic Flute* (1791), the young couple were perpetually in debt. At times the composer turned to teaching to subsidize the pitifully small income he received for the volume of music that was destined to become immortal.

The Grave Situation

The last year of Mozart's life, 1791, was one of his most productive yet many of these compositions reflected his inner sadness. These included: the Piano Concerto in B flat (K. 595), *Concert Rondo* for horn and orchestra (K. 371), the operas *The Magic Flute* (K. 620) and *La Clemenza di Tito* (K. 621), piano and vocal music, and most of his *Requiem*.

Toward the end of the year he fell ill. An unknown patron had commissioned him to write a *requiem*, a mass for the dead. Mozart became obsessed with the feeling that he was writing this for himself. On December 4, he gave detailed instructions to his student, Franz Sussmayr, on how to complete the work. That night he died. Because of the swollen condition of the body, rumors of his being poisoned circulated throughout Vienna.

The basis of the play and film *Amadeus* was that the jealous court composer, Antonio Salieri (1750–1825), was his murderer. It is documented that Salieri was jealous of Mozart's genius and used his position to put obstacles in the younger man's professional path. It is also a fact that when Ignaz Moscheles (1794–1870), a pupil of Beethoven, visited Salieri in October 1823, in a hospital outside Vienna, the old, sick man swore that there was no truth to the rumor that he had poisoned Mozart. Medical research has determined from the description of the symptoms that the cause was a combination of streptococcal infection, kidney failure, cerebral hemorrhage, and broncho-pneumonia.

There are different versions of Mozart's burial, the most popular being that Constanza, because of her lack of finances, would only pay for the cheapest funeral possible, and therefore the body was placed in an unmarked pauper's grave. Added to this is the legend that a sudden storm drove away the few friends who attended. The City of Vienna, however, kept amazingly accurate records of the weather, and December 5 and 6, 1791, were logged as mild and sunny.

As to the burial site, the city's precise bookkeeping could have caused authorities to exhume the body from its marked resting place and transport it to ignominy because Constanza failed to keep up with cemetery maintenance fees. Perhaps to make up for this callousness, many years later the city erected a beautiful memorial statue of the composer near the Vienna Opera House.

We are also fortunate that the Mozarts were a close-knit family who corresponded regularly. These letters have been saved and published, giving us a remarkable view of the life of an eighteenth-century musician and a personal picture of the warm human being who was Mozart.

K1—K600+

Mention of Ludwig von Köchel (1800–1877) must be made in connection with Mozart. This Austrian botanist/mineralogist made it his life's work to chronologically catalogue the composer's more than six hundred compositions—a gargantuan undertaking. Thus the letter K and a number appears after every Mozart work, which is very useful to scholars and does not affect us at all.

COMPOSITIONS: 41 symphonies, 26 string quartets, 27 piano concertos, 20 piano sonatas and fantasias, 42 violin sonatas, 6 violin concertos, concertos for flute, flute and harp, clarinet, bassoon and horn, 40 divertimentos and serenades, 10 quintets for various combinations of instruments, 18 operas, 42 separate arias, 20 canons, 19 Masses and litanies, an oratorio, 4 cantatas, 34 songs, a ballet, plus many miscellaneous instrumental works as well as movements of sonatas and symphonies and other compositions never completed.

Perennial Favorites: Symphonies Nos. 39, 40, 41 ("Jupiter"). Piano Concerto No. 21, known as "Elvira Madigan" from the 1967 Swedish film of the same name, Violin Concerto No. 5, Serenade No. 13, *Eine Kleine Nachtmusik (A Little Nightmusic*—long before Stephen Sondheim).

Keep an eye on that young man, some day he will make a big splash in the world.

—Mozart, on hearing the teenage Beethoven improvise at the piano

CHAPTER SEVEN

Ludwig van Beethoven

The Bridge Over the Generation Gap

Born: December 16, 1770, Bonn, Germany
Died: March 26, 1827, Vienna

Straddling like a giant Colossus with one foot in the Classical Era and the other kicking open the door to the Romantic is the bearer of the most famous name in music: Ludwig van Beethoven.

Historically, Mozart lived and died while Napoleon was still busy fighting inside France, so his music did not reflect the turmoil that began in 1805 when the French dictator started his conquest of Europe. Haydn's long life ended in 1809, amid the din of French bombardment of his beloved Vienna. The lifespan of Ludwig van Beethoven (1770–1827) paralleled that of Napoleon Bonaparte (1769–1821), and the

37

power, strength, and freedom of his music mirror the dramatic events of Napoleon's career.

An Abused Child

Born in Bonn, a small city which two centuries later would enjoy forty years of prominence as the capital of West Germany (1949–89), Ludwig was the second child of a valet's widow and a not terribly talented alcoholic musician in the court of the Elector of Cologne—a position he had slipped into by virtue of *his* talented father, Ludovicus, who emigrated to Germany from the Netherlands.

Hoping the boy would be another Mozart-like prodigy and make a fortune for the family, Ludwig's father subjected him to a harsh tutelage, demanding that he learn violin, piano, and composition. At the age of eleven he became a pupil of the court organist, Christian Neefe. This man helped undo the abuse the boy had suffered, encouraged his musical compositions and, in essence, became his musical father. Beethoven wrote his first three piano sonatas that year. Next, Neefe obtained for the twelve-year-old a position as assistant court organist, which allowed him to earn him a little money. Meanwhile, until he was fourteen, the boy attended public schools in Bonn.

Beethoven's mother, whom he loved and pitied, died when he was seventeen. For the next five years the young man supported his family until his father drank himself to death in 1792.

New Directions

Beethoven's gifted piano playing and compositions began to be noticed by wealthy people. In 1792, with their help, he moved to Vienna, the center of the musical world. He wanted to study with Mozart, whom he had briefly met on a visit to Vienna when he was sixteen, but Mozart died a few months before Beethoven arrived in Austria. Instead, Haydn accepted him as a pupil for music theory. The young genius was expected to "receive Mozart's spirit from the hands of Haydn." The two had a stormy year together, for the great master who broke the rules in his own music was too busy to explain why a student had to obey them.

Beethoven's gift of being able to improvise on any theme endeared him to the public before any of his compositions were ever published. Viennese nobility invited him into their palatial homes to play, and commissioned works for these performances. (Some even had music paper lying around hoping he would leave behind a little gem. He often used the paper, but always remembered to take it with him.) Besides this source of income, he sold works to publishers on a scale according to the composition—so much for a sonata, a little more for a string quartet, and top price for a symphony. After leaving Bonn, Beethoven never worked for anyone again. He was a new breed, a free-lance composer and musician.

The Falling Curtain

By the end of his first ten years in Vienna, Beethoven was in great demand, his fame spreading throughout Europe. At the peak of his performing career a shadow fell across his life. Around 1800, he began to lose his hearing. He contemplated suicide, but caught the infection of the budding Romanticism, shook his fist at Fate, and turned away from people to find comfort in nature. Still "hearing" with his "inner ear," he did not stop composing. He wrote some of his greatest masterpieces when he was completely deaf.

Hero or Tyrant?

European history during the major portion of Beethoven's life was dominated by Napoleon, a charming, workaholic dynamo who was not only a military genius but his own press agent. He made sure that his victories were well publicized by the best writers and artists. His influence was everywhere, since he had a habit of putting his brothers, brother-in-law, and other handy relatives on the conquered thrones of Austria, Prussia, assorted German states, Italian kingdoms, Holland, Portugal, and Spain. He imposed the best achievements of the French Revolution on the rest of the continent in the form of his *Code Napoléon*, which included setting up a parliament with a constitution and a bill of rights, the male vote, common law, and higher education open to all who qualified, regardless of class or religion. No wonder Beethoven along with the rest of the common people considered him a hero.

The Themes of Freedom

As the French and American Revolutions changed the social order of Europe, Beethoven, who truly felt that liberty was man's birthright, infused this new freedom into his compositions, creating dramatic music different from any written before. His Third Symphony, "Eroica," which broke the Classical mold forever, was at first dedicated to Napoleon. But at this point in time the "hero" decided to declare himself Emperor. In disillusionment, the composer tore up the first page of the manuscript with the dedication on it.

The Fifth is the best-known of all symphonies ever written. In World War II it became known as the "Victory" Symphony because the first three notes spell out "V" in Morse code (dot, dot, dot, dash: . . . —).

Embodying Beethoven's communion with nature, the beauty of the Sixth Symphony, "Pastoral," cannot be destroyed even by the cartoon Bacchus and his nymphs and satyrs cavorting in Disney's *Fantasia*. It must be admitted however, that viewing this film will indelibly acquaint children with the great master.

The Seventh is pure power with a sublime haunting slow movement contrasting the energy of the first and the last.

The culmination of the spirit of freedom is most apparent in the final movement of the master's last and perhaps greatest symphony, the Ninth, "Choral," using both chorus and orchestra in the soul-stirring musical setting of the "Ode to Joy" by the famous German poet Friedrich Schiller.

Three Personal Eras

Beethoven's work is divided into three parts: between 1792 and 1802 his compositions were patterned after the works of Haydn and Mozart; 1803 to 1816 marked the period of greater inventiveness, variation, and development of contrasts of tempo and mood from delicacy and tenderness to force and power; and during 1817–1827 he flung aside all classic rigidity and wrote monumental compositions bursting with emotion and personal expression.

The Standard Bearer

Like most innovators, Beethoven was widely criticized. In his later works it was for the "wildness" and "lack of elegance." He made great demands on performers and audiences of his day. He never composed quickly or easily and left notebooks full of sketches showing his struggles to perfection. He was like a musical sculptor hammering away at tones, sometimes taking years on one theme. Nevertheless, the output of the last period of his life set the standard against which serious composers are still measuring themselves.

COMPOSITIONS: 32 piano sonatas, 5 sonatas for cello and piano, 10 sonatas for violin and piano, 17 string quartets, 5 piano concertos, 1 violin concerto, a concerto for violin, cello, and piano, 9 symphonies, an opera, a ballet, 2 Masses, and a magnitude of other chamber and piano music.

A LEGACY

"He who truly understands my music must thereby go free of all the misery which others bear about with them."

—Ludwig van Beethoven

*The only reality in music is the state of
mind which it induces in the listener.*
—Stendhal (1783–1842),
French author

CHAPTER EIGHT

The Romantic Era (1850–1920)

The Romantic period of music was named after the medieval *romances*—stories and poems about heroic people written in the language of the country, rather than Latin which could only be read by scholars and churchmen. In the Baroque and Classical periods music was impersonal and usually focused on or was dedicated to God. *Romanticism* stressed freedom to express personal emotions, not just in music, but also in painting, sculpture, literature, and all the arts.

Reviving the Past

Creative artists made a last stand against the growing mechanization of society. It was a last desperate gasp of fresh air before the Industrial Revolution with its crowded factories and smoke-belching chimneys would pollute the sky and spirit of humanity. Artists wanted to preserve the simple life, quiet villages, flowing crystal rivers, mysterious unexplored forests. Inspiration came from faraway places and times—from legends of swashbuckling knights loving unattainable maidens. In story and song these dreams were never realized, nor were desires fulfilled. This was PROGRAM MUSIC, music that told stories.

Church music was not neglected, either. Monumental sacred works for chorus and orchestra—oratorios, Masses, and requiems—were composed by Beethoven, Schubert, Berlioz, Mendelssohn, Liszt, Saint-Saëns, Brahms, Verdi, Fauré and Dvořák.

Following the legacy of Beethoven, the Romantic composer was no one's employee. He created music for himself, out of his passionate thoughts and feelings, not just for entertainment. The only reality he had to deal with was the insecurity of depending on his living from sales of his music or, if he was also a performer, the income from his concerts.

A New Audience

The Romantic audience no longer consisted solely of nobility. The wealthy new middle class of merchants and businessmen and their families began attending concerts. Performances were no longer limited to the salon, concert hall, or opera house. Since the invention of the piano in 1709, for which Mozart created a whole new range of compositions, music-making moved into the home. Most houses had a piano or harmonium (a small organ) in the parlor, and the children, especially girls, of the household were expected to be able to play. This tradition remains entrenched to this day in the upper middle class, to the delight and income of music teachers. Composers wrote works for these budding artists ranging from the intensive repetitive exercises of Johann Baptist Cramer (1771–1858), Muzio Clementi (1752–1832), and Carl Czerny (1791–1857), whose *School of Velocity* is still visited upon hapless piano pupils, to the beautiful and challengingly difficult *études* (studies) of Chopin and lofty *Transcendental Études* of Liszt.

Women in the Limelight

For the first time concert careers were open to women. Clara Wieck, who became the wife of Robert Schumann, was an outstanding pianist. Her first public performance was at age nine. She also composed many piano pieces, including a concerto, a trio, cadenzas for the concertos of Mozart and Beethoven, and several songs. In France, Cecile Chaminade (1857–1944) also achieved prominence as both composer and pianist— she made her debut at the age of eight. Her works include a comic opera, a ballet, orchestral suites, songs and light salon music. "The Flatterer" and "Scarf Dance" are usually included in most collections of piano music.

A Conservatory Is Not Just a Greenhouse

With so much interest in music, major schools were being established all over Europe and the United States. Conservatories had existed in Italy since the Renaissance, but these were mostly orphanages stressing music training. The new institutions were open to applicants on the basis of talent. One of the earliest was the Conservatoire National de Musique in Paris (1795). This was followed by conservatories in Prague (1811), Brussels (1813), Vienna (1821), London (The Royal Academy of Music, 1823), and Leipzig (1843), which was founded and directed by Felix Mendelssohn. The Leipzig Conservatory became a model for many others in the world, especially the United States, where Oberlin (1865), the New England Conservatory (1867), Cincinnati (1867), and the Peabody Institute in Baltimore (1868) were among the first music schools to flourish as the country shook off the chains of the Civil War.

See It In Print

The earliest music publishers were Breitkopf and Härtel, established in Leipzig in 1719. Also in Germany were Peters (1814) and Schott (1773); in Italy, Ricordi (1808), in France, Durand (1869), in England, Novello (1811), and G. Schirmer (1861) in the United States. All of these publishing houses are still in business.

On Their Toes and Dirty Dancing

Ballet as we know it today also reached its peak during the Romantic period. Paris, home of the ballet—which is why all ballet terms are in French—was temporarily challenged by the establishment of Russian ballet schools in Moscow and St. Petersburg, and by the Royal Danish Ballet. However, many famous Russian choreographers such as Fokine, ballet dancers such as Pavlova and Nijinsky, and the impressario Diaghilev moved to France before the 1917 Revolution, making Paris once again the world center of ballet.

The waltz was elevated to the concert stage as Chopin enchanted salon audiences with his ethereal creations. Tchaikovsky wrote grand orchestral waltzes for his ballets, suites, his opera *Eugene Onegin*, and the third movement of his Fifth Symphony. Berlioz had set the example earlier with the second movement of his *Symphonie fantastique* titled, "A Ball." Brahms's very original contributions are his *Liebeslieder Waltzes* for voices and piano duet. But it took Josef Lanner, Johann Strauss, Sr., and Johann Strauss, Jr.—the "Waltz King"—to trip the waltz off the stage. In the traditional dances—minuet, gigue, quadrille, etc.—partners, as in square dancing, barely touch. Now society had to get over the shock of seeing men and women with their arms around each other!

Other dances for couples infiltrated the social scene. From middle and eastern Europe came the mazurka, the polka, and the polonaise. Although group dancing did not die out, dances for paired couples became the most popular until the jitterbug, the twist, and rock 'n' roll once again took the closeness out of dancing.

Musical Melting Pot

Music, which had been monopolized by German, Austrian, French, and Italian composers, now flowed in from all parts of Europe: Chopin (Poland), Liszt (Hungary), Tchaikovsky and the "Russian Five" (Balakirev, Borodin, Cui, Moussorgsky, Rimsky-Korsakov), Grieg (Norway), Sibelius (Finland), Smetana and Dvořák (Bohemia), Balfe, Sullivan, Delius, and Elgar (England), Gottschalk, Joplin, and MacDowell (U.S.) all contributed to the rich tapestry of the Romantic period.

The Storm King

Opera reached new heights. The man who revolutionized the form was Richard Wagner (1813–83), whose work many musicians initially refused to play because of its opposition to established principles and which many people would not even listen to. He also made history with his *Ring Cycle* of four mythic operas which takes three days to perform.

Meanwhile, Italian opera peaked with the more traditional but highly dramatic and melodic masterpieces of Verdi and Puccini.

Fin de Siècle

The end of the Baroque period marked the beginning of realistic progress. The first railway was opened in England in 1825, the telegraph tapped its first message in 1836, the camera snapped its first likeness in 1839. The Romantic era witnessed Alexander Graham Bell saying "Mr. Watson, come here, I want you" on his first telephone in 1877, Mr. Edison lighting up New York City in 1878, and the internal combustion engine paving the way for horseless carriages.

By the end of the century, composers also moved in the direction of *realism*. In France, Fauré, Satie, Debussy, and Ravel blended with the Impressionist school of art, trading in passion for sophistication and elegance. In Germany, Bruckner and Mahler wrote huge symphonies with dissonant chords that would take another generation for listeners to get used to.

By the beginning of the twentieth century, the Wright Brothers got off the ground, opening the skies even as political storm clouds darkened them. A period which began with exuberance about life and love ended with brooding nostalgia as people realized they were coming to the end of an age of innocence. The high principles of the Romantic era evaporated in the smoke of the cannons of World War I.

CHAPTER NINE

The Romantic Composers

The men who followed in the giant footsteps of Ludwig van Beethoven each left their mark in the fertile field of the Romantic Era. Here are the most prominent.

Carl Maria von Weber

Born: December 18, 1786, Eutin, Germany
Died: June 5, 1826, London, England

Son of a musician and a singer/actress, and nephew of Mozart, Weber also had parents who tried to mold him into a prodigy. For a while he studied with Michael Haydn, brother of Franz Joseph. His first opera was produced when he was fourteen. At eighteen he was made conductor of the Breslau Theater, but the musicians resented his youth, so he was forced to leave in 1806. His next position was with Duke Eugen of Wurtemberg, who had an excellent little orchestra. A projected piano tour had to be cancelled due to the Napoleonic Wars. From 1813–1816 Weber was conductor of the Prague Opera Theater. In 1817 he married Caroline Brandt. His operas and other works were gaining recognition, but the tuberculosis he had inherited from his mother began to take its toll. Instead of heeding his doctor's advice to take a year of rest, he accepted more concert engagements and opera commissions. He went to London in April of 1826 to conduct twelve performances of his new opera, *Euryanthe*, and gave several piano concerts. But in his weakened condition his health failed rapidly and he died in that city in June. He was honored by a ceremonial funeral, and in 1844 his coffin was moved to Dresden, where Wagner delivered the eulogy.

Apart from Beethoven in his later works, Weber is considered the first Romantic composer. He set German music free from Italian influences. Along with Beethoven and Schubert he demonstrated the possibilities of the piano, which were expanded upon by Mendelssohn, Chopin, and Liszt. His orchestrations paved the path for Berlioz and Wagner.

COMPOSITIONS: 2 symphonies, 8 operas, including *Der Freischütz, Euryanthe* and *Oberon*, 2 clarinet concertos, many songs, and much piano and chamber music.

Most Popular: *Invitation to the Dance*, an orchestral piece orchestrated in 1841 by Hector Berlioz and made into a ballet, and *The Spectre of the Rose* (1911), danced by Nijinsky.

Franz Schubert

> *Whom the gods love, die young.*
> —Old Proverb

Born: January 31, 1797, Leichtenthal near Vienna
Died: November 19, 1828, Vienna

Schubert was a true son of Vienna and, aside from a few trips into the countryside, never left the city. His father was a schoolmaster and his mother a cook. His early training in music consisted of violin, organ, theory, and singing lessons. At age eleven, his lovely voice gained him admittance into the Vienna Court School choir, known as the *Konvikt*, where he received one of the best educations available at the time. The school orchestra was excellent and he quickly worked his way up from second violin to assistant conductor.

In 1811, he began to study with Antonio Salieri (1750–1825)—who did *not* murder Mozart, but was music director of the court and for a while one of Beethoven's teachers.

At fifteen Schubert began writing the *Lieder* that were to make him the first great composer of a new musical form—the nineteenth-century Romantic German Art Song. His first symphony was written at sixteen and the following year he wrote a Mass.

Schubert was dismissed from the choir when his voice changed at the age of sixteen. Not good enough at any instrument to be a performer, and exempt from military service because he was only 5 feet 1¼ inches tall, he entered a teachers' college for a year, after which he became an assistant at his father's school.

He continued composing during this time and made three friends who literally saved his life—Josef von Spaun, Franz von Schober, two young law students, and Johann Vogl, whose operatic singing voice was failing, but who found a new career in performing Schubert's songs. They realized his greatness, helped him financially and did everything they could to publicize his work. Von Spaun even sent some of Schubert's musical settings of Goethe's poems to the influential man himself, but they were never acknowledged.

Of the 150 songs he wrote in 1815, "The Erlkönig," with its theme of a child succumbing to the Erlking (Death) while riding at night in his father's arms, was an instant success. Like his subsequent songs, the words, melody, and accompaniment form a mini-drama with voice and piano merging in equal importance.

Perhaps because Beethoven—whom Schubert admired—was the center of the musical limelight, the young composer's star never had a chance to shine in his own time. In 1826, when the first public concert of his works took place in Vienna, the German papers were full of praise, while the local reviewers ignored it!

In the final year of his short life (1828), Schubert became ill, but managed to write his last (Ninth) Symphony in C, the "Great," the F minor Fantasy for Piano Duet, and his most popular song, "Ständchen" (Serenade).

Schubert was a pallbearer at Beethoven's funeral, and a scant year later was laid to rest next to his idol.

Like Bach and von Weber's, Schubert's five hundred compositions "died" with him and were found in odd places years later, through the efforts of Schumann and Mendelssohn. They were published in confusing order, and it was not until 1951 that Otto Erich Deutsch put together a catalogue which did for Schubert what Köchel did for Mozart. Schubert's sketchbooks, like Beethoven's, show him to be a tireless worker always striving for perfection.

COMPOSITIONS: 9 symphonies, 15 string quartets, 1 quintet, 21 piano sonatas, 11 impromptus, 7 masses, 600 songs, 15 stage works, and much other orchestral, chamber, and piano music.

Most Popular: Symphony No. 8 ("The Unfinished"), Fifth, Sixth, and Ninth Symphonies; *The Wanderer Fantasy* for piano; song cycle: *Die schöne Müllerin* (*The Fair Miller's Wife*) and *Die Winterreise* (*Winter Journey*). Songs: *An die Musik* (*To Music*), *Hark, Hark, the Lark, Who Is Sylvia?, Der Erlkönig* from the spooky ballad by Goethe, *Die Forelle* (*The Trout*), and the *Trout Quintet* based on this song.

Hector Berlioz

> *Every composer knows the anguish and despair occasioned by forgetting ideas which one has no time to write down.*
> —Hector Berlioz

Born: December 11, 1803, near Grenoble, France
Died: March 8, 1869, Paris

Whatever anguish France's greatest symphonic composer may have had over lost ideas, he made up for by being one of the leaders of the Romantic movement, a brilliant critic, a powerful conductor, and the father of modern orchestration.

During Berlioz's boyhood Napoleon was busy conquering most of Europe. By the time Berlioz was an adult this "glory" had faded. The social and national energy generated by the French Revolution and stirred to new intensity by Napoleon's victories was now channeled into the Romantic movement. Born within a few years of one another, Delacroix led the Romantics in art, Victor Hugo in literature, and Berlioz in music.

Young Hector was expected to become a doctor like his father. At nineteen he went to Paris to study medicine, but after two years, his love of music and aversion to the dissecting room prompted him to switch schools to the Paris Conservatory. While there he proved to be a difficult student, always rebelling against his "old-fashioned" teachers, especially the director Cherubini. By 1830, after three submissions, Berlioz's definite ideas in composition earned him the Prix de Rome. This entitled him to three years' study in the Italian capital, but after eighteen months, homesickness took him back to Paris where he found a job as a music critic to support himself while composing.

He began to organize and conduct concerts throughout Europe and Russia. In France, however, his outspoken criticism and avant-garde style of music was too violent for audiences. Nevertheless, the greatest contemporary composers—Chopin, Liszt, Mendelssohn, Schumann, Wagner—became his friends, and he influenced all of them.

His was the original PROGRAM MUSIC. His compositions told a story or painted a picture. He wrote works based on Shakespeare's *Romeo and Juliet, Hamlet, The Tempest* and *King Lear. The Damnation of Faust* came from Goethe's drama. *Les Troyens (The Trojans)*, about the destruction of Troy, is an opera of the grand design later emulated by Wagner. The cast is so huge and production so difficult that it is rarely staged. His *Requiem* and *Te Deum* are also on a large scale.

In 1827 Berlioz saw a production of *Hamlet* and fell in love with Shakespeare and Harriet Smithson, the Irish actress who played Ophelia. From this came his most-played composition, the *Symphonie fantastique* (1830). It was the first symphony to show the revolutionary impact of Beethoven. Calling for a huge orchestra—the composer would have liked 220 musicians—the theme of the beloved (*l'idée fixe*) runs through all five movements. The first begins traditionally with a slow section ("Reveries"), leading to the main faster section ("Passions"). The second movement, "A Ball," depicts the beloved amid festivity. For the first time a waltz was used in a symphony. (Fifty years later Tchaikovsky inserted a lovely waltz in his Fifth Symphony). The third movement paints a rural scene reminiscent of Beethoven's *Pastoral Symphony*. The fourth and fifth movements are the lover's nightmares. First he dreams he is marching to the scaffold, and, finally, he sees his beloved participating in a grotesque witches' sabbath which culminates in the ominous *Dies Irae*, the chant for the dead. Amazingly, Berlioz' dramatic form of courtship won the fair lady. They were married in 1832, but their stormy relationship ended in 1841.

In Russia, twelve thousand people attended one of his concerts. The young Russian composers, among them Rimsky-Korsakov and Moussorgsky, idolized Berlioz and patterned their music after his. Not until 1856 was he honored in his own country. Made a member of the French

Institute, he was awarded a yearly sum of money which allowed him to give up his job as a critic.

Berlioz was also a talented writer. His treatise on orchestration (1844) is still used. His *Evenings in the Orchestra* (1854) and *Memoirs* (1870) give us a perfect picture of European music in his era. By the time of his death in 1869, he was recognized as one of the founders of modern music.

COMPOSITIONS: Besides those already mentioned: *Harold in Italy*, a tone poem (sometimes called a symphony) for viola and orchestra; operas: *Benevuto Cellini, Beatrice and Benedict*; overtures: *Waverly, The Corsair, Roman Carnival; Les Nuits d'été (Summer Nights)*, six songs for mezzo-soprano or tenor with piano accompaniment, which he later orchestrated; *L'Enfance du Christ (The Childhood of Christ)*, an oratorio whose delicacy and gentleness is a complete departure from his usual dramatic style.

Felix Mendelssohn

> *There was actually a composer who was not born in poverty, whose parents didn't want him to become a doctor or a lawyer, who was loved, happy, and successful. You might not know his name, but you know his Wedding March.*
>
> —Dr. Anne Gray

Born: February 3, 1809, Hamburg
Died: November 4, 1847, Leipzig

Born into a wealthy banking family, Felix was the grandson of the Jewish philosopher Moses Mendelssohn, known as the "German Socrates" for his belief in the immortality of the soul and his efforts to delete the division between Jews and Christians. The Mendelssohns converted to Protestantism when Felix was seven, adding Bartholdy to their family name.

Living in this privileged environment, the boy was given the best training on the piano, viola, and in music theory. He appeared in public at the age of ten and started composing at twelve. In 1819, his setting of Psalm 19 was sung by the Berlin *Singakademie*. Other early compositions were sonatas, piano quartets, and string symphonies.

Among the eminent visitors to his parents' salon was the great German poet Goethe. The seventy-two-year-old man and the twelve-year-old boy formed a bond of friendship.

After studying Shakespeare in German, Mendelssohn wrote the Overture to *A Midsummer Night's Dream* at age seventeen. The rest of this lovely incidental music, including the Wedding March, was not completed until seventeen years later.

In March, 1829, he conducted Bach's *St. Matthew's Passion*—the first time the oratorio had been heard since the composer's death eighty years before. The same year Mendelssohn made the first of ten trips to England. To great acclaim, he gave the premiere performance of Beethoven's "Emperor" Concerto in that country. He also toured Scotland and was inspired to write the *Hebrides,* or *Fingal's Cave,* Overture. From 1830–31, he traveled through Italy and composed his most popular symphony, No. 4, the "Italian."

He returned to Paris in 1831, and to London in 1832 and 1833, after which he accepted a conducting post in Düsseldorf from 1833–35, where he concentrated on Handel's oratorios, which inspired him to write his own, *St. Paul* (1836) and the popular *Elijah* (1846). He returned to Leipzig and conducted the famed Gewandhaus Orchestra from 1835–45, showcasing the works of Bach, Beethoven, Weber, Schumann, and Berlioz. During this time (1843), he founded the Leipzig Conservatory, with Robert Schumann as one of his associates. It became the leading German music school.

He somehow managed to find time to marry the daughter of a French Protestant clergyman and father five children.

Proud of the fact that he never neglected his students, Mendelssohn composed only during summer vacations, giving us the *Ruy Blas* Overture, the "Scotch" Symphony (No. 5), the Piano Trio in C minor, and the instantly successful Violin Concerto in E minor.

The only times he was not comfortable were when he was intermittently employed by the king as composer and choirmaster in Berlin, but good came of even this in that the rest of the *Midsummer Night's Dream* music was written there in 1843.

Mendelssohn also had a fine reputation as an organizer and was hired to put on festivals in the Lower Rhine and in Birmingham, (England). His last visit to England was in 1847 when he played for Queen Victoria and Prince Albert. On his return he was mistaken for Dr. Mendelssohn, a political activist, and detained at the Prussian border. After he was released, he learned of the death of his beloved sister, Fanny, herself a pianist and composer. Run down from overwork, this shock set off a series of strokes. He died a few months later.

Mendelssohn was truly a gifted man. Besides his musical talent, he had an amazing memory and was a superb pianist, a good violist, an excellent organist, and an inspiring conductor; he was also a fine painter and a clever writer with much literary knowledge. He was generous to other musicians and aspired to elevate the popular taste of audiences.

The eminent conductor Hans von Bülow claimed Mendelssohn to be the most complete master of form since Mozart. After a Classical apprenticeship, this composer became a true Romanticist, finding inspiration for his orchestral music in art, nature, and history. He invented the CONCERT OVERTURE—creating almost a symphonic poem—raising the form above a mere introduction to a larger work. The sea is a recurring theme in his work—*Calm Sea and Prosperous Voyage, The Hebrides, The Fair Melusine*. His music is clear, graceful, lyrical, and has great strength—as in his Fifth Symphony, the "Reformation"—but is never revolutionary.

COMPOSITIONS: 12 early string symphonies, 5 symphonies, 5 overtures, 2 piano concertos, *Rondo capriccioso* for piano, 2 violin concertos, many chamber works, including the Octet in E flat for strings, much piano music, notably eight books of *Songs Without Words*, 2 oratorios, many songs and part-songs for choir, and organ music: 6 sonatas, 3 preludes and fugues, *Andante and Variations* in D.

Robert Schumann

> It is music's lofty mission to shed light
> on the depths of the human heart.
> —Robert Schumann

Born: June 8, 1810, Zwickau, Germany
Died: July 29, 1856, Endenich, near Bonn

The son of a bookseller, Schumann heard very little music in his parents' home. He studied with a town musician who could only give him elementary knowledge, but from this he managed to write a few compositions and learn the piano. He also loved literature and could not decide between the two careers when he entered Leipzig University. His father died when he was sixteen and his mother insisted that he attend law school. He also studied music under Frederick Wieck until his mother found out and transferred him to Heidelberg University. Not doing any better there, he was sent to Italy. When he was twenty, he wrote her explaining his decision to make music his life's work. With Wieck's help, he got his mother to give in, and jokingly referred to this as the end of the "Twenty Years' War."

Back in Leipzig he practiced strenuously to make up for lost time. This included putting a mechanical device on the ring finger of his right hand to strengthen it. Instead, he crippled himself and killed his career as a concert pianist. He now turned his full attention to composition and studied with Heinrich Dorn, a prominent conductor and composer of the day.

In order to publicize his work, Schumann founded *Die Neue Zeitschrift für Musik* in 1834. In this periodical he was able to fulfill his literary talent and he remained the editor for ten years, setting high standards for musical criticism. He also called attention to new composers such as Berlioz, Chopin, Mendelssohn, and later, Brahms. His aim, like Mendelssohn's, was to stimulate and improve the tastes of the audience.

Throughout his twenties Schumann also wrote some of his finest piano music: *Carnaval,* a set of pieces imitating the styles of several composers, *Symphonic Études, Fantasie* and *Scenes from Childhood.* Franz Liszt recognized his genius, and Mendelssohn became his close friend.

Schumann tried moving his magazine to Vienna, but culture there had stagnated since the deaths of Mozart, Haydn, Beethoven, and Schubert. After six months he returned to Leipzig. Two good things came out of this attempt: He wrote a charming piece called *Faschingsschwank aus Wien* (Viennese Carnival) and he discovered Schubert's Ninth Symphony in C major, which he called the "Great," and which had never been performed.

Schumann had fallen in love with the young Clara Wieck and after waiting many years, asked for her hand in marriage, but Papa did not want his daughter to marry a poor, unknown composer and ruin her already-blossoming career as a concert pianist. It took four more years and a bitter court case, but in 1840, shortly after Clara's twenty-first birthday, she and Robert wed. While waiting, Schumann had poured his love into music, writing over a hundred art songs, which placed his work on a level with the *Lieder* of Schubert.

They had an idyllic marriage. Clara performed her husband's work all over Europe. Even having eight children did not deter them from traveling as far as Russia, where Schumann also conducted his First Symphony, the "Spring."

In 1843 Schumann helped Mendelssohn found the Leipzig Conservatory. He taught there for a while, but found the job too wearing on his health. In 1844 he moved to Dresden, where he studied Bach's manuscripts, wrote his Second Symphony, and became friends with Richard Wagner. He felt inspired to write his only opera, *Genoveva* (1848), using German tempo markings instead of the traditional Italian. It was not a success.

The last period of Schumann's life contained both triumphs and defeats. In 1850 he took the post of conductor in Düsseldorf. Happy at first, he wrote his beautiful Cello Concerto and his lively Third Symphony, the "Rhenish." But his conducting skills were not up to the position and between 1852–53 his health and spirits began to deteriorate, causing him to resign. In 1853 he met young Brahms and launched his career by calling him a genius in an article in the *Neue Zeitschrift*. In 1854 Schumann suffered hallucinations and dreaded the possibility of becoming insane. He attempted suicide by throwing himself in the Rhine, but was rescued by a fishing boat and taken to an asylum where he remained for two years. He died in the arms of his wife during one of her visits.

For the remaining forty years of her life, Clara played her husband's music all over Europe. She also composed, was on the faculty of the Frankfurt Conservatory, and remained a lifelong friend of Brahms.

Schumann is considered the most romantic of the Romantics. His music is full of youth and exuberance without ever being bombastic. It holds out to mankind a message of life and love.

MAJOR COMPOSITIONS: 4 symphonies, 3 overtures. Concertos: 1 each for piano, violin, cello. Much chamber and piano music: *Album for the Young, Scenes of Childhood, Album Leaves, Novelettes, Arabeske, Träumerei (Dreaming), Aufschwung (Soaring), Carnaval*, etc. Song cycles: *Dichterliebe (Poet's Love), Frauenliebe und Leben (Women's Love and Life)* and many others. *Part-Songs* for mixed choirs. *Requiem* for chorus, and orchestral and other choral works.

Frédéric Chopin

> *No one has ever created richer harmonies, more powerful or delicate melodies or such brilliant arpeggios for this instrument—truly, Chopin is the "Poet of the Piano!"*
>
> —Universal opinion

Born: March 1, 1810, Zelazowa Wola, near Warsaw, Poland
Died: October 17, 1849, Paris

His father was a Frenchman teaching in Poland. His Polish mother was a cultured woman. Chopin showed early musical promise, and in 1817 began lessons with famed instructor Wojciech Zwyny (1756–1842). At a recital the following year the eight-year-old played the difficult piano concerto of Bohemian composer Adabert Gyrowetz (1763–1850). By age ten he had already written several compositions. His first rondo was published when he was fifteen and still in high school. The years 1826–29 were spent at the Warsaw Conservatory, during which he wrote his *Krakowiak Rondo*. He performed his Piano Concerto in F minor in Vienna in 1829 and Warsaw in 1830. Later that year he performed his Concerto in E minor.

Chopin left Poland at the age of twenty to concertize in Prague, Dresden, and Vienna. When he heard that the Russians had captured Warsaw (1830), he refused to play in that country again. He never returned to Poland, but filled his music with love for his native land, introducing mazurkas, polonaises, and other Polish dances and songs to Western Europe. Legend has it that he carried with him a small container of Polish soil.

In 1831, already acclaimed for his salon recitals and his early compositions, he settled in Paris and pursued a successful career performing and teaching. Here he was soon surrounded by the greatest writers, artists, and composers of the day, including Balzac, Heine, Bellini, Delacroix, Berlioz, Liszt, and Schumann—the latter proclaiming, "Hats off, gentlemen! A new genius!" Chopin's frail handsomeness, sensitive playing, and courteous manner placed him constantly in demand by the highest society.

Of his several romantic affairs, the most significant was with the novelist who called herself Georges Sand and scorned convention by wearing men's clothes. Her real name was Baroness Aurore Dudevant. She had married the baron in 1822 and separated from him in 1831, the same year Chopin arrived in Paris. She had already had several liaisons before becoming intimate with Chopin. Some say her attraction to him was mostly maternal. Whatever it was, it lasted from 1838 to 1847, and coincided with Chopin's most creative and productive period. His music was published simultaneously in Paris, Leipzig, and London.

When the Baroness broke up the relationship, Chopin's health—he had been battling tuberculosis since 1836—began to deteriorate. In need of money, he went to England in 1848, concertizing in Manchester, Glasgow, and Edinburgh before he collapsed and went back to Paris to die. Three thousand people attended his funeral at the famous Madeleine church. It is said that, following his last request, the container of Polish soil was poured upon his coffin.

No other composer devoted himself so exclusively to the piano. In his two romantic concertos, the orchestra is merely an accompaniment to the piano. His few other long works include three piano sonatas—the one in B flat minor contains the celebrated Funeral March—a sonata for cello and piano, and the *Andante Spianato* and *Grande Polonaise*. His short, solo works include 31 mazurkas, 14 polonaises, 19 waltzes, 14 nocturnes—a dreamy form created by the Irish composer, John Field (1782–1837)—24 preludes, 27 etudes, 4 ballades, 4 impromptus, marches, variations, 17 Polish songs, *Bolero, Berceuse, Barcarolle, Polonaise-fantasie*.

His melodies, unusual chords, and innovative harmonies influenced Liszt, Wagner, Fauré, Debussy, Grieg, Albéniz, Tchaikovsky, Rachmaninoff, and many other composers.

His life story was fantasized in the 1944 movie *A Song to Remember*, starring Cornel Wilde and Merle Oberon. Another version, *Impromptu*, was filmed in 1990, with Judy Davis and Hugh Grant. Chopin's music has been featured in many other films. His poignant Étude Opus 10 No. 3 was made into a popular French song of the thirties entitled "*Tristesse*" (Sadness). The cream of Chopin's music was distilled into the ballet *Les Sylphides*, produced in St. Petersburg in 1907, choreographed by the great Michael Fokine, with Anna Pavlova among the dancers. The opening measures of the *Military Polonaise* were played over and over on Radio Warsaw to bolster the nation's spirit as Hitler's army was approaching the capital. When the station went dead September 1, 1939, the people knew their country was once more in captivity.

Chopin's compositions continue to be played more than any others for the piano.

Franz Liszt

Liszt came on stage, shook his mane,
lifted his hands high and came crashing
down on the keys. Strings snapped,
great volumes of tone filled the air, and
a new world of pianistic color and
excitement was discovered as the king
of virtuosos swept up and down the
keyboard. . . . His recitals sent the
ladies into a Bacchanalian frenzy.
                    —Harold Schonberg (1915–),
                    The Great Pianists

Born: October 22, 1811, Raiding, Hungary
Died: July 31, 1886, Bayreuth, Germany

Son of a steward on one of the Esterházy estates, Liszt studied piano
with his father until the age of nine, by which time he showed so much
talent that a group of noblemen raised the funds to send him and his
family to Vienna to study with Carl Czerny. There his playing was
praised by Schubert and Beethoven. When he was twelve his father took
him to Paris, but the Conservatory did not accept him because the
director, Luigi Cherubini (1760–1842) disliked foreigners* and child
prodigies. This marked the end of his piano lessons, but the boy
continued to study composition.

Paris became Liszt's home between his many concert tours. His
friends were young writers and composers who took part in the Romantic movement: Victor Hugo, Hector Berlioz, Robert Schumann, Fred-
eric Chopin, and Niccolo Paganini, whose dazzling violin technique
spurred Liszt to strive for the same effects on the piano. He did this in
his *Hungarian Rhapsodies*, concert études and piano concertos.

Liszt became a legend both for his fantastic playing and his flamboyant lifestyle. In 1833, he fell in love with the already married Countess
Marie d'Agoult. They lived together until 1844, with homes in Italy and
Switzerland. (Of their three children, Cosima became the wife of Hans
von Bülow in 1857. This student of Liszt went on to become a respected
pianist and conductor. In 1869, Richard Wagner fell in love with
Cosima. Von Bülow unselfishly divorced her so she could marry the
passionate opera composer.)

* Cherubini was born in Italy!

After years of concertizing throughout Europe and Russia, where Liszt met the (also already married) Princess Carolyne Sayn-Wittgenstein, in 1848 he was given the full-time conducting post at the court of Weimar. In the decade he lived there with the Princess, he made Weimar a great music center, writing his major works: the *Faust* and *Dante* Symphonies and 12 symphonic poems—a form he introduced consisting of one-movement dramatic works telling a story. He also conducted new operas by Wagner, Berlioz and Verdi.

From 1861–69 he turned to religion and lived in Rome at the Villa d'Este. In 1865 he was given the title Abbé—a minor priest. He composed much liturgical music at this time, including the oratorio *Christus* and his *Missa Solemnis*. His organ works rank with those of César Franck.

From 1869 on, he returned to concertizing, spending his time between Rome, Weimar, and Budapest. The last five years of his life marked a new phase of composition in which his harmonies anticipated the Impressionism of Claude Debussy. In 1886, he made a jubilee tour to Paris and London to celebrate his seventy-fifth birthday. Returning to Weimar for the Bayreuth Festival, he became ill and died a few weeks later.

From all reliable accounts, Liszt was the greatest pianist who ever lived. Besides his own works, his repertory included almost everything from Scarlatti onwards. He invented the modern piano recital. He composed some of the most difficult piano music ever written, especially his *Transcendental Études*. His piano transcriptions of operas and other major works have never been surpassed. He wanted to make the piano sound like an orchestra, and extended chords, harmonies, and tempos that led the way to modern music.

His character was a contradictory combination of romantic and realistic, and his restless intellect was combined with ceaseless creativity. His generosity extended from teaching deserving pupils without a fee to playing benefit concerts for such causes as flooded Hungarian towns and the building of a monument to Beethoven in his birthplace, Bonn. He championed younger composers, notably Wagner. He was the leader of the "New German School," which alienated him from the Romantics like Brahms and Schumann, a process of progress inevitable in all the arts.

MOST FAMOUS PIANO COMPOSITIONS: 3 books of *Années de Pèlerinages* (Years of Pilgrimage), 3 *Liebesträume, Mephisto Waltz, Concert Études,*

20 *Hungarian Rhapsodies* (most of which he also orchestrated), Sonata in B minor, 2 Piano Concertos.

The 1960 movie *Song Without End*, starring Dirk Bogarde as the composer and Capucine as the Princess, takes the usual liberties with Liszt's life story, but is worth seeing for its elegance and, of course, the music.

Johannes Brahms

> *My musical credo is in the key of E flat major . . . which has three flats*: Bach, Beethoven, Brahms!*
> —Hans von Bülow, German pianist, conductor, composer (1893–94)

Born: May 7, 1833, Hamburg
Died: April 3, 1897, Vienna

Musicianship was in the family. His father was a double bass player in a theater orchestra. Brahms took piano lessons from age seven and at thirteen studied composition with Edward Marxsen, an exceptional teacher. From his father he learned how to play dance music on the violin, cello, and horn and to make arrangements for brass bands. He helped bring in money by playing at theaters and taverns at night—an experience that showed him the seamy side of life at an early age. He was fifteen when he gave his first public piano recital.

By the time he was twenty, his ability to transpose (switch from the written key to another) at sight brought him to the attention of the Hungarian violinist Eduard Remenyi. The virtuoso asked the young man to be his accompanist on a concert tour. Through this Brahms not only became acquainted with the gypsy music that would be translated into his twenty-one *Hungarian Dances*, but also met the great violinist Josef Joachim who would become his lifelong friend and to whom he would dedicate his brilliant, and only, violin concerto. Through Joachim he met Franz Liszt, who did not recognize his genius, and Robert and Clara Schumann, who did. Robert publicized his work in his music magazine and Clara played it in her many recitals throughout Europe.

Although Brahms's reputation as a pianist grew, he had trouble

* Called b's in German.

gaining recognition as a composer. His First Piano Concerto, now part of the popular repertoire, was not appreciated when he performed its premiere in Leipzig in 1859, because the style seemed so traditional and the public expected the "fireworks" of Liszt. It was his *German Requiem*, a non-religious work sung in German instead of the usual Latin, on which he worked from 1857–68, that earned him the international honor and financial security he deserved.

A perfectionist, Brahms took fifteen years to write his First Symphony, which was premiered in 1876 when he was forty-three. Its beauty and form definitely established him as the successor to Beethoven. It also inflamed the "battle" that was going on between supporters of the Weimar School led by Liszt and Wagner, who considered theirs "the music of the future," and the traditional Leipzig School represented by Mendelssohn, Schumann, and Brahms, whose spokesman was the influential Austrian critic Eduard Hanslick (1825–1904).

Brahms did not lead a dramatic life. He never attained his desire to conduct the Hamburg Philharmonic, but had temporary positions directing other choruses and orchestras, including those of Vienna, where he settled permanently in 1868.

Although he refused an honorary music doctorate from Cambridge, he did accept a Doctor of Philosophy degree from the University of Breslau in 1881, and wrote the *Academic Festival Overture* for the occasion.

In his personal life he concealed a shy, sensitive nature behind a mask of sarcasm and rude manners; yet he was generous to talented young musicians and helped the Czech composer Dvořák gain recognition.

When Robert Schumann was committed to an asylum, leaving Clara with seven children to support, Brahms moved into their house for two years. He helped take care of the children while Clara toured. A great many letters passed between them. Clara was fourteen years older than Johannes and apparently had no wish to be married again, but they remained lifelong friends. He never married. In 1896, when she lay dying, he assuaged his grief by writing the haunting *Four Serious Songs*. Shortly afterward, it was discovered that he had cancer. On March 7, 1897, he managed to attend a performance of his Fourth Symphony. At the end, the audience and the orchestra stood and applauded their tearful farewell. Less than a month later he was gone.

Brahms's style is considered traditional, but it bears his own unique sound. The form may be Classical and composed with technical perfection, but the warmth and lyricism is pure Romantic.

COMPOSITIONS: 4 symphonies, 2 piano concertos, 1 violin concerto, 1 double concerto for violin and cello, much chamber music, orchestral serenades, and variations, volumes of piano music, including lovely *Liebeslieder* (lovesongs), waltzes, intermezzi, and rhapsodies. Songs and song-cycles: He was another important composer of the German art song. Choral: *A German Requiem, Song of Destiny (Schicksalslied)*, and others.

Pyotr (Peter) Ilyich Tchaikovsky

> *I have striven to render in music all the anguish and the bliss of love.*
> —Pyotr Ilyich Tchaikovsky

Born: May 7, 1840, Votkinsk, Russia
Died: November 6, 1893, St. Petersburg

The best known of all Russian composers was born in the Ural Mountains of European Russia, where his father was a mining engineer. A sensitive child, he began to study piano but did not show any great talent. When he was ten, his family moved to St. Petersburg and sent him to the School of Jurisprudence. He did not want to part from his mother. Traumatically for him, she died when he was fourteen. He graduated from school at nineteen and became a law clerk in the Ministry of Justice. He remained there for four years, but during that time became increasingly involved in music, studying theory and composition with the eminent Anton Rubinstein. In 1863 he resigned his post to concentrate full time on music and entered the newly founded St. Petersburg Conservatory, where he spent the next two years.

Nicholas Rubinstein had just established the Moscow Conservatory and took a chance on the young composer, hiring him as a professor of music theory. Tchaikovsky retained this post for twelve years, composing all the while.

At this time the Russian Five—Mily Balakirev, Alexander Borodin, César Cui, Modeste Mussorgsky, and Nicolai Rimsky-Korsakov—were expounding their nationalism and trying to get away from the western European influence in Russian music. They chided Tchaikovsky for not following their lead.

The composer was on the verge of collapse between his workload and his tumultuous personal life. In 1877, in an effort to rid himself of the stigma of his homosexuality, he married a young music student who was even more emotionally unstable than he. After nine nightmarish weeks, during which he tried to catch pneumonia by throwing himself into the Moskva River, they separated. (He only caught a cold.) At this darkest of his many dark periods, a godsend occurred in the form of Nadezhda von Meck, the mother-in-law of his niece. This wealthy woman, who in the 1880s would hire Debussy to teach her children during summer vacations, now sent Tchaikovsky money to travel to Switzerland, France, and Italy, plus an annual subsidy—an arrangement lasting thirteen years during which they never met, but carried on a continuous correspondence. Despite his depression, he was able to write his most successful opera, *Eugene Onegin*, and the Fourth Symphony, which he dedicated to Madame von Meck.

Tchaikovsky met with an amazing amount of failures. His now so-popular Piano Concerto in B flat minor written for Nicholas Rubinstein was rejected by the artist as being "unplayable." His glorious Violin Concerto intended for Leopold Auer met the same response. The critical reaction to the 1877 premiere of *Swan Lake* was that the music was too symphonic for ballet. Even *Sleeping Beauty* and *The Nutcracker* were not successful at their first performances. Most ballet music up to this time had been a series of mediocre tunes strung together. Posterity would prove that Tchaikovsky raised the stature of ballet music to such a level that since 1900 serious composers such as Stravinsky, Khatchaturian, Prokofiev, Copland, Bernstein, and others have aspired to write for this genre.

Outside of Russia, Tchaikovsky was much in demand to conduct his own works, and made several tours of Europe. His fame spread to the United States. In 1891 he was invited to the dedication of New York's Carnegie Hall. He shared four concerts there with famed conductor Walter Damrosch. He also conducted in Philadelphia and Baltimore, where his co-conductor was operetta composer Victor Herbert. He was taken on sightseeing tours of Washington, D.C., and Niagara Falls and wrote glowingly in his diary of his American experience.

On returning to Russia he wrote his final symphony, the Sixth, to which his brother Modeste gave the title *Pathétique*. The composer conducted the first performance in St. Petersburg, October 28, 1893. Within nine days he was dead. It has always been believed that he died from drinking unboiled water during a cholera epidemic in the city. Recent evidence indicates that he was "tried" by a "court of honor" from his old school regarding his sexual behavior and given the "sentence" to commit suicide. Whatever the reason, it was a waste of a tremendous genius.

Fortunately for us, his credo was to write something every day, so that in the span of about twenty-five years he produced what was to be an impressive legacy of compositions.

Those who claim Tchaikovsky's music is too sentimental or morbid have not probed deep enough to realize the imagination and skill in its structure. To counter the accusation of "The Five," that his was not truly national music, it can be said that it was as Russian as the mixture of Russian, German, and French ideas which formed the culture of his time. Igor Stravinsky, who based his ballet *The Fairy's Kiss* on Tchaikovsky themes, said, "He was the most Russian of us all."

COMPOSITIONS: 6 symphonies, 2 piano concertos and other piano music, 1 violin concerto, 3 ballets, several operas—but only two still performed: *Eugene Onegin* and *Pique Dame (The Queen of Spades)*—tone poems, serenades, overtures, *Overture-Fantasie: Romeo and Juliet*, chamber music, suites, choral works, many songs.

A nation creates music—the composer
only arranges it.
        —Mikhail Glinka (1804–1857)

CHAPTER TEN

Men With a Country:
The Nationalists

Renaissance music and early opera derived mainly from Italy. With Bach, Handel, Gluck, Haydn, and Mozart dominating the scene during the seventeenth and eighteenth centuries, German influence pervaded music for the next two hundred years. In the middle 1800s as Romanticism stressed personal feelings, composers from other countries felt the need to express their own traditions. The use of folksongs and dances in symphonic music and historical events as subjects for operas, ballets, and program music led to the creation of a Nationalistic movement which continues to the present.

Chopin introduced Polish mazurkas and polonaises to Western Europe. In Russia, five composers, Balakirev, Cui, Mussorgsky, Borodin and Rimsky-Korsakov sought to develop a style free from Western influences and, in turn, influenced their contemporaries and those who came after them. Bohemia found its voice in Smetana, Dvořák, and Janáček. Hungary was represented by Liszt and later Dohnányi, Kodály, and Bartók. France ran the gamut from the romanticism of Franck, Gounod, Massenet, Lalo, Bizet, Saint-Saëns, Chabrier, and Fauré, the impressionism of Debussy and Ravel, and the eccentricity of Satie to the modernism of Poulenc, Milhaud, Honegger, d'Indy, Chausson, Roussel, and Ibert. Spain is represented by Albéniz, Granados, de Falla, Turina, and Rodrigo. Grieg *is* Norway. Sibelius *is* Finland. England, which had not produced any major composers since Purcell and the transplanted Handel, came alive with Sullivan, Elgar, Delius, Vaughan-Williams, Holst, Walton, Britten, and a large group of lesser known composers. Villa-Lobos of Brazil and Alberto Ginastera of Argentina put South America on the musical map. North America's contribution came from Gottschalk, Joplin, Ives, Gershwin, Copland, Menotti, Barber, and Bernstein, among others.

The Russian Five

Mikhail Glinka's opera, *A Life for the Tsar* (1836), planted the seed of Russo-nationalism. He inspired a group of composers who called themselves "The Five" and whose aim was to develop a pure Russian style. The leader was MILY BALAKIREV (1837–1910), who at the age of eighteen came from the provinces to St. Petersburg with firsthand knowledge of folk music. Apart from his fantasy *Islamey*, very little of his music is performed today, but he influenced the other four—Cui, Mussorgsky, Borodin and Rimsky-Korsakov—and to a certain extent, Tchaikovsky.

CÉSAR CUI (1835–1918) was a military engineer who became a composer as well as a writer. In journals, newspapers, and his book *Music in Russia* (1880), he put into words the nationalistic principles the Five were trying to convey in their music. Ironically, he is now mostly remembered by a short piano piece called *Orientale*.

MODEST MUSSORGSKY (1837–1881) was an officer in the St. Petersburg Guards when he met Cui and Balakirev. Although he was proficient on the piano, he had not studied harmony or composition, so took lessons from Balakirev. His life was marked by constant personal conflicts. He resigned his army commission in 1858. After the emancipation of the serfs in 1861 he had to spend two years helping manage the family estate. Next he worked in the Ministry of Communications, all the while continuing to compose. He began to drink after his mother's death in 1865. By 1867 he was dismissed from the ministry and spent the summer at his brother's house where he wrote one of his most famous compositions, (*St. John's*) *Night on Bald* (or *Bare*) *Mountain*, which Disney animated in *Fantasia*.

Of Mussorgsky's operas, only orchestral excerpts from *The Fair at Sorochinsk* (or *Sorochintsy Fair*) and *Khovansh(t)china* are popular concert favorites. The majestic *Boris Godunov*, however, is produced in its entirety all over the world. One of the few operas with a bass in the leading role, it brought the great Russian basso Fyodor Chaliapin (1873–1938) to world attention. This opera led the way for young Italian composers Mascagni and Leoncavallo in their search for realism.

Mussorgsky's most-played work is *Pictures at an Exhibition*, a set of piano pieces inspired by the paintings of his friend Victor Hartmann, which is superb program music, enabling the listener to "see" what he is hearing. It was orchestrated by Ravel in 1922.

Death came to Mussorgsky from alcoholic epilepsy, March, 1881. His many unfinished compositions were edited and completed by Rimsky-Korsakov. No composer with so little musical education ranks with Mussorgsky in influence on other composers, among them Debussy, Satie, de Falla, and Copland.

ALEXANDER BORODIN (1833–1887) was the illegitimate son of a Georgian prince. By sixteen he could play piano, violin, and cello. At twenty-eight, after qualifying in medicine, he took the post of lecturer at the St. Petersburg Medical Academy. His scientific research and writings made him an authority in the field of chemistry. He fulfilled the other love of his life, music, when he met Balakirev in 1862. He began to compose and made several concert tours as a pianist. He also managed to find time to marry (happily) and establish a School of Medicine for Women in 1872. He lectured there until his death on February 28, 1887, which ironically came in the midst of a party celebrating his return from a successful concert tour in Germany.

His clear style, sensitive harmonies, and rich orchestral colors are found in his major works, which include 2 symphonies, 2 string quartets, a tone poem, *On the Steppes of Central Asia*, 11 songs, and the opera, *Prince Igor* (also completed by Rimsky-Korsakov), from which the *Polovtsian Dances* are his most heard work. The crème of his music was cleverly woven into the 1953 Broadway musical *Kismet*. A recording of this is an excellent way to become acquainted with the most beautiful themes of this composer. The film version of *Kismet* was made in 1955.

NICOLAI RIMSKY-KORSAKOV (1844–1908) was born into an aristocratic family. He began piano lessons at six, entered the St. Petersburg Naval School at twelve, but continued to study piano. At twenty-three he met Balakirev, who introduced him to Cui, Mussorgsky, and Borodin, and encouraged him to compose. Upon graduation from the Naval School Rimsky-Korsakov was obliged to take a cruise around the world (1862–65). On his return he started composing his First Symphony, which he did through instinct since he had not studied harmony or theory. He taught himself both, and became an excellent theorist. In 1871 he began teaching at the St. Petersburg Conservatory, numbering among his students such future luminaries as Glazunov, Liadov, Arensky, Ippolitov-Ivanov, Gretchaninov, and Stravinsky. He resigned from the navy in 1873, but accepted a position as inspector of marine bands until 1884, when the post was abolished.

Besides completing the compositions of his deceased colleagues, Rimsky-Korsakov wrote fifteen operas which are seldom heard outside Slavic-speaking countries. His most popular works are the orchestral suites arranged from his operas *Le Coq d'Or* and *Tsar Sultan*, which contains the violin dazzler, "Flight of the Bumble Bee." "The Song of India" from the opera *Sadko* has become a popular piano piece. Other great concert favorites are *Scheherazade*, a suite from stories out of the *Arabian Nights, Capriccio espagnol, Russian Easter Overture* and the overture to his opera *May Night*. His very listenable Second Symphony, *Antar* (1897), deserves more exposure.

The Intermediate Generation

There followed a group of composers—all but one students of Rimsky-Korsakov—who were, unfortunately, relegated to second-class status because they arrived on the scene *after* the zenith of the Russian Nationalists and *before* the nucleus of modern Russian composers who would make such an impact on the twentieth century.

ANATOL LYADOV (1855–1914) followed the precepts of "The Five," but procrastination prevented him from gaining greater stature. His tone poems, *The Enchanted Lake, Baba Yaga, Kikimora*, and a piano piece, *The Music Box*, written between 1909 and 1914, show his sense of flowing orchestral color and enjoyed continued popularity. From 1878 he taught at the St. Petersburg Conservatory, with Prokofiev as one of his students.

MIKHAIL IPPOLITOV–IVANOV (1859–1935), after studying at the St. Petersburg Conservatory from 1875–1882, was active as an opera conductor as well as teacher at the Moscow Conservatory from 1893; he became director there after the Communist Revolution. His works, written in the style of Rimsky-Korsakov, include operas, chamber music, and orchestral pieces. His name survives with the well-known suite *Caucasian Sketches* (1895).

ANTON ARENSKY (1861–1906) became professor of harmony and counterpoint at the Moscow Conservatory from 1882–95, after which he succeeded Balakirev as director of the Imperial Chapel at St. Petersburg, 1895–1901. He wrote one opera, songs, a piano trio, and other melodic piano compositions. His main fame rests on his Suite for Two Pianos, with its exciting Waltz movement.

ALEXANDER GLAZUNOV (1865–1936) was the most prolific of the group. His first symphony was performed by Balakirev when Alexander was sixteen. A few years later he met Liszt at Weimar and heard Wagner's music. He taught at the St. Petersburg Conservatory in 1899, becoming director from 1905 until he left Russia in 1928. Dmitri Shostakovich was one of his students. Glazunov visited the United States in 1929, then made Paris his home for the rest of his life.

The bulk of his compositions—9 symphonies, 2 piano concertos, a violin concerto (usually in the repertoire of every major soloist), a saxophone concerto, and some chamber music—were written before World War I. His most-played works are excerpts from his ballet *Raymonda*, the tuneful suite from his other ballet *The Seasons*, and two lovely *Concert Waltzes*. With his blend of nationalism, virtuosity, and lyricism he represents the bridge back to the reconciliation of Russian and European music. Currently, there is a resurgence of interest in Glazunov's music.

VASSILY KALINNIKOV (1866–1901), although dogged by poverty, was fortunate to find a good teacher in Simon Kruglikov, with whom he studied in Moscow. In 1892 he met and was encouraged by Tchaikovsky, who had *his* publisher bring out some of the young composer's work. Suffering from tuberculosis, Kalinnikov sought the warmth of Yalta on the Black Sea. There Rachmaninoff found him living in such terrible conditions that he sent him money and saw to it that his two symphonies were published. The first was successful enough to be performed in Vienna and Berlin. The second had its premiere a year later in Kiev in 1898. His style, with its folk-like themes, shows the influence of Borodin.

Ironically, immediately after his death, Kalinnikov's widow was offered ten times the amount of money he had ever received to have the rest of his work published. This included the lyric tone poem *The Cedar and the Palm*, incidental music to *Tsar Boris*, and 2 Intermezzi for Orchestra. Recent CDs have been issued featuring most of his music. It has been predicated that if his life had not been cut short at thirty-five, Kalinnikov would have become a major Russian composer.

ALEXANDER SCRIABIN (1872–1915) was born in Moscow, on January 6, to his lawyer father and pianist mother. A prodigy, Alexander was in the same piano class as Rachmaninoff, under Zverev. At the Moscow Conservatory (1888–92), his teachers were Taneyev and Arensky. He taught piano at the Moscow Conservatory (1898–1903), but became bored and went to Switzerland. During his U.S. tour (1905–1906), his music was heard by conductor Serge Koussevitzky, who became a champion of his work. In Brussels, in 1908, Scriabin came under the influence of theosophy and mysticism. He now regarded his music as the "supreme ecstatic mystery." This is reflected in his Fourth Symphony (*Poem of Ecstasy*). He toured Russia with Koussevitzky's orchestra in 1910, and the following year performed his own compositions with the Concertgebouw Orchestra of Amsterdam, under Willem Mengelberg. In 1914, Scriabin visited London to give recitals and to solo in his own Piano Concerto at a concert which featured his Fifth Symphony (*Prometheus*), under the direction of Sir Henry Wood. On returning to Russia for another tour, he became ill and died in Moscow on April 27, from an infected tumor on his lip.

Chopin and Liszt influenced his early compositions. Later he developed the "mystic" chord, a series of fourths—C, F♯, B♭, E, A, D—a floating dissonance putting Scriabin on the threshold of atonality. Of his many piano compositions, the Étude in C♯ minor has been a favorite showpiece. Recently, there has been renewed interest in his music.

REINHOLD GLIÈRE (1875–1956) dovetailed the "Intermediate Generation" when he studied at the Moscow Conservatory (1894–1900) with Arensky, Taneyev, and Ippolitov-Ivanov. From 1913–20 he was Director of the Kiev Conservatory with Prokofiev and Khatchaturian among his pupils. Surviving the turbulent flow of history in his country, his work was nationalistic enough to find approval with the new Soviet regime after the 1917 Revolution. In addition to composing, Glière appeared regularly as a pianist and conductor. His compositions include three symphonies of which the third, *Ilya Murometz* is an international favorite. Four string quartets, 2 operas, a harp concerto, a cello concerto, 123 songs, 175 piano pieces, and much chamber music make up his considerable output. Of his two ballets, the overture to *The Bronze*

Horseman is a concert regular, but it is the suite from *The Red Poppy* which is his most popular work.

Bohemia (Czechoslovakia)

BEDŘICH SMETANA (1824–1884), considered the father of Bohemian music, had difficulty gaining recognition in his early struggling years. He tried to establish a music school in Prague, but it was a financial failure. The political climate of the city was in turmoil between those who wanted independence and those who were content to remain under Austrian rule. This added to his personal tragedy of the deaths of three of his four daughters. Seizing an opportunity, Smetana moved to Sweden to become director of the Göteborg Society of Classical Music. In the next five years he introduced audiences to the "new" music of Mendelssohn, Liszt, and Wagner, and began composing. His wife died in 1859 and he remarried. By 1861, following the defeat of the Austrians by Napoleon III, there was a reawakening of Czech culture which inspired Smetana to return to his native country. He finally met success with his first two operas. Of the six he wrote, *The Bartered Bride* (1866) contains the lively melodies and toe-tapping polkas that have become orchestral standards.

In 1874 he introduced Antonin Dvořák to the public by conducting the young composer's Symphony in E flat Major. Smetana's own major compositions are *Ma Vlast* (*My Country*), a cycle of six symphonic poems, the most famous of which is *Vltava* (*The Moldau*), depicting the course of the river from its source in the mountains down its 270-mile course through Prague. He also wrote ten brilliant Czech dances for piano and some choral works. The last movement of his string quartet, *From My Life* (1876), suggests the piercing whistling in his ears which began to haunt him. He became unbalanced enough to warrant being put into an asylum in April 1884, where he died a month later. As a national composer he was much loved for the patriotic spirit of his music. His use of history, legends, folklore, scenery, etc., gave the Czech people a new musical identity.

ANTONIN DVOŘÁK (1841–1904) started as a viola player in the band that became the Provisional Theatre Orchestra, first conducted by Wagner and from 1866 by Smetana. He became friends with Brahms, who saw to the publishing of some of his work. Dvořák had a successful career, especially with foreign performances. He was well received in

England and wrote his Seventh Symphony (1885) for the Philharmonic Society of Birmingham. He also received an honorary doctorate from Cambridge. He visited Russia in 1890. In 1891 he taught at the Prague Conservatory. From 1892–95 he was director of the National Conservatory in New York. During this time he composed his excellent String Quartets in F and E flat, the Cello Concerto and the *New World Symphony*, his Ninth and last. While in the U.S. he spent the summers in Spillville, Iowa, home of many Czech farmers. His house still stands there. He returned to Prague and fulfilled his dream of writing a successful opera, *Rusalka*, in 1901.

Despite all his awards and honors, Dvořák remained a modest man, loyal to his Czech nationality. He admired Classical composers like Mozart, Haydn, Beethoven, and Schubert and was attracted to aspects of Wagner's style and, to a certain extent, emulated the symphonic form of his friend Brahms. His music is full of folk rhythms and his style is rich and eloquent. His much-played compositions include 9 symphonies, a piano concerto, a violin concerto, a very popular cello concerto, 5 symphonic poems, 2 Slavonic rhapsodies, 2 sets of foot-stomping *Slavonic Dances*, a set of lively *Legends*, rich chamber and choral music, including a *Requiem*.

LEOŠ JANÁČEK (1854–1928) was twenty-five when he enrolled in the Leipzig Conservatory after having spent his younger years as a schoolteacher and choral director in Brno. He returned there in 1881 and married one of his students. Besides immersing himself in Moravian folk music, he founded an organ school and edited a musical journal. He started composing operas and orchestral suites, but it was *Jenůfa*, an opera on which he worked from 1894–1903—it had its Prague premiere in 1916—that made his name known outside Czechoslovakia. Well into his sixties, Janáček composed three more operas between 1919 and 1925. This creativity may have been inspired by his pride in the newly acquired independence of his country after World War I. He was awarded a doctorate from Masaryk University on his seventieth birthday. His famous *Sinfonietta* was written in 1926.

His later style is very modern, the orchestration striking and sometimes quite harsh. Although he was first known as an instrumental composer, Janáček is now regarded as one of the most original opera composers of the twentieth century.

JOSEF SUK (1874–1935) not only studied composition with Antonin Dvořák, but married his daughter. His early works, such as the tuneful *Serenade* in E flat for strings, were naturally influenced by Dvořák, but following the trend of the early twentieth century, he turned to a more complex harmonic style, sometimes bordering on atonality. His best works are on CDs. The Czech violinist Josef Suk (1929–), is his grandson.

BOHUSLAV MARTINŮ (1890–1959) was born in the bell tower of the village church in Policka, where his father was a watchman. His first violin studies were at age seven with the local tailor. In his teens he went to the Prague Conservatory (1906–09), the Prague Organ School, and played in the second violin section of the Czech Philharmonic. The year 1923 saw him in Paris taking private lessons with Albert Roussel (1869–1937). His progressive compositions became known in Europe. In 1932, his String Sextet won the Elizabeth Sprague Coolidge award.

Martinů fled the June 1940 German invasion of Paris, and reached New York via Portugal in 1941. After the liberation of Czechoslovakia in 1945, he was unable to accept the offer of a teaching position at the Prague Conservatory, but later became a visiting professor at Princeton (1948–51). Despite spending most of his life abroad, Martinů 's music reflected the spirit of his homeland. In his lyric work, *Memorial to Lidice*, he immortalized the martyrdom of all the men and boys over the age of sixteen who had been executed by the Nazis in the 1943 village massacre. In 1953, the composer returned to Europe, spending the remaining years of his life in Switzerland. Twenty years after his death, his remains were returned to the family masoleum. Martinů 's centennial was celebrated in 1990 throughout his homeland. His huge volume of works includes opera, ballets, orchestral, vocal, and chamber music.

Poland

After Chopin, Polish music lay dormant until the giant leap by several composers into the modern era.

IGNACE JAN PADEREWSKI (born Kurylowka, November 18, 1860; died, New York, June 29, 1941) was a pianist, composer, and statesman. A child prodigy, he studied at the Warsaw Music Institute in Berlin, and with Polish pianist Theodor Leschetizky (1830–1915) in Vienna. He started composing at the age of six. In 1988, his internationally famous piano career began with an extensive concert tour, including Europe, South Africa, Australia, New Zealand, and North and South America. During the summers he composed, producing the opera *Manru* (1892–1901), the Symphony Op. 24, and the *Fantaisie* polonaise Op. 19 for the piano and orchestra and the Piano Concerto (1888)—all typical of the late Romantic Polish national school. His most famous piano miniature is his *Minuet in G.*

Paderewski worked tirelessly for the Polish cause during World War I and became Prime Minister and Foreign Minister of the first government when Poland became an independent nation in 1919. In 1922 he returned to his music career, his recitals raising much money for war victims. He sponsored several competitions which are perpetuated by the Paderewski Foundation. In 1937 he appeared in the British film *Moonlight Sonata*, showcasing his talent. From 1936–38, he supervised a complete edition of the works of Chopin, which was published in Warsaw. He died in New York, June 29, 1941, when heartbreakingly his country was once again enslaved—this time by the Germans during World War II.

KAROL SZYMANOWSKI (born: Ukraine, October 6, 1882; died: Switzerland, March 29, 1937) came from a well-to-do family, which, like many other wealthy Poles, owned land in this part of Russia. His early musical promise sent him to study in Warsaw in 1903. He lived in Berlin 1905–1908 and, influenced by Richard Strauss, wrote his first symphony there. Returning home, Szymanowski's work began to be championed by other Polish musicians, especially pianist Arthur Rubinstein, and violinist Paul Kochansky, who inspired his first violin concerto. After travelling in Europe he became director of the Warsaw Conservatory (1926–30) revolutionizing its teaching methods. *Stabat Mater* (1928) was his first national triumph. In 1933–34 the composer toured Europe as a solo pianist, but his continued battle with tuberculosis put an end to his career.

Four symphonies, two violin concertos, orchestral, chamber and a large number of piano and vocal works show the characteristics of the twentieth-century composer graduating from "Impressionism" to experimenting with tonality and unusual rhythms. His return to Poland, influenced by Chopin, inspired his nationalism. The opera *King Roger* (1920–24) is considered the composer's best work.

WITOLD LUTOSLAWSKI (born: Warsaw, January 25, 1913) studied in his birthplace and worked as a pianist in cafés from 1939 to 1945, meanwhile writing musical works in a folk song style. After 1956, the influence of Webern surfaced as he briefly used the twelve note system. He proceeded to an aleatory style combined with traditional harmonic patterns. This is evident in his Second (1967) and Third (1983) symphonies, concertos for cello (1970), oboe, and harp (1980), and settings of

French verse with chorus. Lutoslawski has been internationally active as a teacher and conductor of his own music.

KRZYSZTOF PENDERECKI (born: Debica, November 23, 1933) attended the Krakow High School for Music (1955–58) where he became a teacher and its director in 1972. He taught at Yale School of Music from 1975. An avant-garde composer, his experiments with sound include sawing wood, rustling paper, knocking, screeching, hissing, clacking typewriters, and other original effects from singers and conventional instruments. Some of these were put to artistic use in his *St. Luke Passion* (1966). Of his orchestral, chamber, and choral works, the most famous is *Threnody for the Victims of Hiroshima* for 52 strings (1960).

HENRYK MIKOLAJ GÓRECKI (1933–) began formal music studies in his twenties in his native Poland. During the 1960s, he travelled to Paris and Darmstadt (Germany), meeting prominent proponents of postwar serialism like Pierre Boulez and Karlheinz Stockhausen. By 1965, he was moving away from dissonance and immersing himself in Catholicism and folk song studies. The political climate of his country hindered his recognition, and after he resigned a teaching post in 1979, his compositions were boycotted. This gave the composer a chance to refine his work without the pressures of performance schedules.

A gradual international following with champions in the West, such as conductor Dennis Russell Davies and the Kronos String Quartet, swelled to adulation after the 1992 release of Górecki's Third Symphony (1976) on Nonesuch with soprano Dawn Upshaw. This emotionally powerful work is an amalgam of a fifteenth-century Polish prayer, (Mary mourning the death of Christ), the opening lines of the Polish *Ave Maria* carved in a Gestapo cell by an eighteen-year-old female prisoner, and a Polish folksong portraying a mother's anguish over her son killed in battle ("He lies in his grave and I know not where . . ."). Commissions are now pouring in from all over the world.

Hungary

The length of Liszt's life, seventy-five years, cast his shadow over more than a generation of composers, musical trends, and historic events. His influence was felt everywhere in music circles and especially in his native Hungary where three major composers took up the flag of musical nationalism when he relinquished it in 1886.

ERNO (ERNST) VON DOHNÁNYI (1877–1960) after studying at the

Budapest Academy (1894–97) gained immediate success as an international pianist—ranked among the greatest—and composer. From 1905–15 he taught at the Berlin Hochschule. In 1919 he returned to Budapest as director of the Conservatory, teaching, conducting, composing and concertizing. One of his pupils was Georg Solti, one of the foremost conductors of our time. In 1931 von Dohnányi became the director of the Hungarian radio, but returned to the Hochschule in 1934. He settled in the United States in 1949.

Considered one of the chief architects of twentieth-century Hungarian music, his work contains a blend of Liszt's virtuosity and Brahms's orchestration. Besides championing the music of his fellow countrymen Kodály and Bartók, von Dohnányi's influence was far-reaching. He wrote 3 operas (1912, 1922, 1929), 2 symphonies (1901, 1944), 2 piano concertos (1898, 1947), 2 piano quintets (1895, 1914) 2 violin concertos (1915, 1950), a violin and a cello sonata, 3 string quartets (1899, 1906, 1926) and piano music including 4 rhapsodies. His most popular composition is *Variations on a Nursery Song* (1914). His grandson, Christoph, born in Berlin in 1929, is also a prominent conductor, having led the Frankfurt and Hamburg Opera Orchestras, the London Philharmonic, and, since 1984, the Cleveland Symphony.

ZOLTÁN KODÁLY (1882–1967) grew up in a musical atmosphere with his father playing violin and his mother, piano. In 1900 he entered Budapest University and the Liszt Academy of Music, studying with János Koessler, teacher of von Dohnányi and Bartók. He graduated in 1905 and began a collaboration with Bartók, collecting and transcribing folksongs. Traveling to Bayreuth, Salzburg, Berlin, and Paris gave him a wider view of music styles. He brought the music of Debussy back to Bartók, with whom he worked side by side. Their first quartets were played in companion concerts in 1910, marking the entrance of twentieth-century Hungarian music.

Kodály's melodic inspiration confined itself to Hungarian material. His compositions are finely crafted and harmonically smooth. They include three operas of which the one based on folk hero *Háry János* is most popular as a suite. He also wrote much choral, chamber, and orchestral music. His typically ethnic *Dances of Galánta*, the province where he was raised, is also one of his most played works. Another of his contributions is a method, named after him, for teaching music to children.

BÉLA BARTÓK (1881–1945) began lessons with his mother, who raised the family after his father died when Béla was eight. In 1894 they moved to Bratislava where the boy attended the Gymnasium (High School) at which von Dohnányi was an older student. Bartók studied piano and began composing. In 1898 he was accepted at the Vienna Conservatory, but followed von Dohnányi to the Budapest Academy (1899–1903), taking piano from Istvan Thoman, a pupil of Liszt, and composition with János Koessler. Here Bartók absorbed the music of Wagner and Richard Strauss. In 1903 his symphonic poem *Kossuth* showed the influence of Strauss while retaining the Hungarian elements of Liszt. In 1904 he began a career as a pianist, performing his own "Lisztian" virtuoso showpieces. In 1907 he was appointed Thoman's successor at the Academy.

The authentic Magyar folk music elements as well as the influence of Strauss and Mussorgsky began emerging in his music. After World War I the styles of Stravinsky and Schoenberg could be detected in the more complex music of his two violin sonatas (1921–2).

Bartók was now gaining international esteem. His first piano concerto in 1926 uses the piano as a percussion instrument, like a xylophone. His search for new sounds and rhythms continue in the next two string quartets.

Divorced and remarried in 1923, Bartók and his wife left war-torn Europe in 1940 and settled in New York, where he never felt at home. Finances were shaky and so was his health, but he managed to write the exciting *Concerto for Orchestra* in 1943 and his Third Piano Concerto in 1945 to leave his widow with an income. The vitality of his music insures its continued success.

Israel

PAUL BEN-HAIM (1897–1984) was born in Munich, where he studied at the Academy. In 1931 he emigrated to Palestine, which was a protectorate of the British Empire until granted its independence in 1949 to become the country of Israel. Ben-Haim assumed his Hebrew name and began composing in a style combining Middle Eastern music and Western tradition. His works include two symphonies written during World War II, concertos for violin (1960) and cello (1962), chamber and choral pieces.

ALEXANDER URIAH BOSKOVICH (1907–1964) was born in Transylvania, Roumania. He studied at the Vienna Academy (1924) and in Paris (1925) with Paul Dukas, Nadia Boulanger and Alfred Cortot. He worked as a conductor and pianist before emigrating to Palestine in 1938, where he taught at the Tel Aviv Academy. His compositions synthesize contemporary style with Jewish traditional music. He wrote his major works in the 1960s—*Daughter of Israel*, a cantata, and *Concerto da camera*. He was music critic for the Israeli newspaper *Ha'aretz* (1955–1964). One of his many students was Shulamit Ran, now a prominent U.S. woman composer.

OEDOEN PARTOS (1907–1977) was born in Hungary where he studied violin with Jenö Hubay (1858–1937) and Zoltán Kodály (1882–1967) at the Royal Academy of Music in Budapest (1918–1924). In 1938 he went to Palestine, becoming first violist in 1956 in what was renamed the Israel Philharmonic. In 1951 he became director of the Tel Aviv Academy of Music. He was the soloist at the premieres of his three viola concertos. In 1971 he went to the Netherlands, experimenting with thirty-one-tone scales proposed by Dutch mathematician Christiaan Huygens. He won the UNESCO prize in 1952 for his symphonic fantasy *Ein Gev*. His enormous output includes much orchestral, chamber, piano, and vocal music.

JOSEF TAL (1910–) studied with Paul Hindemith, among others, at the Berlin Hochschule für Musik. He emigrated to Palestine in 1934 and became a piano and composition instructor at the conservatory in Jerusalem (1936). The conservatory was renamed the Israel Academy of Music in 1948, and Tal served as director until 1952. He was head of the musicology department at the Hebrew University and director of the Israel Center of Electronic Music. He appeared as pianist and conductor with the Israel Philharmonic and with orchestras in Europe. In 1971 Tal was awarded the State of Israel Prize. In 1975 he received the Arts Prize of the City of Berlin, and in 1982 was made a fellow of its Institute of Advanced Studies. His vast amount of compositions include choral works to Hebrew texts, 3 symphonies, 5 piano concertos (No. 4 and No. 5 with tape), ballets, operas, and chamber music.

MORDECAI SETER (1916–) was born in Russia. He went to Palestine at age ten and then to Paris, where he completed his studies with Dukas and Boulanger (1934–37). Returning to what was now Israel in 1951, he taught at the University of Tel Aviv until his retirement as professor emeritus in 1985. His honors include Prix d'Itale (1962), the Israel State Prize (1965), and the A.C.U.M. (1983). His style is influenced by Jewish liturgical chants and serialism. Compositions include *The Daughter of Jeptha* for orchestra (1965), and *Jerusalem*, a symphony for chorus and orchestra (1966).

JAKOB GILBOA (1920–). Born in Czechoslovakia, Jakob grew up in Vienna and went to Palestine in 1938. He studied composition with Tal in Jerusalem, and Ben-Haim in Tel Aviv (1944–47), after which he went to Germany to study new music with Karlheinz Stockhausen (1928–) and other electronic avant-garde composers. His music is a blend of oriental and Eastern Mediterranean idioms, lyrical yet ultra-modern.

TZVI AVNI (1927–) was born in Germany and emigrated to Palestine in 1935, studying with Mordecai Seter at the Tel Aviv Academy of Music, from which he graduated in 1958. He also took private orchestration lessons with Paul Ben-Haim. In the summer of 1963, Avni came to the Berkshire Music Center in Tanglewood to study with Aaron Copland and Lukas Foss. He also studied electronic music at Columbia University in New York. From 1961 to 1975 he was the director of the Central Music Library in Tel Aviv and taught electronic music at the Rubin Academy in Jerusalem. Avni was the chairman of the Israel League of Composers (1978–1980). In 1986 he was awarded the A.C.U.M. prize for his life's work.

MARK KOPYTMAN (1929–) studied at the Moscow Conservatory and taught at several music institutes in his native Russia before emigrating to Israel, where he joined the Rubin Academy of Music in Jerusalem in 1974. He was also a guest professor at the University of Pennsylvania in 1985.

NOAM SHERIFF was born in Tel Aviv in 1935. He studied composition with Ben-Haim (1949–57) and also at the Hochschule für Musik in Berlin (1960–62). He taught at the Jerusalem Academy of Music from 1966, and at the National Academy in Tel Aviv in 1967. His modern atonal style is based on Jewish folk rhythms.

AMI MAAYANI (1936–). A native-born Israeli (sabra), he studied privately with Ben-Haim (1956–1960), at the same time taking courses in architecture in Haifa. Like Tzvi Avni, he worked on electronic music with Ussachevsky at Columbia University in the 1960s. His works use Near Eastern elements, and include orchestral and choral compositions. He is best known for his Harp Concerto No. 1 (1960) and the *Toccata* (1961).

Norway

EDVARD GRIEG (1843–1907), considered the voice of Norway, received his first music lessons from his mother, from whom he learned the folksongs of his country. At fifteen, on the advice of Norway's foremost violinist, Ole Bull, he was sent to study at the Leipzig Conservatory. Here he started to compose in the style of Schumann and Mendelssohn. In 1864 he met the nationalist Rikard Nordraak, who encouraged the composer to popularize Norwegian music. In 1867 he married his cousin Nina Hagerup, a soprano, who inspired and interpreted many of his songs. He settled in Christiania, (Oslo) where he taught and composed. Asked by the playwright Henrik Ibsen to write the incidental music to his play *Peer Gynt,* it turned out to be one of Grieg's greatest compositions and made him a national figure. In 1874, Grieg received a pension from the government which left him free of financial worries. His music was admired by Liszt, Brahms, and Tchaikovsky. He was also honored in England, where he met Delius and Grainger and received music doctorates from Cambridge (1894) and Oxford (1906).

Although he never wrote large forms such as symphonies or operas, the lyrical quality of Grieg's music was masterfully styled with great emotional depth. His largest work is his Piano Concerto in A minor—considered the most popular of *all* piano concertos. Liszt played it at sight from the manuscript in 1870. Grieg's other works include *Norwegian Dances, Lyric Pieces,* concert overtures, songs, chamber music, and much piano music. Besides the concerto, if one were pressed to choose the most outstanding compositions, they would be the *Holberg Suite* for strings, the two poignant *Elegiac Melodies* ("Heartwounds" and "The Last Spring"), and, in both piano or orchestral arrangement, the joyous *Wedding Day at Troldhaugen* (the name of his house outside Bergen). Uniquely, it may be said that *everything* Grieg wrote is beautiful—the life's work of a happy, fulfilled man.

Scandinavia

Several other composers emerged form Scandinavia. One of the earliest is JOHAN HELMICH ROMAN (1694–1758), who studied in England and met Handel. He was the first Swedish composer of real significance. He toured Europe 1735–37, and founded Stockholm's first public concerts. His writings include sacred music, songs, orchestral suites, symphonies, concertos, and chamber works.

One of Grieg's contemporaries in Norway was JOHAN SVENDSEN (1840–1911) who began his career as a violin virtuoso. Like Grieg, he also studied at the Leipzig Conservatory, where he became interested in composition. Grieg considered his first symphony strongly national. Svendsen traveled to Paris and Bayreuth where he met Liszt and became friends with Wagner. He also visited London before returning to his homeland to conduct the Christiania Music Society Concerts (1872–77) and continue composing. His works include 2 symphonies, a cello concerto, a violin concerto, 4 Norwegian Rhapsodies, *Carnaval à Paris,* songs, chamber music, and his most-played composition, *Romance* for violin and orchestra. He contributed to the culmination of nationalism in Norway.

CHRISTIAN SINDING (1856–1941) was stylistically Grieg's heir in his lyrical piano pieces and songs, but after studying at the Leipzig Conservatory (1874–78) and spending time in Germany he absorbed much of that culture through the influence of Wagner and Richard Strauss. He also taught at the Eastman School of Music in Rochester, New York, from 1921–22. He enjoyed fame in his lifetime, received a government pension, and produced a large number of compositions including an opera, 4 symphonies, a piano concerto, 3 violin concertos, and chamber pieces. His bravura solo, *Rustle of Spring,* has made Sinding known to every piano student.

CARL NIELSEN (1865–1931) was a notable Danish composer who studied at the Copenhagen Conservatory (1884–86), toured Europe in 1890–91 and produced his first symphony in 1892 in the style of Brahms. From 1889–1905 he was a violinist in the Danish court orchestra. He became an international figure and conducted his works abroad. His unusual harmonies, progressive tonality (pieces ending in a different key from which they began) characterize the dramatic style of his compositions: 2 operas, 6 symphonies, violin, flute, and clarinet concertos, songs, choral music, chamber music, piano and organ music. Excerpts from his second opera, *Maskarade* (1906), and his *Little Suite* (1888) are the most familiar.

HUGO ALFVÉN (1872–1960), a Swedish composer and violinist, spent from 1887 to 1890 in the Stockholm Conservatory, while also studying art. He was Director of Music at the University of Uppsala from 1910–39. His five symphonies, choral works and songs show the painter's subtlety in harmony and timbre. Alfvén burst upon the American public when his Swedish Rhapsody, *Midsummer Vigil,* which he wrote in 1903, suddenly became a popular tune in the 1950's.

KURT ATTERBERG (1887–1974) another Swedish composer, was at the Stockholm Conservatory from 1910 to 1911. Although he worked in the patent office from 1912 to 1968, he managed to compose 6 symphonies, 5 operas, 5 concertos, and other works. He was also a writer and music critic in the *Stockholms Tidningen* from 1910 to 1957, and served as secretary for the Royal Academy of Music from 1940 to 1953. His music is tunefully orchestrated and deserves more international recognition. His *Suite Pastorale* is delightful!

DAG WIRÉN (1905–1986) studied in Stockholm and Paris. First considered neo-classical—a twentieth-century version of the Baroque style with which many modern composers countered the excessive orchestration of Romanticism—from 1944 Wirén used "Metamorphosis technique and constructed his compositions from a single cell or set of cells. Although Sweden was neutral during World War II, in 1940 he wrote a radio opera, *Blått, gult röt* (1940), inspired by Winston Churchill's "Blood, Sweat and Tears" speech which buoyed British spirits in the dark days when London was being bombed night after night and it looked as though Hitler would invade the country. Wirén is considered the most modern Scandinavian composer.

LARS-ERIK LARSSON (1908–1986), after studying at the Stockholm Conservatory 1925–29, went to Vienna and Leipzig, then conducted for Swedish radio 1937–54. He taught at the Stockholm Conservatory 1947–59 and Uppsala University 1961–66. His variety of style ranges from post-Sibelius to neo-classical. His compositions include 3 symphonies, a saxophone concerto, a violin concerto, 12 concertinos, 3 concert overtures, a serenade for strings, and 3 string quartets. His lovely light music to Shakespeare's *A Winter's Tale* has been released on a compact disc. This is a composer worth getting to know.

Finland

JEAN SIBELIUS (1865–1957) is known as the voice of Finland. Composing before he received any technical instruction, he made up for this by quitting law school after one year (1885–86) to study at the conservatories of Helsinki, Berlin, and Vienna. From 1892 to 1897 he taught at the Helsinki Music Institute. Inspired by the patriotic feelings which were sweeping the country in protest to Russian domination (Finland had been a grand duchy of Russia until 1917), he composed a choral symphony, *Kullervo*, based on the national folk epic, *Kalevala*. His tone poem *Finlandia* (1899) was banned by the Czar because it aroused such fervor in the people.

Stylewise, it took Sibelius another decade to emerge from the powerful influence of Tchaikovsky, but his masterful orchestral technique and innate formal structure reflected Brahms. Meanwhile, he wrote the tuneful *Karelia Suite* (1893) and four Legends from the *Kalevala*, both featuring the folk hero Lemminkäinen. His Violin Concerto written in 1903 was his farewell to nineteenth-century Romanticism. Its warm second movement reflects his visit to Italy. After this he developed his own distinctive style in which fragments of themes evolve to complete melodies which lead to powerful, triumphant climaxes. By using the melodic and rhythmic patterns characteristic of Finnish folk poetry and music, he created his own unique nationalism.

In 1897 the Finnish government voted to give Sibelius a pension for life, leaving him free to compose, which he did until the 1920s. He did some traveling in the early years, to England in 1905, and again after World War I in 1921 and 1923. In America he conducted his tone poem *The Oceanides* commissioned by the Norfolk, Connecticut, Festival in 1914. The last thirty years of his life were spent receiving admirers from abroad and honors from his own country. In 1904 he bought land outside Helsinki and built a house where he lived the rest of his life with his wife and five daughters.

His influence was felt in Scandinavia, England, and America, but was resisted in France and Germany. His major compositions: 7 symphonies, 1 violin concerto, many tone poems, chamber, piano music, choral music, and songs were balanced by a great number of light works and theater music. Most popular are his Second and Fifth Symphonies, the Violin Concerto, the *Karelia Suite, Finlandia, Suite Mignonne, The Swan of Tuonela,* incidental music to Shakespeare's *The Tempest*, the tone poem *Tapiola,* and *Valse Triste*. Sibelius is the voice of the north, sometimes brooding and tragic, yet often sunny and warm.

AULIS SALLINEN (1935–), born in Salmi, studied at the Sibelius Academy in Helsinki (1955–60), was managing director of the Finnish Radio Orchestra for the next ten years, and taught at his alma mater from 1963 to 1970. He was the first person to receive the government-bestowed title Professor of Arts for Life (from 1981). In 1983, with Polish composer Krzysztof Penderecki, he won the Withuri International Sibelius Prize. In the 1970s he turned from his avant-garde style of the previous decade and concentrated on opera—*The Horseman* (1876), *The Red Line* (1978) and *The King Goes to France* (1984)—using as sources Orff, Janáček, and Shostakovich. Sallinen has also written ballets, symphonies, concertos, and chamber and vocal music.

France

After sharing the Baroque limelight via Lully, Rameau, and Couperin, French music lurked in the shadow of the German classicists until Belgian born CÉSAR FRANCK (1822–1890) became one of the first Romantic composers to return France to the forefront of the musical scene.

From touring his native Belgium as a pianist at the age of eleven, Franck went to Paris to study in 1835. At the Conservatory from 1837 to 1842, he concentrated on composition; after graduation, he made the French capital his home. In 1858 he became organist of the church of Sainte-Clotilde where his outstanding improvisational skill caused Liszt to compare him to Bach. At a time when the French concentrated only on opera, Franck, appointed professor of organ at the Conservatory in 1872, taught his pupils—among whom were the young composers d'Indy, Chausson, Duparc, Pierné, and Widor—the greatness of the instrumental music of Bach and Beethoven.

Although Franck was made Chevalier du Légion d'Honneur in 1885, his compositions were not really appreciated during his lifetime, except by his pupils, who worshipped him. His major compositions were written after the age of fifty, his greatest after sixty; the only real public success he had was the String Quartet, performed in the last year of his life. All of which did not affect his rather saintlike character.

Franck's style, with its rich, chromatic harmonies stemming from years of improvisation on the organ, is unmistakable. His only Symphony in D minor and his *Symphonic Variations* for Piano and Orchestra are now standards. His tone poems *Les Éolides, Le Chasseur maudit* (The Accursed Hunter), *Les Djinns,* and *Psyché*, have several recordings, but not enough performances. His oratorio, *Les Beatitudes*, took him ten years (1869–79) to complete. Among other choral, chamber, organ, and piano works is his lovely song *Panis angelicus* and the flowing Sonata for Violin and Piano, which has also been arranged for cello and piano and flute and piano.

CHARLES GOUNOD (1818–1853) like Franck studied at the Paris Conservatory—he won the Prix de Rome in 1839—and became an organist with a thought to the priesthood, an idea he abandoned in favor of devoting himself to composition. Of his many works—operas, oratorios, church music, and miscellaneous pieces—he is mainly remembered for two of his operas, *Faust* (1859) and *Romeo and Juliet* (1867); the *Ave Maria*, which he adapted as a song from Bach's C Major

Prelude from the *Well-Tempered Clavier*, and the *Funeral March of a Marionette*, known to a generation as the theme of Alfred Hitchcock's murder-mystery television show. His pleasant Symphony No. 1 in D gets too rare a hearing.

JACQUES OFFENBACH (1819–1880) was born in Cologne, but attended the Paris Conservatory and made his home in France, where he became a conductor of the Theatre Français. Of his ninety operettas, the best-known is *The Tales of Hoffman*, featuring the famous *Barcarolle*.

EDOUARD LALO (1823–1892), after his conservatory training became a violinist and teacher in Paris in the 1850s. He showed great interest in chamber music at a time when opera dominated the musical scene. By the 1870s he had established his immortal niche with the lovely *Symphonie espagnole*, a five movement violin concerto (1874). There is also a vigorous Cello Concerto (1877). His ballet score *Namouna* (1881) is known through the orchestral suites arranged therefrom. The overture to his opera *Le Roi d'Ys* (1888) is a concert favorite.

GEORGES BIZET (1838–1875) was admitted into the Paris Conservatory at the age of ten, and studied under Gounod and Jacques Halévy (remembered for his opera, *La Juive*). He married Halévy's daughter Geneviève in 1869. Bizet became a brilliant pianist, writing many compositions for that instrument. The duet, *Jeux d'enfants* (Childrens' Games) enjoys continuing popularity in orchestral form. The best-known of his many songs is *The Maids of Cadíz*. In 1855, while still at the Conservatory, Bizet wrote his lively Symphony in C which was not unearthed for its premiere until 1935! Of his other compositions the tone poems *Roma* and *La Patrie* are very tuneful, but his operas were not well received.

After his death, popular orchestral suites were made from *L'Arlesienne* (The Girl from Arles) and *The Fair Maid of Perth*. *The Pearl Fishers* (1863) is recently enjoying a revival. The beautiful tenor-baritone duet from this opera has been "elevated" to the status of a "popular song" by being featured in the 1981 Australian film *Gallipoli*, as well as being arranged for woodwinds on the compact disc *Voices for Winds*.

The supreme irony of Bizet's life was its premature end due to two heart attacks brought on in part by his depression over the cool reception of his masterpiece, *Carmen*. Shocked by the "obscenity" of the raw passion, jealousy and lurid characters, critics condemned the work at its premiere, March 3, 1875. The composer died exactly three months later on June 3 not knowing that, despite the critics, audiences flocked to see the opera thirty-seven times in that year alone, from which time it has kept its place as the most popular opera in the world.

CAMILLE SAINT-SAËNS (1835–1921) began composing at the age of six. Five years later at his first public concert he played a Mozart and a Beethoven piano concerto and was compared to the prodigy Mozart by such composers as Gounod, Rossini, and Berlioz. He studied with Halévy after entering the Paris Conservatory in 1848. From 1857–75, in his position at the famed Paris church, the Madeleine, Liszt hailed him as the world's greatest organist. He also taught at the École Niedermeyer, where Fauré was one of his pupils. In 1871 he co-founded the *Societé Nationale de Musique* to promote French orchestral music.

Composing prolifically for most of his eighty-six years, Saint-Saëns imparted to his music the French elements of clarity, elegance, and graceful harmonies. His tremendous output of operas, choral, orchestral, piano, organ, and chamber works provide a vast field to explore. Of his twelve operas, only *Samson and Delilah* remains in the international repertoire, although the overture to *La Princesse jaune* (The Yellow Princess) is on recordings. His Third Symphony, the "Organ," is his most popular. There are five piano concertos with the Second the favorite. From his five violin concertos, the Third is the most played, while two shorter works: the *Havanaise* and *Rondo Capriccioso* are standards for violin virtuosos. His other well-known compositions are *Carnival of the Animals*, each segment of which playfully depicts a different form of wildlife, and the *Danse Macabre*, which is more humorous than morbid in its bone-rattling rhythm. *Omphale's Spinning Wheel* is his most-liked tone poem. Awarded many honors, the composer wrote on musical, scientific, and historical topics and traveled throughout Europe, North Africa, the United States, and South America, concertizing to within the last few months of his long, successful life.

EMILE WALDTEUFEL (1837–1915) was another student at the Paris Conservatory. He gained his fame as a society pianist and director of court balls, as well as composing 250 dances, including the famous *España, Estudiantina*, and *Skaters* waltzes.

EMMANUEL CHABRIER (1841–1894) was a largely self-taught composer and pianist who studied law and worked for the Ministry of the Interior until 1880. His friends included the poet Verlaine, the Impressionist painter Manet, and composers Fauré, Chausson, d'Indy, and Duparc, who encouraged his music. A fervent admirer of Wagner, he patterned his opera *Gwendoline* after the master. Only orchestral excerpts are heard from this today, as with his other opera, *Le Roi malgré lui.* His *Marche Joyeuse* and the sparkling rhapsody, *España*, are concert favorites. Chabrier's vibrant rhythms and bold harmonies inspired subsequent composers, particularly Ravel.

JULES MASSENET (1842–1912) entered the Paris Conservatory at eleven, studying under Ambrose Thomas (1811–1896) the latter known mainly for his opera *Mignon.* Massenet won the *Grand Prix de Rome* in 1863. A wealth of compositions, including 22 operas, 7 oratorios and cantatas, orchestral music, and 200 songs, has left us with *Manon* and *Werther* still in the operatic repertoire; the scintillating suites: *Scènes pittoresques, Scènes Alsaciennes,* and *Le Cid,* the piano piece, *Élégie,* and, from his opera *Thaïs,* the hymnlike *Meditation,* a jewel of a violin solo.

GABRIEL FAURÉ (1845–1924), one of the most influential musicians of his time, studied under Saint-Saëns from 1854–1866, following the composer's footsteps by becoming choirmaster, in 1877, and then organist at the Madeleine, 1896–1905. Professor of composition at the Paris Conservatory in 1896, he was its celebrated director from 1905 to 1920. His pupils included Ravel, Enesco, Schmitt, and Nadia Boulanger, who was to become one of the greatest teachers of composition to many American composers, and the first woman to conduct major orchestras.

Fauré's delicacy and elegance of style is lined with an inner strength and emotional appeal which pervades his myriad output. His piano music, bearing titles of nocturnes, impromptus, preludes, barcarolles, and waltzes, are reminiscent but quite distinctive from Chopin. He is regarded as the French master of song—he wrote ninety-six—the most famous of which is *Après un Rêve* and the cycle *La Bonne Chanson.* His chamber and choral music display traditional roots unfolding with a poignant original melodic line. Although he wrote no major orchestral works, his *Ballade* for piano and orchestra is a gem of a "miniature" concerto. His best-known compositions are his suites, *Masques et Bergamasques, Peléas et Mélisande,* and *Dolly* orchestrated from a piano duet; the flowing piano piece *Pavane,* which has also received an enriching arrangement for orchestra and optional chorus; the lovely *Cantique de Racine;* and the sublime *Requiem.*

GABRIEL PIERNÉ (1863–1937) from the age of eight studied organ with Franck, whom he succeeded as organist at St. Clotilde (1890–98), and composition with Massenet. From 1910 to 1934 he enjoyed a high reputation conducting the *Concerts Colonne,* which championed young French composers. He composed incidental and chamber music, including the lyrical *Concert Piece for Harp and Orchestra* (1901), an oratorio, *The Children's Crusade* (1902), some operettas, and the ballet *Cydalise and the Satyr* (1923), from which comes the main piece he is known for: "The Dance of the Little Fauns." His compositions, written in a clear style with overtones of Franck and Debussy, are worthy of more recognition.

THE IMPRESSIONISTS

CLAUDE DEBUSSY (1862–1918) was one of the most original composers in the world of music. At nine he began piano lessons with a former pupil of Chopin, then entered the Paris Conservatory at age eleven to study theory and composition until 1884. He constantly rebelled against the set music rules and searched for new chords and melodic lines. Two summer trips in 1880 and 1881 to teach the children of Baroness von Meck, Tchaikovsky's patroness, exposed Debussy to the "wild" and "different" music of the Russian Five. He also traveled to Bayreuth and came temporarily under the spell of Wagner's music. Returning to the Conservatory, he further irritated his teachers by writing dissonant harmonies and strange chord progressions. Despite this he managed to win the Prix de Rome in 1884 for his sentimental cantata, *The Prodigal Son*, but only stayed in that city two out of the three years the prize awarded. It was here that he wrote his cantata *La damozel élue (The Blessèd Damosel)*.

Returning to Paris he joined the group of poets, writers and Impressionist painters—Verlaine, Baudelaire, Mallarmé, and Monet—who were advancing new techniques in the arts. An indelible influence entered Debussy's music as a result of visiting the Paris World's Fair of 1889, for which the Eiffel Tower was built. Here the composer was not only fascinated by the subtle paintings and decorated vases of Japan, but became entranced by the sounds of the Javanese *gamelan*, an Asian ensemble consisting of various combinations of gongs, xylophones, metallophones, drums, bowed and plucked strings, a flute or oboe, small cymbals, and singers—the music written in the five- or seven-tone scale.

Now Debussy's true style evolved as he blended chords together to make new chords, resurrected medieval modes and pentatonic or whole tone scales. Like the Impressionist school of art which diffused realistic shapes, creating instead just the outlines or "impressions" of an object, so the subtlety and floating tone of Debussy's music creates an impression upon the listener. In his 1903 tone poem *La Mer*, we hear the

"Dialogue of the Wind and the Sea" and sense "The Play of the Waves" undulating towards the shore. In the 1894 idyll, *L'Après-Midi d'un faune*, we are transported into a dreamy summer afternoon. In 1912 famed ballet dancer Vassily Nijinsky performed the sensual ballet he choreographed for this work and "scandalized" audiences. Other impressionistic orchestral works include the symphonic suite *Printemps* (Spring), *Nocturnes* (Clouds, Festivals, Sirens), *Images,* Rhapsody for Saxophone and Orchestra, *Danses Sacrées et Profanes.*

His opera *Pelléas et Mélisande*, which took him ten years to write, goes back to the true meaning of opera—"drama in music"—but was not well received because it lacks arias and a ballet, and the orchestra underscores the voice.

Most of his piano music, which even the composer admitted "terrifies the fingers," is constantly performed, especially the two *Arabesques, La Cathédrale engloutie* (*The Sunken Cathedral*), *The Girl With the Flaxen Hair, Valse, Reverie,* the *Children's Corner* suite, and the *Suite Bergamasque*, whose last movement is the famous *Clair de Lune.* The *Petite Suite* for two pianos also has a well-orchestrated version. Other piano works are 12 preludes, 12 études, *Estampes, Pour le Piano, L'Ille joyeuse,* and *Images.* Poetic titles abound, like "Gardens in the Rain," "Reflections on the Water," and "Steps in the Snow."

Songs and other choral and chamber music are part of Debussy's prodigious output. His friendship with Erik Satie produced orchestral arrangements of the eccentric composer's *Gymnopédies*, and there are piano transcriptions of the music of Gluck, Schumann, Wagner, Raff, Saint-Saëns, and Tchaikovsky.

Debussy's personal life was filled with financial and emotional crises. His craving for luxury had him constantly in debt, and he was known for his tempestuous love affairs. Feeling established by 1899, he married a country girl, Rosalie Texier, but left her in 1904 for the sophisticated divorcée Emma Dardac, whom he married in 1905 after his divorce. They had a daughter nicknamed Chouchou for whom he wrote the *Children's Corner* and *La Boîte a Joujoux* (*The Box of Toys*) ballet. Sadly, she died at the age of fourteen. Debussy learned that he had cancer in 1909. During the last nine pain-ridden years he wrote the majority of his chamber works. He died during the World War I bombardment of Paris. Another bombardment intruded upon his quiet funeral. The papers, full of war news, paid scant attention to his passing. It was some time before the world realized it had lost one of its greatest composers.

Besides achieving his own distinctive style, Debussy led the way for moderns such as Messiaen, Webern, Bartók, and Stravinsky. He was an innovator who revolutionized piano and orchestral forms. Beneath the translucent delicacy of his compositions lies a solid structure, but like a true Impressionist, he left us music filled with glowing colors, gossamer textures, and shimmering light.

MAURICE RAVEL (1875–1937) was born in Southern France near the Spanish border, the descendant of a Swiss father and a Basque mother. His family moved to Paris when he was small and he started playing the piano at the age of six. He entered the Paris Conservatory at age fourteen, staying there for sixteen years. One of his teachers was Fauré. During this time he wrote *Shéhérazade* for voice and orchestra, much piano music, including the popular *Pavane pour une infante défunte* (*Pavane for a Dead Princess*), *Jeux d'eau* (*Fountains*), the five pieces which make up *Miroirs* (*Mirrors*), a sonatine, and his only string quartet. He tried five times (1900–1905) for the Prix de Rome. This failure to award Ravel, who had already proven himself an outstanding composer, caused such a scandal that the director was forced to resign. Ravel left the conservatory to become a freelance musician.

In the following nine years he turned out a Piano Trio, the haunting *Rapsodie espagnole, Alborado del gracioso (The Morning Song of the Jester),* orchestrated from one of his *Miroirs, Gaspard de la Nuit,* a set of three difficult piano pieces, many songs, the fairy tale *Mother Goose Suite,* a duet he later orchestrated, a short opera *L'Heure espagnole, Valses nobles et sentimentales,* and *Daphnis and Chloe,* written for Diaghilev's *Ballet Russe* (1912), which he later arranged into two orchestral suites.

When World War I began Ravel tried to enlist as an aviator, but looked so frail he was turned down; he became an ambulance driver instead. Under fire in battle he was hospitalized because of ill health.

His war service over, he returned to composing. His set of piano pieces *Le Tombeau de Couperin*, honoring François Couperin, is based on baroque musical forms. As he did for many of his other piano works, he subsequently orchestrated it. After his "rival" Debussy died, a group of young composers calling themselves "Les Six"—Auric, Durey, Milhaud, Honegger, Tailleferre, and Poulenc—began to take over the French musical scene, making Ravel the "old master" in his middle forties. He wrote a tribute to his contemporary, *Le Tombeau de Claude Debussy* (1920), for violin and cello.

A shy man, Ravel held no official position and did very little teaching. The English composer Ralph Vaughan Williams studied with him for three months. Thanks to an arrangement with Durand publishers, Ravel lived well, composing about one carefully crafted new work each year.

One of his few compositions written directly for orchestra was *La Valse* (1920), a vibrant work evoking the nostalgia of glittering ball-rooms filled with dancers swirling in joyful abandon until the music builds with strident chords to depict the decline of society after WWI, signaling the change of mood to despair and tragedy. *La Valse*, the apotheosis of the waltz form, was also arranged for solo piano and two pianos, and a one-act ballet version was performed by different companies in 1928, 1929, 1951, and 1958. His magnificent orchestration of Mussorgsky's *Pictures at an Exhibition* was done in 1922.

Ravel's later years produced a lyric fantasy, *L'Enfant et les Sortilèges*, the orchestral version of the dainty *Menuet antique, Tzigane*, a virtuoso piece for violin and orchestra, chamber music, songs, and his popular masterpiece, the breathtaking *Boléro*, which was also made into a ballet.

From 1922–28 the composer toured Europe and the United States, conducting and playing his own music. Already fascinated by the black jazz musicians in Paris, when in New York Ravel frequented the Harlem night clubs to hear more of this music which he then incorporated into his own works, as well as the Orientalism he, like Debussy, absorbed from the 1889 Exposition.

His two piano concertos were not written until 1931. One he wrote for Austrian pianist Paul Wittgenstein, who lost his right hand in the war, is for the left hand alone; the other is an exuberant, vivacious work written, according to Ravel, "in the spirit of Mozart and Saint-Saëns."

Although Ravel is consistently paired with Debussy, the composers' styles are quite different. Debussy took much of his inspiration from nature; Ravel from dances of the past and present, from Spain and distant lands. While Debussy reveled in new, vague forms, Ravel's modern harmonies had classical roots. Exceptional clarity marked his orchestrations. He was also considered one of the great innovators in writing for the piano. While not passionate, Ravel's music is elegant, colorful, sometimes witty, and always polished like a fine jewel.

One of a Kind

ERIK SATIE (1866–1925) rebelled even more than Debussy against rigid rules of composition during the one year he studied at the Paris Conservatory. In 1888 he became a pianist at the cabaret *Chat Noir* in Mont-martre, the same year he composed the works he is most known for, the *Gymnopédies*, named after the slow athletic dances of ancient Greece, and the *Gnossiennes*, (1890) in which he abandoned bar lines to achieve a flowing unaccented rhythm. In 1891 he joined the mystic Christian Rosicrucian sect for which he composed music in a medieval style. From 1905–08 he became a student again, this time in the Schola Cantorum as a pupil of d'Indy and Roussel. From 1910 onwards he was a "cult" for the younger composers, *Les Six*, who were drawn to his eccentric titles—*Three Pieces In the Form of a Pear, Dessicated Embryos, New Cold Pieces*, etc.—and even wilder musical directions, such as "Light as an egg" or "Like a nightingale with a toothache." In 1915, a meeting with poet-novelist-librettist Jean Cocteau (1889–1963) led to their col-laboration on the ballet *Parade* for Diaghilev, in which jazz rhythms, an airplane engine, a typewriter, a siren, and a steamship whistle are used in the instrumentation.

In the art world Satie made fun of the Impressionists and associated himself with the Dadaists and the Surrealists, members of the literary and artistic movements which protested against all aspects of estab-lished Western culture.

Satie is a genre unto himself; his compositions are original in their simplicity, with quiet blocks of chords that move slowly and strangely, proving that music does not have to be loud to be heard. His main aim was to free French music from German heaviness, and basically he succeeded. His influence is apparent in his contemporaries, Debussy and Ravel, in the younger generation, Poulenc, Milhaud, Honegger, Auric, and in American composers Aaron Copland, Virgil Thomson, and the avant-garde John Cage.

Spain: A Distinctive Style

THE RENAISSANCE

The *vihuela*, forerunner of the guitar, drew together a prolific group of Renaissance Spanish composers: Luis Milán (*c*1500–*c*1536), Luis de Narváez (1500–*c*1555), Miguel de Fuenllana (*c*1500–*c*1579), Diego Pi-rador (*c*1508–*c*1557), Enrique de Valderrábano (mid-sixteenth century) and, after them, Gaspar Sanz (1640–1710), by which time the guitar had replaced the ancient instrument. Their work and published music books are back in the repertoire thanks to the revival of interest in the classical guitar begun in the 1920s by Andrés Segovia (1893–1987).

ZARZUELA

Another early form of Spanish music was the *zarzuela*, a light opera with music and spoken dialogue. The first zarzuela was written in 1629. In the eighteenth century the more satirical *tonadilla*, a type of cantata, became popular. It was not until the nationalistic movement of the nineteenth century that the zarzuela once again came into its own.

FLAMENCO

Flamenco music emerged in the middle of the nineteenth century. Originating in Andalusia in the south, the term may have been derived from the bright colored flamingo-like costumes worn by the gypsies who performed this vibrant music involving a loud, harsh, gutteral type of singing, heel-tapping, dramatically posed and whirling dancing accompanied by rapid arpeggios and flourishes on the guitar.

MOST FAMOUS COMPOSERS

This period also established a definite national style as represented by a new generation of composers who contributed the unique stamp of Spanish rhythm and color to classical music.

ISAAC ALBÉNIZ (1860–1909) studied in Paris, Leipzig, and Brussels, with Liszt, Dukas, and d'Indy among his teachers. He settled in Paris in 1893 and came under the influence of Fauré, Debussy, and Ravel. But it was composer/musicologist Felipe Pedrell (1841–1922) who inspired Albéniz to turn to Spanish folk music. From 1880 the young composer toured and played his own piano compositions. He wrote 250 between 1880 and 1892.

His bold harmonies and evocative instrumentation are given full reign in his masterpiece *Iberia*, a set of twelve piano pieces published in four volumes. This was later lavishly orchestrated by violinist/conductor Enrique Arbós (1863–1939). Albéniz's other major piano work, *Suite española*, was orchestrated by Spanish conductor Rafael Frühbeck de Burgos (1933–). Albéniz was one of the most important figures in Spanish music creating a national style especially in piano literature.

One of his most avid interpreters for the past half century has been Spanish pianist Alicia de Larrocha (1923–).

ENRIQUE GRANADOS (1867–1916) studied with Pedrell in Barcelona, going on to Paris (1887–89) as the piano student of the famed Charles de Beriot (1833–1914). Returning to Barcelona, Granados founded the Society of Classical Concerts in 1900 and his own piano school, *Academia Granados*, in 1901. He was a brilliant pianist. His poetic and elegant style is evident in his piano pieces, songs, and orchestral music. His greatest success is his piano suite *Goyescas*, composed from his impressions of Goya paintings. He later expanded this into an opera. Granados and his wife were drowned when the English Channel liner *Sussex* was torpedoed by a German U-boat during World War I.

MANUEL DE FALLA (1876–1946) also studied with Pedrell in Madrid. Creating his own Spanish folk music, he won the Madrid Academy of Fine Arts prize for his two-act folk opera *La vida breve* and was also awarded a prize for his piano compositions. In 1907 he went to Paris, where he came under the influence of Dukas, Debussy, and Ravel. In 1915 de Falla wrote the ballet-pantomime *El amor brujo*, from which comes the famed "Ritual Fire Dance." The hauntingly delicate yet powerful *Nights in the Gardens of Spain* comes closest to a piano concerto (1916), followed in 1919 by his most successful ballet *The Three-Cornered Hat*, produced by Diaghilev in London. The music from both of de Falla's major ballets has been arranged into popular orchestral suites.

He composed chamber, choral, and other piano music. His *Seven Popular Spanish Songs* have been performed by almost every leading soprano. When de Falla was invited to conduct a series of concerts in Buenos Aires in 1939, the dictatorship of Franco in his homeland and the onset of World War II in the rest of Europe, both of which began in the same year, contributed to the composer's decision to settle in Argentina.

JOAQUIN TURINA (1882–1949) studied in Seville and Madrid, then went to Paris to the Schola Cantorum (1905–13) where he studied composition with d'Indy. He became associated with de Falla and returned to Spain with him in 1914. Turina taught at the Madrid Conservatory from 1931. His works include operas, songs, orchestral compositions, and chamber, piano, and guitar music. The most well-known are *La procesion del rocio* (1912), *Danzas fantasticas* (1920) and *La oracion del torero* (1925). He also wrote music critiques. The only major Spanish composer to write a symphony, Turina had a style more modern than his predecessors, but containing the same grace and national feeling.

JOAQUIN RODRIGO (1902–), blind from the age of three, studied in Valencia, and then Paris with Dukas (1927). Encouraged by de Falla, he wrote concertos for violin, harp, flute and guitar(s). His *Concierto de Aranjuez* for guitar and orchestra (1939) established him as a major Spanish composer.

ANDRÉS SEGOVIA (1893–1987) taught himself the guitar, made his debut at the age of sixteen, and subsequently toured all over the world. He reinstated the guitar as a concert instrument with his arrangements of Bach, Handel, and the Spanish Baroque masters. His contemporaries—de Falla, Turina, Rodrigo—wrote music for him, as did Mexican composer Manuel Ponce (1882–1948), and Italian-American Mario Castelnuovo-Tedesco (1895–1968), whose beautiful Guitar Concerto (1939) vies with Rodrigo's *Concierto de Aranjuez* as one of the finest written for this instrument. The year 1981 marked the founding of the Segovia International Guitar Competition, and the bestowing of his title Marquis of Salobreia by King Juan Carlos II. In 1985 Segovia received the Gold Medal of the Royal Philharmonic Society of London.

FERNANDO SOR (1780–1839), FRANCISCO TÁRREGA (1852–1909), and FEDERICO MORENO TÓRROBA (1891–1982) should also be mentioned for their major contribution to Spanish guitar literature.

Of Segovia's followers, including many guitarists from England and America, one of the most unusual is the ensemble known as the ROMERO FAMILY OF THE GUITAR. CELEDONIO (1913–), born in Málaga, studied there and at the Madrid Conservatory. After making his debut at age ten, he concertized all over Europe. He married Angela Gallega Molina, a voice student at the Málaga Conservatory. Their three sons, CELIN (1940–), PEPE (1944–), and ANGEL (1946–), began performing with their father in the 1960s. (The family settled in California in 1957.) In 1990, Celin's son, Celino (1969–), replaced Angel in the quartet. They also perform as soloists and in duos. In 1967, their friend Joaquin Rodrigo wrote the dramatic *Concierto Andaluz* for the Romero family.

Celedonio Romero has composed over 120 compositions for guitar: solo, and with orchestra, including nine concertos for one, two, or four guitars. He has received a multitude of world honors, including those from the King of Spain and the Pope.

MUSICA ESPAÑOL INTERNACIONAL

With the body of orchestral music plus its native instrument the guitar, Spanish music is always exuberant, identifiable, and tuneful. Composers of other lands have come under its spell, as witnessed in *Rapsodie espagnole* and *Boléro* by Ravel, *España* by Chabrier, *Le Cid* by Massenet, *Capriccio espagnol* by Rimsky-Korsakov, *Symphonie espagnole* by Lalo, and the setting in Spain of Bizet's masterpiece opera, *Carmen*, to name a few.

England: The English Renaissance

After the prominence of early composers John Dunstable (*c*1385–1453), John Taverner (*c*1490–1545), Thomas Tallis (*c*1505–1585), William Byrd (1543–1623), Thomas Morley (1557–1603), Thomas Campion (1567–1620), John Dowland (1563–1626), Henry Purcell (1659–95), Thomas Arne (1710–1778), William Boyce (1711–1779), and the naturalized Handel (1685–1759), the music of England, like that of France, was put on hold for almost a hundred years until the liturgical works of Sir John Stainer (1840–1901), of which the oratorio *The Crucifixion* (1887) is still performed in churches. Concurrently, at the other extreme, was the collaboration of Gilbert and Sullivan, which from 1871 to 1896 gave the public a set of unique light operas that have become a continuing cult with a devoted following on both sides of the Atlantic.

SIR ARTHUR SULLIVAN (1842–1900) was the son of an Irish bandmaster at Sandhurst, the British equivalent of West Point Military Academy. In 1854 he became a Chorister of the Chapel Royal, and was the first holder of the Mendelssohn Scholarship at the Royal Academy of Music in 1856. He studied at the Leipzig Conservatory (1858–61), after which his early concert works led to festival commissions and conducting posts.

It was not until he collaborated with playwright William Schwenk Gilbert (1836–1911) in a series of light operas satirizing Victorian manners and politics that Sullivan's fame was assured. Richard d'Oyly-Carte, the impresario who had brought playwright and composer together, leased the Savoy Theatre for exclusive performances of these operas, which led to devotees being called Savoyards. After a string of successes: *Trial by Jury* (1875), *The Sorcerer* (1877), *H.M.S. Pinafore*

(1878), *The Pirates of Penzance* (1879), *Patience* (1880–81), *Iolanthe* (1882), *Princess Ida* (1883), *The Mikado* (1884–5), *Ruddigore* (1886), *The Yeomen of the Guard* (1888), and *The Gondoliers* (1889), the two men ended their relationship after a violent quarrel.

Ironically, Sullivan felt these parodies were "beneath" him and continued writing "serious" music which, aside from the lighthearted *Overture Di Ballo*, the song *The Lost Chord*, and the immortal hymn *Onward Christian Soldiers*, is rarely performed.

Sir Arthur, knighted in 1883, continued to be much in demand after the break with Gilbert and was kept busy composing and conducting until his health failed from over-expending himself. In his last years he met Elgar, whose career was just beginning. Sullivan died on St. Cecilia's Day (named for the patron saint of music), November 22, 1900.

An orchestral suite from the one-act ballet *Pineapple Poll* (1951), as arranged by conductor Sir Charles Mackerras, contains the crème of Sullivan's music from the operas and is a delightful way to become acquainted with G&S.

Following Sullivan the spirit of British nationalism evolved in a new generation of composers. The most prominent of these were Sir Edward Elgar, who epitomized the Edwardian Age, Frederick Delius, with his pastoral romanticism, and Gustav Holst, who led the way to a more modern yet still English style. But it was Ralph Vaughan Williams (1872–1958) who dominated the English musical scene for over half a century, serving as mentor for a large group of his contemporaries who added their contributions to the British repertoire. The best known among the latter being William Walton (1902–1983), and Benjamin Britten (1913–1976).

SIR EDWARD ELGAR (1857–1934), son of a music shop owner, showed an early interest in music. From the age of sixteen he worked as a violinist, organist, bassoonist, teacher, and conductor. His compositions at this time reflected the influence of Schumann and Mendelssohn. Until his *Imperial March* was conducted at the Crystal Palace for Queen Victoria's Diamond Jubilee in 1897, he was virtually unknown outside the Midlands of England. It was his *Enigma Variations* (1899)—each variation portraying a friend of his—which catapulted him to international fame.

During the years from 1901 to 1914 the composer received his greatest acclaim. Number 1 of a set of five *Pomp and Circumstance Marches* made Elgar a household name. This march has been used at almost every U.S. school graduation for decades. King Edward VII suggested that it be set to words and the "alternate" British national anthem, *Land of Hope and Glory*, was born.

The composer was knighted in 1904 at forty-seven years of age, became Master of the King's Musick in 1924, and was made a baronet in 1931. After his wife died in 1920, Elgar composed very little, but made many priceless recordings of his works, the most celebrated being his violin concerto with sixteen-year-old Yehudi Menuhin (1932).

Of an abundance of compositions—orchestral, choral, chamber music, songs and theater music—his best-known works, besides *Enigma* and *Pomp and Circumstance*, are the *Cockaigne Overture* (1901), *Dream Children* (1902), *Wand of Youth Suites* Nos. 1 and 2 (1907 and 1908), *Nursery Suite* (1931), *Spanish Ladies Suite*, *Bavarian Dances* (1897), *Chanson de Matin*, *Chanson de Nuit* (1897), *Salut d'Amour* (1889), and the poignant *Sea Pictures* (1897–99) a song cycle for mezzo-soprano and orchestra. His major compositions include a Violin Sonata, a String Quartet, both dated 1918, the Violin Concerto (1909–10), Symphony No. 2 (1903–11), and the celebrated Cello Concerto (1918–19).

A combination of imperial nobility, spirituality, and nostalgia mark Elgar's style. His major works have been compared to Bruckner's, with their combination of extrovertism and introspection. He could be called the Father of English Nationalism in Music.

FREDERICK DELIUS (1862–1934), whose music-loving father was absolutely opposed to his son pursuing a career in music, tried to please him by entering his father's wool trade, but had no aptitude for it. In 1884 he went to Florida to manage an orange plantation, but spent his time studying with a Jacksonville organist, and set himself up as a violin teacher. He also took an organist position in New York. By 1886 his father permitted Delius to enter the Leipzig Conservatory. After two years he moved to Paris, becoming one of the "Bohemian" group with Gauguin, Ravel, Munch, and Strindberg in his circle. On vacation in Norway in 1897, he met Grieg and formed a lasting friendship with him. In 1897 he married artist Jelka Rosen and with the exception of World War II (1914–18), which he spent in England, lived the rest of his life in France.

Delius's reputation on the Continent was greater than in his native country until 1907, when his music began to be performed there. In 1922 he developed a progressive paralysis due to the syphilis he had contracted in Paris in the 1890s. By 1926 he was blind and helpless. For the last six years of his life he was able to compose with the help of Eric

Fenby (1906–), a young English musician who consequently made it a major part of his life's work to perpetuate the composer's memory in writings and in working for the Delius Trust. Delius died in France in June 1934, but was reinterred in England in May 1935.

It has been observed that his chromatic harmonies caught the spirit of Chausson, Debussy, Strauss, and Mahler, but the overall impression of Delius's music is a pastoral lyricism which is easy to enjoy right from the first hearing.

Of his great output of compositions, some of the most delightful are the *Florida Suite* (1886), *On Hearing the First Cuckoo in Spring* (1912), *Brigg Fair* (1907), *In a Summer Garden* (1911), and orchestral excerpts from his operas *Irmelin*, *A Village Romeo and Juliet*, *Fenimore and Gerda*, and *Koanga* from which the ebullient dance *La Calinda* was taken. *La Calinda* is also one of the movements of the *Florida Suite*.

GUSTAV HOLST (1874–1934), of Swedish descent, was trained as a pianist by his father, a music teacher, who later sent him to the Royal Academy of Music to study composition under Sir Charles Stanford. He left there in 1898, having formed a lifelong friendship with Vaughan Williams, which included their critiquing each other's compositions. In 1903 Holst became music teacher at a girls' school in Dulwich and in 1905 at St. Paul's Girls' School, an appointment he retained the rest of his life and for which he wrote his famous *St. Paul's Suite* for strings (1912–13).

Of an enormous body of compositions ranging from orchestral, chamber, piano, much choral music and songs, his best-known composition is *The Planets* (1914–16), a suite of seven movements based on astrological associations, such as "Mars, the Bringer of War," "Jupiter, the Bringer of Jollity," etc. The music may be considered far ahead of its time in that many outer space films including *2001: A Space Odyssey* and *Star Wars* employ themes extremely reminiscent of *The Planets*.

Holst's daughter, IMOGEN (1907–1984), was educated at St. Paul's, and also studied at the Royal Academy. During World War II she organized the Encouragement of Music and the Arts. From 1952 for several years she directed and was assistant to Benjamin Britten at the Aldeburgh Festivals. She conducted her father's works and authored his biography and other books about him, Britten, and Byrd. In 1975 she was made Commander of the Order of the British Empire.

RALPH VAUGHAN WILLIAMS (1872–1958), following in the wake of Elgar, led the revival of English music in the twentieth century with Holst and others contributing alongside. In England he studied at

Cambridge and the Royal Academy with Stanford. In Berlin, Bruch was his teacher, and in Paris, Ravel.

He began collecting English folk-songs in 1902, and his early music was mostly songs, *Linden Lea* being one of the most beautiful. His studies with Ravel in 1913 caused the production of major works, including the soulful *Fantasia on a Theme of Thomas Tallis* (an early English composer, 1505–1585) and *A London Symphony* (1914).

Although he was over military age, Vaughan Williams served in World War II. Afterwards he was active in every phase of English musical life, conducting, teaching, writing essays, composing, and encouraging young musicians. His singular style with its characteristic folk-song modal harmonies graduated from pastoral and visionary to a later period of desolate bleakness which found expression in his Sixth Symphony, the film music for *Scott of the Antarctic* (1947–48), and the *Sinfonia Antarctica* (1949–52), an expansion of the film score. His Ninth and final symphony returns to his contemplative vein.

He tackled many genres, from symphonies to operas to a myriad of other orchestral, chamber, piano, choral, and vocal works. His writing for British films began with the 1940 World War II spy thriller, *49th Parallel.* To single out two compositions from his enormous repertoire seems almost sacriligious, nevertheless to acquire a taste for Vaughan Williams the ethereal Romance for Violin and Orchestra, *The Lark Ascending* (1914–20), and the well-known *Fantasia on Greensleeves* (1934) should be first on your list.

SIR WILLIAM WALTON (1902–1983) lived for a while with the poets Osbert, Sacherell and Edith Sitwell, which resulted in his composition *Façade* (1921), a set of instrumental accompaniments to Edith's recitation of her poetry. Its "jazziness" caused quite a furor, marking Walton as an *enfant terrible.* His later works, however, fundamentally romantic and lyrical, progressed in a full circle from the influences of Stravinsky and Honegger in his *Portsmouth Point Overture* (1925) to Prokofiev in his Viola Concerto (1928), to Sibelius in his First Symphony (1931–5), to Elgar in his Violin Concerto (1939). From a large output encompassing opera, orchestral, chamber, piano, organ, choral works and song cycles, Walton is best known for his film music, especially Sir Laurence Olivier's Shakespeare productions of *Henry V*, *Hamlet*, and *Richard III*, as well as *Orb and Sceptre* (1953), the coronation march for Queen Elizabeth II.

BENJAMIN BRITTEN (1913–1976) as a boy studied with Frank Bridge, and entered the Royal Academy of Music in 1930. In 1935 he worked for the General Post Office Film Unit with the poet W.H. Auden, writing music for short documentaries. He was a brilliant pianist and conductor. Many of his compositions were written for specific performers such as the cellist Mstislav Rostropovich, and singers Dietrich Fischer-Dieskau, Janet Baker, and his lifelong companion, tenor Peter Pears, for whom he wrote many operatic and vocal roles. From 1939–1942 Britten, Pears, and Auden lived in New York, where his first opera *Paul Bunyan* was written and his Violin Concerto and *Sinfonia da Requiem* were performed in Carnegie Hall under British conductor Sir John Barbirolli. Returning to England, Britten settled in Aldeburgh, Suffolk, founding the Aldeburgh Music Festivals where, like his predecessors Vaughan Williams and Holst, he shared his great interest in the work of amateur musicians.

His opera, *Peter Grimes*, which premiered June 7, 1945, is a landmark in English music, establishing Britten as one of the foremost modern opera composers of our time. His other most produced operas are *The Rape of Lucretia* (1946), *Albert Herring* (1947), *Billy Budd* (1951), and *Death in Venice* (1973). Of his many orchestral, chamber, choral, vocal, and piano works, the two suites *Soirées Musicales* (1936) and *Matinées Musicales* (1941)—both arrangements of the works of Rossini—are among his most tuneful. Otherwise, his style is modern and at times abstract and needs getting used to by those whose ears are attuned to the Romantic. Britten's immortality is assured, however, by his Variations and Fugue on a theme of English Baroque composer Henry Purcell: *The Young Person's Guide to the Orchestra* (1946), in which he demonstrates the four instrument families of the symphony orchestra.

To complete the picture of this phenomenal "renaissance," mention must be made of the large group of other composers, both predecessors and contemporaries of these major voices of British nationalism.

SIR HUBERT PARRY (1848–1900) was a pioneer revitalizing influence on English music in the nineteenth century. He taught at the Royal Academy from 1883, taking over from founder Sir George Grove in 1894. Of his five symphonies, suites, oratorios, cantatas, motets, and songs, his niche in music history is assured by his setting of William Blake's poem *Jerusalem* (1916), which belongs to the class of patriotic songs such as Elgar's *Land of Hope and Glory*. Its stirring theme was featured in the 1981 film *Chariots of Fire*.

SIR CHARLES STANFORD (1852–1924), whose pupils included Vaughan Williams, Bliss, Ireland, and Holst, was also one of the principal figures in the late nineteenth century beginnings of this renaissance.

Apart from his church music little of his prolific output is performed today.

SIR EDWARD GERMAN (1862–1936) wrote much incidental music for Shakespeare's plays and is best remembered for the sprightly dances from *Henry VIII* and his lyrical patriotic operetta *Merrie England* (1902). He was considered a successor to Sullivan.

SIR GRANVILLE BANTOCK (1868–1946) was another major figure in the British renaissance who promoted the music of his contemporaries as well as championing Sibelius, whose Third Symphony is dedicated to him. His own compositions were much performed at the beginning of the century, with a revival now in progress.

FRANK BRIDGE (1879–1941) studied with Stanford and was the teacher of Britten. His early music resembles Delius's, but after World War II underwent a striking change, showing the influence of Schoenberg while still maintaining its English flavor.

SIR HAMILTON HARTY (1879–1941) conducted the Hallé Orchestra of Manchester from 1920–33, molding it as one of the finest in Europe. He is remembered for his modern orchestrations of Handel's *Water Music* and *Fireworks Music.*

JOHN IRELAND (1879–1962), also a student of Stanford, composed a large amount of chamber music, songs, a piano concerto with jazzlike interludes, tone poems, and overtures. He is best known for the suite Charles Mackerras arranged from his music to the 1946 film *The Overlanders.*

PERCY GRAINGER (1882–1961) was born in Melbourne and studied there before going to the Hoch Conservatory in Frankfurt (1894–1900), where he was in the company of English composers Balfour Gardiner (1877–1950), Roger Quilter (1857–1953), and Cyril Scott (1879–1970). His piano teacher was the virtuoso Ferruccio Busoni (1866–1924). Percy settled in London in 1901, where he met Grieg, who invited him to Norway to study his piano concerto. Grainger became its most notable interpreter. For the next decade, besides having a successful career as a concert pianist, he travelled widely with a cylinder recorder, collecting folksongs. Among his prime discoveries were the *Londonderry Air* ("Danny Boy") and *Brigg Fair*, which his good friend Frederick Delius arranged as a rhapsody. An eccentric and unconventional man, Percy's marriage to Ella took place on stage during the intermission of a concert at the Hollywood Bowl, August 9, 1928. His music is untraditional, using polytonality, freedom of rhythm, and unusual instrumentation. Grainger settled in the United States in 1915, becoming a citizen in

1919. He made several trips to Australia to help in the establishment of the Museum in Melbourne bearing his name. He is best known for his myriad lighter compositions, which he called "fripperies": *Molly on the Shore* (1921), *Shepherd's Hey* (1922), *Handel in the Strand,* (1930), *Mock Morris,* plus choral works, and piano and instrumental versions of his songs. His larger compositions are generating renewed interest.

SIR ARNOLD BAX (1883–1953) was a brilliant pianist and prolific composer of vocal, chamber, piano, and orchestral music, including seven symphonies now only intermittently performed. His most-played works are his ethereal tone poems, *The Garden of Fand* (1916), based on the legend of the Irish heroine whose garden was the ocean, and *Tintagel* (1919), the fabled location of King Arthur's Camelot. Bax was Master of the King's Musick from 1942 until 1953. His autobiography, *Farewell, My Youth* is one of the best books written by a composer.

LORD BERNERS (Sir Gerald Tyrwhitt-Wilson) (1883–1950), baronet, besides being a gifted composer was also a painter, author, and diplomat. While an honorary attaché in Rome he took lessons with Stravinsky. His best known work is the ballet *The Triumph of Neptune* (1926), some of which was arranged by Walton, and his film score of Charles Dickens's *Nicholas Nickleby* (1946).

GEORGE BUTTERWORTH (1885–1914), educated at Eton and Oxford, began collecting folksongs, which led to a friendship with Vaughan Williams. His well-known rhapsody *A Shropshire Lad* (1913) and the idyll *On the Banks of Green Willow* plus the rest of his few compositions suggest a great talent which was cut short by his untimely death at the Battle of the Somme during World War I. Vaughan Williams's *A London Symphony* is dedicated to him.

ERIC COATES (1886–1957) was the master of English light classical music. His orchestral suites, marches, and songs are all easy listening delights. The most famous are the suites *London* (1932), with its immortal "Knightsbridge" March, and *London Again* (1936), the dreamy piece *By the Sleepy Lagoon* (1939), and the lovely song *Bird Songs at Eventide.*

SIR ARTHUR BLISS (1891–1975) was considered Elgar's successor. His style expresses his feelings for drama and atmosphere. His output includes concertos for piano (1935), violin (1955), and cello (1970), songs, and choral, chamber, and piano music. His most familiar music is the ballet *Checkmate* (1937) and the score from Alexander Korda's early science-fiction film based on H.G. Wells's *Things to Come* (1936), which predicted war in 1940 and rocketships to the moon.

PETER WARLOCK (1894–1930) edited works of the first Elizabethan era under his real name Philip Heseltine. As composer Peter Warlock he wrote many songs ranging from the starkly desolate to the amorous and charming. A friend of Lambert and Delius, about whom he wrote a book, Warlock was largely self-taught, yet had great technical skill and sensitivity. The two names he used may have indicated a split personality, which teetered from alcoholic joviality to neurotic self-analysis. He took his own life. Despite the preponderance of vocal compositions, he is best remembered for his whimsical *Capriol Suite* (1926), whose six movements are based on old French dances.

GERALD FINZI (1901–1956) taught at the Royal Academy in the 1930s. His music shows the influence of Elgar and Vaughan Willliams, but his individuality lies in his songs, many of which are settings of poems by Hardy. It is these which are considered a valuable contribution to English twentieth century music.

RICHARD ADDINSELL (1904–1977) wrote mainly for films. His romantic *Warsaw Concerto* for the 1941 movie *Dangerous Moonlight* (American title: *Suicide Squadron*) is considered one of the most popular pieces of film music ever written.

CONSTANT LAMBERT (1905–1951) studied at the Royal Academy with Vaughan Williams. His original works put him with Walton in the league of the new generation of composers. As an author, his 1934 book *Music Ho! A Study of Music in Decline* was an important, provocative commentary on music of the time. He was also the narrator of Walton's *Façade* with Edith Sitwell. The first English composer to receive a commission from Diaghilev, for his *Romeo and Juliet* (1926), Lambert took a leading part in the establishment of British dance in his position as musical director of the Vic-Wells Ballet from its founding in 1931 until 1947. His best known work is the one-act ballet *Horoscope* (1938).

SIR MICHAEL TIPPETT (born: London, January 2, 1905) studied with his mother, one of the original suffragettes. He entered the Royal College of Music in 1923, studied composition with Charles Wood and conducting with Adrian Boult and Malcolm Sargent. He then became music director for a work camp, an experience which left him a pacifist. In 1932, he began his long affiliation with Morley College, committed to the education of London's underprivileged. Here he led what became the South London Orchestra. When the college was nearly destroyed in the October 1940 bombing raids, Tippett registered as a conscientious objector. Because he refused his war time assignment, in 1943 he was sentenced to three months in Wormwood Scrubbs prison. Tippett resigned from Morley in 1951 to devote more time to composition and accepted a job as commentator for the BBC.

Tippett's first masterpiece was the Concerto for Double String Orchestra (1938–39). This was followed by the oratorio *A Child of Our Time* (1938–41), based upon the true incident of a Polish teenager who shot a German official to avenge the death of his parents, thereby causing vicious retaliation by the Nazis on the Jews. Next came the opera *The Midsummer Marriage* (1955), establishing his mastery of stage composition. He wrote four symphonies (1944–1977), a *Fantasia on a Theme of Handel* for piano and orchestra (1931–41), a *Fantasia Concertante on a Theme of Corelli* for string orchestra (1953), a Piano Concerto (1953–55), a Concerto for Orchestra (1962–63), and a Triple Concerto for small string trio and orchestra (1978–79). Writing his own librettos, he produced three later operas: *King Priam* (1962), *The Knot Garden* (1970), *The Ice Break* (1977), and *New Year* (1989), which was premiered by the Houston Opera.

Already recognized in the 1950s as being one of the major symphonic and operatic composers of our time, Tippett was honored as a Commander of the Order of the British Empire (C.B.E.) in 1959, knighted by Queen Elizabeth in 1966, and received honorary membership in the American Academy of Arts and Letters in 1973.

His music, combining the Baroque heritage with jazz rhythms and blues, are in three style periods: the first, tuneful and somewhat neoclassic; the second, modern and strident; and the third, broad, varied, showing the culmination of technical mastery.

MALCOLM ARNOLD (born: Northampton, October 21, 1921) studied at the Royal College of Music (1937–40). He was a trumpet player in the London Philharmonic Orchestra (1940–42), the BBC Symphony Orchestra (1945), and returned to the London Philharmonic as principal trumpet in 1948, after which he left to devote himself to composition. His work is influenced by Berlioz, Sibelius, and Walton. He wrote nine symphonies between 1952–1982, two ballets, choral, chamber, and piano music, and both serious and light pieces, including *A Grand Grand Overture* (1956), with the orchestration including three vacuum cleaners, a floor polisher, and four rifles. His best-known works are the concert overtures *Beckus the Dandipratt* (1948), and *Tam O'Shanter* (1955), and two sets of *English Dances* (1951). He also wrote scores for many films, including *The Bridge On the River Kwai* (1957).

SIR PETER MAXWELL DAVIES was born in Manchester in 1934 and

attended the Royal Manchester College of Music. In the 1960s, he taught music in England, studied with Roger Sessions at Princeton, and lectured around the world with the UNESCO Conference on Music in Education. He also was composer in residence at the University of Adelaide, Australia. In 1967, he organized the Pierrot Players (renamed The Fires of London in 1970), playing programs of very modernistic works. After making his home in the isolated Orkney Islands, in 1977 Davies organized the annual St. Magnus Festival, which attracted attention despite the remoteness of the location. In 1979 he was awarded an honorary doctorate from Edinburgh, and was named Composer of the Year by the Composers' Guild of Great Britain. He was commissioned to write a symphony for the Boston Symphony Orchestra for its 1981 centennial. In 1985, he was named composer in residence and associate conductor in Glasgow (Scotland). In 1987, he was knighted. Davies' style includes innovative combinations such as medieval chants and twentieth-century serialism.

Mexico

Far across the Atlantic, three men rose to musical prominence in Mexico.

MANUEL PONCE (born: Fresnillo, December 8, 1882; died: Mexico City, April 24, 1948) began his career as a pianist, church organist, and composer during his boyhood. He studied in Mexico City, Bologna, and Berlin. He taught at the Mexico City Conservatory 1909–15 and 1917–22, assuming the directorship in 1934–35, with periods of travel to Havana 1915–17 and Paris 1925–33, where he was influenced by Dukas and other French composers. He founded a music journal 1936–37, and was the first Mexican composer to research Creole and Meztiso folklore. He wrote a concerto for violin, 2 concertos for piano, 24 preludes, 5 sonatas, and over 100 sentimental songs and piano pieces. His *Concierto del Sur* (1941) for guitar, was popularized by Segovia and *his* followers.

CARLOS CHÁVEZ (born: Mexico City, June 13, 1899; died there, August 2, 1978) studied with Ponce (1910–14) and also taught himself. He traveled in Europe (1922–23) and to New York (1923–34), living there from 1926 to 1928 and forming a close association with Cowell, Copland, and Varèse. Returning to his homeland, Chávez became a great influence on cultural life. He co-founded and was director of the

Mexico Symphony Orchestra (1928–48), director of the National Conservatory (1928–33), founder/director of the National Institute of Fine Arts (1947–52) and director of composers' workshops (1960–65). Considered a master of orchestration, his output includes 7 symphonies, concertos for piano and violin, an opera, *The Visitors*, and 2 Aztec ballets, *El fuego nueve* (1921) and *Los cuatros soles* (1925). Although he did not make use of folk music, his style is nevertheless nationalistic.

SILVESTRE REVUELTAS (born: Santiago Papasquiaro, December 31, 1899; died: Mexico City, October 5, 1940) studied in Mexico and at the Chicago College of Music (1918–20, 1922–24). He was a freelance violinist and conductor until Chavez appointed him assistant conductor of the Mexico Symphony Orchestra (1929–35). He also taught violin and chamber music at the National Conservatory, then went to Spain during the Civil War. Like Chavez, he did not use folk music, but composed bold, colorful, vigorous music, turning to atonalism in 1930. His compositions include *Esquinas* (1930), *Colorines* (1932), *Homenaje a Garcia Lorca*, chamber and film music. Most well-known is *Sensamaya* (1938), which was influenced by Stravinsky's *Rite of Spring*.

South America

The two most famous composers of South America are Heitor Villa-Lobos and Alberto Ginastera.

BRAZIL

HEITOR VILLA-LOBOS (born: Rio de Janeiro, March 5, 1887; died: there, November 17, 1959) was taught cello by his father. In his teens he played in cafes and later in the Rio Opera and Symphony orchestras, where he absorbed the influence of Stravinsky and Strauss. He became friends with Darius Milhaud, who was attached to the French embassy in Rio at the time. In 1921 he met one of the world's greatest pianists, Artur Rubinstein, who played some of his works. He traveled to Europe 1923–24 and spent 1927–30 in Paris, where he met Milhaud again. During this time he wrote more of his *Choros*, luxuriant Brazilian "impressions"—not folk music, but rather the "flavor" of his country and its music. On his return to Brazil in 1930, the spell of Satie and the trend to neoclassicism resulted in his brilliant *Bachianas Brasileiras*, a set of nine pieces in Baroque forms interwoven with the same Brazilian elements. No. 2 of these, *The Little Train of the Caipira*, is an excellent musical portrait of the small train chugging up the mountains. No. 5 with the soprano voice used as a wordless instrument accompanied by cellos, is sheer innovative beauty.

In 1945 Villa-Lobos founded the Brazilian Academy of Music in Rio de Janeiro, and did other valuable work to reform musical education. He also wrote 12 symphonies (1916–57), 17 string quartets (1915–57), suites, songs, and piano and guitar music.

ARGENTINA

ALBERTO GINASTERA (born: Buenos Aires, April 11, 1916; died: Geneva, June 25, 1983), studied at the National Conservatory (1936–38). One of his first and very popular works is his ballet *Panambí* (1940). His best-known ballet, *Estancia*, followed in 1941, when he was also appointed to the staff of the National Conservatory. He lived in New York (1945–47), during which time he attended Copland's course at Tanglewood. Thereafter his life was divided between Argentina and abroad—he was not in favor with Juan Peron, who was President 1946–55 and 1973–74. In 1963 Ginastera became Director of the Center for Advanced Music Studies in Buenos Aires. In 1971 he settled in Geneva.

Until the mid-1950s his music was essentially nationalistic like Bartók's, de Falla's, and Stravinsky's; then he became very modern, using serialism involving the twelve-tone system of Schoenberg. These elements are prominent in his operas, *Don Rodrigo* (1964), *Bomarzo* (1967), and *Beatrix Cenci* (1971). His other works include two piano concertos (1961, 1972), the *Cantata para América mágica* for soprano and percussion (1960), and three string quartets (1948, 1958, 1973). His most-played compositions are orchestral exerpts from his ballets *Panambí* and *Estancia*.

United States

Early American music has a British heritage. Music for the colonists consisted largely of hymns and anthems. The best known colonial composer, WILLIAM BILLINGS (1746–1800), was self-taught and made a living publishing songbooks for religious and recreational purposes. His music centered on religion and patriotism. Some of his works became marching songs for George Washington's army. He knew Paul Revere and Samuel Adams. His most famous composition is the hymn tune

"Chester," which was used in the last movement of the *New England Triptych* (1956) by modern American composer William Schuman (1910–1992) who also wrote a *William Billings Overture* (1944).

The next generation of American composers studied in Europe, absorbed the influences of the Old World, returned to their homeland, and infused their music with New World culture—folksongs, Negro spirituals, blues, jazz, ragtime, and other idioms—to create classical music that was distinctly American.

LOUIS MOREAU GOTTSCHALK (born: New Orleans, May 8, 1829, died: Tijuca, Brazil, December 18, 1869) went to Paris at thirteen and studied with Hallé and Berlioz. His piano debut in 1844 was praised by Chopin himself, and his style of playing was compared to the Polish composer-pianist—a great compliment, indeed. By nineteen, having produced compositions filled with reminiscences of his native New Orleans—*Bamboula, La savane* and *Le bananier*—he became a household name in Europe. He was hailed as the New World's first musical representative. After tours of Switzerland, France, and Spain (1850–52) he made his New York debut. Concertizing in the U.S. during 1853–56, he wrote more crowd pleasers, including the popular *The Last Hope*. The years 1857–61 were spent in the Caribbean, where Gottschalk wrote some of his finest works: *Souvenir de Porto Rico* and his first symphony, *Night in the Tropics*. A second tour of America produced *The Dying Poet*. He lived his last years in South America giving us the charming *Pasquinade*, the *Grande scherzo*, and the *Grande tarantelle* for piano and orchestra. Gottschalk's flashy, syncopated, tuneful style, was a precursor for ragtime and the use of jazz in classical forms.

GEORGE WHITEFIELD CHADWICK (born: Lowell, Massachusetts, November 13, 1854; died: Boston, April 4, 1931) studied in Leipzig (1876–79) and Munich (1879–80), after which he returned to his native Boston where he became a teacher, organist, and choral conductor. In 1897 he was made director of the New England Conservatory, a position he held until his death. Characteristic of the "New England School," his music was a mixture of German classicism and French influence. A versatile composer, he wrote 3 operas, 3 symphonies, and other orchestral works. He is best known for his melodious *Symphonic Sketches* (1895–1904).

JOHN PHILIP SOUSA (born: Washington, D.C., November 6, 1854; died: Reading, Pennsylvania, March 6, 1932) was trained as a violinist but had playing knowledge of the piano and various wind instruments. He was apprenticed to the United States Marine Band when he was only thirteen. After a five-year hitch, Sousa left to play violin in theater orchestras, including that of the touring French composer Offenbach. At the age of twenty-six, in 1880, he was appointed leader of the Marine Band, the oldest of such bands and the official band of the President of the United States. The Marine Band was a typical service aggregation when Sousa arrived, but with drilling, rehearsing, and demand for perfection, Sousa made it into the best in the nation. To add to its repertoire, he ordered new music from Europe as well as writing his own compositions. By 1892, his reputation was so great that he left to form his own concert band.

Sousa's band, usually about sixty musicians, had the finest wind players in the country. They made four European concert tours (1900–05) introducing Sousa's marches and American "ragtime." In 1910 they went on a world tour. A natural showman, the composer demanded military bearing, spotless uniforms, and white gloves. He believed in playing what audiences wanted to hear, but he also introduced many people—in the days of primitive phonographs, and before radio—to their first taste of Wagner, Dvořák, Tchaikovsky, and others. His programs also featured operatic overtures, especially those of Rossini, Von Suppé, and Verdi, as well as soprano solos, showpieces for his cornet and trombone soloists, and, of course, his own more than 100 marches and excerpts from his eleven light operas. Sousa also wrote waltzes, dance music, suites for band and orchestra, and a symphonic poem, *The Chariot Race*, based on *Ben-Hur*.

Sousa inspired the invention of the *sousaphone*, a type of tuba whose bell can be turned to aim sound in any direction. His book, *Through the Years with Sousa*, was published in 1910. In 1928, he wrote his autobiography, *Marching Along*. Deservedly called "The March King," his *Stars and Stripes Forever*, *Washington Post*, *El Capitan*, *Semper Fideles*, *Liberty Bell*, *King Cotton*, *Hands Across the Sea*, etc., are still the most popular items in all the band repetoire. Tuneful and vibrant, they are expertly written to bring out the rich band sound, amply fulfilling the composer's credo that "A good march should make a man with a wooden leg step out."

EDWARD MACDOWELL (born: New York, December 18, 1860; died: New York, January 23, 1908) entered the Paris Conservatory in 1876 and the Frankfurt Conservatory in 1879. In 1881 he taught piano at the Darmstadt Conservatory. He visited Liszt in Weimar and on the great master's recommendation had his *First Modern Suite* and First Piano Concerto published. By 1884 German firms had published ten of his compositions. From 1885–88 he lived in Wiesbaden. He returned to the

Johann Sebastian Bach
(1685-1750)

George Frideric Handel
(1685-1759)

Franz Joseph Haydn
(1732-1809)

Wolfgang Amadeus Mozart
(1756-1791)

Ludwig van Beethoven
(1770-1827)

Franz Schubert (1797-1828)

Felix Mendelssohn (1809-47)

Frédéric Chopin (1810-49)

Richard Wagner (1813-83)

Giuseppe Verdi (1813-1901)

Johannes Brahms (1833-97)

Peter Ilyich Tchaikovsky
(1840-93)

Giacomo Puccini
(1858-1924)

Gustav Mahler (1860-1911)

Maurice Ravel (1875-1937)

Aaron Copland (1900-90)

USA in 1888, settling in Boston. He was the soloist for his First and Second Piano Concertos in Boston and New York in 1889. Mac-Dowell's romantic style derived from Schumann, Liszt, and Grieg, and established him as a leading figure in American music. Of his output of orchestral, piano, and vocal music, his concertos are still performed and recorded, and the perennial favorites "To a Wild Rose" and "To a Water Lily" from his *Woodland Sketches* (1896) are usually included in piano albums.

ETHELBERT NEVIN (born: Edgeworth, Pennsylvania, November 25, 1862; died: New Haven, Connecticut, February, 1901) studied in Pittsburgh, Dresden, and Berlin. Despite intermittent ill-health, he gave piano concerts in Pittsburgh and wrote sentimental piano pieces and songs. His most famous are *Narcissus* (1891), for piano, and "The Rosary" (1898), a song which sold over six million copies over the next thirty years.

SCOTT JOPLIN (born: near Marshall, Texas, or Shreveport, Louisiana, November 24, 1868; died: New York, April 1, 1917) played the piano in brothels in St. Louis and Chicago, before settling in New York. He became known as the "King of Ragtime" with compositions such as *Maple Leaf Rag*, *The Entertainer*, and many others. He wrote two ragtime operas which were failures during his lifetime. Championed by American pianist and musicologist Joshua Rivkin, ragtime experienced a revival in the 1970s. The Paul Newman/Robert Redford film *The Sting* (1973) brought Joplin's music to an even larger audience. In 1976, the black composer received a posthumous Pulitzer Price.

CHARLES IVES (born: Danbury, Connecticut, October 20, 1874, died: New York, May 19, 1954) was the first prominent modern American composer. He did not study in Europe, but after graduating from Yale in 1898 moved to New York to become an insurance clerk as well as an organist. In 1907 he and a friend opened their own insurance company, while Ives continued working long hours on his music, to the detriment of his health. Far ahead of his time, Ives' music is full of polytonality, with whole tone scales, dissimilar rhythms, different keys, and multiple tunes juxtaposed within a single work. His output—1910–18 being the most prolific period—was enormous. His symphonies, orchestral, choral, piano, chamber music and songs abound with American themes— jazz elements, hymn tunes, patriotic songs and quaint titles such as *Central Park in the Dark, In the Good Old Summertime, Lincoln the Great Commoner* and *Some South-Paw Pitching*. His music is an acquired taste.

JOHN ALDEN CARPENTER (born: Park Ridge, Illinois, Feburary 28, 1876; died: Chicago, April 26, 1951) like Ives combined music with a successful business career. He studied piano and theory at Harvard, and had some lessons from Elgar in Rome in 1906. His compositions include 3 ballets, 2 symphonies, a tone poem, violin concerto, string quartet, piano quintet, and songs. His most-performed work is the humorous four-movement orchestral suite, *Adventures in a Perambulator* (1915), describing a baby's eye view of sights from his "buggy": "The Policeman," "The Hurdy Gurdy," "The Lake," and "The Dogs."

ERNST BLOCH (born: Geneva, July 24, 1880; died: Portland, Oregon, July 15, 1959) studied at the Brussels Conservatory (1897–99) and in Frankfurt (1900). He went to Paris in 1903 and composed the symphonic poem *Winter—Spring* (1904) and the opera *Macbeth* (1910). While these reflected the influences of Mussorgsky, Debussy, and Strauss, his trademark modality and frequent shifts of tempo and key signature were already evident. In 1916 Bloch moved to the United States, taking American citizenship eight years later. He taught in New York until 1920, then became the first director of the Cleveland Institute of Music (1920–25). From 1926–30 he headed the San Francisco Conservatory. The next nine years were spent in Geneva and Rome, but with the onset of World War II he returned to America, settling in Oregon.

Besides his major works, which include *Voice in the Wilderness* (1936) for cello and orchestra, his violin concerto (1938) and the Symphony in E flat (1954–5), the major portion of Bloch's output reflects his Jewish heritage: The *Israel* Symphony (1912–16), *Three Jewish Poems* (1913), *Psalm 22* (1914), *Shelomo* (1916), the sacred service *Abodath Hakodesh* (1933), *Suite Hebraique* (1953) and *Bad Shem* (1923) for violin and piano, or orchestra. His best-known composition is the *Concerto Grosso No. 1*, for strings and piano (1924–25).

CHARLES WAKEFIELD CADMAN (born: Johnstown, Pennsylvania, December 24, 1881; died: Los Angeles, December 30, 1946) was an organist and music critic besides being a composer. He specialized in American Indian music, which he used in his own works. His *Shanewis* ("The Robin Lady"—based on a Native American legend) was the first American opera to be performed at the Metropolitan two seasons in a row (1918–19). Of his other operas, symphonies, orchestral compositions, and over 180 songs—all in traditional nineteenth-century style— he is best remembered by the delicate song "At Dawning."

CHARLES TOMLINSON GRIFFES (born: Elmira, New York, September 17, 1884; died: New York, April 8, 1920) was a pupil in Berlin (1903–

07) of the "real" Engelbert Humperdinck (1854–1921), who wrote the opera *Hansel and Gretel.* On his return to America (1908) Griffes took on what would become a lifetime teaching position at a boys' school in Tarrytown, New York. His fairly large body of work—orchestral, dramatic, vocal, piano, and chamber music—was just beginning to be recognized before he died. Besides the French Impressionist influence, Japanese and American Indian themes are found in his compositions. The most-played compositions are his languorous *The White Peacock* (1918) and the symphonic poem *The Pleasure Dome of Kubla Khan,* after the poem by Samuel Taylor Coleridge.

AMERICAN MODERNS

Next came a succession of American composers whose music embraced twentieth-century trends, some of them daringly avant-garde in the breaking up of accepted forms of composition.

DEEMS TAYLOR (born: New York, December 22, 1885; died: New York, July 3, 1966) was music critic for the *New York World* 1921–25, music advisor to CBS in 1936, and well known for the narration of New York Metropolitan Opera broadcasts and New York Philharmonic concerts. He was also the narrator for Disney's *Fantasia.* Commissioned by the Met, he wrote the operas *The King's Henchman* (1926–27) and *Peter Ibbetson* (1930–31). His most-heard work is the orchestral piece *Through the Looking Glass* (1922).

FERDE GROFÉ (born: New York, March 27, 1892, died: Santa Monica, April 3, 1972) was a violist in the Los Angeles Philharmonic 1909–19. His work as an arranger came to the notice of Paul Whiteman, who engaged him to orchestrate symphonic jazz, including Gershwin's *Rhapsody in Blue* (1924). He began composing in the popular symphonic style, leaving us with the lovely but too little played *Mississippi Suite* and the immortal *Grand Canyon Suite,* whose premiere in 1931 was conducted by Arturo Toscanini.

WALTER PISTON (born: Rockland, Maine, January 20, 1894; died: Belmont, Massachusetts, November 12, 1976) majored in composition at Harvard (1919–24) then went to Paris to study with Dukas and Boulanger. He returned to Harvard, becoming a renowned theory teacher (1926–60). He is the author of three important textbooks, *Harmony* (1941), *Counterpoint* (1947), and *Orchestration* (1955). His clear style of music reflects the neoclassism of Stravinsky, Fauré, and Roussel. Of his many orchestral and chamber works, Piston's most-performed work is the music from his ballet *The Incredible Flutist* (1938).

WILLIAM GRANT STILL (born: Woodville, Mississippi, May 11, 1895; died: Los Angeles, December 3, 1978) went to Oberlin Conservatory (1917–18) and studied privately with Varèse (1922–25) and Chadwick at the New England Conservatory (1922). He played the violin, cello, and oboe in various orchestras and in the 1920s was an orchestrator for Broadway musicals, radio shows and Paul Whiteman's band. (Which premiered Gershwin's *Rhapsody in Blue*). Still's *Afro-American Symphony* (1930) was the first by a black American to be played by a major orchestra. He also wrote four other symphonies, operas, orchestral, choral and piano music, and songs.

HOWARD HANSON (born: Wahoo, Nebraska, October 28, 1896; died: Rochester, New York, Feburary 26, 1981) won the American Prix de Rome (1921) and spent three years at the American Academy in that city. One of his teachers was Respighi. On his return he became director of the Eastman School of Music in Rochester, New York, a post he held for forty years. An influential teacher, he established festivals which, since 1925, have premiered hundreds of works by American composers. Hanson was known as the American Sibelius because his music contains a similar blend of the romantic rooted in tonality. His output includes six symphonies, tone poems, and choral and chamber music. His opera *Merry Mount* (1934) and his Symphony No. 2 (*Romantic*) are his best-known compositions.

ROGER SESSIONS (born: Brooklyn, New York, December 28, 1896; died: Princeton, New Jersey, March 16, 1985) began his musical studies early and wrote an opera at thirteen. He attended Harvard (1910–15) and Yale (1915–17), and became a member of the faculty at Smith College (1917–21) while studying privately with Ernst Bloch (1880–1959). He became that composer's assistant at the Cleveland Institute (1921–25). Between 1927–33 Sessions lived in Florence, Rome, and Berlin. He returned to the U.S. to teach at Boston University (1933–35), Princeton (1935–45), Berkeley (1945–51), Princeton again, (1953–65), and the Juilliard School of Music (1965–80). His pupils included a new generation of American composers. Sessions's music—symphonic, orchestral, choral, chamber, and piano—contains the main international twentieth-century elements.

VIRGIL THOMSON (born: Kansas City, Missouri, November 25, 1896; died: New York City, September 30, 1989) was educated at Harvard

(1919–23), during which years he spent 1921–22 in Paris, where he studied with Boulanger and met Satie and Les Six. From 1925–40 he was again in Paris, where Stravinsky was an important influence. He also met the unconventional writer Gertrude Stein, with whom he collaborated on two operas, *Four Saints in Three Acts* (1934) and *The Mother of Us All* (1947). For fourteen years after his return to New York in 1940, Thomson was music critic for the *Herald Tribune*. His elegant writing and discriminating ear made him one of the top critics in the country. Thomson's body of compositions was rooted in Americana, but with the flavor of Satie's influence. Besides his operas, there are 2 ballets, 3 symphonies, 2 suites, a cello concerto, and chamber and vocal music. His most enduring works are his film scores for *The Plow that Broke the Plains* (1936), *The River* (1937), and *Louisiana Story* (1948).

HENRY COWELL (born: Menlo Park, California, March 11, 1897; died: Shady, New York, December 10, 1965) began to play the violin at age three and composed at eleven without formal training. In 1913 he devised a piano technique known as *clusters*, a method in which adjacent notes are played with the forearms or the flat of the hand. With one hundred compositions already to his credit, he began formal music studies in 1913 with Charles Seeger, who encouraged him to write down his unorthodox approach. Cowell did so in a book called *New Musical Resources* (1919). He pioneered different uses of the piano, such as plucking the strings or muting them with cardboard or metal. Cowell also invented a new method of notation and the *rhythmicon*, an electric instrument which could reproduce his complicated rhythms. He became interested in music of other cultures and combined Indian, Persian, and Oriental instruments with Western ones. In 1936 he reverted to American roots with his *18 Hymns and Fuging Tunes*. In his last fifteen years he returned to clusters and other unconventional modes. His 140 orchestral works, including 21 symphonies, many concertos, 170 chamber and 60 choral works, plus 200 piano pieces, operas, and film music, put him in the forefront of avant-garde composers.

ROY HARRIS (born: Lincoln County, Oklahoma, February 12, 1898; died: Santa Monica, California, October 1, 1979) studied in Los Angeles and Berkeley, and took private lessons with Arthur Bliss before going to Paris (1926–29) to study with Boulanger. He gained recognition as this country's leading symphonist when Serge Koussevitzky conducted his First Symphony in Boston (1934). His third symphony (1937) was equally well received. His modern style is distinctively

American—infused with hymn tunes, folk and patriotic themes. Harris taught at Juilliard, Cornell, UCLA, and California State University, Los Angeles.

GEORGE ANTHEIL (born: Trenton, New Jersey, July 8, 1900; died: New York, February 12, 1959) caused a furor in Europe in the 1920s with his *Airplane Sonata, Mechanisms*, and the *Ballet Mechanique* which used 8 pianos, 8 xylophones, 2 doorbells, car horns, anvils, and the sound of an airplane propeller. He returned to the U.S. in 1933, wrote film scores from 1936 on and gradually became more conservative in his later output of 6 symphonies, 3 operas, a piano and a violin concerto, and vocal, chamber, and piano music. He also made a study of the glandular abnormalities of criminals and wrote detective stories and a "Dear Abby" type of column.

MARC BLITZSTEIN (born: Philadelphia, Pennsylvania, March 2, 1905; died: Fort-de-France, Martinique, January 22, 1964), son of a wealthy family, studied at the Curtis Institute (1923–25), in Paris (1926) with Nadia Boulanger, and Berlin (1927) with Schoenberg. He returned to America during the Depression, met Berthold Brecht in New York and began to write for the popular theater. His most successful work is his "play in music," *The Cradle Will Rock* (1937), which has to do with labor relations. His major concert work is the *Airborne Symphony* (1946) for soloists, men's choir and orchestra about the air victory against Germany—he served with the U.S. Air Force in England from 1942–45. Blitzstein also wrote 2 ballets, 5 operas, a piano concerto and theater and film music. He was the first composer to develop the American vernacular speech style in theater music.

PAUL CRESTON (born: New York, October 10, 1906; died: San Diego, California, August 24, 1985), whose original name was Joseph Guttoveggio, was self-taught yet wrote much instrumental and choral music in a strong vital style with Impressionistic harmonies and full orchestration, beginning with his First Symphony in 1940. His output included concertos for saxophone, harp, tuba, and accordion, as well as chamber, choral, and piano music. He was organist at St. Malachy's Church in New York from 1934–67.

ELLIOTT CARTER (born: New York, December 11, 1908) enjoyed the friendship of Charles Ives from age sixteen and through the latter's recommendation studied at Harvard with Piston and Holst (1926–32) after which he went to Boulanger in Paris (1932–35). From early neo-classical works he shook off the Stravinsky influence and plunged into

Schoenberg and Varèse-like avant-garde style in ballets, orchestral, chamber, piano, and vocal compositions.

SAMUEL BARBER (born: West Chester, Pennsylvania, March 9, 1910; died: New York, January 23, 1981) played the piano and cello at age six. He studied voice (baritone) and composition at the Curtis Institute (1924–32) and won acclaim in 1931 for *Dover Beach*, from the poem by Matthew Arnold, written for string quartet with himself as soloist. In 1935 he won a Pulitzer Scholarship and in 1936 the Prix de Rome. His first symphony was premiered there in 1936. Famed conductor Arturo Toscanini conducted the first performances of his first *Essay for Orchestra* (1937) and the sublimely beautiful *Adagio for Strings*, which has made Barber's name immortal. Over the years American premieres of his works in New York, Boston, and Philadelphia were conducted by all the greats: Bruno Walter, Serge Koussevitzky, Erich Leinsdorf, Dimitri Mitropoulos, Eugene Ormandy, and Zubin Mehta. Of his operas, *Vanessa* (1958) was more successful than *Antony and Cleopatra*, which he wrote for the opening of the Met at Lincoln Center in September 1966. His Romantic style with its melodic elegance was a direct contrast to the dissonant musical experiments of the 1930s. Most of Barber's works continue to be performed today. Favorites include the overture to *The School For Scandal* (1933), the Violin Concerto (1941), *Knoxville: Summer of 1915* (1948), for soprano and orchestra, and music from the ballet *Souvenirs* (1955).

WILLIAM SCHUMAN (born: New York, August 4, 1910; died: New York, February 15, 1992) studied at Columbia University in 1933 under Roy Harris. His first symphony established him as a serious composer. His second was performed in Boston by Koussevitzky, who became his champion. Schuman taught at Sarah Lawrence College (1935–45), became president of Juilliard (1945–61), and the first president of the new Lincoln Center of the Performing Arts. Besides one opera, *The Mighty Casey* (1953), he wrote 6 ballets, 10 symphonies, and orchestral, choral, piano, and chamber music. His music is vigorously modern and sometimes layered—that is, using different instrumental groups at different tempos. He received many honors.

ALAN HOVHANESS (born: Somerville, Massachusetts, March 8, 1911) studied at the New England Conservatory and later taught at the Boston Conservatory (1948–52) after which he settled in New York. His early music is Romantic, but by 1943 his Armenian ancestry began to show in his compositions. In the 1950s he traveled abroad and incorporated experimental styles. The 1960s witnessed his interest in Japanese and Korean music. In the 1970s he returned to a more Western style. Much of his work is religious in nature. His compositions number over 300, including symphonies, operas, orchestral, choral, and chamber music. One of Hovhaness's unique creations is *And God Created Whales*, for hump-backed whale solo (on tape) and orchestra. His most famous compositions are *Fantasy on Japanese Woodprints* (1965) for xylophone and orchestra, and *Mysterious Mountain*, a haunting orchestral piece.

GIAN-CARLO MENOTTI (born: Cadegliano, Italy, July 7, 1911) spent most of his life in the USA and is considered an American composer. He studied at the Milan Conservatory (1924–27) and on Toscanini's advice, at the Curtis Institute in Philadelphia (1928–34), where his co-student Samuel Barber became a close friend. He later taught there from 1945– 55. Opera was Menotti's first love—he wrote two before he was fifteen—and his first success was his comic one-act opera *Amelia Goes to the Ball*, conducted by Fritz Reiner in 1937 and staged by the Met the following year. Next came the radio opera *The Old Maid and the Thief* (1939). The chamber opera *The Medium* (1946), an atmospherically sinister supernatural tragedy, and *The Telephone* (1947) a comedy, ran as a pair on Broadway for 211 performances (1947–48). The *verismo* ("true to life") *The Consul* (1950), dealing with the plight of refugees, and *The Saint of Bleecker Street* (1954) were also well received. *Amahl and the Night Visitors* (1951) was the first opera written for television. Menotti's small body of orchestral work is eclipsed by his operas, for which he wrote his own librettos. He also provided the libretto for Barber's opera *Vanessa* in 1957. Menotti achieved his goal of bringing opera to the Broadway theatergoer. In 1958, he founded the Festival of Two Worlds in Spoleto, Italy, which he directed until 1967.

JOHN CAGE (born: Los Angeles, California, September 5, 1912; died: August 12, 1992), was the grand old man of avant-garde music. He traveled through Europe (1930–31), then studied with Cowell in New York (1933–34) and Schoenberg back in his native Los Angeles in 1934. He developed his atonal (unkeyed) system at this time. In 1937 he moved to Seattle and founded a percussion school. He began to use electronic devices such as variable speed turntables in 1939, and invented the "prepared piano" by placing various objects (rubber bands, paper clips, etc.) between the strings of a concert grand to create percussive effects. He moved to San Francisco in 1939, to Chicago in 1941, and to New York in 1942, all the while writing for dance companies using the prepared piano and percussion. He also wrote concert works using these effects.

Through the 1950s and '60s Cage wrote "indeterminate" music, where the decision of the soloist of a composition replaces that of the composer. His *Imaginary Landscape 4* (1951) is scored for twelve radios operated by two performers, one changing the stations while the other works the volume controls. He used taped sounds, plants, shells, environmental sounds, and silence (*4' 33"*, 1952), and staged "jamborees of haphazardness." He has lectured in Europe and this country and has had much influence on younger musicians and artists.

MORTON GOULD (born: New York, December 10, 1913) studied at the Institute of Music and Art in his native New York, was a member of the staff of Radio City Music Hall, and worked for NBC and CBS. A brilliant orchestrator, his compositions blend popular American idioms and jazz in formal structures. Of many television and film scores, some chamber and much orchestral music, the best-known are his *Latin American Symphonette* (1940) and the ballet *Interplay* (1943). He has served as President of ASCAP since 1986.

NORMAN DELLO JOIO (born: New York, January 24, 1913) studied at Juilliard (1939–41) and with Hindemith at Yale (1941). Son of an organist and choir director, he was influenced from childhood by Gregorian chant and Italian opera. He was organist at St. Ann's Church, New York, 1934–40, and music director of the Loring Dance Players 1941–43. He held various teaching positions and became professor of music at Boston University in 1972. He wrote several ballets, including some for modern dance innovator Martha Graham. His gift for opera is displayed in three whose subject is St. Joan. Catholic church music, jazz, and a bold melodic line characterize his orchestral, choral, and chamber music. He may be best remembered for his vibrant incidental music to the television series *Air Power* in the 1950s.

DAVID DIAMOND (born: Rochester, New York, July 9, 1915) studied at the Cleveland Institute of Music (1927–29), the Eastman School of Music in his home town (1930–34), with Roger Sessions in New York City (1935), and then went to study with Boulanger in Paris (1936–37), where he met the French philosophical writer André Gide (1869–1951) as well as Ravel, Stravinsky, and Roussel, who were to influence his contrapuntal style. He won the Juilliard Award in 1937, Guggenheim Fellowships in 1938 and 1941, and the American Academy in Rome Award (1942). He lived in Florence from 1952 to 1965, then became head of the composition department of the Manhattan School of Music 1965–67. *Elegy in Memory of Ravel* was written in 1938. He also wrote a song cycle, *L'Âme* (the soul) *of Debussy*. His neoclassic lyricism swung toward serialism (twelve-tone music) after the 1950s. His body of compositions include 11 symphonies, concertos, 11 string quartets, choral music, and songs. The *Rounds* for strings (1944) is widely performed.

Lukas Foss (born: Berlin, August 15, 1922, original name Fuchs) is an American composer of German parentage. He studied in Berlin and Paris before coming to America in 1937. Here he went to the Curtis Institute, and then became a student of Koussevitzsky and Hindemith at Yale (1939–41). He was pianist for the Boston Symphony (1944–50), worked in Rome (1950–52), taught at UCLA (1953), then became conductor of the Buffalo Philharmonic (1963–70) and the Brooklyn Philharmonic (1971), introducing much new music. Like Diamond, Foss's early music was neoclassical, turning to modern improvisations, including electronics, in the 1950s. He conducted the Milwaukee Symphony from 1981 to 1986. His works include three operas, of which *The Jumping Frog of Calaveras County* (1950) is based on the Mark Twain tale. There is also a ballet, *The Gift of the Magi* (1945), from the Guy de Maupassant short story. Choral, chamber, and orchestral works make up the rest of his output.

Ned Rorem was born in Richmond, Indiana, 1923, studied in Chicago and at the Curtis Institute and Juilliard. He worked in New York as a copyist to Virgil Thomson, and lived in Morocco and Paris from 1949 to 1958. His *The Paris Diary of Ned Rorem* (1966) is an entertainingly candid autobiography. After winning several awards and fellowships, he taught at the Universities of Buffalo (1959–61) and Utah (1965–67). His studies in France with Milhaud, Auric, and Poulenc are evident in their influence in his music, especially his songs, for which he is considered one of the foremost American composers. His works, some of which contain a modified serial technique, include operas, symphonies, concertos, chamber and choral music, and many songs.

Gunther Schuller (born: New York, November 22, 1925) is the son of a violinist in the New York Philharmonic. He studied at the Manhattan School of Music and became principal horn player in the Cincinnati Symphony in 1943. He joined the New York Metropolitan Orchestra (1945–57), taught horn at the Manhattan School (1951–59), was associate professor of music at Yale (1964–67), an innovative president of the New England Conservatory (1967–77), and supervised contemporary music at Tanglewood from 1965, as well as being joint art director at the Berkshire Music Center since 1970. His music is a combination of the influence of Webern and Stravinsky with strong jazz elements. His output includes two operas, a ballet, instrumental and chamber works, and five Shakespeare songs for baritone and orchestra.

PHILIP GLASS (born: Baltimore, Maryland, January 31, 1937) studied at Juilliard, and in Paris with Boulanger (1964–66). There he also worked with Indian sitar virtuoso Ravi Shankar and, on his return to New York in 1967, continued his studies with Alla Rakha. This influenced his style of *ostinato*, a repetitive pattern of slow change. He formed his own ensemble to perform this music and has appeared with them internationally. Since 1975 most of his compositions have been for the theater, gaining fame with the Metropolitan Opera staging of his *Einstein on the Beach* (1976). Glass has become one of the most popular serious American composers; he performs also in rock and jazz. In 1992 he received a commission from the Met for an opera on Columbus to celebrate the 500th anniversary of the explorer's discovery of America.

STEVE REICH (born: New York, October 3, 1936) graduated with honors in philosophy from Cornell (1957). He studied both at Juilliard (1958–61) and Mills College (1962–63), where Milhaud was one of his teachers. After working at the San Francisco Tape Music Center (1964–65), he moved to New York, where in 1966 he began performing with his own ensemble, composed mostly of percussionists. Reich became one of the principal composers of *minimal music*, developing a style of changing *ostinato* patterns that, played on two or more tape recorders, gradually get out of phase with one another. *Drumming* (1971) is a ninety-minute elaboration of a single rhythmic cell. Gradually Reich added harmonic change to his music, and, in the 1980s, melody. At this time, he released his scores for public performance, having previously reserved them for his own ensemble. His interest in Balinese and African music is reflected in the *Desert Music* (1984), which features larger orchestral and choral forces. *The Four Sections* premiered in 1987. *The Cave*, in collaboration with video artist Beryl Korot, is a new kind of musical theater incorporating video footage in sequence with live music. It was premiered in Vienna in May 1993. The title refers to the place where Abraham and his family are buried. Since Jews trace their lineage to his son Isaac, and the Moslems to Ishmael, the site is the only place on earth where both religions come to worship.

JOHN CORIGLIANO (born: New York, Feburary 16, 1938), whose father was a violinist, studied at Columbia with Giannini and Creston, then worked in radio and television. His brilliantly orchestrated works are characterized by tonal harmony and a romantic style. *The Naked Carmen* (1970) is called an "electric rock opera." *A Figaro for Antonio* (1985), was commissioned by the Met. He has also written orchestral music, a Clarinet Concerto (1977), vocal music, and film scores. From 1987–90 he was composer-in-residence of the Chicago Symphony.

JOHN HARBISON (born: Orange, New Jersey, December 20, 1938) studied with Walter Piston at Harvard and in Berlin in 1961. He was a student of Sessions at Princeton, 1961–63, and has taught at MIT since 1969. His style is lucid and lyrical, with operas and large vocal works predominating. He has also written concertos for violin and piano, and chamber music. He has guest conducted throughout the United States, including appearances with the San Francisco and Boston symphony orchestras.

ARNOLD ROSNER, born in New York in 1945, has been composing since he was nine. His music bypasses gimmicky trends and is a synthesis of old and new, serenity and passion—sometimes violence—infused with spirituality and mysticism. His output of over one hundred compositions ranges from simple solos, songs, and sonatas to massive scores for orchestra, chorus, and wind band. Among his works are *A MyLai Elegy*, *Music de Clavecin*, *De Profundis*, *A Gentle Musicke*, various Latin choral works, Judaic music (*And He Sent Forth a Dove*, *Kaddish*, from *Three Elegiac Songs*), Buddhist compositions (*Five Ko-ans for Orchestra*), piano and cello sonatas, concerti grossi, string quartets, and *Gematria*, for full orchestra, based on mystic Hebrew numerology.

JOHN ADAMS, born Worcester, Massachusetts, Feburary 15, 1947, studied at Harvard with Roger Sessions among others, and started teaching at the San Francisco Conservatory in 1972. His interest in electronics (*Onyx*, 1976) turned to minimalism with the influence of Steve Reich. His works include *Shaker Loops* (1978) for seven strings, *Harmonium* (1981) for orchestra and choir, *Grand Pianola Music* (1982), and operas based on contemporary events: *Nixon in China* (1987), and *The Death of Klinghoffer* (1991).

Other composers falling into the modern experimental genre are Milton Babbitt (1916–), George Rochberg (1918–), William Kraft (1923–), Mel Powell (1923–), Leonard Rosenman (1924–), a pupil of Schoenberg whose film music includes *East of Eden* (1954) and *Rebel Without a Cause* (1955), Earle Brown (1926–), who was associated with John Cage, Morton Feldman (1926–87), George Crumb (1929–), Morton Subotnik (1933–), Roger Reynolds (1934–), Terry Riley (1935–), and William Bolcom (1938–).

These composers have evolved and interwoven a rich tapestry of music from European Romanticism to Americana to avant-garde serialism; they continue to develop a unique brand of nationalism.

The American Masters

Standing out like the three Bs in Europe are three masters whose compositions contain the native elements which personify the core of American music, including the versatile combining of classical and popular repertory.

GEORGE GERSHWIN, original name Gershovitz (born: Brooklyn, New York, September 26, 1898; died: Hollywood, July 11, 1937), was the son of Russian Jewish immigrants. At sixteen he worked as a "song plugger" for Remick music publishers, which meant that if someone wanted to buy a piece of sheet music, the plugger played it so that the customer could hear how it sounded. He wrote his first song in 1916 and his first Broadway musical, *La La Lucille*, in 1919. His theory teacher was Edward Kilenyi. He also studied with Henry Cowell, among others. For the next fourteen years, a Gershwin musical was an annual fixture on Broadway: *Lady Be Good!*, 1924; *Oh Kay!* 1926; *Strike Up the Band*, 1927; *Funny Face*, 1927; *Girl Crazy* 1930. The lyrics were usually written by his brother Ira. In 1924 Gershwin became famous in the concert hall when he converted jazz idioms to classical music in his tremendously successful *Rhapsody in Blue*. This led the way to more serious music, the Piano Concerto in F (1925), the tone poem *An American in Paris* (1928), the *Second Rhapsody* (1931), the *Cuban Overture* (1931), the folk opera *Porgy and Bess* (1935), and the three piano preludes.

In 1936, Gershwin went to Hollywood to write for films such as *The Goldwyn Follies* (1938). Of his hundreds of songs embodying the spirit of the 1920s and 1930s which have become classics, the favorites are: *Swanee, The Man I Love, Embraceable You, I Got Rhythm, 'S Wonderful, Fascinatin' Rhythm, Loved Walked In* and *Summertime*. All his music is vibrant and easy to listen to. Dead at the age of thirty eight, from a brain tumor, Gershwin, had he lived longer and studied more formally, obviously would have been a great symphonic composer.

AARON COPLAND (born: Brooklyn, New York, November 14, 1900, died: New York, December 2, 1990) was Nadia Boulanger's first full-time American student in Paris (1921), but he made it his life's work to get the European flavor out of his music. He introduced jazz elements into his work until 1930. His distinctive style is best heard in *El Salon Mexico* (1936), an orchestral fantasy based on popular Mexican tunes, and his ballet music from *Billy the Kid* (1938), *Rodeo* (1942), and *Appalachian Spring* (1944). He also wrote music for films: *Of Mice and Men* (1939), *Our Town* (1940), *The Red Pony* (1948), and *The Heiress* (1949), for which he won an Academy Award. The *Fanfare for the Common Man* and *A Lincoln Portrait* for speaker and orchestra, both written in 1942, plus arrangements of *Old American Songs* (1950–52), are among his most popular "Americana" compositions. His chamber and instrumental works tend to be more complex, leading by the 1960s toward serialism.

Copland toured the world as an ambassador for his country's music. With Roger Sessions he founded a series of concerts (1928–31) promoting new American works. He also established a publishing company and the American Composers' Alliance (1937). The embodiment of American music, Copland was honored throughout his long life. He received the Pulitzer Prize for Music (1944), the Gold Medal of the American Academy (1956), the Presidential Medal of Freedom (1964), and the Congressional Medal of Honor (1977).

LEONARD BERNSTEIN (born: Lawrence, Massachusetts, August 25, 1918, died: New York, October 14, 1990) was one of the most familiar conductor-composer-pianists in American history. He went to Harvard (1935–39) and the Curtis Institute of Music in Philadelphia (1941), where he studied conducting under the renowned Fritz Reiner (1888–1963) conductor of the Pittsburgh, Chicago, and New York Metropolitan Orchestras from 1938–63. In the summers of 1940–43 Bernstein was at Tanglewood, the summer music school in the Berkshire Mountains of Massachusetts, and became assistant to Serge Koussevitzky (1874–1951), maestro of the Boston Symphony from 1924–1949. Artur Rodzinski (1892–1958) conductor of the New York Philharmonic, invited the gifted young man to be his assistant (1943–44).

Bernstein became an overnight sensation with his storybook premiere, November 1943, when he stepped in to conduct the New York Philharmonic when the guest conductor, famed international maestro Bruno Walter (1876–1962), was taken ill. "Lennie" was promoted to sole conductor of the Philharmonic from 1958 through 1969, the first

American to hold this prestigious position. Bernstein achieved an international reputation guest conducting in Israel, Vienna, and La Scala, Milan, among many other orchestras. A gifted pianist, Bernstein often conducted from the keyboard. His innovative televised Children's Concerts in the 1960s made him a familiar personality to millions of viewers.

His compositions run the gamut from serious Mahler/Stravinsky-like symphonies with names like *Jeremiah* (No 1. 1942) and *The Age of Anxiety* (No 2. 1949), to Broadway musicals, the most famous of which is *West Side Story* (1957), a modern gang version of the Romeo and Juliet plot. This was made into a movie in 1961. His other musicals are *On the Town* (1944) featuring the ballet *Fancy Free*, *Wonderful Town* (1953), and *Candide* (1956), based on Voltaire's satire, whose overture is played regularly as a symphonic piece, with the rest of its sparkling tunes somewhat neglected. Bernstein also wrote chamber, orchestral, and choral music, two operas, *Trouble in Tahiti* (1952) and *A Quiet Place* (1983), and the dramatic film score for *On the Waterfront* (1954). Like Gershwin, he brilliantly bridged the gap between concert hall and theater.

Land of the Free and the Silver Screen

Always the land of opportunity, the United States has drawn European composers throughout history. Dvořák was director of the National Conservatory in New York (1892–95), and spent summers in Spillville, Iowa. Tchaikowsky conducted at Carnegie Hall in 1891, Mahler in 1910. Sibelius visited in 1914. Schoenberg settled in Los Angeles in 1934. Wars and political turmoil in Europe sent composers like Rachmaninoff, Stravinsky, and many others to seek freedom on our shores. Hollywood also attracted many talents.

Austrian-born ERICH WOLFGANG KORNGOLD (1897–1957) wrote music for such memorable Errol Flynn swashbuckling epics as *Captain Blood*, *The Prince and the Pauper*, *The Adventures of Robin Hood*, *The Sea Hawk*, and *The Private Lives of Elizabeth and Essex*, as well as orchestral works, including a lovely violin concerto.

FRANZ WAXMAN (1906–1967), born in Poland, worked in Berlin and Paris before coming to the United States. His film credits include *Sunset Boulevard*, *Peyton Place*, and *The Spirit of St. Louis*.

MIKLÓS RÓZSA was born in Budapest, April 18, 1907, and lived in Paris and London, where he wrote for Korda films (1936–42).

He emigrated to America in 1940 and composed for MGM from 1942 to 1962. His credits number Alfred Hitchcock's first U.S. thriller, *Spellbound*, the Ronald Colman *film noire*, *A Double Life*, and the Roman history extravaganzas, *Quo Vadis* and *Ben-Hur*. His style integrated his native Hungarian folk idiom with the essence of Hollywood, while his "serious" music, concertos and chamber works, combine dissonance and strong rhythms into symphonic form.

Born in New York, June 29, 1911, BERNARD HERRMANN has contributed many fine film scores. He studied at Juilliard and worked at CBS from 1934, conducting the Columbia Broadcasting Symphony Orchestra from 1942 to 1959. He also conducted in London. His movie credits include *Citizen Kane* (1940), *Psycho* (1959), and *Fahrenheit 451* (1966). His other works are a cantata, *Moby Dick* (1938), and an opera, *Wuthering Heights* (1952).

VICTOR YOUNG (born: Chicago, August 8, 1900; died Palm Springs, California, November 10, 1956) was an accomplished violinist by the age of six. He studied at the Warsaw Conservatory and made his debut with the Warsaw Philharmonic. Returning to Chicago, he became musical director at the Central Park Theatre. In the 1920s and 1930s he was a violinist and arranger with Ted Fiorito's orchestra. Young was a conductor/arranger in New York before going to Hollywood, where movie music became his field for the rest of his life.

Of the more than 350 films with which he was associated, the most popular are *Reap the Wild Wind* (1942), *For Whom the Bell Tolls* (1943), *Golden Earrings* (1947), *Samson and Delilah* (1949), *The Greatest Show on Earth* (1952), *The Quiet Man* (1952), *Shane* (1953), *The Country Girl* (1954), and *Around the World in Eighty Days* (1956).

Other notable film composers include MAX STEINER (1888–1971), whose most famous scores were for *The Informer* (1935), *Now Voyager* (1942), *Since You Went Away* (1944), and *Gone With the Wind* (1939); DIMITRI TIOMKIN (1899–1979): *Lost Horizon* (1937), *High Noon* (1952), *the High and the Mighty* (1954), etc.; DAVID RAKSIN (1912–), who collaborated with Charlie Chaplin on the music for *Modern Times* (1936), and whose other scores include *Forever Amber* (1947), *The Bad and the Beautiful* (1952), and his masterpiece, the haunting theme "Laura," from the film of the same name; ELMER BERNSTEIN (1922–), *The Ten Commandments* (1956), *The Magnificent Seven* (1960), *To Kill a Mockingbird* (1962), *The Great Escape* (1963), *Hawaii* (1966), *Airplane!* (1980), *Ghostbusters* (1984), and *Lost in Yonkers* (1993); and JERRY GOLDSMITH (1929–), whose large output contains *Freud* (1962),

Planet of the Apes (1968), *Patton* (1970), *MacArthur* (1977), *Rambo* (1985), and *Total Recall* (1990).

The enormous talent pool of all these composers has enriched American culture and served to draw the nations of the world ever closer together in the universality of music.

A Man for All Countries

ALBERT SCHWEITZER (born Kayersberg, Germany, January 14, 1875; died Gabon, September 4, 1965) was a philosopher, organist, scholar, physician, and humanist. His music studies began as a child. In 1896 he became organist of the Bach Concerts in Strasbourg. He received Ph.D.s in philosophy (1899) and theology (1900) at the university. The same year he was ordained as a curate of the Church of St. Nicholas in Strasbourg. He joined the university faculty in 1902, completing his M.D. in 1912. Concurrently he was organist of the Bach Society in Paris (1905–13). He also explored the psychology of sound in Berlin, gaining fame as an authority on organ construction. His best known work, *Johann Sebastian Bach* (in French, 1905; in German, 1908), emphasized the deeply religious nature of Bach's music and set the accepted unadorned way of playing his music.

As a theologian, Schweitzer expounded different views of the New Testament with his books *The Quest for the Historical Jesus* (1906) and the *The Mysticism of St. Paul the Apostle*. His first trip to Lamboréné, French Equatorial Africa (now Gabon), was in 1913; there he set up a jungle hospital. Interned in France during part of World War I because he was German, Schweitzer used the time to write two volumes of philosophy, *The Decay and the Restoration of Civilization* and *Civilization and Ethics*. Far ahead of his time, he advocated reverence for life, blaming lack of love and compassion as decayers of society.

He returned to Africa in 1924 and, in spite of floods, pestilence, and lack of trained help, built a hospital which over the years cared for thousands of natives, including lepers. To raise money, he frequently came back to Europe to lecture and give organ recitals. He visited the United States in 1949. As one of the world's foremost thinkers, he won the Nobel peace price in 1952—thus far the only professional musician to be so honored.

CHAPTER ELEVEN

Modern Music

Western music has been evolving for a thousand years.

Initially purely vocal, the single-voiced chant gave way to complex polyphony, or choral singing. This combined with instrumental accompaniment gave rise to early opera.

Gradually instrumental works took their place beside vocal. In the chamber music of the 1600s instrumental trios replaced vocal madrigals, in turn to be phased out in the 1700s by the string quartet—a form that has retained its popularity to this day.

Music to More Ears

The invention of the piano in 1709 created a revolution of its own, creating not only the most popular instrument for composers and performers, but the main means of bringing music into the home, until the advent of radio two hundred years later.

Meanwhile, orchestras grew from the few winds and strings of the 1700s to the large ensembles of Wagner, Liszt, and Berlioz in the 1800s to the modern symphony orchestras affiliated with every major city in the world. Music has become big business.

Reflection of the Times

Each generation of composers feels the need to perpetuate the life of their era. In the years before World War I (1900–1913) many discoveries overturned long-held theories. Sigmund Freud developed psychoanalysis and explored the subconscious mind. Albert Einstein's theory of relativity revolutionized our view of the universe. In art, Picasso distorted human figures and objects, while Kandinsky presented a completely abstract world. Music followed the trends as composers experimented with new techniques. The advent of the machine age, the accelerated tempo of living, the invention and perfecting of electronic instruments, and the unlimited potential of the computer have all found their way into music.

New Sound Waves

Sowing the seeds of this new harvest were some of Germany and Russia's greatest composers. Their roots were Romantic, but they introduced new sounds which audiences, musicians, and critics at first found hard to accept. Only the ensuing years attested to their greatness and the shape of things to come.

ANTON BRUCKNER (born: Ansfelden, September 4, 1824; died: Vienna, October 11, 1896) was the son of a village schoolmaster. Although showing great musical talent, he received no expert teaching until age eleven. After his father's death in 1837, he was sent as a choirboy to the St. Florian monastery, where he also studied organ, violin, and theory. In 1840 he trained in Linz as a schoolmaster, but continued organ lessons and became so expert that he returned to St. Florian as a teacher and organist. During these years he wrote masses and other sacred works. In 1855, he went to Vienna, where he studied counterpoint with the leading theorist, Simon Sechter; the same year he was appointed organist at Linz Cathedral. His studies continued until he was forty. In 1865, he met Wagner in Munich at the premiere of *Tristan and Isolde* and they developed a lifelong friendship.

In Vienna, the Philharmonic rejected Bruckner's First Symphony (1866, revised 1891) as "wild," the Second (1872, revised 1876) as "nonsense," and "unplayable," and the Third (1877, revised 1889) as "unperformable." His most successful, and still the most popular, is his Fourth, the *Romantic* (1874, revised 1880 and 1888). Dedicating his Third Symphony to Wagner put Bruckner in the middle of hostilities between the supporters of Brahms and those of Wagner. In 1883, while working on the Adagio of the Seventh Symphony, Bruckner heard of the death of his idol and immediately designated the coda as "funeral music for the Master."

In 1868, after Sechter's death, Bruckner replaced him as theory teacher at the Vienna Conservatory. In demand as an organist and improvisor, he played in Paris at Notre Dame (1869), and the new Albert Hall in London (1871).

Well-meaning friends often urged him to cut and re-orchestrate his work, and unfortunately the composer listened to them; as a result, at his death many of his creations were left in a state of chaos. Since 1934, under the editorship of Robert Haas (1886–1960) and, since 1954, Leopold Nowak, (1904–), the International Bruckner Society has attempted to piece back together Bruckner's original intent.

In the last five years of his life, the composer finally received the financial rewards and honors he deserved. His childlike religious faith and personal modesty have been misinterpreted as peasant-like and simpleminded, but the creator of such complex symphonies with their contrapuntal intricacies, melodic beauty, and magnificent orchestration could not fit such a description. He started late in life, yet mastered a technique which only now is recognized as following the Austrian tradition of Schubert. This removes the stigma that his symphonies were Wagner-like monsters.

His output includes ten symphonies, the first being designated as "No. 0," much religious and choral music, and two quintets. His Fourth Symphony is the most familiar.

HUGO WOLF (born: Slovenj Gradec, March 13, 1860; died: Vienna, February 22, 1903) idolized Wagner, and, as a music critic for the *Wiener Salon Blatt* (1884–87), made many enemies for his dislike of Brahms. As a composer, his originality lay in the concept of compiling his work in songbooks representing a particular poet or other source, such as folk music, nature, national settings, humorous, religious, or erotic themes, e.g., 51 poems of Goethe (1890), *Spanisches Liederbuch* (1891), and *Italianisches Liederbuch* (1892). Basically a romantic, Wolf also wrote chamber and choral works, two operas, a symphonic poem, and his most famous composition, the *Italian Serenade* (1892).

GUSTAV MAHLER (born: Bohemia, July 7, 1860; died: Vienna, May 18, 1911) began piano lessons at age six and gave a public recital in 1870. He entered Vienna Conservatory in 1875. His life was split into two careers, composer and conductor. His conducting career began in 1886 in Leipzig, with subsequent posts in Prague, Budapest, Hamburg, and Vienna. His opera interpretations were brilliant. In January 1887, taking over the *Ring* cycle after famed conductor Artur Nikisch was taken ill, Mahler established himself as a genius. It was said that he conducted "like a fanatic monk."

In 1902, he entered a somewhat tempestuous marriage with Alma, daughter of the artist Anton Schindler (at one point he even consulted Freud on their relationship). The death of his elder daughter Maria in 1907 left him distraught. A perfectionist—he often re-orchestrated works that had already been performed—he wrote nine symphonies and six song cycles during vacations between opera seasons. He often used voices and choruses in his symphonies.

In 1907, he came to the United States as principal conductor of the Metropolitan Opera and New York Philharmonic, earning a then enormous salary of $30,000 a year. He conducted his final concert, February 21, 1911, while suffering from a high fever. The diagnosed bacterial infection, so easily taken care of nowadays by antibiotics, was then incurable. He sailed for home and died in Vienna a few days later.

Mahler was a Romantic composer, yet the unconventional forms of his symphonies included mystic passages, contrasts of childlike simplicity, and psychological insights. The ability of his music to relate to the complexities of modern life appealed both to audiences and the radical young composers Schoenberg, Berg, and Webern, among others, whose work he encouraged and whose idol he became.

His works, full of personal feeling, are large-scale, with long movements and requiring many performers. His early compositions celebrate his love of the countryside, and sing of nature. The later ones change to moods of longing, loneliness, and desolation. The rich orchestration glows with the sounds and tone color of each instrument. His harmonies follow the Austro-German tradition of Beethoven and Wagner. Like Mozart and Beethoven, Mahler yearned for the brotherhood of man.

It took until the 1940s for Mahler to be heard outside Austria and Germany. This was through his friend, the great conductor Bruno Walter (1876-1962), who conducted the composer's work throughout Europe and brought it to America when he lived here during World War II.

The lyricism of the First Symphony, subtitled, *Titan*, and the sublimeness of the *Adagietto*, the third movement of the Fifth, are the best introduction to this great composer.

RICHARD STRAUSS (born: Munich, June 11, 1864; died: Garmisch-Partenkirchen, September 8, 1949) was the son of Franz Strauss, a horn player in the Munich court orchestra. He began piano lessons at four, started composing at six, and took violin lessons at eight. He studied theory privately, beginning in 1875, but never went to a conservatory, finishing his regular education at Munich University. He wrote his first symphony and string quartet at age sixteen. Both were performed in Munich in 1881. The following year his *Serenade* for winds was performed in Dresden, which led to a commission from famed conductor Hans von Bülow, to whom he became an assistant for the Meiningen Orchestra (1885); he succeeded von Bülow a month later. He left Meiningen in 1886, visited Italy, then obtained important posts in Munich, Bayreuth, Weimar, Berlin, and Vienna. The excellence of his conducting received universal admiration.

Strauss married soprano Pauline De Ahna in 1894 and wrote many songs for her as well as being her accompianist.

His compositions reflected the influence of Berlioz, Liszt, and Wagner, to whom he was considered a successor, and many of his orchestral pieces were modeled after Liszt's descriptive tone poems. His success, at twenty-five, with *Don Juan* (1889), made him Germany's most important young composer. He continued writing in this programmatic form with *Death and Transfiguration* (1890), *Till Eulenspiegel's Merry Pranks* (1894–5), *Thus Spake Zarathustra* (1896), *Don Quixote* (1898), and the autobiographical *A Hero's Life* (1899). His other orchestral works are the *Domestic Symphony*, which premiered during a visit by Strauss to New York in 1904, and his last full-scale work, the *Alpine Symphony* (1915), which uses alphorns, cowbells, and wind and thunder machines. Near the end of his career he wrote the Second Horn Concerto (1942) and *Metamorphosen* (1945) for 23 strings, a lament for the destruction of culture through the World War II bombing of German opera houses.

At the turn of the century, Strauss concentrated on opera. *Salomé* (1905) and *Elektra* (1909) shocked audiences with their "obscene" treatment of biblical and classical subjects. Both deal with deranged female obsessions, feature sensual dancing, imply abnormal sexuality, and lead to violent climaxes and gruesome deaths—all the while pressing the female voice to dramatic extremes. His most popular work, *Der Rosenkavalier* (1911) had a triumphant premiere at Dresden and has remained in the repertoire of leading opera houses ever since. *Ariadne auf Naxos* (1912) and *Die Frau ohne Schatten* (1919) are also regularly performed.

From 1933–35, he was made president—without his seeking it—of the State Music Bureau by the new Nazi regime. Also, he once conducted at Bayreuth when Toscanini refused. Prohibited from working with his Jewish librettist Stefan Zweig, as well as protecting his Jewish daughter-in-law, Strauss was put under surveillance. He and the authorities coexisted in cautious toleration. During World War II he lived mostly in Vienna, continuing to compose. After the war he moved to Switzerland (1945–9) and did not return to his country villa in Garmisch-Partenkirchen until he was cleared of any Nazi collaboration. He visited London in 1947, conducting his own works and attending concerts conducted by his English champion, Sir Thomas Beecham. The composer died shortly after worldwide celebrations of his eighty-fifth birthday.

Living during the transition from Romantic to Modern, Strauss felt that music should express emotion and tell a definite story. A master of musical description and Wagnerian counterpoint, he drew new sounds out of the orchestra which are by now familiar and accepted by today's audiences.

MAX REGER (born: Upper Palatinate, March 19, 1873; died: Leipzig, May 11, 1916) had a career as professor of composition at the University of Leipzig, as well as being an internationally known conductor and pianist. He was prolific and his many compositions adhered strictly to "absolute" music—a term used by German Romantics for "pure" music, independent of words, drama, or other meaning—the complete opposite of "program" music. Reger saw himself continuing the tradition of Bach, Beethoven, and Brahms, infused with his own complex themes and great energy. His output includes orchestral, chamber, organ, piano, vocal, and choral music.

OTTORINO RESPIGHI (born: Bologna, July 9, 1879; died: Rome, April 18, 1936), went to Russia in 1900, where he played viola in the St. Petersburg Imperial Opera and studied with Rimsky-Korsakov, who influenced his own style. Professor of composition at Rome's Saint

Cecilia Conservatory from 1913 to 1926, he then toured the U.S. as a conductor and pianist. One of the masters of modern Italian music, his melodic harmonies and colorful orchestration pervade his compositions, the best known of which are *The Fountains of Rome* (1916), and *The Pines of Rome* (1924), the latter featuring the innovation of using a recording of a nightingale singing. He also arranged the music of Rossini in a suite, *Rossiniana* (1925), and a ballet, *La Boutique Fantasque* (1919).

PAUL HINDEMITH (1895–1963) was concertmaster in the Frankfurt Opera Orchestra (1915–23)—with time out for serving in the German Army (1915–17)—and violist in the Amar String Quartet (1922–29), which played only modern music. From 1927 to 1937 he taught composition at the Berlin Hochschule für Musik. When Hitler came to power, the Nazis banned his music because he refused to stop playing music written by Jews. Beginning in 1934, he made three visits to Turkey to help establish the Ankara Conservatory. In 1937, he emigrated to the United States, where he became naturalized in 1948, was a professor at Yale (1940–53), and lectured at Harvard. After World War II, he again concertized in Europe, and received the prestigious $35,000 Sibelius Award in 1954.

Hindemith is known for *Gebrauchsmusik*, designed for audience participation, and *Hausmusik*, for amateur performance. His style interweaves neo-Classical, Baroque, Romantic, and Modern. Of his enormous amount of works in all forms, his masterpiece is his opera *Mathis der Maler*, whose interludes he arranged into a successful symphony.

The French Modernists

Aside from Debussy and Ravel, for whom musicologists have reserved a special category, there are several noteworthy composers who carried the spirit of French nationalism into the twentieth century. The group who called themselves *Les Six* disbanded in the 1920s, but continued composing and developing distinctive styles.

Although never a part of the group, ERNEST CHAUSSON (1855–1899) may be considered one of the modernists. Trained in law, he turned to music, studying under Massenet and Franck at the Paris Conservatory. His friends included Mallarmé, Debussy, the Spanish composer Albéniz, and the great pianist Alfred Cortot. Chausson died prematurely in a cycling accident, but left a large body of work, of which the best-known piece is the languorously lovely *Poème* for violin and orchestra.

VINCENT D'INDY (1851–1931) was another conservatory student of Franck, and a Wagner enthusiast. He played percussion in the Colonne orchestra before co-founding the *Schola Cantorum* for the study of church music. By 1900 this became a general music school, with the composer as sole director from 1911. He taught there for the rest of his life. His pupils included Satie, Auric, Roussel, and Turina. He assisted the violinist-conductor Charles Lamoureux, who founded a popular concert series which introduced Wagner's music to Paris. While championing Debussy at one end of the spectrum, d'Indy revived the music of Monteverdi, Gluck, Rameau, and Bach at the other. From his impressive number of compositions, he is best known for his *Symphony on a French Mountain Air*.

PAUL DUKAS (1865–1935) studied at the Paris Conservatory from 1881–89, coming under the influence of Franck; he later taught there. Debussy and d'Indy were his friends. The style of his main claim to fame, the symphonic scherzo *The Sorcerer's Apprentice* (1897), influenced both Debussy and Stravinsky. His perfectionism caused a limited output. His second best-known work is an exotic ballet *La péri* (1912), from which we occasionally hear the "Fanfare."

ALBERT ROUSSEL (1869–1937) after a naval career as an officer gravitated to music, studying at the Schola Cantorum with d'Indy from 1898 to 1908, beginning to teach there in 1902. In 1909 he toured India and Indo-China, writing a Hindu ballet, *Padmavati*, from this experience. His style ranges from the brilliance of Ravel to an astringent modern intensity. Later works reverted to the neo-classical. His extensive output includes 4 symphonies, an orchestral suite, a piano concerto, orchestral, chamber, and piano music, 20 songs, and 3 ballets, of which *Bacchus et Ariane* is his best-known work.

ARTHUR HONEGGER (1892–1955), a Swiss who was born in France, entered the Paris Conservatory in 1911. He went to Switzerland for the one-year compulsory military service (1914–15), then came back to Paris. Originally a member of *Les Six*, he became disenchanted with their "flippancy" and returned to the guidelines of Bach and Beethoven, although his wide-ranging harmonies and rhythmic propulsion is thoroughly modern. During World War II he lived in seclusion, refusing every Nazi offer to conduct music on the German-controlled radio in France. He visited the United States in 1929 and 1947 as guest conductor of major orchestras, and taught at the Tanglewood Summer Festival. Out of the bulk of his dramatic music, including radio and film scores, his representation of a locomotive in *Pacific 231* brought his name to prominence in 1924. He also wrote many chamber works. Of his orchestral music which includes five symphonies and a violin concerto, the tranquil symphonic poem *Pastorale d'Été* (1921) is recommended as a get-acquainted piece.

JACQUES IBERT (1890–1962), after studying at the Paris Conservatory and winning the Prix de Rome in 1919, returned to that city to become director of the French Academy from 1937 to 1955, and the assistant director of the Paris Opera and Opera-Comique from 1955 to 1957. His suave style has overtones of Debussy, Poulenc, and Stravinsky. He wrote comic operas, ballets, chamber music, songs, and orchestral music, of which the 1922 triptych *Escales* (*Ports of Call*) and the lively *Divertimento* (1930), as well as the piano piece *Le petit âne blanc* (*The Little White Donkey*) are his best known compositions.

FRANCIS POULENC (1899–1963) began composing at the age of seven. At fifteen he was introduced to Satie, Auric, and others, and by 1917 joined the *Nouveaux Jeunes*, a group of young composers designated *Les Six* by music critic Henri Collet. The Six gave concerts together, their music drawn from "Parisian folklore"—street bands, music halls, and circus bands. Part of Poulenc's style reflects these influences. Stravinsky on hearing his music recommended him to impresario Diaghilev. The result was one of his most famous compositions, *Les Biches* (1923), written for the Ballets Russes. It is full of the brittle sophistication of the 1920s, interlaced with the jazz idiom. The *Adagietto* contrasts in a romantic lyricism that dominates Poulenc's later works, especially after his many recitals with French baritone Pierre Bernac.

From 1935 onwards a change in his personal and spiritual life is reflected in a great deal of religious music, culminating in the opera *Dialogues of the Carmelites* (1955), which has had recent revivals in Houston (1989) and San Diego (1990), and is performed often at the Met in New York. The rest of his output encompasses dramatic works including incidental music for 11 plays and 5 film scores, plus choral, vocal, chamber, and instrumental music. Of his many works for the keyboard, including the organ, the Concerto for Two Pianos in D minor is a favorite.

DARIUS MILHAUD (1892–1974) entered the Paris Conservatory in 1909, studying with Dukas, Widor and d'Indy. From 1917–19 he was attaché to the French Legation in Rio de Janiero. Returning to Paris in 1919, he became one of *Les Six*. The year 1922 saw him in America, concertizing his piano works. Milhaud inherited the leading position in French music after the death of Ravel in 1937. He left German-occupied France in 1940 at the outset of World War II, remaining in the U.S. until 1971, teaching at Mills College in Oakland, California, and concurrently at the Paris Conservatory from 1947 to 1971. The onset of crippling arthritis did not interfere with his composition or teaching. He continued to do both from a wheelchair until his death in 1974.

His prodigious number of compositions includes 9 operas, chamber and vocal music, 11 ballets—one of which, the fun-filled *Le boeuf sur le toit* (1919), put him on the international musical map—theater music, 6 symphonies, other orchestral works, the most popular of which is the *Suite provençale*, 3 violin concertos, a viola and a cello concerto, 5 concertos and other piano pieces, including the lively *Scaramouche* for two pianos.

Before and Behind the Iron Curtain

SERGEI RACHMANINOFF (born: Semyonovo, Russia, April 1, 1873; died: Beverly Hills, March 28, 1943) entered the St. Petersburg Conservatory in 1882. In 1892 he wrote the *Prelude* in C sharp minor, which became his most celebrated composition, and for which he never received royalties. His first opera, *Aleko*, was produced in Moscow in 1893 and was praised by Tchaikovsky. His First Piano Concerto and First Symphony, however, were rejected, sending the composer into deep depression. His therapy and hypnosis sessions with Dr. Nikolai Dahl, who was also an amateur musician, resulted in the beautiful Second Piano Concerto—probably the universally most-performed work in this genre.

He visited the United States in 1909, premiering his Third Piano Concerto in New York. He returned to Russia in 1912, but with the Bolshevik Revolution in October of 1917, as an aristocrat and landowner, he found himself in danger and managed to escape via an invitation for a concert tour of Scandinavia. He was the last performing artist to obtain a visa to leave Russia legally. After writing an article criticizing the new regime, his music was banned in his homeland until 1933.

From 1918 on, Rachmaninoff lived mainly in New York, although still traveling to Europe to perform. With the advent of World War II, despite failing health he began an American tour in the winter of 1942–43, with the proceeds going to war relief. After playing in Knoxville, Tennessee, on February 15, he became seriously ill and died March 28 at his home in Beverly Hills.

Considered one of the world's greatest pianists for his great clarity of technique, he wrote many compositions for the instrument, one of the most popular being the *Rhapsody on a Theme of Paganini* (1934). His orchestral and chamber music, piano pieces and songs reflect the unfettered freedom of the Romantic modern without the harshness and stridency characteristic of some of his national contemporaries confined behind the (former) "Iron Curtain."

IGOR STRAVINSKY (born: near St. Petersburg, Russia, June 17, 1882; died New York, April 6, 1971) was the son of a leading opera basso. He studied with Rimsky-Korsakov (1902–08) who, along with Tchaikovsky, Glazunov, and Borodin greatly influenced his early work, which included an opera, *The Nightingale* (1914) and the orchestral suite *Fireworks* (1909). These were heard by the impresario Diaghilev and resulted in an immediate commission to write the music for his ballet *The Firebird* (1910). Its success was followed by that of *Petrouchka* (1911), written in a more modern style than the lushness of *Firebird*. But it was the music to the ballet *The Rite of Spring*, with its biting savage rhythms, constantly changing tempos, and wild new orchestral sounds—coupled with Nijinsky's unorthodox choreography—that really caused a riot at the Paris opening in 1913. Fights broke out in the audience between those who liked it and those who didn't, while critics cried, "Hideous noises!" "Obscene!" and, "No relation to music!" (*Rite* is now an accepted masterpiece.)

With the Russian Revolution of 1917 barring his return, Stravinsky became a French citizen in 1934. It was not until 1962 that he made a triumphant visit to his homeland, and was honored as one of the greatest composers of the century.

In 1920 another style change—to the neoclassic—resulted in the ballet *Pulcinella*, written on graceful themes of Pergolesi (1710–1736). In the 1930s Stravinsky wrote large instrumental works, including a violin concerto (1931), a concerto for two pianos (1935) and the *Dumbarton Oaks* (1938) concerto for orchestra. With war breaking out in Europe, Stravinsky came to America in 1939, bought a home in Hollywood, and became an American citizen in 1945. Besides major works like the Symphony in C (1940), the Symphony in Three Movements (1945) and the Concerto for Strings in D (1946), he got involved in other facets of American life, composing the *Circus Polka* (1942) for the elephants in the Ringling Brothers Circus, the *Ebony Concerto* (1945) for clarinetist/ dance bandleader "Woody" Herman, and ballet music for the Broadway show *The Seven Lively Arts* (1944).

The late 1940s were devoted to the opera *The Rake's Progress*. At this time the composer met American conductor Robert Craft (1923–), a devotee of ultra-modernists Webern, Schoenberg, and Berg. Through Craft's influence Stravinsky developed a personal serial style which is evident in the religious works he wrote when he was in his seventies. He continued to compose into his mid-eighties, also conducting concerts, making recordings, and writing books. A key figure in mirroring the evolution of styles in twentieth-century music, whatever style he used the work is always recognizable as Stravinsky. The orchestral music from *Firebird*, *Petrouchka*, and *Rite of Spring* remain his most-played compositions.

SERGEI PROKOFIEV (born: Sontsovka, April 27, 1891: died: Moscow, March 5, 1953) learned piano at age three from his mother, and wrote an opera at nine. After studying with Glière (1902), he entered St. Petersburg Conservatory (1904) as a student of Liadov and Rimsky-Korsakov. He was considered an ultra-modern *enfant terrible*, which pleased his brash personality, since he refused to accept all the early rejection of his music and eventually got someone to publish his work. Like many of the audiences of today, most people hated the "cacophony" of his music, while some of the critics saw its potential.

He met Diaghilev in London (1914) but World War I interfered with plans for a ballet, whose already-written music became the *Scythian Suite*. His first symphony, the *Classical* (1917) is a brilliant modern reincarnation of Haydn. Prokofiev visited the United States in 1918, appearing in New York as solo pianist in his own works. His opera *Love For Three Oranges* was commissioned by the Chicago Opera and performed in 1921.

In 1920 Prokofiev moved to Paris, where he wrote three ballets for Diaghilev and had several of his works conducted by Serge Koussevitzky, another exile. Prokofiev, however, chose to return to Russia in 1933, and plunged into film music, *Lieutenant Kije* (1934) and *Alexander Nevsky* (1938) being the most familiar. His ballets *Romeo and Juliet* (1935), *Cinderella* (1934), and *The Stone Flower* (1948–50) are among the most popular in orchestral suite versions. Despite the success of his Fifth Symphony (1944) Prokofiev, along with Stravinsky, was among those condemned for "formalism" (1948). He was forced to "confess" his "shortcomings" in an open letter to the Union of Soviet Composers.

His enormous output—operas, symphonies, concertos, suites, chamber, choral, and piano music, and songs—regarded so horribly dissonant and avant-garde in his youth, is now accepted as twentieth-century style with Romantic roots. *Peter and the Wolf* (1936) for narrator and orchestra is an entertaining method of teaching children about the four instrument families. News of Prokofiev's death was kept from the public for several days because it occurred on the same day as Josef Stalin's.

ARAM KHACHATURIAN (born: Tbilisi, Armenia, June 6, 1903; died Moscow, May 1, 1978) planned to be a biologist, but at age nineteen began studying the cello in Mosow. Prokofiev arranged the Paris performance of his 1932 trio. His First Symphony was a success (1935), as was his piano (1936) and violin (1940) concertos. His Second Symphony and Cello Concerto came under the same 1948 cloud of official disapproval, and, like Prokofiev, he switched to the safety of writing film music. In the fifties he was allowed to travel, and toured Europe and Latin America conducting his own works. Concert favorites are the orchestral suites arranged from his ballets *Gayane* (1942) and *Spartacus* (1954). Khachaturian's style reflects the colorful vitality of his Armenian heritage. Not as harshly modern as some of his contemporaries, his music continues the link of the nationalist tradition of the St. Petersburg school.

DMITRI KABALEVSKY (born: St. Petersburg, December 30, 1904; died: Moscow, February 27, 1987) moved to the capital in 1918 to study at the Scriabin Institute (1919–22). From 1922 to 1925 he was a piano teacher and played for silent movies. The years 1925–29 found him at the Moscow Conservatory studying composition. His First Piano Concerto made him famous within Russia. When the Union of Soviet Composers was formed in 1932, Kabalevsky helped organize the Moscow branch, holding various administrative positions and writing articles on Soviet music and composers. He became a professor at the Moscow Conservatory from 1935 to 1939, all the while composing prolifically, including significant pieces for young musicians. His Third Symphony was a requiem for Lenin. He joined the Communist Party in 1940 and wrote patriotic works during World War II. His post-war compositions reflect the "socialist realism" prescribed by official policy. Of his sizable output in opera, choral, orchestral, chamber, piano music, and songs, he is mainly known in the West for his overture to the opera *Colas Breugnon* (1938) and the suite from *The Comedians* (1940). In keeping with the party decree in 1948, his music maintained a lyrical idiom. As a spokesman on cultural policy, Kabalevsky occupied an important role in Russian music.

DMITRI SHOSTAKOVICH (born: St. Petersburg, September 25, 1906; died: Moscow, August 9, 1975) at age nine studied with his mother, a professional pianist, and then at the Petrograd Conservatory (1919–25). His First Symphony was his graduation piece and gained him immediate international attention at age twenty. Living throughout the Communist regime, he was a believer in Russian socialism and felt that his music should serve the state. He wrote for stage, films, and ballet, the "Polka" from *The Age of Gold* (1927–30) being one of his best-known pieces. His opera *Lady Macbeth of the Mtsensk District* (1936) was successfully produced, but got him into trouble with the government. Under the circumstances, he withdrew his Fourth Symphony, which was in rehearsal, and wrote his most popular, the Fifth, which he meekly inscribed: "A Soviet artist's practical creative reply to just criticism." This was well received. After that he stayed away from the theater and between 1938 and 1953 wrote 5 more symphonies and 4 string quartets, and taught composition at the Leningrad (now back to its original name, St. Petersburg) Conservatory. In 1940 he won the Stalin Prize for his Piano Quintet. In 1943 he settled in the capital, becoming professor at the Moscow Conservatory. In 1948, along with Prokofiev, Khachaturian, and others, Shostakovich was again in disgrace, being accused of "formalism," a term coined by the authorities to define music which in their opinion was too modern and discordant. He was fired from his teaching post and did not regain it until 1960. When Stalin died in 1953, regulations eased a little. He wrote his Tenth Symphony, which initiated the final period (twenty-two years) of his career. He visited England in 1958 and 1974, becoming a friend of Benjamin Britten. In 1969 he had a massive heart attack which left him in fragile health for the rest of his life.

Looked upon as one of the greatest twentieth century composers, Shostakovich's style is marked by great emotional intensity. He goes from the savage to the sublime, using solo instruments in their highest and lowest registers, building themes into a mosaic imbued with humor and parody, sometimes to the point of the bizarre. His 15 symphonies, 15 quartets, ballets, operas, choral, chamber, and piano compositions are all considered masterpieces—it is just a matter for the Romantic ear to become attuned to them.

A New School of Musical Thought

Living at the same time as the German and Russian pioneers were three Viennese composers who literally broke all traditional sound barriers.

ARNOLD SCHOENBERG (born: Vienna, September 13, 1874; died: Los Angeles, 1951) began violin lessons when he was eight, and composed a few pieces for the instrument. Because his parents could not afford it, he had almost no formal musical education until 1895 when the composer Alexander von Zemlinsky (1871–1942) befriended him and gave him instruction in counterpoint. (He married Zemlinsky's sister in 1901.) His early works were Romantic, but modeled after Mahler and Strauss. His first successful work, a string sextet later arranged for string orchestra, *Verklärte Nacht* (*Transfigured Night*, 1899) continues to be his most-played composition. The music in the chromatic style of Wagner—short motifs developed at length with climax building upon climax—was later used in Antony Tudor's ballet *Pillar of Fire*. This, and his *Gurrelieder*, a choral composition for five soloists, narrator, eight-part mixed chorus, and an immense orchestra, plus Strauss's recommendation got Schoenberg a teaching post at the Stern Conservatory in Berlin. He returned to Vienna in 1903, where he met Mahler and also acquired the pupils Anton Webern and Alban Berg, who would follow his radical new methods to the extent of being known as the Second Viennese Music School—the first being Haydn, Mozart, and Beethoven.

In his compositions from 1903 to 1907 chromatic harmony was experimented with to its limits. By 1908 he had done away with a key center and achieved *atonality*. In 1909 his *Three Piano Pieces* and the song cycle *The Book of Hanging Gardens* (*Das Buch des hängenden Gärten*) shocked audiences with its dissonance, while others recognized the emotional intensity displayed in the works and the crossing of a new frontier. Like Freud, Schoenberg explored the world of fears and dreams. An accomplished artist (he had taken lessons from Kandinsky) he also became an Expressionist musically—projecting his feelings directly into his work. In 1911 he published a masterful book, *The Theory of Harmony*, with the modest disclaimer, "This book I have learned from my pupils." In 1912 came *Pierrot lunaire*, a work for reciter and chamber ensemble—its premiere provoking more hostility. His next set of works, appearing in 1923, introduced the "twelve-tone scale," his technique for organizing atonal music, which became known as "serial." At the same time he was still writing in traditional forms. In 1923, his wife Mathilde died, and a year later he married Gertrud Kolisch, sister of the virtuoso violinist, Rudolf Kolisch. Their daughter Nuria married Italian composer Luigi Nono, another serial composer.

In 1925 Schoenberg was invited to teach at the Prussian Academy of Arts. He remained there until 1933, when he was dismissed by the Nazis for his Jewish heritage, even though he had converted to Lutheranism in 1898. He went to Paris and then emigrated to the United States, settling in Los Angeles. He taught first at the University of Southern California and then at UCLA (1936–44), influencing a generation of young American composers. When he became a naturalized citizen he officially changed the spelling of his name, using the *oe* instead of the *o* with an *umlaut*, or two dots over the *ö*. He also returned to the Jewish faith. In 1938 he wrote a setting of the prayer *Kol Nidre* for rabbi, chorus, and orchestra. In the next eighteen years he varied his style from twelve-tone serialism and also produced some of his largest works: the Fourth String Quartet, a String Trio, a Violin Concerto, the Second Chamber Symphony, and the *Ode to Napoleon* (1942). *A Survivor from Warsaw* (1947) is a harsh composition graphically depicting the inhumane treatment of Jews in the Polish concentration camps. He also wrote several religious pieces, including the oratorio *Jacobleiter*, which he never finished, and the opera *Moses and Aron*, of which only two of the three acts were completed. This was produced after his death and proved greatly moving.

Schoenberg died in 1951, leaving behind important theoretical books, especially *Style and Idea* (1950), some well-executed paintings, including excellent self-portraits, and the twelve-tone controversy he started. He did more to change the sound of music of the twentieth century than any other composer. Foreseeing the reaction of those who opposed him and would eventually come around, he said, "Time is a great conqueror. He will bring an understanding of my works."

ANTON VON WEBERN (born: Vienna, December 3, 1883; died: near Salzburg, September 15, 1945), after early tuition from his mother, a pianist, and other studies, he entered the University of Vienna in 1902, where he earned a Ph.D in 1906 for his dissertation on the Dutch Renaissance master Heinrich Isaak. He then became a pupil of Schoenberg (1904–08), which began his close friendship with fellow student Alban Berg. In 1908 he wrote his *Passacaglia for Orchestra* in Brahmsian style. During this time he supported himself by conducting operettas at Bad Ischl, Teplitz, Danzig, Stettin, and Prague. From 1918 to 1922 he was active in Schoenberg's Society for Private Performances, which permitted no critics to attend.

After World War I Webern took charge of the Vienna Workers' Symphony Concerts (1922–34). Meanwhile, he was conductor and music advisor to Austrian Radio (1927–38). At the same time he commuted to London to conduct for the BBC (1929–36)—the main place his music received any recognition during his lifetime (during World War II, the

Nazis considered it Bolshevistic). His workers' organizations were dissolved by the Nazis in 1934, and in 1938 he lost his radio job. He lived through the war years in seclusion in a suburb of Vienna. After their son was killed in an air raid, the Weberns moved to their daughter's house near Salzburg. Several months after the war, during the postwar American occupation, not realizing there was a curfew, Webern stepped out of the house to smoke one evening, and was shot to death by an American military policeman.

One of the triumvirate of the Second Viennese School, Webern's particular contributions were the symmetrical forms and divisions of the twelve-tone row and his approach to serial organization. He had an obsession for brevity—one of his pieces is only six measures long—and although his entire output lasts only about three hours, the *avant-garde* generation of European composers used his music as a focal point.

ALBAN BERG (born: Vienna, Feburary 9, 1885; died: there, December, 24, 1935) had little formal music education until he took composition lessons with Schoenberg. He entered the artistic circle of Vienna with Webern, the poet Peter Altenberg, and the painter Kokoschka—all dominated by Mahler. In May 1914, Berg attended the premiere of Georg Büchner's play *Wozzeck*, and immediately saw it as an opera. He worked on this during his World War I military service and finished it after the war in 1921. The opera was sharply criticized in Berlin and Prague, but welcomed in America. The wide leaping melodic lines, rhythmic problems, and use of *Sprechstimme* (half-song, half-speech), which caused such difficulty for musicians of the time, are now taken in stride. *Wozzeck* is also known for its inclusion of a passacaglia with variations, a rhapsody, and several symphonic sections. Berg's second opera *Lulu* (1928–35), was interrupted by the composition of his Violin Concerto, which was his last complete work, dedicated "to the memory of an angel," referring to the death of Manon Gropius, the young daughter of architect Walter Gropius, who had married Mahler's widow. *Lulu* was left with the last act sketched out but unorchestrated at the composer's death. The plot is even more violent than *Wozzeck*, tracing the heroine's rise in society through her successive relationships, and then her descent into prostitution and eventual death at the hands of Jack the Ripper.

Although embracing the twelve-note or "dodecaphonic" method, Berg's style was nearer to Mahler than Schoenberg. Nevertheless, when two of the five *Altenberg Songs* with orchestra were performed in Vienna in March 19, 1913, the rest of the concert was abandoned due to the ensuing riot. Today his music is considered the most listenable of the three members of the Second Viennese School because it is not truly atonal and thus is able to evoke an emotional response from the listener.

Breaking New Sound Barriers

The crop of ultra-modern composers coming after the Second Viennese School appear to be trying to outdo each other in breaking traditions and writing music so complicated that the popular guess is that conductors include such works in their programs to 1) lift themselves from the ennui of "war horses," 2) dazzle the critics, 3) challenge the ability of the musicians, and 4) "educate" the audience, which usually applauds out of politeness but is relieved the "lesson" is over. It is not music that can be hummed after leaving the auditorium.

Since the 1920s, composers have been divided into the vanguard of experimenters and the conservatives who preserve tradition yet whose style is still recognizable as modern. Among the former group:

OLIVIER MESSIAEN (1908–1992) blended Indian and Oriental ideas in his novel rhythmic interpretations of bird and animal sounds, gave new dimension to organ music with use of special acoustic reverberations, and produced abstract and atonal music with rich, chromatic harmonies.

French-born American composer EDGARD VARÈSE (1883–1965) became a pioneer in electronic music in the 1950s, combining tape recordings and orchestra.

Also beginning in the 1950s, in West Germany, KARLHEINZ STOCKHAUSEN (1928–) layered sonically altered tapes, producing ear-bending electronic sounds. By the 1970s he was considered a "spiritual guide" for the new generation. He influenced American composers like TERRY RILEY (1935–), STEVE REICH (1936–), PHILIP GLASS (1937–), and JOHN ADAMS (1947–) into developing *Minimalism*, a style of repetitive, patterns of slowly evolving melody—music that requires a great deal of patience and open-mindedness on the part of the listener.

Holding Onto the Past

In the conservative group, sometimes called Neo-Romantic, music forms of the past such as Baroque dances and concerti grossi are being recreated. Symphonies, concertos, suites, and string quartets have never gone out of style. Sergei Prokofiev (1891–1953), Paul Hindemith (1895–1963), Francis Poulenc (1899–1963), Dmitri Shostakovich (1906–77), Benjamin Britten (1913–1976), Samuel Barber (1910–1981), and Gian-Carlo Menotti (1911–) among the many, wrote within traditional parameters, even though their styles are unmistakably of the twentieth century.

The New Romanticism extends to the generation of American composers born in the 1930s, John Corigliano, Arnold Rosner, Jacob Druckman, Joan Tower, and Ellen Taaffe Zwilich, whose individual and eclectic styles still manage to hold the interest of the concertgoer.

Looking into the Future

Universities are playing a vital role in creating new audiences through music appreciation courses, as well as grooming future musicians and composers. Many have their own orchestras and electronic studios. Their sponsorship of cultural events and employment of composers and music scholars has placed them in the patron role once belonging to the church and aristocracy.

Another modern trend finds women becoming more active as composers, conductors, music educators, soloists, and orchestra musicians.

Radio—especially FM classical music stations—television, video, CDs, tapes, and the rapidly-being-phased-out LP records put a vast scope of music within the reach of almost everyone.

The use of computers is revolutionizing the very act of writing music.

As to what the future holds for classical music? Predictably, there will always be resistance to experimentation. In past eras, audiences consistently demanded the most recent works. In the twentieth century, concert programs and ticket sales show preference for the time-polished favorites of the past, especially from the Romantic era. In the end, when novelties have worn off, that which endures through wars, political upheaval, society-changing inventions, and the forging of new frontiers in outer space is music which best expresses the human experience: music which touches our hearts.

*Music is about humanity, not the
gender of the composer. . . .*
—Ellen Taaffe Zwilich

CHAPTER TWELVE

Women Composers
Through the Centuries

B eginning with SAPPHO (*c*600 B.C.)—who besides writing exquisite
poetry (Sapphic Odes), also composed wedding songs, elegies, hymns,
and other music—women composers have existed throughout the ages.
Many of them positioned in a high place in society were of historical
importance. In our time, with the increasing momentum of acceptance
of gender equality, research by authors such as Judith Lang Zaimont,
Joan Weiner LePage, Karen Pendle, and Christine Ammer, and organizations such as the National Women Composers Resource Center in San
Francisco, the International Congress on Women in Music in the Los
Angeles area, American Women Composers, Inc., in Washington, D.C.,
and the International League of Women Composers in New York, as
well as many others both here and in Europe, is producing an ever
growing volume of books, recordings, and performances of the works
and contributions of women, past and present.

In the early part of this century, the eminent British conductor, Sir
Thomas Beecham (1879–1961) declared, "There are no women com-

posers, there never have been and, possibly, there never will be." This opinion, reflecting centuries of mindset of the "inferiority" of women, stifled, buried and otherwise kept much talent from coming to fruition.

According to British composer Dame Ethel Smyth (1858–1944), it all began in the Garden of Eden when Eve piped a tune on a hollow reed and Adam told her to stop making such a horrible noise, adding, "Besides, if anyone is going to make it, it's not you, but me."

The Bible has not been tolerant either. "Let the women keep silence in the churches . . ." (I Corinthians 14:34). Ecclesiastes 12:4 warns, "All the daughters of music shall be brought low."

In 1686, Pope Innocent XI declared, "Music is completely injurious to the modesty that is proper to the female sex, because they become distracted from the matters and occupations most proper to them. . . . No woman . . . under any pretext (should) even learn music (or) . . . play any sort of musical instrument." (This edict was renewed in 1703 by Clement XI.)

Moses Mendelssohn, the philosopher grandfather of Felix and Fanny, expounded the family attitude: "Moderate learning becomes a lady, but not scholarship. A girl who has read her eyes red deserves to be laughed at."

Showing a little more understanding, Edward Clark in his *Sex in Education* (1908) underlines the fundamental reason which has always been the shackler: "Women might be able to equal or even outstrip men intellectually, but since biology has dictated that such intellectual development would be at the cost of their reproductive functions, it is to be condemned on biological grounds."

Sidney Lanier in an 1898 article, "The Orchestra Today," struck a more positive note: "The superior daintiness of the female tissue might finally make the woman a more successful (instrument) player than the man."

Despite eons of prohibition and prejudice, there has emerged a core of women who have made their voices, instruments, and music heard. They commanded respect in their own time and along with the current generation of composers are regaining the limelight that once was theirs.

Hildegard of Bingen (1098–1179)

In past centuries the main requirement for a woman to engage in intellectual pursuits was to be born into aristocracy. Hildegard, tenth child of a prominent family, was placed into a convent at the age of eight—a not unusual procedure with superfluous daughters. By 1136 she was in charge of her own abbey at Bingen. From 1160–79 she traveled along the Rhine preaching and explaining the visions which had been coming to her since she was eleven.

Like Bach, Beethoven, and other artistic geniuses, the abbess believed her talents to be God speaking through her. She inspired the monk Bernard de Clairveaux to present to the Pope her series of visions regarding freeing the Holy Land from the Saracens. Hildegard was officially recognized as the prophetess of the Crusades and considered responsible for this turning point in European history. For the rest of her long life, she continued to be consulted by popes, emperors, kings, and archbishops. She combined in one person the ancient arts of prophecy and healing with the creative talents of literature and music. Besides her treatises on theology and natural history, her *Materia Medica* is still the sourcebook on medieval medicine. Her compositions forever changed the direction of music with the legacy that music gives added power to prayer—a concept intimately embraced by Christianity and other religions.

(Named for her, the Hildegard Publishing Company is devoted to publishing the work of women composers.)

Women of the Renaissance

Four centuries rolled by before more women composers were heard from. In England, ANNE BOLEYN (c1507–1536), the ill-fated second wife of Henry VIII, besides being an accomplished lutanist and singer, composed several ballads, the most famous being "O Death Rock Me Asleep," written in the Tower of London as she awaited her execution. This song is regarded as the first example of a vocal work with independent instrumental parts. Her highly educated daughter ELIZABETH I (1533–1603), who ascended the throne in 1558, composed hymns and songs and in 1549 set to music the songs of Margaret of Navarre.

In Italy, the most prominent Renaissance woman composer was FRANCESCA CACCINI (1587–1640), eldest daughter of composer Giulio Caccini (1546–1618)—a member of the Camerata and the Medici court. As well as composing songs and dramatic entertainment, she was a virtuoso singer, lutanist, and harpsichordist, and founded a music school in 1618. Performing with her two daughters, for over twenty years Caccini was the highest paid singer at the court.

Her *La Liberazione di Ruggiero*, produced in Florence in 1625 for the visit of Prince Sigismund of Poland, is believed to be the first Italian opera written by a woman. It was also the first Italian opera seen outside Italy when it was performed in Warsaw in 1682.

Women of the Baroque Era

Also in Italy, BARBARA STROZZI (1619–1664), daughter of poet/dramatist Giulio Strozzi, was able to showcase her exceptional voice in the Academia degli Unisoni, founded by her father in 1635. She received great recognition for her eight volumes of secular vocal chamber music published between 1644 and 1664, the year of her death in Venice. She was one of the most prolific composers of the early Baroque.

ISABELLA LEONARDA (1620–1704) was not a performer. Encased in the convent of St. Ursula of Novara, she became mother superior in 1686. Her formal music studies led to a lifetime of composition of much sacred choral music, plus a set of trio sonatas written at the age of seventy-three. In 1696 her Sonata for Solo Violin and *continuo* put her among the first Italian women to compose in the new Baroque instrumental styles.

(Leonarda Records, devoted to releasing the works of women composers, is named in her honor.)

ANTONIA BEMBO, born in Venice, went to Paris around 1690. On a salary from King Louis XIV, she lived at the convent of Notre Dame des Bonnes Nouvelles and devoted herself to composing, dedicating her works to the "Sun King." Most of her compositions—sacred pieces and an opera—are preserved in the National Library in Paris.

ELISABETH CLAUDE JACQUET DE LA GUERRE (1666–1729) had the advantage of being the daughter of Claude Jacquet, instrument-maker, organist, and harpsichordist to Louis XIV, and living in a court where culture reigned in the music of Couperin, the ballets of Lully, and the theater of Molière. The king himself undertook her education. In 1677, a French journal referred to her as "the child wonder who sang the most difficult pieces at sight, and who could also accompany and compose little pieces in all keys." She was called the Marvel of France.

She married Marinde de la Guerre. Her works—harpsichord pieces, cantatas, a ballet, and an opera *Cephale et Procris* (1694)—were performed at court. In 1704, after the deaths of her husband and son, she organized organ concerts and harpsichord recitals and was much in demand in the salons held in elegant homes. When Elisabeth died in 1729, the king struck a medal in her honor.

The Classical Period

In the era of Gluck, Salieri, Haydn, Beethoven, and Schubert, several women came to prominence.

ANNA AMALIA, Princess of Prussia (1723–1787), as the youngest sister of Frederick the Great (1712–86) lived in a court which vied with Louis XIV's in nurturing musical and literary culture, even having French writer-philosopher Voltaire (1694–1778) in its employ. After studying harpsichord, piano, organ, violin, and counterpoint, the princess wrote her main compositions past the age of forty, in a style similar to that of Karl Philipp Emanuel Bach (1714–88). An important patron of music, her soirées included musicians from all over Germany. Her entire library remains preserved in a Berlin museum.

ANNA AMALIA, Duchess of Saxe-Weimar (1739–1807), was named after her royal aunt. Married at seventeen to the eighteen-year-old Duke Ernst August Konstantin of Saxe-Weimar, she was left with two infant sons after he died two years later. From 1758–75 until her eldest son took over, Duchess Anna Amalia acted as regent. Meanwhile, both she and her children studied composition. Goethe, a frequent guest at the Weimar court, wrote poetry and libretti for her *singspiels* (song plays).

During this period Gluck was introducing opera in Germany, and music was dominated by Haydn and Mozart.

MADDALENA DI LOMBARDINI SIRMEN (c1735–c1800) studied voice at Venice Conservatory, where she was the favorite violin pupil of Giuseppe Tartini (1692–1770), renowned for inventing a new style of bow, discovering what he called a "third sound," and composing the "Devil's Trill" Sonata.

From 1768–85, she toured Italy, France, England, and Germany, performing her own compositions and also appearing in turn as a harpsichordist, singer, and violinist. Her popularity rivalled the equally favored violinist Pietro Nardini (1722–93), also a student of Tartini. She married German violinist and composer Ludwig Sirmen.

MARIANNE VON MARTINEZ (1744–1812) took harpsichord lessons with a poor tenant who lived in the same apartment house in Vienna—

Franz Joseph Haydn. Another tenant, court poet and opera librettist Pietro Metastasio, arranged for her to study with the great Italian opera singer and composer Nicola Porpora (1686–1768). She also studied composition, and by the 1760s was writing large church works—symphonic Masses, oratorios, motets, and choral litanies—as well as much piano music. (Mozart wrote his Piano Concerto in D major for her.)

When Emperor Joseph II ascended the throne (1775), he reinvoked the ancient rule against women singing in church, after which Martinez wrote no more Masses. Meanwhile, her fame had spread to Italy, where she was admitted to the Accademia Filarmonica of Bologna in 1773.

When Metastasio died in 1782, leaving his large estate to Martinez, she conducted musical soirées which Haydn and Mozart often attended. In 1796, Martinez opened a singing school in her home, producing many fine female singers. Both Martinez and Haydn made their last public appearance to hear Salieri conduct Haydn's oratorio *The Creation*, on March 27, 1808. A well trained and serious musician, Martinez was a significant composer.

MARIA THERESIA VON PARADIS (1759–1824), daughter of the Imperial Secretary, was the namesake of her godmother, the Empress Maria Theresa, who personally undertook the musical education of the child, who became blind at the age of two. The empress reigned from 1740 until her death in 1775, when she was succeeded by her son, Joseph II. Von Paradis studied with Salieri, who dedicated his organ concerto to her, and met Mozart, who wrote his Piano Concerto No. 18 for her.

Having memorized over sixty piano concertos, she spent the years 1783–1808 touring throughout Europe with her mother and librettist Johann Riedlinger, who had devised a wooden pegboard using different shapes for note values which enabled the blind woman to compose.

In 1808 after the death of her father, von Paradis founded and headed the Institute for Music, specializing in singing and piano. Her works include cantatas, songs, piano pieces, 2 operas, an operetta, a melodrama, 2 piano concerti, a piano trio, 16 piano sonatas, and 2 piano fantasies. Much of this music has been lost. Remaining are a sonata for piano and violin, a piano toccata, a Sicilienne for piano and violin, and various vocal compositions. She was highly respected.

AND THERE WERE OTHERS. . . . .

With the rise of the new middle class and its voracious demand for music and other forms of entertainment, women in the arts enjoyed more freedom. In Germany, singer actress CORONA SCHRÖTER (1751–1802) was employed as a chamber musician in the Weimar Court, where as a friend of Goethe she composed, to his libretto, the *singspiel Die Fischerin*, plus forty other songs. In Paris, actress, singer, pianist, and harpist JULIE CANDEILLE (1767–1836) composed operas, *singspiels*, and instrumental chamber music.

Women and the Romantic Spirit

The Romantic era (1830–1900) represented a period of turning away from the rigidity and structure of Classicism, with new freedom of thought and emotion in all the arts: literature, painting, architecture, and especially music, in what is considered its Golden Age. Caught up in the tide with their male counterparts—Beethoven, Schubert, Schumann, Mendelssohn, Liszt, Chopin, Brahms, et al.—several women also wrote music reflecting this spirit.

LOUISE REICHARDT (1779–1826), daughter of the Chapel Master of the court of Frederick the Great, was only eight when her songs appeared in her father's anthologies. She grew to have a profound effect on the musical life of Hamburg. Although not permitted to conduct in public, Reichardt trained and rehearsed the large mixed chorus for the city's Music Festival, where *Messiah* and the Mozart *Requiem* were given before audiences numbering six thousand. Besides teaching and conducting oratorios, she translated Latin texts into German, wrote *lieder* in the style of Schubert, and published two books of sacred songs.

MARIA SZMANOWSKA (1789–1831) was born in turbulent times in her country's history, with Russia, Prussia, and Austria annexing most of Poland, and Napoleon creating the Duchy of Warsaw. Acclaimed throughout Europe, Szymanowska eventually made her home in St. Petersburg, where she was named pianist of the Imperial Court in 1822. Ahead of her time in facing modern challenges, she married, divorced, retained custody of her three children, and still had a highly successful career. A victim of a cholera epidemic, she died in 1831 at age forty-two.

Her compositions, classified as *salon music*, were refined and elegant. Later in the century salon music evolved into the equivalent of modern "elevator music," as amateurs and commercial composers churned out pieces for mass consumption catering to the advent of pianos in the homes of the new middle class.

Of over 113 piano pieces, her mazurkas, preludes, etudes, nocturnes, and polonaises were models which Chopin, who attended her concerts, later enhanced in his own style.

LOUISE DUMONT FARRENC (1804–75), after studying with contemporary greats Ignaz Moscheles (1794–1859) and Johann Nepomuk Hummel (1778–1837), entered the Paris Conservatory at fifteen, already a proficient pianist. Between 1825–39, Farrenc wrote most of her piano works, including thirty etudes in all major and minor keys. Praised by Schumann, these became required study for all conservatory piano students. The orchestration of her three symphonies impressed Berlioz.

In 1842, she began her thirty-year teaching career at the Paris Conservatory—the only woman to hold such a post for so long. In 1861 Dumont-Farrenc was the first person to win the Prix Chartier Académie des Beaux-Arts for her chamber music. (She won again in 1869.) Subsequent winners were Franck, Lalo, and Fauré. The year 1861 also marked the beginning of a joint effort with her husband in authoring a twenty-three-volume anthology of seventeenth- and eighteenth-century music, Le Tresor des Pianistes, which made history and established Louise as a scholar in addition to her importance as a composer, teacher, and performer. Widowed in 1865, she completed the work in 1874.

The popularity of Farrenc's compositions forced the Conservatory to raise her salary to the level of male professors. Living during the full bloom of French Romantic composers—Franck, Bizet, Saint-Saëns, Chaminade, Dukas, et al.—Louise Dumont Farrenc enjoyed a success women composers are still striving for over a century later.

CLARA (WIECK) SCHUMANN (1819–1896) was one of the major musical figures of her era. Raised by a strict father, who gave her lessons from the age of six in piano, violin, singing, theory, harmony, and counterpoint, she became a superb musician. From performing in their home, a center for musicians, writers, and publishers, she made her first public appearance in 1828 at the Leipzig Gewandhaus. The same year marked the publication of her Opus 1: four polonaises.

Acclaimed throughout Europe as a gifted child prodigy, Clara spent the next decade concertizing, composing, and basking in the admiration of such notables as Goethe, Mendelssohn, Chopin, Paganini, and Liszt. Her work was published by major houses in Paris, Vienna, and Leipzig. In 1838, after her second Viennese tour, Clara was appointed Klavier Virtuosin (piano virtuoso) to the Austrian court and was honored with a poem entitled Clara Wieck and Beethoven.

In 1831, a piano student named Robert Schumann came to live with the Wiecks. He fell deeply in love with Clara, but waited until she was old enough before asking her father for permission to marry. When permission was refused, it took a long hideous court battle until they were able to marry on September 12, 1840. Eight children (one died in infancy) came from the happy union. Touring even during her pregnancies, Clara's career never faltered.

In 1853, young, unknown Johannes Brahms came to live with the Schumanns. He remained an integral part of Clara's life, helping her cope with Robert's mental collapse the following year and his death in an asylum in 1856. Brahms looked after the children while she continued dazzling the world—even in far off Russia—playing Robert's music, and sometimes her own. Always dressed in mourning, Clara instituted the tradition of orchestra members and conductors wearing black. She was also one of the first to play without music, thereby setting the precedent that soloists memorize their parts.

In 1873, her father died, and later two of her children. From 1879–93 Madame Schumann was the principal piano teacher at the Hoch Conservatory in Frankfurt. Her last public appearance was in that city in 1891, performing Brahms's *Variations on a Theme by Haydn*. She "retired," teaching in her home for the rest of her long life.

Clara considered herself first an artist, second a mother, and third a composer. History has thus far viewed her as the wife of Robert Schumann and the object of Brahms's affection, and recognizes her consummate artistry as a pianist. Recently, thanks to the efforts of writers like Nancy Reich and Pamela Susskind, Clara Schumann *the composer* has begun to receive the recognition she deserves. Her Piano Trio (Opus 17, 1846) and romantic Piano Concerto in A minor are on CD.

FANNY MENDELSSOHN HENSEL (1805–47) was born in Hamburg into an artistic, intellectual family. Her grandfather was the renowned Jewish philosopher Moses Mendelssohn. Sunday concerts were a tradition in their home, attended by the elite in the world of culture.

From their mother's musical background (Lea Mendelssohn had studied with a student of J.S. Bach), Fanny and Felix were steeped in Mozart and Beethoven, the reason their compositions span from Baroque and Classical forms—cantatas, oratorios, chorales, preludes, and fugues—to the styles of their own period—*Lieder*, songs without words, and piano music.

The year 1829 saw Fanny's happy marriage to painter Wilhelm Hensel, and 1830 marked the birth of her only child, Sebastian. Her husband was very supportive of her composing.

An accomplished pianist, Hensel confined herself to home concerts except for her only public appearance in February, 1838, performing one of her brother's piano concertos. During her brief life—she died of a stroke at age forty-two—Fanny's talents were not encouraged by the men in her family, and as a dutiful daughter she did not press for the publication of her more than four hundred compositions, some of which only saw daylight when brought out within albums of her brother's works. They are preserved in a Berlin Archive.

PAULINE VIARDOT GARCIA (1821–1910), born to opera singers Manuel and Joaquina Garcia, at age seven was already accompanying her father's singing lessons. Besides singing in recitals with her famous sister, Maria Malibran, from 1836–38 Pauline studied with Franz Liszt, who encouraged her to become a concert pianist. Not only was she successful in this field, but in 1839 made her debut as an opera singer, and was hired as the prima donna by director Louis Viardot for the Italian Opera season in Paris. In 1840 Garcia married Viardot, twenty-one years her senior, who gave up his post to devote himself to furthering his wife's career.

From 1843–58 she toured throughout Europe and Russia. In 1849 Meyerbeer wrote his immensely popular opera *La Prophète* for her. In 1859, at the invitation of Hector Berlioz, she gave 150 performances as Eurydice in his revival of Gluck's *Orpheus*.

Viardot-Garcia retired from opera in 1862, but continued to give recitals. In 1871 she and Louis left Germany because of the Franco-Prussian War and returned to Paris where for the next five years she taught singing at the Conservatory and in her home.

As a composer Viardot-Garcia wrote operettas, over one hundred songs and arranged for voice various selections of Handel, Schubert, Chopin, and Brahms. In 1904 at the age of eighty-three she wrote a grand opera in the French tradition.

Her happy forty-three-year marriage (Louis died in 1883) produced four children, all good musicians. Her daughter Pauline Marie Heritte-Viardot (1841–1919) was both a singer and composer. Her son Paul was a composer and a violinist. Her other two daughters were concert singers.

The Viardot home was a center for musicians, artists, and writers. Hers was a most sought-after class in the Conservatory. Schumann wrote his Opus 24 song cycle for her, Brahms, his *Alto Rhapsody*. Saint-Saëns created his opera, *Samson et Delilah* for her to sing the leading role, and Fauré dedicated his songs Opus 4 and 7 to her. The famous

Russian author Ivan Turgenev (1818–1883) practically lived in the household and wrote libretti for her operettas. Writers Georges Sand (Madame Dudevant) and Alfred de Musset were her friends. Adding to her accomplishments, she helped launch the careers of Charles Gounod (1818–93), Jules Massenet (1842–1912), and Giacomo Meyerbeer (1791–1864).

Talent and Triumph — Black Women

Despite the long history of racial bias, especially in the South, several black women, by virtue of talent and faith, managed to overcome two enormous barriers: that of their skin color and their gender. . . .

FLORENCE SMITH PRICE (1888–1953), born in Little Rock, Arkansas, spent her youth in a milieu of hostility. By 1906 state lawmakers had established all-white primary elections and segregated all schools. For entrance to the New England Conservatory, her mother, of partly white ancestry, to avoid prejudice, wrote Mexico as Florence's birthplace. At the Conservatory, Price wrote a string quartet and a symphony.

At nineteen, Florence returned to Arkansas, took over the music department at Shorter College, married, and had children. She moved to Chicago in 1927, to escape increasing Southern race riots. In 1933 her Symphony in E minor was performed by Frederick Stock (1872–1942) and the Chicago Symphony at the Chicago World's Fair "Century of Progress" Exposition, making her the first black woman to have a work played by a major orchestra. In 1935 she returned to Little Rock for a highly successful concert of her music. Eleanor Roosevelt was in the audience in November, 1940, when the composer conducted her Third Symphony and played her Second Piano Concerto with the Michigan WPA orchestra in Detroit. The First Lady congratulated Price on her contribution to music.

Deeply religious, Price's style, rooted in traditional harmony, is infused with the rich heritage of Afro-American rhythms. Arrangements of spirituals, art songs, piano and organ and band music comprise a teeming repertoire which includes 3 piano concertos, a violin concerto, concert overtures, *Abraham Lincoln Walks at Midnight* for chorus and orchestra, and a string quartet, *Suite of Negro Dances. Two Traditional Spirituals* (1949) was dedicated to black contralto Marian Anderson, who had made Price's *Songs to a Dark Virgin* a great success. Her music was being played in Europe, and Florence was preparing for a trip there when she became ill and died on June 3, 1953.

Following in her footsteps, other black women rose to musical prominence. UNDINE SMITH MOORE (1904–1989), drawing on her roots, wrote choral compositions and arrangements of spirituals. Following the European art song form, she also explored twelve-tone writing. She co-founded the Black Music Center during her forty-five years (1927–72) at Virginia State College. Her oratorio, *Scenes from the Life of a Martyr* (*to the Memory of Martin Luther King, Jr.*) was nominated for a Pulitzer Prize in 1982.

EVELYN PITTMAN (1910–) studied with Nadia Boulanger. She founded the Evelyn Pittman Choir, which performed during the 1930s and 1940s. Her many choral compositions, showing the influence of black church music, include *Rich Heritage*, a collection of songs and stories about eminent blacks (two editions, 1944, 1968); *Cousin Esther*, a folk opera performed in Paris (1957); and *Freedom's Child* (1972), an opera about Martin Luther King, Jr.

MARGARET BONDS (1913–1972) studied with Florence Price in Chicago and Roy Harris and Djane Lavoie-Herz in New York, where several of her popular songs were published.

In 1934 she was the soloist and Florence Price conductor in a performance of her Piano Concerto in F minor. From the 1940s to the 1960s, Bonds appeared with the Chicago Symphony, Chicago Woman's Symphony, New York Symphony, and other orchestras. She formed the Margaret Bonds Chamber Society to present black musicians in works of black composers. Winner of many awards, her over two-hundred compositions show the influence of jazz and blues infused with original melodies in spiritual style. Her best known work is *The Negro Speaks of Rivers*, the setting of Langston Hughes's first published poem. In 1967, Bonds moved to Los Angeles, devoting the rest of her life teaching music to inner city children. In 1972, a few months before her death, the Los Angeles Philharmonic under Zubin Mehta premiered her *Credo* for chorus and orchestra.

JULIA PERRY (1924–1979) launched into composition with her Juilliard master's thesis, *Chicago*, a secular cantata. In Paris she won the Boulanger Grand Prix for her Viola Sonata. In 1957, she conducted a series of concerts in Europe under the sponsorship of the U.S. Information Service. After suffering a paralytic stroke in 1971, Julia recovered enough by the end of the decade to resume composing. Her early works incorporated black musical idioms. In the 1950s Perry turned from vocal to instrumental compositions. By 1971, she had written 12 symphonies, a requiem *Homage to Vivaldi* (1959), an opera, *The Symplegades*, about the Salem witchcraft trials, an opera-ballet based on Oscar Wilde's fable "The Selfish Giant," *Bicentennial Reflections* (1977), and a *Suite for Brass and Percussion* (1978).

LENA MCLIN (1929–), a teacher and choir director, has written masses, cantatas, anthems, operas, songs, arrangements of spirituals, piano, orchestral, and electronic music. Her work incorporates traditional black idioms and twentieth-century blues, gospel, jazz, and rock. *The Torch Has Been Passed,* for a cappella chorus, is based on President Kennedy's plea for world peace. *Free at Last* is a cantata about Martin Luther King, Jr.

MARY RUDD MOORE (1940–) studied with Nadia Boulanger. She has written symphonic, chamber and vocal works.

TANIA LEON (1944–), from Cuba, co-founded the Dance Theater of Harlem (1966). Musical director of *The Wiz* (1978) and other Broadway shows, she has been resident composer at the Lincoln Center Institute and assumed that post at Yale in 1993. On the faculty of Brooklyn College since 1985, her compositions show the influence of Cuban rhythms and American jazz idioms. *Carabale* was premiered in 1992 for the Cincinnati Symphony centennial, and an opera is planned for the Munich Biennale in 1994.

The Second New England School

Led by John Knowles Paine (1839–1906) of Harvard, and George Whitefield Chadwick (1854–1931) of the New England Conservatory, the "school," centered in Boston, included Arthur Foote (1853–1937), Edward MacDowell (1860–1908), and John Alden Carpenter (1876–1951). (The first school originated with William Billings [1746–1800], "Father of New England Music.") Four women were accepted into this group.

CLARA KATHLEEN BARNETT ROGERS (1844–1931) entered the Leipzig Conservatory at age twelve. She enjoyed a successful operatic career before settling in Boston and joining the faculty of the New England Conservatory in 1902. Besides several books on singing, she wrote a well-received number of art songs, a scherzo, a cello sonata, and piano pieces.

HELEN HOPEKIRK (1856–1945), born in Scotland, also studied in

Leipzig. Besides her career as a concert pianist, in 1905 she published her collection of *Seventy Scottish Songs*, based on the folk music of her native land.

MARGARET RUTHVEN LANG (1867–1972) studied violin and composition in Munich (1886), and orchestration with George Chadwick and Edward MacDowell. She wrote songs and light orchestral pieces. On her one-hundredth birthday, she was honored by Erich Leinsdorf and the Boston Symphony.

AMY MARCY CHENEY BEACH (1867–1944) made her piano debut with the Boston Symphony at age sixteen. The same year she married Dr. Henry Beach, twenty-four years her senior, which gave her a privileged position in Boston society. She was celebrated as the foremost woman composer of her day, and Amy Beach Clubs sprang up all over the country. She was the first American woman to succeed in writing large scale orchestral works. Her Piano Concerto in C# minor (1900) was dedicated to the famous Caracas-born opera singer-pianist-composer Teresa Carreño. Numerous songs, piano pieces, a violin sonata, and chamber and sacred music are among Beach's many compositions. After the death of her husband in 1910, she toured Europe until the outbreak of World War I. Ending a "black-out" of nearly half a century, her work is attracting renewed recognition. Her Romantic *Gaelic* Symphony and Grand Mass are now on CDs.

Into the Twentieth Century

After Amy Beach, more American women composers entered the national spotlight. MABEL DANIELS (1878–1971), the first woman admitted to a score reading class at the Munich Conservatory, also studied with George Chadwick (1854–1931) rooting her style in the Romantic New England School. In 1908, the Boston Pops performed her *In the Greenwood*. Of her major works, *Exultate Deo* (1932), *Deep Forest* (1937), and *A Song of Praise* (1954) made her the first woman to have three different compositions played by the Boston Symphony.

MARY HOWE (1882–1964) entered the Peabody Conservatory in 1900. As a pianist, she performed in Europe and at the White House for Presidents Taft and Teddy Roosevelt. She met Amy Beach and Premiered her *Suite for Two Pianos* with Anne Hull. Her most successful compositions were *The Chain Gang Song*, premiered in 1925 with 275 voices and the New York Symphony. Her tone poem *Sand*, played by the Philadelphia Orchestra in 1934, was praised by its conductor Leopold Stokowski for its new use of staccato.

In 1930 Howe helped raise $40,000 to establish the National Symphony of Washington, D.C. The year 1933 marked a year's study with Nadia Boulanger. After two decades of composing, she was given, in 1952, an all-Howe program by the National Symphony. In 1954, guest at a concert of her music by the Vienna Symphony, Mary received a standing ovation, unheard of for a foreigner, and a woman! Her works were featured at her eightieth birthday celebration attended by over two hundred guests. Among her last tributes was an honorary doctorate from George Washington University.

MARION BAUER (1887–1955) gained fame as teacher, composer, and music critic. In 1906 she traded English lessons for harmony instruction from Nadia Boulanger—making her the first of an entire generation of American composers who would study with this genius. A strong supporter of contemporary American music, Bauer was the only woman on the executive board of the American Composers Alliance, founded by Aaron Copland in 1937. Besides her compositions, she collaborated on several music history books, including *20th Century Music* in 1933. In 1951, she was honored with an all-Bauer concert in New York's Town Hall.

RUTH CRAWFORD (SEEGER) (1901–1953) was the first woman to win a Guggenheim Fellowship to study in Europe (1930). An accomplished pianist, she was considered an outstanding composer, in the same peer group as Charles Ives (1874–1954) and Henry Cowell (1897–1965) of the early twentieth-century American avant-garde movement. After her 1931 marriage to Charles Seeger, she collected and arranged several hundred folksongs from recordings in the Archives of the Library of Congress.

Politically active in the social issues of her day, Crawford raised four children during the Depression. Her stepson, Pete, and her daughter Peggy, gained renown as folk singers.

ELINOR REMICK WARREN (1900–1991), after studying with Frank LaForge, one of the world's greatest accompanists, toured with illustrious opera singers Lucrezia Bori (1887–1960), Richard Crooks (1900–72), and Lawrence Tibbett (1896–1960). Warren was soloist at the Hollywood Bowl in 1923, and with the Los Angeles Philharmonic in 1926.

Warren's first large work, *The Harp Weaver*, for women's chorus, baritone soloist and orchestra, was premiered at Carnegie Hall in 1936. In 1940 the Los Angeles Philharmonic premiered her *Legend of King*

Arthur, a choral symphony. It was broadcast nationwide, and the country was intrigued that a beautiful young wife and mother was writing music serious enough to be played by a major orchestra. A huge success, half a century later it was recorded on a Cambria CD.

Warren continued to compose and perform into the 1980s. Although her music has been played internationally, the composer lived most of her life in Los Angeles.

Also from the West, RADIE BRITAIN (1903–) followed the path of her peers, studying in Europe and spending summers at the MacDowell Colony. Much of her music reflects her Southwestern origins, incorporating cowboy tunes and Mexican rhythms. She was the first woman to receive the Juilliard Publication Award for her *Heroic Poem*, and has received many honors from the National League of American Penwomen.

MIRIAM GIDEON (1906–), after studying with Marion Bauer and Roger Sessions among others, is known for sacred music stemming from her Jewish heritage.

LOUISE TALMA (1906–) spent seventeen of her summers in France perfecting her piano technique, then had the direction of her life changed when Nadia Boulanger heard one of her pieces and encouraged her to become a composer. After studying with Boulanger, Talma became the first American woman to teach at Fontainebleau.

The bulk of her work—spanning from 1939 to the 1990s—is choral, including *In Praise of a Virtuous Woman* (1991) and *Psalm 115* (1992). Talma was the first woman to win the Sibelius Medal for composition (London 1963), the first woman to have twice been awarded a Guggenheim Fellowship in composition, the first American woman to have her work, *The Alcestiad*, staged at a major opera house in Europe (Frankfurt, 1962), and the first woman to be elected to the American Institute of Arts and Letters.

JULIA SMITH (1911–), whose 1933 doctoral dissertation has become a standard reference work on Aaron Copland, was the pianist for Frederique Petrides' Orchestrette Classique. In her thirty-year performing career, Smith has given much exposure to Copland's piano music. In her own music she incorporates the musical idiom of her native Southwest: hoedowns, rodeo songs, and Mexican elements.

VIVIAN FINE (1913–) from age twelve to seventeen studied with Ruth Crawford, one of the first women to compose atonal music. In 1932, Fine went to New York, where she became well known as a modern dance accompanist. This led to writing ballets for the companies of

Doris Humphrey, Charles Weidman, Hanya Holm, José Limón, and Martha Graham. Fine's many compositions include the operas *The Women in the Garden* (1978), *Uliana Rooney* (1992), and many orchestral works. Fine has taught at Bennington College 1964–87, New York University, and Juilliard.

RUTH SCHÖNTHAL (1924–) was the youngest student ever accepted by the Stern Conservatory in Berlin. In 1938, her family fled Hitler and went to Stockholm where, after three years, they once again had to escape—this time to Mexico, where Ruth studied with Manuel Ponce. Paul Hindemith heard her play and arranged for her to study with him at Yale.

Her work is a unique blend of European traditions and contemporary techniques. In 1983, the first of her annual trips back to Germany resulted in *Nachklange (Reverberations)*, for timbred piano, reflecting the composer's distress over the havoc wrought by Hitler. It was chosen for "Education for Peace through Music" programs in the German Schools. The premiere of her anti-war cantata *The Young Dead Soldiers* (1987) was attended by an audience of 2,000. Her CDs include *Portrait of the Artist as an Older Woman*, and *Fragments from a Woman's Diary*. Schönthal continues her career as a Master Piano Teacher.

JEANNE SINGER (1924–) enjoyed fifteen years of piano study with the great Nadia Reisenberg and continues a thirty-year career as soloist with chamber ensembles. She uses the works of modern women poets for her extensive output of contemporary *lieder*. Among many awards, she has won the International First Prize from the Composers Guild for *To Stir a Dream* (1989). *To Be Brave*, dedicated to Raoul Wallenberg (1912– 1947), the Swedish diplomat who risked his life saving 100,000 Jews in World War II, is on a 1993 CD.

MARGA RICHTER (1926–) came to national attention in the 1950s with her *Sonata for Piano; Concerto for Violas, Cellos and Basses; Transmutation*; and *Two Chinese Songs*. The paintings by Georgia O'Keeffe inspired the series *Landscapes of the Mind* I, II, III (1970s). *Blackberry Vines and Winter Fruit* was recorded by the London Philharmonic on Leonarda (1989). Recipient of numerous honors and awards, Richter is also an accomplished pianist and teacher.

URSULA MAMLOCK (1928–), born in Berlin, emigrated to New York in 1941, studying with the renowned George Szell. Her work has been compared to Elliott Carter's. *Der Andreas Garten* (1986), depicting the tranquility of a garden growing above California's earthquake fault, received the Opus One 50th Anniversary Award.

NANCY VAN DE VATE (1930–), founder in 1975 of the International League of Women Composers, utilizes *sound-mass*, a concept which minimilizes the importance of pitch, in preference to dynamics, timbre, and texture. *Journeys* (1981–84) and *Chernobyl* (1987) illustrate this technique.

POZZI ESCOT (1933–), born in Lima, was named Laureate Composer of Peru at age twenty-three. Affected by the events of World War II, she composed *A Triology* (1962–64): *Lamentus, Cristhos, and Visione*, as a tribute to the six million martyrs of the concentration camps. In 1975, Escot was named one of the five outstanding women composers whose works were performed by the New York Philharmonic under the direction of Sarah Caldwell. (The others were Grazyna Bacewicz, Ruth Crawford, Thea Musgrave, and Lili Boulanger.)

On the faculty of the New England Conservatory, Escot is president of the International Hildegard von Bingen Society and figures prominently in European contemporary musical events.

KATHERINE HOOVER (1937–), an accomplished flutist, originated the *Festivals of Women's Music* in New York City (1978–81). In 1981, her *Psalm 23* was performed by a 400-voice choir and orchestra at the Cathedral of St. John the Divine. *Eleni: A Greek Tragedy* premiered in 1987. She has written numerous orchestral and works for solo instruments, especially the flute.

BARBARA KOLB (1939–) made musical history by becoming the first American woman to win the Prix de Rome in composition (1969–71). Performances of her works by major orchestras include those of the New York Philharmonic, under Pierre Boulez, and the Boston Symphony, under Seiji Ozawa. She composed the tape collage score of the Italian film *Cantico*, which won first prize at the 1983 American Film Festival. In 1986, Kolb completed a music theory instruction course for the blind and physically impaired for the Library of Congress. Her *Millefoglie*, for chamber ensemble and computer tape, was awarded the Kennedy Center Friedheim Award in 1987. In March 1992, an all-Kolb program was presented at Kennedy Center. Her works have been performed throughout Europe. She is published by Boosey and Hawkes.

JUDITH LANG ZAIMONT (1945–), after study at Juilliard, toured the country (1960–67) giving duo-piano recitals with her sister Doris. The year 1971 was one of prizes: The International Gottschalk Competition Gold Medal for *Man's Image and His Cry*, the Delius Competition, a fellowship to study at the MacDowell Colony, and a Debussy Scholarship to Paris, where she composed *Concerto for Piano and Orchestra*.

Chroma—Northern Lights, in honor of the Statue of Liberty's centennial, won first prize in the 1986 National Competition for Chamber Orchestras.

Her voluminous output ranges from orchestral to chamber, vocal, and choral works. Her *Annotated List of 20th Century Repertoire for the Piano* is a standard resource in piano teaching. She is editor of *The Musical Woman* (Greenwood Press, 3 volumes, 1983, 1987, 1991)—a critically acclaimed series covering the worldwide contribution of women to music.

Zaimont continues a distinguished teaching career with the post of Professor of Composition at the University of Minneapolis–Twin Cities (from 1992).

At the Forefront

The many women composers through the centuries who forged their way into what has been historically a man's milieu each left a paving stone upon the path for those to follow—not that this eased the way. Everyone mentioned in this chapter (and many others) made a vital contribution to the music literature but, as in all fields, there are those who through talent and circumstances reach the top. In the latter part of the twentieth century, four women have scaled the heights.

JOAN TOWER (1938–), raised in Bolivia, Chile, and Peru, where her father was a geologist, studied with many piano teachers before her family returned to America in 1945. In 1978 she formed the Da Capo Chamber Players. In 1979, her first orchestral work, *Sequoia*, was premiered by Zubin Mehta with the American Philharmonic for the televised United Nations Day Celebration. Leonard Slatkin, with the St. Louis Symphony, took *Sequoia* all over the world on his tour, catapulting her to further fame. In 1985, Tower became composer in residence for the St. Louis Symphony. In 1986, *Silver Ladders* won the $150,000 Grawemeyer Award. Her 1988 Clarinet Concerto won the Naumburg Prize. The triple orchestra commission (St. Louis, Chicago, and New York Philharmonic), for *Concerto for Orchestra*, was premiered in 1991. Futher recognition for Tower was gained by her four *Fanfares for the Uncommon Woman*. Her ballet *Stepping Stones* was premiered April, 1993, by the Milwaukee Ballet.

ELLEN TAAFFE ZWILICH (1939–), born in Miami, moved to New York in 1964, studying with the great violinist Ivan Galamian. From

1965–72, she played in the American Symphony Orchestra under Leopold Stokowski. In 1975, Zwilich made history by becoming the first woman to receive a doctorate in composition from Juilliard. Roger Sessions and Elliott Carter were among her teachers. In 1983, she again made history by being the first woman to win a Pulitzer Prize in music with her Symphony No. 1. In 1986, Zwilich received the Arturo Toscanini Music Critics' Award for the New World recordings of her Symphony No. 1, *Celebrations for Orchestra*, and *Prologue and Variations* for string orchestra. In 1988, Zubin Mehta and the New York Philharmonic premiered *Symbolon*, in Leningrad (St. Petersburg).

Commissions for other symphonies and concertos poured in: Concerto for Trombone and Orchestra from the Chicago Symphony under Sir Georg Solti (1988), Concerto for Oboe and Orchestra from the Cleveland Symphony with Christoph von Dohnányi (1990). In 1991, the Boston Symphony, under Seiji Ozawa, premiered Concerto for Flute (1989), Violin, and Cello (1991) and Quintet for Clarinet and String Quartet (1990). Concerto for Bassoon was premiered May 1993, by Lorin Maazel and the Pittsburgh Symphony. The Third Symphony had a February 1993 premiere under Kurt Masur, celebrating the 150th anniversary of the New York Philharmonic.

SHULAMIT RAN (1949–), born in Tel Aviv, Israel, at age eight, had her songs performed by a children's choir on the radio. Nadia Reisenberg, on a visit to Jerusalem, arranged for the then fourteen-year-old Shulamit to receive a full scholarship to the Mannes College of Music in New York. There Ran studied piano with Reisenberg and composition with Norman Dello Joio. Auditioning for Leonard Bernstein for his Young People's Concerts, she played her own composition, *Capriccio* for piano and orchestra, and was chosen to perform with the New York Philharmonic on the televised series in 1963.

Between 1968–73, Ran toured America and Europe. In 1971, she premiered her *Concert Piece* with the Israel Philharmonic under Zubin Mehta. She joined the faculty of the University of Chicago in October 1973. After the success of her Concerto for Orchestra (1988), conducted by Daniel Barenboim, he named Ran to succeed John Corigliano to become the second composer in residence for the Chicago Symphony.

Among Ran's numerous awards, fellowships, and commissions, a landmark was established when her second string quartet, *Vistas*, became the first commission in this country given to a Soviet chamber ensemble, the Taneyev Quartet of St. Petersburg. Her First Symphony, commissioned by the Philadelphia Orchestra, made her the second woman to win the Pulitzer Prize in music (1991). The same composition won the 1992 Kennedy Center Friedheim Award. Christoph von Dohnányi and the Cleveland Orchestra included her *Concert Piece for Piano and Orchestra* on two American tours (1991, 1993), culminating in Carnegie Hall. The year 1993 has *Legends*, a work honoring the centennials of both the Chicago Symphony Orchestra and the University of Chicago, with Daniel Barenboim conducting the premieres.

Ran's compositions are published by Theodore Presser Co., Carl Fischer, and the Israeli Music Institute.

LIBBY LARSEN (1950–), raised in Minneapolis, began her career composing operas during her coffee breaks while working as a secretary. This encouraged further study. In 1973, with Stephen Paulus, she co-founded the Minnesota Composers' Forum, a support group whose concept has been widely copied. In 1983, the two were appointed composers-in-residence for the Minnesota Orchestra under Sir Neville Marriner.

Larsen's body of compositions draws from a variety of modern styles. *The Atmosphere as a Fluid System*, a virtuostic challenge, was showcased by flutist Eugenia Zukerman. *Coming Forth the Day* (1986), on the theme of war and peace, integrated the writings of Jihan Sadat (widow of the assassinated Egyptian President), who narrated the premiere. Her seventh opera, *Frankenstein, The Modern Prometheus* (1990), commissioned by the Minnesota Opera Company, is a multimedia blockbuster combining singers and orchestra with innovative audio and video technology. *Ghosts of an Old Ceremony* (1991), a glimpse of pioneer women, features nine dancers. The *Marimba Concerto After Hampton*, (1992), honors Lionel Hampton, one of the greatest exponents of the instrument. The work was commissioned by a consortium of twelve American orchestras. Larsen has also written film and television scores.

Among the international interpreters of her work are Zubin Mehta, Leonard Slatkin, Sir Neville Marriner, Catherine Comet, and JoAnn Falletta. Winner of numerous awards, the composer is married and has a daughter, Wynne, born in 1986.

International Women

Just as music is a universal language, so genius, inspiration, and the desire to compose know no boundaries. Long before jet travel, women composers traversed the globe, some starting from as far away as

Australia and South Africa. Drawn to Europe and America, they contributed to the treasure chest of music, intermingling their culture and widening the horizons of style, form, and melody.

British music had not had a great exponent since Henry Purcell (1659–95)—Edward Elgar (1857–1934) did not achieve public recognition until 1897—and there were certainly no women in the field, other than performers. ETHEL SMYTH (1858–1944) changed all that. At age seventeen she taught herself orchestration from Berlioz' *Treatise on Instrumentation*. At nineteen she went to Europe and met Brahms, Clara Schumann, Grieg, Dvořák, Tchaikovsky, and violinist Joseph Joachim.

Returning to England, her powerful Mass in D (1891), performed by the Royal Choral Society at the Royal Albert Hall, was compared to the choral works of Bach, Beethoven, and Brahms.

Smyth made history at age forty-six when, in 1903, the first opera by a woman reached the stage of the New York Metropolitan. (The ovation was said to have lasted ten minutes.) Her best known opera, *The Wreckers*, set on the Cornish coast of England, is the predecessor of Benjamin Britten's *Peter Grimes* with its characterization of the sea.

From 1910–12 Ethel interrupted her career to join the suffragist movement with Emmeline Pankhurst. Smyth's *March of the Women* became their anthem. In 1913 she composed *The Boatswain's Mate*, in a style similar to Gilbert and Sullivan's, using the *March of the Women* in the overture. The same year she began to hear ringing in her ears. By the end of World War I she realized that she was going deaf. Despite this, she continued composing.

In 1922, Smyth was named Dame Commander of the British Empire (the female equivalent of being knighted). Her increasing deafness led to a new career. She wrote ten books, mostly biographical, full of wit and brilliant portraits of many notables of her day, including Queen Victoria.

Several other women achieved recognition in England in the early part of the century. REBECCA CLARKE (1886–1979) became the first woman in a professional orchestra when she joined the Queen's Hall Light Orchestra (1912). In 1916, she established herself as a violist and composer in America.

GRACE WILLIAMS (1906–77), known for her *Fantasia On Welsh Nursery Tunes* (1941) and *Sea Sketches* (1947), made an important contribution to Welsh music.

CÉCILE CHAMINADE (1857–1944) was part of the rising tide of French nationalism, which included Franck, Saint-Saëns, Chabrier, and d'Indy. It was the era in which Paris audiences flocked to the *Concerts Populaires* and the *Concerts Colonne,* whose orchestras numbered one hundred musicians. A prolific composer of over 350 compositions, she made her American debut in 1908 conducting her *Concertstück* with the Philadelphia Orchestra.

Published by the most prestigious companies in Europe, Chaminade enjoyed great popularity during her long life. She was the first woman awarded the order of *Chevalière de la Légion d'Honneure,* one of France's highest decorations. During World War II, the composer lived in neutral Monte-Carlo, where she died in 1944. Her most performed work, *Concertino for Flute and Orchestra,* is now on CD.

LILI BOULANGER (1893–1918) at age five audited her sister Nadia's Conservatory classes in organ, piano, and composition. At age eight she made her public debut as a violinist (1901). The year 1904 marked her debut as a pianist. By 1909, along with music studies at home, Lili began composing, arranging psalms for soloist and orchestra. She also mastered the harp and the cello. The years 1911 to 1913 were devoted to intensive study for the Prix de Rome. Despite stiff competition, including organist Marcel Dupré (1886–1971), Lili won the prize for her cantata, *Faust et Hélène;* she was the first woman to win the Paris Conservatory's highest recognition, which dates back to 1803.

After years of suffering, Lili died at twenty-five, leaving behind a remarkable ten-year output of skillled and imaginative works. Despite the war, newspapers on both sides of the Atlantic gave considerable space to her passing.

AUGUSTA HOLMÈS (1847–1903) numbered Richard Wagner, Franz Liszt, and César Franck in her circle of acquaintances. Her music, in the French vocal tradition, was heard at the *Concerts Populaires,* the Paris Exposition of 1889, and the Paris Opera in 1895.

ALMA MAHLER (1879–1964) composed only five songs during her marriage to Gustav (nineteen years her senior). One of them, *Ansturm* ("Assault"), with its theme of sexual desire, is probably the earliest work by a woman dealing with such a subject.

GERMAINE TAILLEFERRE (1892–1983) entered the Paris Conservatory at age twelve. Later she became part of Les Six. Her music—chamber and piano works, songs, operas, ballets, and film scores—were influenced by her orchestration teacher, Maurice Ravel.

MARGARET SUTHERLAND (1897–1984), born in Australia, studied in London and Vienna, then returned to Melbourne to help build a complex used for major international art events. A composer, teacher, and chamber music pianist, she was awarded an honorary doctorate by the University of Melbourne for her dedication to the cultural life of the city.

PRIAULX RAINIER (1903–86), from South Africa, studied violin in London at the Royal Academy and composition in Paris (1937) with Nadia Boulanger. The rhythmic structure of her compositions is based on African music and dance.

CLAUDE ARRIEU (1903–), born Marie Louise Simon in Paris, studied at the Conservatory under Paul Dukas, where she won the first prize for composition in 1932. Her copious output includes a symphony, many concertos, chamber, vocal, and piano music, an oratorio, a requiem, four ballets and an opera. Beginning in 1946, she wrote over seventy radio and film scores.

ELISABETH LUTYENS (1906–), daughter of distinguished architect Edward Lutyens and Lady Emily Litton, went to Paris to study Impressionism, but on her return to London began to compose in the serial technique of Anton Webern, which isolated her from her English contemporaries. After thirty years of excellence in the avant-garde genre, Lutyens finally received recognition and was made a Commander of the Order of the British Empire in 1969.

ELIZABETH MACONCHY (1907–), a student of Vaughan Williams, also studied on the continent. Her Piano Concerto was premiered in 1930 by the Prague Philharmonic, the same year Sir Henry Wood conducted her suite, *The Land*, at his Promenade Concerts.

The turmoil of World War II, marriage, children, and a long battle with tuberculosis restricted her activities, but she continued composing. Her output includes three one-act operas, a mass, many orchestral, chamber, and choral works, and music for children's voices. Her major accomplishments are the fourteen string quartets written between 1933 and 1984.

Maconchy was made a Dame in 1977, and a Daughter of the British Empire in 1987. Her daughter, Nicola LeFanu (1947–), is also a prize-winning composer.

GRAZYNA BACEWICZ (1909–69) studied at the Warsaw Conservatory with Szymanowski, then went to Paris for studies in composition with Nadia Boulanger, and violin with Carl Flesch. From 1936 to 1938, she played principal violin in the Polish Orchestra. Despite the hardships of the German occupation during World War II, Grazyna married, had a daughter, and gave refuge to war victims. Her secret concerts kept Polish culture alive, and helped raise money for relief funds. Her first major success came after the war, with the *Concerto For String Orchestra* (1948), for which she won the Polish National Prize. The American premiere in Washington, D.C., established Bacewicz as an important composer. Most of her music is neoclassical, but in the 1960s, under the influence of Lutoslawski, she began using avant-garde serial techniques. Besides four symphonies, a concerto for orchestra, concertos for viola and cello, a piano quintet, and a ballet, she wrote much violin music, including seven string quartets, sonatas, and concertos. She died, greatly honored, in Warsaw, January 17, 1969.

PEGGY GLANVILLE-HICKS (1912–) was born in Melbourne and studied there and in London with England's top names in music: Ralph Vaughan Williams, composition; Arthur Benjamin, piano; Constant Lambert and Malcolm Sargent, conducting. In 1936, she studied with Nadia Boulanger in Paris. Her first big success came in 1938 with Sir Adrian Boult directing her *Choral Suite* at the International Society of Contemporary Music (ISCM) Festival in London. In 1940, she moved to New York, where she served as director of the Composers' Forum, organized contemporary music concerts, and was a respected music critic for the New York *Herald Tribune*. Her compositions include ballets, operas, concertos for flute and piano, chamber works, vocal music, and film scores. *Letters from Morocco* (1953), for tenor and orchestra, reflecting her interest and travels in North Africa, was premiered by Leopold Stokowski. *Transposed Heads*, with a libretto by Thomas Mann, was the first opera commission awarded to a woman and produced in 1954 by the Kentucky Opera Company.

In 1961, Glanville-Hicks moved to Greece, producing another opera, *Nausicaa*. *Sappho*, for the San Francisco Opera (1963), also drew on Greek material. In 1975, the composer returned to her homeland and set up a highly successful Asian Music studies program at the Australian Music Centre.

BETSY JOLAS (1926–), born in Paris, came to America when her family returned in 1939 after World War II broke out. At age fifteen she was an accompanist on piano and organ, as well as a chorister in the Dessoff Choir. As a student at Bennington College she composed a full Mass. Her *Motet* I, *To Everything There is a Season* was performed at her graduation, and later at Carnegie Hall.

In 1946 Betsy returned to France to study with Messiaen and Milhaud. She married a French doctor in 1949 and became the mother of three children, all the while continuing to compose. Editor (1955–65) of the French Radio-Television periodical, *Écouter Aujourd'hui* (*Listen*

Today) Jolas came in contact with the most important musicians in France. Recipient of many honors, her music reflects her choral background, incorporating influences from French Renaissance composers, Impressionism, and serialism.

THEA MUSGRAVE (1928–), born near Edinburgh, was another in the illustrious stream of students of Nadia Boulanger. In 1959 she came to America, where she studied with Aaron Copland, met Milton Babbitt (1916–), a serialist and early experimenter with electronic synthesizer music, and became acquainted with the music of Charles Ives.

From 1958–65 Musgrave was a visiting lecturer at London University. In 1970, she returned to the United States and married violist Peter Mark, general director and conductor of the Virginia Opera Company.

In 1976, she became the first woman to conduct her own composition, *Concerto for Orchestra*, with the Philadelphia Orchestra. In 1977 she made her New York City Opera conducting debut in a performance of *The Voice of Ariadne*. The same company produced her *Mary, Queen of Scots* in 1981.

Her work includes operas, ballets, and orchestral, chamber, vocal, and choral music. Her unique contribution is "dramatic abstract," in which solo instruments take on a theatrical role, sometimes requiring players to move around the stage.

Experimental International

An international group of women composers continues to contribute to the ever-growing repertoire of new music:

From Russia, SOFIA GUBAIDULINA (1931–) combines avant-garde influences with her Tartar origins and religious traditions. Her orchestral piece *Stufen* (*Steps*) won first prize in the 1975 Seventh International Composers Competition in Rome. In 1987 her work as a whole received a prize from the Prince Pierre de Monaco Foundation.

ALICIA TERZIAN (1938–), from Argentina, is one of the most dynamic composers of Latin American new music. She lectures on the avant-garde at universities and conservatories throughout the world.

Australian-born JENNIFER FOWLER (1939–) has written in the avant-garde style of *indeterminacy*—which leaves players to work out the details of their performance.

New Zealand's ANNEA LOCKWOOD (1939–) challenges the line between sound and noise, adapting environmental applications of taped

Jessye Norman (1945-)
mezzo-soprano

Thomas Hampson (1955-),
baritone

Yehudi Menhuin (1916-),
violinist

Isaac Stern (1920-),
violinist

Yo-Yo Ma (1955-),
cellist

Jean-Pierre Rampal (1922-),
flutist

Richard Stoltzman (1942-),
clarinetist

Wynton Marsalis (1961-),
trumpet

Bella Davidovich (1928-),
pianist

Gustavo Romero (1965-),
pianist

The Janáček String Quartet

Leipzig Gewandhaus Orchestra

Sir Georg Solti
(1912-)

Leonard Bernstein
(1918-90)

Kurt Masur (1927-)

Iona Brown (1941-), directing the Academy of St. Martin-in-the-Fields

sounds. Her compositions also include improvisation and *musique con-crète*.

From Sydney, ALISON BAULD (1944–) moved to London to study with Lutyens. Acting experience and an interest in the dance are infused in her works, most of which involve voice and drama.

GILLIAN WHITEHEAD (1941–) studied in London with Sir Peter Maxwell Davies. Her diverse style reflects her native New Zealand Maori influences, the impressionism of Debussy and serialism of Webern. Her operas *Tristan and Iseult* (1975) and *The King of the Other Country* (1984), as well as her chamber and solo pieces, have been well received.

MARTA PTASZYNSKA (1943–), along with her contemporaries Witold Lutoslawski and Krystof Penderecki, are the representatives of modern Polish music. She studied with Nadia Boulanger in Paris and at the Cleveland Institute in the U.S.A. Her impressive output in a variety of styles, including sonic devices and light projections, is played by major symphonies throughout the world. One of her most popular works is the Concerto for Marimba (1985).

NICOLA LEFANU (1947–), daughter of composer Elizabeth Maconchy and William Lefanu, has taught in London and Australia, and is considered one of Britain's leading contemporary composers.

DIANA BURRELL (1948–), educated at Cambridge, made an impact in 1980 with her *Missa Endeliente*, and continues composing in her distinctive dramatic style.

The music of ELENA FIRSOVA (1950–) was first heard outside Russia in 1979, when her settings of Petrarch's sonnets were performed in Venice, Paris, London, and Cologne. Much of her music is based on the work of Russian poets such as Pasternak, Mayakovsky, and Tsvetaeva. Her *Autumn Music* (1988) has been performed by the Women's Philharmonic.

KAJIA SAARIAHO (1950–), born in Helsinki, is one of Finland's best-known contemporary composers. *Vers le blanc* (*Towards the Void*) is the computer piece which established her international reputation. Her other experimental works include *Verblendungen* (*Bedazzlement*, 1984) for orchestra and tape, *Jardin Secret* I, II, and III, and *Lichtbogen* (*Arcs of Light*, 1986).

JUDITH WEIR (1954–), from Cambridge, England, attained international recognition with *A Night at the Chinese Opera* (1986–87). Her strikingly original music is infused with her Scottish heritage, making use of bagpipes, traditional dances, and folk songs. Her interest in the medieval has led to compositions utilizing the Icelandic *King Harald* sagas, fifteenth- and sixteenth-century Spanish texts, and Serbo-Croatian folksongs.

Women and New Music

Influenced by modern trends, many women composers are exploring the outer limits of contemporary music with experimentation and innovation, aided by continuously advancing electronic and computer technology.

Beginning early in the century, NETTY SIMONS (1918–) turned from the traditional to *aleatory* (in which the elements of the music are determined by the performer rather than the composer) and *graphic scores*, which use linear graphs and verbal instructions instead of regular notation.

JEAN EICHELBERGER IVEY (1923–) experimented in the early 1960s with electronic sounds and twelve-tone music. Her *Pinball* (1965) is a pinball machine in action with bells, rattles, and clicks. This is *musique concrète* (music made up of taped real-life sounds, as devised in the late 1940s in Paris by Pierre Schaeffer and Pierre Henry).

In 1969 Ivey founded the Electronic Music Studio at the Peabody Conservatory, where she combined electronic music with live performance, as in her *Testament of Eve*, featuring a soprano debating with the taped, disembodied voice of the devil; it was premiered by the Baltimore Symphony in 1976.

WENDY CARLOS (1939–), working with Robert Moog in 1964, established the synthesizer as a musical instrument by developing a method of creating electronic versions of orchestral sounds. Her historic 1968 recording, *Switched On Bach*, is now on CD. *Timesteps*, used in the filmscore of *A Clockwork Orange* (1971) and the background score for the sci-fi film TRON (1982) are examples of the merging of orchestral and synthesizer sounds. Working with digital synthesis through a computer, Carlos has discovered limitless possibilities, as in *Cosmological Impressions* and *Digital Moonscapes*, released in 1984. In 1987, eight pieces entitled *Beauty and the Beast* drew on a new array of sounds, some from third world instruments; this is now on CD.

Other women composing in this genre are the Schoenberg scholar DIKA NEWLIN (1923–), LUDMILA UHLEHLA (1923–), composer of *Elegy for a Whale*, complete with taped whale sounds; keyboard expert

EMMA LOU DIEMER (1927–); LAURIE SPIEGEL (1945–), who devised GROOVE, (Generating Real-Time Operations On Voltage-controlled Equipment); SUSAN CIANI (1945–), who wrote the film scores for *The Stepford Wives, Help, Help, the Gobolinks,* and *The Incredible Shrinking Woman*; DARIA SEMEGEN (1946–); and HILARY TANN (1947–).

Multimedia Performance

Some composers showcase their own work, performing their compositions with their own staging and special effects. One of the first to gain prominence in this field was PAULINE OLIVEROS (1932–), who employs theatricality, audience participation, dancers, actors, musicians, and experimentation with video, electronic, and taped music. Her involvement with Asian culture led to the development of a sonic awareness she calls Deep Listening. Plans are underway for a global celebration of her work in the year 2001.

Following in her footsteps are dancer, actress, singer MEREDITH MONK (1942–); LAURIE ANDERSON (1947–), who devises her own instruments; JOAN LA BARBARA (1947–), developer of a vocal technique in which the voice is heard both during the inhalation and exhalation of breath; and BETH ANDERSON (1950–), who creates "text-sound" pieces with tapes and dancers (living sculptures).

Forging the Future

New generations of women composers are constantly adding to the contemporary repertoire. Among these are LORI DOBBINS (1958–), who has had her work performed by many contemporary music groups; AUGUSTA READ THOMAS (1964–), who, composing since childhood, has produced a constant flow of compositions in major orchestral, chamber, and choral forms; and, one of the youngest to gain recognition, DALIT HADASS WARSHAW (1974–), who orchestrates "by instinct" and has had performances of compositions, many based on biblical texts—with libretti by her brother Hilan (1977–)—played by major symphonies, including the New York and Israel Philharmonic orchestras under Zubin Mehta.

One Size Fits All

Almost half a century ago Sophie Drinker pointed out the obvious in her *Music and Women* (1948): "It [music] requires for its composition . . . the same germ of emotional and artistic potency—the same capacity for symbolic thinking—that is required for the development of musical imagination at any time."

In other words, there is no age, size, weight, or gender delineation required to create music. Like Mozart, many of the women in these pages began composing at a very young age. Circumstances permitted some to rise to the top during eras when their sex was considered no more than chattel. Sappho noted, "We are oppressed by fears of oblivion," but optimistically forecast, "Someone, I tell you, will remember us."

The enlightenment of the Renaissance and the new freedom of the Romantic movement is reflected in the music of women. Robert Henderson wrote in the *Daily Telegraph* (1987), "Mostly debarred from adequate and essential sources of education, the wonder is that they [women composers and performers] yet managed to achieve so much."

The quest for equality and recognition continues as we approach a new millenium. At least we have come a long way from the philosophy in Ben Sira's *Book of Wisdom* (c190 B.C.) who cautioned: "Consort not with a female musician lest thou be taken in by her snares."

CHAPTER THIRTEEN

The First Instrument

The most important musical instrument in existence is the human voice. More music has been composed for this instrument than any other. Pictures and writings tell about music 4000 years B.C. Primitive man intoned chants to unseen gods long before any formal languge was spoken.

Vocal sounds are made by forcing air from the lungs through a set of muscles in the throat, the vocal cords. The quality of a singer's voice depends on what happens after the sound leaves the vocal cords. Cavities in the body and head act as resonators. Use of the throat, tongue, jaw, lips, and ribs affects the tone.

Vocal Ranges

SOPRANO

From the Italian *sovrano*—in English, *sovereign* or chief—this is the highest female voice. There are three main categories.

Coloratura: The highest range, requiring the ability to sing in an agile manner.

Lyric: Light and flexible, with a pleasant, bright quality.

Dramatic: A strong, powerful voice as required by Wagner heroines.

Some of the most famous sopranos, past and present: Licia Albanese, 1913– (Italy); Elly Ameling, 1938– (Netherlands); June Anderson 1950– (U.S.); Victoria de los Angeles, 1923– (Spain); Kathleen Battle, 1948– (U.S.); Montserrat Caballé, 1933– (Spain); Maria Callas, 1923– 77 (Greece); Regine Crespin, 1927– (France); Geraldine Farrar, 1882– 1967 (U.S.); Eileen Farrell, 1920– (U.S.); Kirsten Flagstad, 1895–1962 (Norway); Mirella Freni, 1935– (Italy); Amelita Galli-Curci, 1882–1963 (Italy); Mary Garden, 1874–1967 (England); Maria Jeritza, 1887–1982 (Czechoslovakia); Dame Kiri Te Kanawa, 1944– (New Zealand); Dorothy Kirsten, 1917–1992 (U.S.); Lotte Lehmann, 1888–1976 (Germany); Lotte Lenya, 1898–1981 (Austria); Jenny Lind, 1820–87 (Sweden); Dame Nellie Melba, 1861–1931 (Australia); Zinka Milanov, 1906–89 (Yugoslavia); Aprille Milo, 1958– (U.S.); Grace Moore, 1901–47 (U.S.); Carol Neblett, 1946– (U.S.); Birgit Nilsson, 1918– (Sweden); Lily Pons, 1898–1976 (France–U.S.); Rosa Ponselle, 1897–1981 (U.S.); Mado Robin, 1918–1960 (France); Anneliese Rothenberger, 1924– (Germany); Leonie Rysanek, 1926– (Austria); Bidu Saÿao, 1902– (Brazil); Elisabeth Schwarzkopf, 1915– (Germany); Beverly Sills, 1929– (U.S.); Dame Joan Sutherland, 1926– (Australia); Eleanor Steber, 1916–1990 (U.S.); Renata Tebaldi, 1922– (Italy); Dame Maggie Teyte, 1888–1976 (England); Helen Traubel, 1899–1972 (U.S.); Carol Vaness, 1952– (U.S.).

MEZZO-SOPRANO

The female voice between the soprano and alto. The title role of *Carmen* requires this range.

Among the most famous mezzos: Marian Anderson, 1902– 93 (U.S.); Dame Janet Baker, 1933– (England); Rose Bampton, 1909– (U.S.); Grace Bumbry, 1937– (U.S.); Rosalind Elias, 1931– (U.S.); Kathleen Ferrier, 1912–53 (England); Marilyn Horne, 1929– (U.S.); Christa Ludwig, 1928– (Germany); Nan Merriman, 1920– (U.S.); Jessye Norman, 1945– (U.S.); Regina Resnik, 1922– (U.S.); Ernestine Schumann-Heink, 1861–1936 (Czechoslovakia); Frederica von Stade, 1945– (U.S.); Rïse Stevens, 1913–92 (U.S.); Blanche Thebom, 1918– (U.S.); Jennie Tourel, 1899–1973 (Canada); Shirley Verrett, 1931– (U.S.).

ALTO OR CONTRALTO

The lowest normal female voice. The range is approximately two octaves upward from the E or F below middle C. From the Latin, *altus*, high, it originally referred to a high male voice, or counter-tenor.

TENOR

The highest male voice. Normal range: one octave below and one octave above middle C. The word comes from the Italian *tenore*, to hold, derived from medieval plainsong when the tenor held the melody and other voices sang counterpoint.

Counter-tenor (male alto): A very high voice, often *falsetto*, i.e., reaching higher than the normal tenor range.

Heldentenor, German for a voice of heroic quality necessary for Wagnerian roles. *Tenor di forza* in Italian.

There are also *tenore buffo*, who specialize in comic roles, and *tenore di grazia*, light, graceful, and lyric tenors.

Most famous tenors, past and present: Peter Anders 1908–54 (Germany); Carlo Bergonzi, 1924– (Italy); Jussi Björling, 1911–60 (Sweden); Hans Peter Blochwitz, 1949– (Germany); José Carreras, 1946– (Spain); Enrico Caruso, 1873–1921 (Italy); Franco Corelli, 1921– (Italy); Placido Domingo, 1941– (Spain); Nicolai Gedda, 1925– (Sweden); Beniamino Gigli, 1890–1957 (Italy); Gary Lakes, 1950– (U.S.); Richard Leech, 1957– (U.S.); John McCormack, 1884–1945 (Ireland); James McCracken, 1926–88 (U.S.); Lauritz Melchior, 1890–1973 (Denmark); Luciano Pavarotti, 1935– (Italy); Jan Peerce, 1904–84 (U.S.); Tito Schipa, 1889–1965 (Italy); Leo Slezak, 1873–1946 (Austria); Giuseppe di Stefano, 1921– (Italy); Ferruccio Tagliavini, 1913– (Italy); Richard Tauber, 1891–1948 (Austria); Richard Tucker, 1913–75 (U.S.); Jon Vickers, 1926– (Canada); Fritz Wunderlich, 1930–66 (Germany).

BARITONE

The male voice lower than a tenor and higher than a bass. Normal range: two octaves upward from the A a tenth below middle C. The word comes from the Greek for "heavy tone."

There is also a *bass-baritone*, a voice sharing the characteristics of each range. Mozart's *Don Giovanni* is an ideal bass-baritone role.

Among the most famous: Dietrich Fischer-Dieskau, 1925– (Germany); Ferruccio Furlanetto, 1949– (Italy); Tito Gobbi, 1913–84 (Italy); Håkan Hagegård, 1945– (Sweden); Thomas Hampson, 1955– (US); George London, 1919–1985 (U.S.); Giuseppe de Luca, 1876–1950 (Italy); Robert Merrill, 1917– (U.S.); Sherrill Milnes, 1935– (U.S.); Hermann Prey, 1929– (Germany); Lawrence Tibbett, 1896–1960 (U.S.); Leonard Warren, 1911–1960 (U.S.).

BASS

The lowest male voice (Italian *basso*). Range: two octaves upward from the E an octave and a sixth below middle C.

Basso buffo, suited to comic roles.

Basso cantante, a lyric, singing bass.

Basso profondo, the lowest you can get!

Among the most famous: Fyodor Chaliapin, 1873–1938 (Russia); Boris Christoff, 1914– (Bulgaria); Simon Estes, 1938– (U.S.); Nicolai Ghaiurov, 1929– (Bulgaria); Jerome Hines, 1921– (U.S.); Alexander Kipnis, 1891–1978 (Ukraine); Ezio Pinza, 1892–1957 (Italy–U.S.); Samuel Ramey, 1942– (U.S.); Cesare Siepi, 1923– (Italy); Giorgio Tozzi, 1923– (Italy); Norman Treigle, 1927–75 (U.S.).

CASTRATI

Male sopranos whose testes were surgically removed in boyhood left them with high, childlike voices projected by adult lung power.

No longer in existence, they were popular in the eighteenth and nineteenth centuries, singing female roles in opera. The favored ones attained stardom and riches. The last castrato, Alessandro Moreschi (1858–1922), sang at the Sistine Chapel in the Vatican until he retired in 1913. Known as the Angel of Rome, his voice may still be heard on recordings.

MUSIC TO THEIR EARS

The kind of vocal sound that is admired varies througout the world. In Europe the smooth flowing *bel canto* (beautiful singing) is favored. Eastern Asia prefers high, thin tones. Spanish flamenco dancers accompany their steps with a range from low harsh sounds to lyrical high notes. Tone quality depends much on the language sung.

Singers have always been of historical importance, from the sirens in Greek mythology, to troubadours and minstrels, church choirs, and choruses of operas and musicals. Top soloists through the ages have enjoyed adulation and wealth. In modern times, radio, recordings, movies, and television have brought the world's most famous voices into our homes. Those voices of the past—lost forever to us—would have reveled in such opportunities.

*Choirs are for people with passable
voices who love to sing, but don't dare
do solos, except in the shower.*
—Dr. Anne Gray

CHAPTER FOURTEEN

Singing Through the Ages

A chorus is a group of singers. Its name is derived from the Greek *choros*, a group that danced and chanted in plays, making comments on the action. A choir is a chorus that sings in church. Choral singing is one of the most popular ways of making music. One does not need to have a solo quality voice. There are mens' choruses, womens' choruses, mixed choruses, school choruses, college glee clubs, and childrens' choruses, the most notable of which is the Vienna Boys' Choir, which tours the world in concert and dates back to 1498.

England and Wales hold choral festivals that bring thousands of singers together. Among the most famous groups in England are the long-established Huddersfield Choral Society and the choirs of King's and St. John's Colleges, Cambridge, Winchester Cathedral, St. Paul's Cathedral, Westminster Abbey, and the Chapel Royal at Windsor Castle. Many European countries have radio ensembles, such as the French National Radio Chorus. Most symphony orchestras and opera companies in the major cities of the world have choruses attached to them.

In the United States, the Mormon Tabernacle Choir, the Robert Shaw

Chorale, and the Roger Wagner Chorale were among the first to set professional standards for what, apart from symphony and opera performances, is usually amateur music-making. Fred Waring and his Pennsylvanians did the same for popular music of the 1930s and 1940s.

Choral music has been composed for every occasion and on just about every subject. Most is written to be sung in four parts—soprano, alto, tenor, and bass. Sometimes these parts are subdivided into eight or more parts. Music written for two choruses answering each other is called *antiphonal*. This type of singing reached its height in Italy around 1600 with the works of Andrea Gabrieli (*c*1510–1586), organist at St. Mark's church in Venice, and his more famous nephew and pupil, Giovanni Gabrieli (1557–1612).

Choral works based on the words of the Catholic Mass have been in existence since the 1300s. Masterpieces in this form have been composed by Palestrina (1525–94), Bach, Mozart, Beethoven, Berlioz, Verdi, and Brahms. Contemporary composer, Leonard Bernstein (1918–1990) wrote a theatrical *Mass*. There is also an excitingly different version of the mass inspired by Latin American popular folk music: the *Misa Criolla*, by Argentinian composer Ariel Ramírez, written in the early 1960s.

Besides opera, the musical forms for chorus include the CHORALE, the CANTATA and the ORATORIO.

CHORALE

The chorale, or simple hymn tune, was first sung in Protestant churches. Martin Luther arranged melodies that could be sung in unison by the whole congregation. Soon German composers began to write chorales giving the sopranos the melody line while the other voice parts sang the harmony. Bach contributed many beautiful compositions in this form.

By 1700, versions of chorales had become so complicated and dramatic that a new form arose called the *cantata*.

CANTATA

A cantata has several sections built around a religious text. It is longer than a chorale, but shorter than an oratorio. Besides choruses there are solos, duets, and orchestral interludes. Bach wrote over two-hundred of them featuring a variety of moods such as adoration, grief, and triumph.

Many were written for particular Sundays in the church year. The most well-known are "Sheep May Safely Graze" and "A Mighty Fortress Is Our God."

ORATORIO

Telling a Biblical or religious story, an oratorio, like an opera, requires soloists and chorus, but unlike an opera is performed in a church or concert hall without scenery, costumes, or dramatic action. Its name is derived from the sixteenth-century meetings held in the small chapel, or oratory, of Filippo Neri in Rome. These meetings featured hymns sung during various parts of the telling of a Biblical story.

An oratorio starts with an orchestral overture. The story is then told by narrators-soloists, who sing in a style of melodic speech called *recitative*. Sometimes the soloists represent characters while the chorus are the crowd or spectators. If the subject is the crucifixion of Christ, the work is called a *passion*.

Beginning in the early 1600s in Italy, the oratorio reached its peak with eighteenth century German composers. Bach poured his strong religious feelings into his *Passions* and his *Christmas Oratorio*. Handel produced twenty grand works in this form, with *Messiah* being the most familiar. King George I was so moved when he heard the "Hallelujah Chorus" that he stood up. Naturally, everyone else had to stand as well. Rising for this chorus has become a tradition to this day.

Haydn wrote *The Creation* in 1797, and Beethoven carried the form into the nineteenth century with his *Christ on the Mount of Olives*. Mendelssohn came later with *St. Paul* (1836) and *Elijah* (1846). Berlioz's *Childhood of Christ* was written in 1854.

Modern composers have also been drawn to the grand scale of the oratorio. The English composer Sir William Walton (1902–1983) wrote *Balshazzar's Feast* in 1931. Arthur Honegger of Switzerland (1892–1955) contributed *King David* (1921) and *Joan of Arc at the Stake* (1934–35). The Russian contemporary, Igor Stravinsky (1882–1971), gave us *Oedipus Rex* in 1926.

Oratorios form the basic repertoire of choirs and choruses. Besides being performed regularly on Easter and Christmas, many of them are sung at annual festivals throughout the world. A new tradition has sprung up in this country with "sing along" versions of *Messiah*, which invites the audience or congregation to participate in the choruses.

CHAPTER FIFTEEN

Opera — The Ultimate Vocal Production

The simplest definition of opera is *drama in music*. The plot and emotions of the characters unfold vocally in stage action with orchestral accompaniment, scenery, and costumes. The *libretto* is the "book," or words of the opera which the composer has set to music.

Early Beginnings

Singing with instruments dates back to ancient times. Greek plays, circa 525 B.C., contained singing accompanied by plucked strings—lutes and lyres—and flutes. *Pastourelles*, little plays about shepherds and shepherdesses containing songs and dances, were featured in the thirteenth century. By the sixteenth century *mascarades*, pageantlike Italian court entertainments combining music and drama, were presented at carnival time. There were also *intermezzi*, vocals and instrumental performances presented between acts of plays. These became more elaborate and so popular that by the end of the 1500s this new musical style, under the name *opera*, shook the foundations of European music and swept the world.

After a few early experiments in music drama, the first true opera was *Orfeo* by CLAUDIO MONTEVERDI (1567–1643), performed in Italy in 1607 (this work is still produced today). The opening of the first public opera house in Venice in 1637 was a great event. For a small fee the public could enjoy what until then had been only for the privileged few. Soon there were sixteen theaters in Venice alone.

By the 1800s more serious and philosophical subjects were emerging in opera, as witnessed in the thought-provoking plots of Rossini's *William Tell* (1829), Halévy's *La Juive* (*The Jewess*, 1835), Bellini's *I Puritani* (*The Puritans*, 1835), and Meyerbeer's *Les Huguenots* (1864).

These lavish spectacles came to be called *grand opera*. Meanwhile, Italy again pioneered a new form, *opera buffa*, or comic opera. GIOACCHINO ROSSINI (1792–1868) was the master of these. In his early years he wrote a new opera every six or eight weeks. The most famous are: *La scala de seta* (*The Silken Ladder*, 1812), *Il signor Bruschino* (1813), *Tancredi* (1813), *L'Italiana in Algeri* (*The Italian Girl in Algiers*, 1813), *La Cenerentola* (*Cinderella*, 1817), *La gazza ladra* (*The Thieving Magpie*, 1817), *Semiramide* (1823) and *William Tell* (1829). Rarely produced today, their tuneful overtures enjoy popularity as orchestral works. *The Barber of Seville*, written in 1816, with its tongue twisting aria, *Largo al factotum*, sung by Figaro the barber, is performed regularly in most major opera houses.

Stars and Spectaculars

Audiences demanded good tunes and gaudy spectacles. Stages were filled with scenery. Gods descended from clouds. Animals—horses, elephants, bears, lions—were paraded on stage. Battles, shipwrecks, erupting volcanoes and other special effects were thrown in whether or not the plot demanded it.

Gradually singers rather than set designers became the stars drawing in the audiences. They dictated to composers, added their own embellishments to the music and even included arias from other operas. *Castrati*, men with boys' voices, became pampered darlings. Italian opera troupes traveled to Austria, Poland, Germany, France and England winning many devotees.

The French Connection

In France, Italian-born JEAN-BAPTISTE LULLY (1632–87) changed the negative attitude of the French court towards opera with his work *Cadmus and Hermione* in 1673. Having worked his way up from teenage kitchen worker and dancer to musical dictator of France under the personal partonage of Louis XIV, "The Sun King," Lully devised a style of singing suited to the French language. In fifteen years he produced fifteen operas, supervising all rehearsals and conducting the forty musicians himself. He was the true father of the modern orchestra and set the pattern for French opera for over sixty years.

JEAN-PHILIPPE RAMEAU (1683–1764) dominated French music in general and opera in particular to the end of his life—and beyond, in that he is still recognized as France's greatest organist and theorist.

Other notable French opera composers are GEORGES BIZET (1838–75), who died three months after the disappointing premiere of what has since become the world's most performed opera, *Carmen*. It has been filmed several times, televised, and transformed into a ballet. A modern version of the plot, *Carmen Jones*, was successfully produced on Broadway in 1945 with an all black cast. This was made into a movie in 1954, starring Dorothy Dandridge (with Marilyn Horne dubbing the singing) and calypso singer Henry Belafonte as *Don José*. There has been a recent revival of Bizet's earlier opera, *The Pearl Fishers* (1863). The superb tenor-baritone duet *"Au fond du temple saint"* was featured in the Australian film *Gallipoli* (1981). The vibrant music from another opera, *L'Arlésienne* (1872), is now heard only in the arrangement of orchestral suites.

HECTOR BERLIOZ (1803–69), an outstanding composer of the Romantic period, wrote several operas. *The Trojans* (1863), after being neglected for over a century has re-entered the repertory of major opera houses. Because of its length, performances are usually split into two evenings.

LÉO DELIBES (1836–91), known for his ballets, contributed *Lakmé* (1883) to the operatic repertoire. Besides the lovely aria "The Bell

Song," in which most sopranos soar to a high E* as the final note, this opera also contains the divine duet *"Viens, Malika . . . Dome epais"* for soprano and mezzo, which was used to lend atmosphere to the movie *Someone to Watch Over Me* (1987).

CHARLES GOUNOD (1818–93) transformed the age-old story of a man selling his soul to the devil in exchange for getting his youth back into the much-performed opera, *Faust* (1859).

CAMILLE SAINT-SAËNS (1835–1921) wrote *Samson and Delilah* (1877), whose aria "My Heart at Thy Sweet Voice" remains a recital favorite. The lively overture is usually all that is still heard from his first opera, *La Princesse jaune* (*The Yellow Princess*, 1872).

JULES MASSENET (1842–1912) composed *Manon* (1884), which enjoys a steady popularity. *Le Cid* (1885) survives as an orchestral suite, and *Thaïs* (1894) has given us the reverent "Meditation," one of the most-played solo pieces in the violin repertoire.

German Geniuses

GEORGE FRIDERIC HANDEL (1685–1759), Bach's contemporary, brought Italian and German opera to London, changing the cool reception of music drama in that country to one of enthusiasm. He wrote operas until 1741, then, finding this unprofitable, turned to the field that made him immortal, the oratorio.

CHRISTOPH WILLIBALD GLUCK (1714–87), another German, laid the foundation for modern opera by having arias and dances as part of the dramatic action rather than being inserted merely for entertainment.

The genius of WOLFGANG AMADEUS MOZART (1756–91) enriched the operatic genre with *The Marriage of Figaro* (1786), *Don Giovanni* (1787), and *The Magic Flute* (1791), to name the most popular of the eighteen operas he wrote.

FRANZ JOSEPH HAYDN (1732–1809) composed light operas for the guests of his employer, Prince Esterházy. There has been mounting interest in recovering them from oblivion.

LUDWIG VAN BEETHOVEN (1770–1827) wrote only one opera, *Fidelio* (1814), which has the distinction of having four overtures. The first

* The Queen of the Night sings five high F's in the course of Mozart's *The Magic Flute*.

three versions, titled *Leonora* Nos. 1, 2, and 3, are performed as separate orchestral works. *Fidelio* has its own overture under the opera's title.

The Giant of the Opera

The towering genius of RICHARD WAGNER (1813–83) overshadowed every other composer with his gigantic four- and five-hour-long operas, their mythical subject matter, and wild, "unplayable" music. Musically and politically he was so controversial that at one point he had to flee the country and live in Switzerland. By 1864, broke and desperate, he was rescued by young King Ludwig II of Bavaria, who wished to be recognized as a patron of the arts. Gradually, Wagner's operas were accepted. The City of Bayreuth, with the backing of private contributors, invited him to build the theater he had been planning for years. Designed with no balconies or boxes like those in the traditional horseshoe shaped houses, the fan-shaped design with the stage appearing to be a continuation of the seats and the orchestra pit hidden from view has become accepted as the most practical for many later auditoriums. In 1876, Wagner was finally able to stage the famous *Ring* cycle, his four mighty mythological operas: *Das Rheingold, Die Walküre, Siegfried* and *Götterdämmerung*. Apart from wartime interruptions, festivals of Wagner operas have been performed there regularly since 1892.

Wagner's other operas include *Rienzi* (1837), *The Flying Dutchman* (1841), *Tannhäuser* (1845), *Tristan and Isolde* (1865), *Die Meistersinger* (1868), his only "light" work, and the final, powerful, *Parsifal* (1882). Written just a few months before his death, this last is a religious work into which he poured his faith.

His personal life was as stormy as his operas. Born in Leipzig, Richard was only a year old when his father died. His sisters and brother were already involved in theater and opera. Wagner's mother, knowing the uncertainties of an artistic career, tried to keep him away from the arts, but his urge was too strong. He studied Shakespeare, Goethe, Dante, Greek myths, and the works of Beethoven. At the University of Leipzig he received his only formal musical training—a six-month course in composition.

Taking a job as a conductor, he married the actress Minna Planer in 1836. In 1857, they went to live on the estate of Otto Wesendonck in Zurich. Wagner fell in love with the man's wife, Mathilde, pouring his feelings into the libretto of *Tristan and Isolde* and composing songs to the poems she had written. Minna left him and they were not reunited until 1859 in Paris. In 1861, she left him for good because he was now in love with Cosima von Bülow, the daughter of Franz Liszt and the wife of one of his best friends, the conductor Hans von Bülow. Minna died in 1866. Cosima bore Wagner two daughters before her marriage to von Bülow was annulled in 1869, the year in which she gave birth to the composer's son, Siegfried. They were married in 1870.

Like other pioneers and innovators, Wagner caused arguments and furors with everything he did—through his thirteen operas, his essays, his books, his autobiography, his lifestyle. What has now become conventional, in his day was revolutionary. He has been the subject of more books and articles than any other composer. He was the embodiment of the Romantic movement and caused music to find new directions. His works are the backbone of German opera, and Bayreuth continues to be his living memorial. There his operas are presented as per his instructions, as they were done first by his widow, then by his son and grandson. Whatever controversy he caused will be forgotten, but his music is secure in history.

Beneath the giant's shadow, a little fairy tale opera has survived—*Hansel and Gretel*, written in 1893 by a man whose *real* name was ENGELBERT HUMPERDINCK (1854–1921).

Not until the twentieth century did Germany find a "successor" to Wagner in RICHARD STRAUSS (1864–1949)—no relation to Johann—who wrote *Salomé* in 1905 and *Elektra* in 1909, both of which are more dissonant than Wagner. The opera of his that is most performed is the lighthearted *Der Rosenkavalier* (1911), featuring beautiful waltzes which have been arranged into two orchestral suites. His later operas, *Ariadne auf Naxos* (1911–12) and *Die Frau Ohne Schatten* (1914–18), are only occasionally produced.

From the Vastness of Russia

Even in faraway Russia opera grew and flourished. MIKHAIL GLINKA (1804–57), known as the "Father of Russian Music," composed the first national operas, *A Life for the Tsar* (1836) and *Russlan and Ludmilla* (1842),

ALEXANDER BORODIN (1833–77) combined the careers of physician and composer. His unfinished opera, *Prince Igor*, was completed by fellow Russian geniuses Nikolai Rimsky-Korsakov (1844–1908) and Alexander Glazounov (1865–1936), leaving us the legacy of the exciting "Polovtsian Dances" frequently heard in concert, sometimes with chorus.

MODEST MOUSSORGSKY (1839–81) wrote what is acknowledged as the supreme Russian opera, *Boris Godunov* (1868–72), which is still performed internationally.

Of the eleven operas of PETER ILYICH TCHAIKOVSKY (1804–93), the most popular are *Eugene Onegin* (1877–78), *The Queen of Spades* (*Pique Dame*, 1890) and *Joan of Arc* (1878).

NIKOLAI RIMSKY-KORSAKOV (1844–1908) combined a naval career and composition. His most noted operas are *Le Coq D'Or* (1906–07), *Sadko* (1894–96) and *The Snow Maiden* (1880–81).

SERGEI PROKOFIEV (1891–53) wrote his most famous opera, *The Love for Three Oranges* (1921), for the Chicago Opera Company. On his return to the Soviet Union he was censured for his "formalism."

DMITRI SHOSTAKOVICH (1906–75) also wrote operas that received Communist censure.

SERGEI RACHMANINOFF (1873–1943) escaped Communism by moving to Dresden in 1906 and later settling in the United States. His operas include *Aleko* (1892) and *Francesca da Rimini* (1900). He is better known for his emotion-stirring orchestral and piano music.

El Cánto Español

Spain introduced the zarzuela, a type of comic operetta with origins dating back to 1644. A wave of nationalism in the late nineteenth century saw composers such as ENRIQUE GRANADOS (1867–1916) produce serious operas like *Goyescas* (1916), and MANUEL DE FALLA (1876–1946) his popular *La Vida Breve* (1911).

In South America, Brazilian ANTONIO CARLOS GOMES (1836–96), had success with his *Il Guarany*, which has played internationally. ALBERTO GINASTERA (1916–83) received acclaim for his *Don Rodrigo*, produced by the New York City Opera in 1966.

Operas Sung in English!

Although England is associated with the satirical, comic and tuneful operettas of Sir William Gilbert and Sir Arthur Sullivan, the country's operatic contributions date back to 1689 when HENRY PURCELL (1659–95) wrote *Dido and Aeneas*. Handel contributed his share of operas for his adopted country until audiences tired of the Italian style and of having to sit through productions in a foreign language.

FREDERICK DELIUS (1862–1934) achieved moderate success with *A Village Romeo and Juliet*, followed by RALPH VAUGHAN WILLIAMS (1872–1958) with *Hugh the Drover* and *Riders to the Sea*, which receive occasional performances.

It is BENJAMIN BRITTEN (1913–76) whose operas show promise of permanence, with *Peter Grimes* (1945), *The Rape of Lucretia* (1946), *Albert Herring* (1947), and *Billy Budd* (1951) being the most produced.

Opera in America

In the United States, composers appear to have the most success with American subjects. One of the earliest was the 1896 production of *The Scarlet Letter* by WALTER DAMROSCH (1862–1950), the German-born American conductor and composer. Ragtime composer SCOTT JOPLIN's (1868–1917) *Treemonisha*, produced in 1911, was revived in the 1970s. DEEMS TAYLOR (1885–1966), composer, author, and critic, scored some success with *The King's Henchman* (1926) and *Peter Ibbetson* (1931). HOWARD HANSON (1896–1981) wrote *Merry Mount* in 1934, and like the fate of many operas, the music has been preserved in an orchestral suite of the same name. DOUGLAS MOORE's (1893–1969) *The Ballad of Baby Doe* (1956), SAMUEL BARBER's (1910–81) *Vanessa* (1956), and *Four Saints in Three Acts* (1934) and *The Mother of Us All* (1947) by VIRGIL THOMSON (1896–1989) are all examples of fairly successful modern American operas.

The best-known U.S. opera is *Porgy and Bess*, by GEORGE GERSHWIN (1898–1937). The all-black production premiered in New York in 1935. Sidney Poitier and Dorothy Dandridge (with voices dubbed) and Sammy Davis, Jr., starred in the 1959 film version. The Met staged a revival in 1987 to mark the fiftieth anniversary of the opera's first performance.

LEONARD BERNSTEIN's (1918–90) *West Side Story* (1957), appears to be transcending its Broadway musical roots and attaining operatic status. The well-executed 1961 movie of this contemporary New York setting of *Romeo and Juliet* starred Natalie Wood with the singing voice of Marni Nixon.

Annual performances of GIAN-CARLO MENOTTI's (1911–) *Amahl and the Night Visitors*, the first opera written for television (December 24, 1951), have become a Christmas tradition.

Italy—The Source

Italy still lays claim to the most prolific operatic composers. GAETANO DONIZETTI (1797–1848) sustains his popularity with *L'elisir d'amore* (*The Elixir of Love*, 1832), *Lucia di Lammermoor* (1835), based on Sir Walter Scott's novel, *The Bride of Lammermoor*, and *La fille du regiment* (*Daughter of the Regiment*, 1840)—a favorite role of retired prima donna Beverly Sills.

RUGGIERO LEONCAVALLO (1857–1919) met instant success with the two-act *Pagliacci* (1892), the story of a clown who kills his unfaithful wife, yet must still go on stage and make people laugh. Legendary tenor Enrico Caruso (1873–1921) immortalized the aria "Ridi, pagliaccio!" (Laugh, clown) from this opera.

The one-act *Cavalleria rusticana* (1840) of PIETRO MASCAGNI (1863–1945) marked the advent of *verismo*—the Italian school of opera realism—and brought the composer immediate international acclaim. The lovely instrumental *Intermezzo* is often heard by itself in concert.

The two short operas are usually paired on a double bill (popularly known as "Pag and Cav").

VINCENZO BELLINI (1801–35) is remembered for *La Sonnambula* and *Norma* (1831), ARRIGO BOITO (1842–1918) for *Mefistofele* (1866), UMBERTO GIORDANO (1867–1948) for *Andrea Chenier* (1896), and ALFREDO CATALANI (1854–93) for *La Wally* (1892), from which the hauntingly beautiful aria *"Ebben? Ne andro lontano"* was interwined in the equally haunting French film *Diva* (1981).

Towering over all other opera composers in creativity, prolific output, and most memorable music are the Italian "giants" Giuseppe Verdi and Giacomo Puccini.

GIUSEPPE VERDI (born: Roncole, October 9 or 10, 1813; died: Milan, January 27, 1901) studied with the church organist in the small town of Busseto at age twelve and became his assistant when he was sixteen. A local grocer, recognizing the boy's talent, offered to pay for his studies in Milan. At first the Conservatory refused to admit him because in 1832 he was already over fourteen. But even when they stretched the rules and gave him an examination, Verdi failed in both piano and music theory. He then studied with a former La Scala opera musician for two years, after which he returned to Busetto, became the town music master, and in 1836 married the grocer's daughter, Margherita Barezzi. He settled in Milan in 1839, where La Scala accepted his first successful opera, *Oberto*. His next, *King for a Day*, was a failure. Tragically, at this time his two infant children and his wife died within a short time of one another. Ready to give up, Verdi felt such bitterness toward the public that from then on he wrote only to please himself.

The next period of Verdi's life saw the production of a series of successful operas, directed by him in major Italian cities—Rome, Milan, Naples, Venice and Florence, as well as Paris and London.

Italy, which had been torn apart by wars and internal strife for more than a thousand years, was seeking national unity. Verdi's powerful operas endeared him to his fellow countrymen. When Italy finally achieved independence from the tyranny of Austria (1861), Victor Emmanuel became king, and the composer was made a member of Parliament and later a senator. He attended the Senate only once, knowing that he could do more for democracy in composition than in debate. Rich and famous, he settled down to enjoy the good life with his second wife, Giuseppina Strepponi, a soprano whom he married in 1839.

The death of Rossini in 1868 led to a proposal that a group of Italian composers honor him by writing a requiem mass, each of them contributing a portion of it. Verdi submitted his part, but the plan collapsed. When the Italian poet, Manzoni, died in 1873, Verdi, this time working alone, wrote a complete *Requiem* for him. This has come to be recognized as one of the great choral-orchestral masterpieces, ranking with those of Mozart and Brahms. At its premiere, despite its beauty, it was attacked for its theatricality, but when Brahms himself came to its defense, the criticism dissipated.

Verdi felt that at his age he should not have to turn out a new opera every other year. He even permitted himself the luxury of writing a string quartet. But he fooled everyone who thought he was too old to go through the strenuous work of writing another opera, and came up with *Otello*, in 1887. A great success, it showed refinement of the composer's technique. With the orchestra he evoked every shade and nuance of the score, yet the instruments never interfere with the voices, so every word is heard clearly. The harmonies are much more subtle and evocative than those of his earlier operas. The superbly written melodies flow together naturally rather than being chopped up into recitatives and arias.

As the world wondered if this was the last of the Verdi operas, the librettist Arrigo Boito (1842–1918), with whom he had collaborated on *Otello*, showed Verdi his condensation of Shakespeare's *Merry Wives of Windsor*. The result was *Falstaff*, premiering at La Scala in 1893, within a few months of the composer's eightieth birthday.

His last composition was a set of four sacred choral pieces. He spent his final years in Milan, showered with honors. His wife died in 1897, and in her honor Verdi established a home for retired musicians. When he died in 1901, he was buried next to her in a simple ceremony that, following his wishes, contained no music. A crowd of 28,000 people lined the streets for his funeral.

The composer was highly articulate. His letters show his knowledge of the theater. He demanded that his librettists give him dramatic texts, not literary masterpieces, explaining to them that one colorful word was worth more than an elegant stanza. He supervised his operas from casting down to every detail of production, always aiming for perfection.

Born the same year as Wagner, for a while Verdi, and his greatness, was obscured by the German's impact on Europe, and the rising popularity of a new Italian opera composer, Giacomo Puccini. That the genius of Verdi has prevailed is evident. His major operas, *Rigoletto* (1850–51), *Il trovatore* (1851–52), *La traviata* (1853), *Un ballo in maschera* (1857–58), *La forza del destino* (1861), and *Aida* (premiered in Cairo for the opening of the Suez Canal in 1870), are constantly being performed by every major opera company in the world.

GIACOMO PUCCINI (born: Lucca, December 22 or 23, 1858; died: Brussels, November 29, 1924) came from a long line of composers. He began his music career as a church organist at age fourteen, but after attending a performance of Verdi's *Aida* he decided to fulfill his desire to write operas. He entered Milan Conservatory in 1880, and studied with Antonio Bazzini (1818–97) and Amilcare Ponchielli (1834–86).

Puccini's first opera was in one-act and entitled *Le Villi* (1882). It was written for a competition and did not even place, but it did catch the attention of the publisher Giulio Ricordi, with whom Puccini would have a lifelong association. After another ill-received opera, *Edgar* (1889), Puccini wrote *Manon Lescaut* (1893), which rocketed him to international success. Interestingly, his next opera, *La Bohème* (1896), directed by a young conductor named Arturo Toscanini, was not a great triumph at its premiere. It is now one of the most famous and loved operas of all time. In 1900, Puccini produced another masterpiece in *Tosca*. For his next endeavor, he was inspired by a one-act play by David

Belasco, *Madame Butterfly*, which he saw in London. Puccini proceeded to write what he felt was his greatest and most technically advanced opera, *Madama Butterfly*. Yet its opening night in February 1904 was a fiasco as jealous rivals of Puccini hired people to sit in the audience to hurl insults and virtually ruin every tender scene with growls and laughter. Despite this, Puccini recast the work in three acts and it was performed in Brescia later that year, where it received the response it deserved. Hailed as a masterpiece, it has risen to almost match *La Bohème* in popularity.

That same year, Puccini married Elvira Gemignani, who had borne him a son eight years before. It was a long time before his next opera, perhaps due to a scandal arising from the suicide of his servant girl. Elvira had accused her of having an affair with her husband. Although the girl's innocence was proven by a court case, the publicity deeply affected the composer, putting his creative talent on hold. Finally in 1910 he wrote *La fanciulla del West* (*The Girl of the Golden West*), also based on a Belasco drama. It was premiered at the Met in New York in 1910. Through its use of Debussian harmony and Straussian orchestration, this work disproved the critics, who claimed Puccini repeated himself in each new opera.

Puccini continued writing, but his next two works were slow to gain popularity. *La rondine* opened in 1917 and was well received, but it is his weakest work, containing no moving lyrical melody. *Il trittico* is a set of three one-act operas which was also premiered at the Met (1918). Of these, the last story, *Gianni Schicchi*, is often performed by itself. For what was to be his last opera, Puccini ventured on new paths. *Turandot*, set in China, has a fantastic, fairy-tale setting, but with realistic human characters. Puccini inserted Chinese melodies in the work and created a new personal style, with dissonance, complex orchestration, and much choral writing. In 1923 Puccini developed cancer of the throat, and despite treatment at a Brussels clinic, it took his life; the opera was left unfinished. Franco Alfano wrote the last scene from Puccini's sketches, and *Turandot* received its premiere at La Scala in 1925 under Toscanini. The audience was awakened to a Puccini they had not expected, and the opera lives on in popularity.

Puccini was a master of melodic lines that infuse his operas with great sentiment and a tenderness few composers can hope to match. He had a mastery of dramatic flair, making his works true "theater." His fine orchestration enabled him to capture the audience with only a few notes, hence his operas contain no overtures, just brief instrumental introductions to set the mood. Puccini was a true artist, responding to influences of other composers from Debussy to Schoenberg. He knew his limitations and never exceeded them. He is quoted as having said, "God touched me with His little finger and told me to write only for the theater. I have followed His command."

Puccini remains the only true successor to Verdi, and his work will undoubtedly continue to move the emotions of operagoers for generations to come.

Opera and History

Because of production expenses, opera reflects the social conditions contributing to its growth. The horseshoe-shaped interior of traditional theatres allows everyone in the boxes to see and be seen. Opera-going was and still is a form of social entertainment. In days gone by, gossiping, eating, drinking, and gambling were an adjunct to the performance. With all this clutter it is amazing that the genre ever reached any artistic heights. That it has must be credited to the composers whose continual input of great music elevated the entire field.

The creators of opera have always had to invent. New sounds, new combinations of instruments, new styles of playing came into being. Thus opera led the way to the composition of the present day orchestra and influenced the makeup of symphonic music.

The history of opera since 1600 has been part of the history of Europe. Opera has always changed in response to changing social conditions. In the last few years most American opera houses feature English subtitles superimposed on a small screen above the stage, making the action completely understandable. This has resulted in attracting new audiences to the grand spectacle of opera.

With the screenings of performances on cable channels such as Bravo and Arts and Entertainment, opera has literally come home!

CHAPTER SIXTEEN

Operettas

They All Lived Happily Ever After

An operetta is literally a merry, tuneful "little opera." The plots are usually sentimental and have happy endings. A few are comic and satirical. There is a good deal of spoken dialogue, making an operetta more like a play with vocal solos, duets, and choruses. But lightness of style does not mean lack of quality. Master composers have written great music for this genre.

Operetta emerged around the middle of the nineteenth century. Social and economic changes saw the middle and working classes becoming more affluent. These people wanted an easier listening alternative to grand opera, and operetta was the answer.

The Fun of Gilbert and Sullivan

In England, Sir William Schwenk Gilbert (1836–1911), a former lawyer turned playwright, and Sir Arthur Seymour Sullivan (1842–1900), a gifted composer-conductor (he wrote "Onward, Christian Soldiers!"), met in 1871. For the next twenty years they collaborated on fourteen humorously satirical operettas—some argue that these are comic *operas*. Richard D'Oyly Carte, an eminent London theater manager, formed a company to produce their works. Today, the ones most performed are *H.M.S. Pinafore* (1878), *The Pirates of Penzance* (1879), *The Mikado* (1885), and *The Gondoliers* (1889).

Gilbert and Sullivan companies have sprung up all over England and the United States and as a result these operettas are performed more often than many other musical stage works. The plots make fun of other operas, English nobility, and politics. Gilbert is a master of clever words and breathtaking tongue-twisting "patter songs." Sullivan's skillful music is so tuneful that the audience always goes home humming happily.

A French Accent

In Paris, Jacques Offenbach (1819–80) was the king of popular music in the 1860s, with a theater of his own where he produced the operettas for which he is remembered: *Orpheus in the Underworld* (1858)—the overture is a standard concert piece—*La Belle Hélène* (1864), *La Vie parisienne* (1866), *La Grande Duchesse de Gérolstein* (1867), and *La Périchole* (1868). His most famous work is the opera, *The Tales of Hoffmann* (1881), from which the "Barcarolle" (Boat Song) is very familiar.

City of Make-Believe

The true home of the operetta, however, is Vienna, where the form originated. Johann Strauss, Jr. (1825–99) found time to write fifteen operettas in addition to his many waltzes, the most well-known being *Die Fledermaus* (*The Bat*) (1874) and *The Gypsy Baron* (1885).

FRANZ VON SUPPÉ (1819–95) wrote thirty operettas whose overtures, *Light Cavalry*, *Poet and Peasant*, *The Beautiful Galatea*, *Fatinitza*, and *Morning, Noon and Night in Vienna*, are perennial concert favorites.

OSCAR STRAUS (1870–1954) wrote over forty operettas, of which *The Chocolate Soldier* (1908), based on George Bernard Shaw's *Arms and the Man*, and *A Waltz Dream* (1907) are still produced.

Hungarian-born FRANZ LEHÁR (1870–1948) gave us the immortal *Merry Widow* (1905), which is respected enough to be performed by major opera companies and has twice been made into a movie, in 1934 with Maurice Chevalier and Jeanette MacDonald, and in 1952 with Fernando Lamas and Lana Turner. Lehár's other most important works are *The Count of Luxembourg* (1909) and *The Land of Smiles* (1929).

Another Hungarian, EMMERICH KÁLMÁN (1882–1953), will be remembered for his Viennese operettas, especially *The Gypsy Princess* and *Countess Maritza*.

Even the sophisticated British composer-playwright Noël Coward came under the spell of Viennese operetta and contributed the touching *Bitter Sweet* to the repertoire in 1929.

Operetta Crosses the Atlantic

Some of the most popular operettas in America were written after 1900 by two Europeans.

RUDOLF FRIML (1879–1972) was born in Prague and came to the U.S. in 1906. His fame rests on *Rose Marie* and *The Vagabond King*, both of which were made into movies starring the singing sweethearts of the 1930s and 1940s, Jeanette MacDonald and Nelson Eddy. Also worthy of mention is *The Firefly*, the 1937 film version of which gave us the perky song "Donkey Serenade," based on Friml's classical composition *Chanson*.

The other composer is Austro-Hungarian SIGMUND ROMBERG (1887–1951), who settled in New York in 1913. His successful operettas include *Maytime* (1911), *Blossom Time* (1921), based on the life of Franz Schubert, *The Student Prince* (1924), filmed in 1954 using the voice of Mario Lanza, *The Desert Song* (1926), filmed in 1953 with Gordon Macrae and Kathryn Grayson, *New Moon* (1928), featuring the glorious song, "Lover Come Back to Me," and *Up in Central Park* (1945), filmed in 1948 with Deanna Durbin, Vincent Price, and Dick Haymes.

The most prolific American operetta composer was Irish-born VICTOR HERBERT (1859–1924). A professional cellist, he played in the Stuttgart court orchestra from 1883 to 1886, in which year he came to this country to join the New York Metropolitan Orchestra. The most memorable of his forty-one operettas are *The Fortune Teller* (1898), *Babes in Toyland* (1903), *Mlle. Modiste* (1905), *The Red Mill* (1906), and *Naughty Marietta* (1910), made into a movie in 1935 that also starred Jeanette MacDonald and Nelson Eddy.

Even Viennese-born famed violinst FRITZ KREISLER (1875–1962), was attracted to the field, collaborating with Victor Jacobi to write an operetta, *Apple Blossoms*, which premiered in New York in 1919.

The Dawn of a New Era

Operettas flourished from the middle 1800s until the 1920s. A new milestone was erected when Jerome Kern's *Show Boat* (1927), with its American setting, (un)royal characters, and colloquial speech, ushered in the era of the American Musical.

CHAPTER SEVENTEEN

Musical Comedy: Blazing the Great White Way

Also known as MUSICAL COMEDY or "Broadway Musical," this is the truly American form of musical theater.

Most of the composers whose names have appeared in lights on Broadway, or "The Great White Way" as the main street of theaters in New York City is called, were already well known for their operettas: Rudolf Friml, Sigmund Romberg, Victor Herbert, George Gershwin, and Leonard Bernstein among them. In the strictly "musicals" field were George M. Cohan, Jerome Kern, Cole Porter, Irving Berlin, Harold Rome, Vincent Youmans, Harold Arlen, Frank Loesser, Frederick Loewe, and Richard Rodgers.

A Way With Words

Not so well-known are the all-important librettists and lyricists whose creative words made these musical comedies so uniquely American.

Harry B. Smith, Guy Bolton, P.G. Wodehouse (the famed English humor novelist), Ira Gershwin (George's brother), E.Y. Harburg, Howard Dietz, and Alan Jay Lerner, who collaborated with Frederick Loewe to write *My Fair Lady*. Two of the most renowned names in this category are Lorenz Hart and Oscar Hammerstein II, both of whom teamed with Richard Rodgers to produce a treasury of the world's most enduring musicals.

Black-Faced Beginnings

The minstrel shows that emerged in the U.S. in the middle of the nineteenth century were a mixture of white and black humor, song and dance. These degenerated into cheap parodies and were replaced by the romantic operettas discussed in the previous chapter.

Yankee Doodle Dandy

Marching into the unreal world of operetta came GEORGE M. COHAN (1878–1942), the "Yankee Doodle Boy" who had grown up in the crude song-and-dance routines of vaudeville. He wrote patriotic, fast-paced shows. His hit songs, "Give My Regards to Broadway," "You're a Grand Old Flag," and "Over There," written for the American troops in Europe during World War I, are still standards.

The Roaring Twenties: Scandals, Follies, and Vanities

Alongside the popular operettas, new musical forms appeared such as revues and follies. The great impresario FLORENZ ZIEGFELD (1867–1932) initiated his *Ziegfeld Follies* in 1907. They were held annually until 1936. By definition, plotless opulent spectaculars, they featured gorgeously gowned and pulchritudinously shaped showgirls and top comedians like W.C. Fields, Eddie Cantor, and Fanny Brice. Contributing were big-name composers such as Irving Berlin, Victor Herbert, and Jerome Kern.

The Broadway stage of the 1920s was dominated by the revue. The Music Box Theater was built for the *Music Box Revues* of Irving Berlin. George Gershwin wrote many numbers for *George White's Scandals* of

1920, 1921, 1922, 1923, and 1924. *Earl Carroll's Vanities* of 1930 and 1931 bordered on the risqué, with lots of girls wearing very little costumes.

The *Garrick Gaieties* of 1925 and 1926 brought together the team of Richard Rodgers and Lorenz Hart, who would collaborate in five smash musicals: *Connecticut Yankee* (1927), *On Your Toes* (1936), *Babes in Arms* (1937), *The Boys From Syracuse* (1938), loosely based on Shakespeare's *The Comedy of Errors*, and *Pal Joey* (1940). The last was made into a movie in 1957 starring Frank Sinatra, Rita Hayworth, and Kim Novak.

Besides Rodgers and Hart, the 1920s brought together the men who were to become masters of the American musical: the Gershwin brothers, Cole Porter, Vincent Youmans, Jerome Kern, and Oscar Hammerstein II.

A Landmark Musical

When Kern and Hammerstein collaborated on Pulitzer Prize-winning author Edna Ferber's novel *Show Boat* (1927), the Broadway musical was elevated to a new artistic level. Instead of caricatures, blacks were featured as suffering, real life people. The characters, black and white, were believable. The showstopping songs, "Only Make Believe," "Bill," "Why Do You Love Me?," "Ol' Man River," have become classics.

Bootleggers, Gangsters, and Hoofers

Meanwhile, history and social conditions were affecting public taste. Silent movies gave way to sound. Busby Berkeley and other directors swept the spectacular revue and dazzlingly costumed showgirls onto the silver screen, with the mobile camera outdoing the boxed-in stage. Ginger Rogers and Fred Astaire danced their way into people's hearts all over America, helping them forget Prohibition, gangsterism, and the Great Depression.

The late 1920s also saw George and Ira Gershwin's humor and sophistication in *Funny Face* (1927), *Girl Crazy* (1930), *Strike Up the Band* (1930), *Of Thee I Sing* (1931)—which won a Pulitzer Prize for playwrights George S. Kaufman and Morrie Ryskind—and *Let 'Em Eat Cake* (1933). Most of these satirized war and American politics. Irving

Berlin's *Americana* (1932) and *As Thousands Cheer* (1933) were also concerned with timely topics.

The Sky's the Story Limit!

As musicals grew up, writers discovered unlimited plot subjects. American history was the basis of musicals like *Knickerbocker Holiday, Bloomer Girl, Oklahoma*, and *1776*. The supernatural was featured in *One Touch of Venus* (1943) and *On a Clear Day You Can See Forever!* (1965), which was filmed with Barbra Streisand in 1970. Serious musicians also got into the act. In *The Seven Lively Arts* (1944), American composer William Schuman wrote the overture, the Russian maestro Igor Stravinsky wrote a ballet score, and the great artist Salvador Dali provided paintings to be enjoyed during intermission.

The Fabulous Fifties!

The late forties and fifties produced gem after gem of musical comedy treasures. The partnership of lyricist ALAN JAY LERNER (1918–86) and composer FREDERICK LOEWE (1901–88) brought us *Brigadoon* (1947), filmed with Fred Astaire and Gene Kelly in 1968; *Paint Your Wagon* (1951, the 1969 film cast included Clint Eastwood); and the huge success, *My Fair Lady* (1956), with Julie Andrews (the leading role in the 1964 movie version went to Audrey Hepburn, with dubbed singing, because Andrews was starring in *The Sound of Music*). In 1958, the pair collaborated for the film *Gigi*, starring Leslie Caron, Maurice Chevalier, and Louis Jourdan. They returned to the Broadway stage on December 1960 with their final smash hit *Camelot*, starring Richard Burton and, again, Julie Andrews. The 1967 film version featured Richard Harris and Vanessa Redgrave. In 1980, the musical was successfully revived, again with Richard Burton, who became indisposed and was succeeded by Richard Harris.

Other musicals of note during this period are *Finian's Rainbow* (1947), with David Wayne as the leprechaun, and Fred Astaire in the same role in the 1968 film; *Kiss Me Kate* (1948), loosely based on Shakespeare's *Taming of the Shrew*, with music by Cole Porter, filmed in 1953 with Howard Keel and Kathryn Grayson; *Fanny* (1954), which starred opera basso Ezio Pinza (the 1960 film version again starred Leslie Caron and Maurice Chevalier, this time with Charles Boyer); *Fiddler on the Roof* (1964), with Zero Mostel, its 3240 performances making it the longest running musical on Broadway in the 1960s (the 1971 film version starred Israeli actor Topol, who had led the London stage version); and *Man of La Mancha* (1965), based on Cervantes' *Don Quixote* and named best musical of the year (the 1972 film version starred Peter O'Toole and Sophia Loren).

The Dynamic Duo

The pair who truly dominated the American musical scene in the 1940s and 1950s were Richard Rodgers and Oscar Hammerstein II, the latter having contributed to a few forgettable shows before gaining recognition writing the lyrics to Rudolf Friml's *Rose Marie* (1924) and Sigmund Romberg's *The Desert Song* (1926). Teaming up with Rodgers enabled Hammerstein to put into words his true feelings for people. The results were *Oklahoma!* (1943), *Carousel* (1945), *South Pacific* (1949), *The King and I* (1951), *Flower Drum Song* (1958), and *The Sound of Music* (1959). All of them have become classics, and all were made into smash hit movies, some with extra songs written for the film versions, adding to this magnificent treasury of music.

A name to be mentioned here is orchestrator-arranger Robert Russell Bennett, who created orchestral suites from the music of *Oklahoma!* and *Carousel*. He also put together two suites from Richard Rodgers' soundtrack score to the television series *Victory At Sea* (1952), after writing almost the entire score from a dozen themes given him by the composer.

A Classical Composer on Broadway

LEONARD BERNSTEIN (1918–1990), composer, author, pianist, and conductor, had a strictly classical education. He sprang to fame in 1943 when Bruno Walter fell ill and, as assistant conductor, "Lenny" took over the New York Philharmonic Orchestra and electrified the audience with his performance.

On the flip side of his classical aspirations was his urge to write popular music. His great successes were *On the Town* (1944), the story of three sailors on leave in New York (the film version in 1949 starred Frank Sinatra and Gene Kelly and included the ballet *Fancy Free*); *Wonderful Town* (1953), from the play *My Sister Eileen*; *Candide* (1956) based on the Voltaire classic; and one of the finest musicals of all time, *West Side Story* (1957), a modern version of *Romeo and Juliet*.

Mod Musicals

STEPHEN SONDHEIM (1930–) gained recognition as the lyricist for *West Side Story* (1957) and *Gypsy* (1959), the story of stripper Gypsy Rose Lee. His own first big hit was *A Funny Thing Happened on the Way to the Forum* (1962). His next successes as both composer and lyricist was *Company* (1970) and *A Little Night Music* (1973), which contains his best-known song, "Send in the Clowns."

His later works increased the challenge to his audiences' ears and intellect. *Sweeney Todd, The Demon Barber of Fleet Street* (1979), has been called the most grisly musical ever presented, since the main character slits his clients' throats in the barber chair and his assistant, Mrs Lovett (played on Broadway by Angela Lansbury), makes the corpses into meat pies. *Sunday in the Park with George* (1984), centering on the painting "A Sunday Afternoon on the Island of La Grande Jatte" by the Impressionist Georges Seurat, deals with the artist's mind, work and mistress, and the people he paints. The plot even moves down to his descendants in America. It ran for 604 performances, with Mandy Patinkin and Bernadette Peters in the leading roles.

Even though several of his efforts have not met with great success, Sondheim has been credited with taking the musical theater to new and interesting places.

A new duo, CLAUDE-MICHEL SCHÖNBERG (1944–), composer, and Alan Boublil, librettist, has given us two recent Broadway blockbusters. *Les Misérables*, based on the Victor Hugo novel, premiered in Paris on September 17, 1980, opened at the Barbican Theatre, London, September 30, 1985, and came to New York's Broadway Theatre, March 12, 1987. Their second hit, *Miss Saigon*, which hit London in 1989 and New York a year later, is a modern version of Puccini's *Madama Butterfly*, set during the Vietnam War, featuring a Vietnamese girl who has a child by an American marine.

Reign of the New King

Today the leader in what can definitely no longer be termed musical "comedy," but musical *theater*, is an Englishman who appears to have conquered the field. ANDREW LLOYD WEBBER was born in England in 1948. At the age of twenty he wrote *Joseph and the Amazing Technicolor Dreamcoat* (1968), a mixture of rock, country, and theatrical styles, based on the biblical tale of Joseph and his coat of many colors. In 1971, Lloyd Webber jolted audiences with *Jesus Christ Superstar* by "humanizing" the title character. *Evita*, in 1976, gave us a musical version of the life of Argentine dictator Juan Perón's controversial wife, Eva, who went from living in abject poverty to becoming first lady of her country. *Cats*, in 1981, based on poems by T.S. Elliot, caught audiences' imagination with the fantastic feline make-up of the characters, the garbage dump stage setting, and the hit song "Memories." The show is still playing somewhere. His masterpiece, *The Phantom of the Opera* (1986), is filled with glorious songs and special effects. It, too, is playing somewhere currently and no doubt will be for years to come. *Aspects of Love*, with a more traditional score, opened in London in 1989, and on Broadway in 1990.

The story line, staging, costumes, choreography, and song style of Lloyd Webber's productions, plus the combination of traditional instruments and electronic music, can safely be said to have taken us over the threshold of yet another era of music entertainment.

CHAPTER EIGHTEEN

Dance: From Cave to Cable TV

Dance music goes back to primitive rituals. Dances accompanied by voice and percussion instruments, usually drums, were used as prayers for good health, good crops, and victory over enemies.

Four Main Types of Dances

There are four main classifications of dance music: RITUAL, as mentioned above; SOCIAL, people dancing in pairs or in groups as in folk and square dancing; EXHIBITION, staged productions such as ballet or modern dance; and CONCERT, dance music performed, without dancers, on individual instruments or by an orchestra, as with the waltzes, polonaises, and mazurkas of Chopin. These categories constantly overlap each other. Tchaikovsky's most famous waltzes are in his ballets as well as suites and symphonies. Many major ballets have been arranged into orchestral suites. The most familiar is *The Nutcracker*.

Social Dancing

Throughout European history, social dances have served as the greatest inspiration for composers. Out of the Renaissance evolved the *pavane*, a processional dance, the *bassedanse*, a gliding dance, the *volta*, a turning dance, and the *galliard*, a leaping dance. These were the basis for instrumental works for small ensembles. The combination of two or more dances became the foundation of the ORCHESTRAL SUITE.

Rather than repeating the same set of notes played during a dance, musicians would make variations while still retaining the essence of the melody. This became translated into the orchestral form THEME AND VARIATIONS. The most famous and tuneful of these are Brahms's *Variations on a Theme by Haydn*, and the *Symphonic Variations* of César Franck. In our century, one of the most important components of jazz is improvised variations.

The Dance Center of the World

Under Louis XIII and Louis XIV, France became the dance center of the world. Court dancing came into fashion, with such names as *allemande, courante, sarabande, gigue, minuet, gavotte, bourrée, rigaudon*, and *passepied* given to the various steps. Of these, the minuet remained at the top of the charts until the 1800s, when it was replaced with the waltz.

The Ethnic Ethos

The Baroque period ended before 1800, and nineteenth-century Europe enjoyed new popular national dances such as the mazurka and polonaise from Poland, the polka from Bohemia, and the new favorite, the waltz, from Austria. Nineteenth- and twentieth-century composers looked increasingly to dance music of their own and other countries for their inspiration. Liszt wrote Hungarian Rhapsodies, Brahms wrote Hungarian Dances, Dvořák wrote Slavonic Dances, and Grieg wrote Norwegian Dances. Bizet, Rimsky-Korsakov, de Falla, Albéniz, Debussy, and Ravel each made wonderful use of Spanish dance rhythms.

Ballet: A New Art Form

First danced by noble amateurs in courtly surroundings, ballet reached the stage by being performed within opera. Until the French Revolution in 1789, most ballets were based on mythical subjects. The first truly Romantic ballet is *La Sylphide*, starring the ballerina Marie Taglioni, who was the first to wear the typical costume—the snug bodice and flaring white muslin skirt known as a *tutu*—and the first to create the technique of toe dancing—dancing on the points of her slippers.

The most famous Romantic ballet, *Giselle*, premiered in 1841, with music by Adolphe Adam. This was followed by the melodic, sparkling music in the ballets of Léo Delibes (1836–91): *La Source* (1866), *Coppelia* (1870), and *Sylvia* (1876). They inspired Tchaikovsky to create his masterpieces: *Swan Lake* (1877), *Sleeping Beauty* (1890), and *The Nutcracker* (1892). These productions, staged by the master choreographer Marius Petipa, creator of the Russian ballet style, temporarily shifted the dance center of the world to Moscow and St. Petersburg.

Ballet in the Twentieth Century

Paris regained her position as the center of the ballet world in 1909 when impresario SERGEI DIAGHILEV (1872–1929) moved his troupe of the finest Russian dancers to the French capital. Passing through his Ballets Russes de Monte Carlo, as he named his company, were such legendary dancers and choreographers as Anna Pavlova, Michel Fokine, Vaslav Nijinsky, Bronislava Nijinska (Vaslav's sister), George Balanchine, and Leonide Massine. Ballets were created to the music of many prominent composers, including Rimsky-Korsakov (*Scheherazade*), Borodin (*Polovtsian Dances*), and the early twentieth-century contemporaries Debussy (*L'apres midi d'un faun*), Ravel (*Boléro*), Prokofiev, and Stravinsky.

Stravinsky's first contribution to the genre was the lush orchestration of Chopin's music for the ballet *Les Sylphides*, choreographed by Fokine. The Russian composer's next masterpieces were *The Firebird* (1910), *Petrouchka* (1911), and the work that caused a near riot with its savage rhythms and unorthodox Nijinsky choreography, *The Rite of Spring* (1913).

Not So Modern Dance

After the death of Diaghilev in 1929, modern dance gave fresh impetus to the dance theater. Isadora Duncan, Martha Graham, and Doris Humphrey created ballets of personal expression, characterization, and storytelling. Modern dance has no set basic steps like classical ballet, but a museum study of Greek dancing figures on urns and in friezes would reveal that there is nothing so really modern about modern dance.

Ballet and Broadway

Ballet continues to flourish. Contemporary composer Aaron Copland (1900–90), gave us *Billy the Kid* (1938), *Rodeo* (1942), and *Appalachian Spring* (written for Martha Graham, 1944); all considered the first authentic American ballets.

Agnes de Mille (1909–), who choreographed *Rodeo*, made musical history with her dream scene in *Oklahoma!*. It was the first time that a ballet sequence furthered the action by exploring the subconscious mind of a character. De Mille became Broadway's most sought after choreographer, adding *Carousel* (1945), *Allegro* (1947), *Brigadoon* (1947), and *Paint Your Wagon* (1951) to her credits.

Pleasant to the ear as well as to the eye.
—Inscription on ornate Renaissance keyboard instrument

CHAPTER NINETEEN

Instruments: The Music Makers

Not content with using his built-in instrument, the voice, as the sole means of making music, from prehistoric times man has devised other ways through the invention of tone-producing tools. Although many no longer exist, a large number of ancient instruments have survived through the efforts of "early music consorts," present-day ensembles specializing in playing Renaissance music using original instruments such as sackbuts, krummhorns, recorders, lutes, and viols. The best known of these groups are those of CHRISTOPHER HOGWOOD (1941–), who founded the Academy of Ancient Music in 1973, and TREVOR PINNOCK (1946–), with his English Concert (1972).

Continuous Improvement

Through the centuries most instruments have benefited from technical improvements especially the piano(forte), today's models of which are a far cry from the first hammer invention of Bartolommeo Cristofori (1655–1731). Valves on brass instruments, woodwind technology, and the tuning mechanism of tympani (kettledrums) have also been updated. The modern electronic organ barely resembles the instrument for which Gabrieli, Bach, and other Baroque composers wrote their grand compositions. The strings are one of the few exceptions, which have not needed updating. In fact, modern violin makers are still vainly seeking the secrets of the late seventeenth- and early eighteenth-century master craftsmen of Cremona—Amati, Guarneri, and Stradivari.

More Than Just a Tool

The main function of a musical instrument is as a tool for producing sound. As such it must obey the laws of acoustics. It has to be just the right shape. Flutes must have their holes drilled a precise distance apart. Violins have to be made of certain kinds of wood to make the fibers vibrate freely.

To make them pleasing to the eye (and to ancient gods) primitive instruments were decorated by carving, painting, gilding, and inlaying them with other woods. Most modern instruments, such as shining brasses, need no enhancement, and master violins have their own built-in beauty.

The Four Divisions

Instruments are classified into four main groups: vibrating strings, or *chordophones*; vibrating air columns, or *aerophones* (woodwinds and brass); vibrating membranes, or *membranophones* (drums with skin heads); percussion instruments that vibrate without strings, air, or membranes—*idiophones* or *autophones* (cymbals, bells, chimes, triangles, xylophones, and celestas). In a symphony orchestra instruments are divided into four "families": strings, woodwinds, brass, and percussion.

The String Family

> *The Strings—akin to the range of the human voice—more than any other instruments, elicit the most personal response from the depths of our spirit.*
> —Zina Schiff, violinist

One of the earliest recorded stringed instruments (3000 B.C. in Sumeria and 1500 B.C. in Egypt) is the LYRE. Related to the harp—in Hebrew a *kinnor*—it is believed to be the instrument played by David. The lyre reached its greatest importance in Greece, where a larger version, the KITHARA, was played by professional musicians. The lyre was made of wood or a tortoise shell, its arms were animal horns supporting a crossbar around which from three to twelve strings were wound, and its sounding board was a piece of skin stretched over the shell.

During the medieval period, the lyre was replaced by the harp and the LUTE. The lute, a long-necked instrument with a flat top and pear-shaped back, is played by plucking. It appeared in Europe in the thirteenth century via Crusaders returning from the Holy Land. It was the favorite instrument of Shakespeare's time (1600). The last pieces written for it were around 1750, just after the death of Bach. There is current interest in a lute revival. Julian Bream (1933–), of England, is one of today's foremost lutanists.

A 2,500-year-old HARP was found buried in an Egyptian tomb. Harps were used in ancient Greece and Rome. It is the national instrument of Ireland and Wales. Its shape is derived from the accommodation of the different lengths of the strings, and has evolved from a few strings stretched on a hunting bow to today's forty-seven-string, seven-pedal model. It is played by plucking the strings from both sides. One or two harps are usually found in an orchestra, even though many major works do not contain a part for it.

The MANDOLIN looks very much like a lute except that it has a deeper bowl and thinner neck. Its four sets of double strings are plucked by a *plectrum*, or pick. The strumming produces the instrument's characteristic tinkling trill. Its delicate tone is just right for playing the love and folk songs of its native Italy. Mozart featured the mandolin in a serenade in *Don Giovanni*. Beethoven wrote a few pieces for it, and Mahler used it in his Sixth Symphony.

The GUITAR has curved sides like a violin and a flat back. Its six strings are made of nylon or metal and are strummed by the fingers of the right hand. Like the lute and mandolin the guitar has a fretted fingerboard. *Frets* are the strips of raised metal across the neck which help the player find the correct pitch by pressing down the strings with the fingers of the left hand.

The history of the guitar goes back 5,000 years to the time when it was played by Egyptian Pharoahs. The Romans brought it to Spain, where by the year 1500 it had become the national instrument. In the same century, Spanish settlers brought the guitar to Mexico.

Boccherini, Paganini, de Falla, Albéniz, and Granados are among the composers who have written for this instrument. But it was the Spaniard Andrés Segovia (1893–1987) who was responsible for the regeneration of interest in the guitar as a classical instrument through his transcriptions of Bach and other composers. Mario Castelnuovo-Tedesco (1895–1968) and Joaquin Rodrigo (1902–), wrote beautiful guitar concertos for him. Segovia also inspired a new generation of classical guitarists, including Julian Bream, *his* protégé John Williams, and the Romero family—father Celedonio and his three sons, Celin, Pepe, and Angel, who, in turn, are now continuing the legacy with *their* sons, notably Celin's son, Celino, currently taking the place of his uncle Angel in the unique quartet.

In the art world, decorated guitars have attracted the attention of painters. Watteau (1684–1721) frequently featured them in his paintings, as did Picasso (1881–1973).

The BANJO was brought to America by African slaves in the form of their *banjar*. On the plantations it was made by stretching a coonskin over a hollowed gourd, attaching a handle to the gourd, and running four strings along its length. It gradually changed to its present form of a skin stretched tightly over a round hoop of wood or metal. Its long fretted neck has five or six strings which are strummed, usually for chord accompaniments. The most popular instrument in the minstrel shows of the 1800s, its syncopated rhythm led to the early form of jazz called *ragtime*, of which black composer SCOTT JOPLIN (1868–1917) was the foremost exponent. Until 1930, when it was replaced by the smoother-sounding guitar, the banjo was a basic member of the rhythm section of dance bands. Nowadays the banjo is mainly heard in "bluegrass" and country and western music.

In the 1930's the guitar replaced the banjo in American jazz groups. The jazz guitar gradually changed shape, becoming electric and then electronic—the basic instrument for rock groups.

The UKULELE, a small four-stringed guitar, originated in Portugal. Brought to America in the 1900s, it became the ideal instrument for accompanying jazz songs in the twenties, but its tone was too small to be part of dance bands. It is the favorite instrument of Hawaiians.

The BALALAIKA has three strings and a wooden body shaped like a triangle. It comes in many sizes and is played by strumming the strings rapidly. Of ancient Tartar origin, it is used mainly in Russia to accompany folk songs and dances. There are also balalaika orchestras which play arrangements of light classical compositions.

The ZITHER, Austria's favorite instrument, consists of forty-five strings stretched over a shallow wooden body. The front five are the melody strings lying over frets; the rest are plucked for accompaniment. Related to the guitar, dulcimer, psaltery, and kithara, the zither is heard today in small ensembles, especially in the fine restaurants of Europe. The instrument was prominently featured in the haunting theme from the spy movie *The Third Man* (1950), starring Orson Welles.

The DULCIMER is of Persian origin and was also transported to Europe during the Crusades. Like the zither it consists of a series of strings stretched across a wooden box. These are struck with small knobbed sticks, producing a pleasant jangling sound. Besides being popular in gypsy music, it is seeing a revival in American folksongs of the southeastern region.

The CIMBALOM, almost identical to the dulcimer, consists of metal strings fastened to pegs set in a wooden box. The player uses padded sticks or wooden hammers to strike the strings. It is the national instrument of Hungary and may be heard in most Eastern European countries. ZOLTÁN KODÁLY (1882–1967) wrote an *Intermezzo* for the cimbalom in the orchestral suite from his opera *Háry János*.

Members of the Orchestra

The VIOLIN is the most popular of all instruments, with more solo pieces written for it than any other except the piano. As the highest range, or "soprano," member of the string family played with a bow, it forms the backbone of the symphony orchestra along with the viola, cello, and double bass. The greatest chamber music has been written for the string quartet: two violins, viola, and cello.

Made from about seventy pieces of various woods—maple, pine, ebony, pearwood, and sycamore—the carefully shaped sections are glued together and varnished. The type of wood determines the price of a violin—from thousands of dollars to under a hundred. The four strings are made of gut, steel, or nylon wound with a thread of fine silver or aluminum and stretched the entire length of the instrument; they are tuned by tightening or loosening the pegs in the neck. A thin curved wooden bridge, notched for the strings, rests on top of the body midway between the *F*-shaped holes. An ebony fingerboard lies under the strings from the pegs down, providing a hard surface for the player to press his fingers in an action called "stopping," which is how the pitch is determined.

The bow is a wooden stick strung with horsehair. It is control of the bow that makes a fine violinist. By changing the amount of pressure on the bow, the player can caress the strings or dig into them. The bow can be drawn smoothly, making connected *legato* tones, or bounced for detached *staccato*.

Besides the ability of the player, the quality of sound of a violin depends upon the kind of wood and the type of glue and varnish, which is why so much research continues into the components of the finest violins ever made, those of the Italian families of Amati, Guarneri, and Stradivari of sixteenth- and seventeenth-century Cremona. Their violins are now worth many millions of dollars.

Some of the great violinists of our time include Fritz Kreisler (1875–1962), Efrem Zimbalist (1889–1985), Mischa Elman (1891–1967), Josef Szigeti (1892–1973), Jascha Heifetz (1901–87), Zino Francescatti (1902–91), Nathan Milstein (1904–92), Erica Morini (1904–), David Oistrakh (1908–74), Yehudi Menuhin (1916–), Oscar Shumsky (1917–), Ruggiero Ricci (1918–), Isaac Stern (1920–), Arthur Grumiaux (1921–1986), Leonid Kogan (1924–82), Ida Haendl (1928–), Christian Ferras (1933–82), Michael Rabin (1937–72), Salvatore Accardo (1941–), Itzhak Perlman (1945–), Young-Uck Kim (1947–), Gidon Kremer (1947–), Kyung-Wha Chung (1948–), Pinchas Zukerman (1948–), and the "younger" generation: Elmar Oliveira (1950–), Zina Schiff (1954–), Nigel Kennedy (1956–), Cho-Liang Lin (1960–), Nadia Salerno-Sonnenberg (1961–), Anne-Sophie Mutter (1963–), Joshua Bell (1967–), Midori (1971–), Gil Shaham (1971–).

The VIOLA is the alto member of the strings. A little larger than a violin, its notes are in a lower register. It is played in the same manner, held under the chin. Usually buried in accompaniment, it was "liberated" by Gluck, who gave the viola important parts in his works. Haydn made it prominent in his string quartets. Mozart played it himself, used two violas in his quintets, and wrote beautiful duets for violin and viola.

Modern composers have written sonatas for it. Scottish-born William Primrose (1903–82), one of the world's greatest violists, brought the instrument to new prominence. Hungarian composer Béla Bartók wrote a concerto for him.

The CELLO (shortened from *violoncello*) is the tenor-bass of the string family. It is so large that the player must be seated with it between the knees. It has a long spike at the bottom which holds it in place on the floor. Resonant in single notes and rich-sounding in plucked chords, it has a shorter bow than the violin, but is played by similar finger stopping action.

In Baroque times the cello was used mostly for accompaniment. Haydn and Mozart gave it running passages, but it was Beethoven who brought out its singing tone, especially in his five sonatas for cello and piano. The Brazilian composer HEITOR VILLA-LOBOS (1887–1959) scored one of his *Bachianas Brasileiras* for eight cellos, and two for eight cellos and soprano. Tchaikovsky featured it prominently in many of his compositions. Cello concertos have been written by Schumann, Dvořák, Saint-Saëns, Elgar, Hindemith, and Barber. The operetta composer, Victor Herbert, originally a cellist in the Stuttgart Court Orchestra, wrote two concertos for his instrument. Bach's six suites for unaccompanied cello are challenging masterpieces. Among the world's outstanding cellists are the Spanish Pablo Casals (1876–1973), Gregor Piatigorsky (1903–76) and Mstislav Rostropovich (1927–), both Russian, Yo-Yo Ma, born in Paris in 1955 of Chinese parents who emigrated to the U.S. in 1962, and Felix Fan (1975–), American born of Taiwanese parents, representing a new generation.

The DOUBLE BASS is the deepest-voiced stringed instrument. It is also known as the bass-viol, contra-bass, and bull fiddle. Six feet tall, it has to be played standing up or sitting on a high stool. The strings are very thick and the bassist must have very strong fingers. The double bass was used mainly for accompaniment, until Beethoven's friend, bassist Domenico Dragonetti, showed the composer what the instrument was capable of, whereupon fast running passages and great leaping lines appeared in Beethoven's Fourth, Fifth, and Ninth Symphonies. Tchaikovsky featured the double bass in the opening of his Sixth Symphony. Schubert let it sing at the beginning of his "Unfinished" Symphony and made it a member of his "Trout" Quintet. The most famous bass solo depicts the elephant in Saint-Saëns' *Carnival of the Animals*.

The double bass replaced the tuba in the jazz bands of the twenties, its plucked pizzicato becoming an indispensable part of the rhythm section.

Serge Koussevitzky (1874–1951), Russian-born conductor of the Boston Symphony from 1924 to 1949, was a virtuoso double bassist.

The Woodwind Family

The oboe sounds like a clarinet with a cold, but it is the instrument the whole orchestra tunes up to.
—Victor Borge (1909–)

The woodwinds consist of the piccolo, flute, oboe, English horn, clarinet, bassoon, contra-bassoon, and saxophone; their non-orchestral members are the recorder, harmonica, accordian, bagpipe, pipe organ, ocarina (sweet potato), and the humble penny whistle.

The two main branches of woodwinds are those whose sounds are made by the player directing his breath across the tip of a tube as with the flute, piccolo, and recorder; and those whose tone comes from setting one or more reeds in motion.

Woodwinds (not necessarily made from wood) have appeared in all parts of the world. Flutes and whistles made from stone, bone, cane, and wood have been unearthed in archaeological digs. Single and double reed instruments were popular in eastern Mediterranean countries thousands of years before Christianity. The Chinese *sheng*, dated 1000 B.C., was a group of reeds with bamboo resonators, blown into by mouth. In Medieval and Renaissance Europe whole families (*consorts*) of woodwinds developed: recorders, *cromornes* (crumhorns or krummhorns), *shawms* (predecessors of the oboe), *bombardons*, which became *fagottos*—evolving into bassoons—and the *chalumeau*, a crude forerunner of the clarinet.

In The Orchestra

The FLUTE and its little brother the PICCOLO are the only orchestral woodwinds played by blowing across the mouth of the instrument. Originally made of wood, silver was the most common material used until contemporary virtuoso soloists Irish James Galway, French Jean-

Pierre Rampal, and American Eugenia Zuckerman made golden flutes a status symbol.

Composers have written for the flute since the 1600s. Johann Quantz (1696–1773), the favorite musician of Frederick the Great; although his works are rarely heard today, has the distinction of having written over 500 pieces for the instrument. Bach's contribution is the Suite in B minor for Flute and Strings. Handel and Haydn wrote flute concertos, and Mozart's Flute and Harp Concerto (K. 299) is one of his loveliest. Beethoven, Mendelssohn, and Tchaikowsky have prominent flute passages in their works, and Impressionist French composers Debussy and Ravel infuse its cool tones to color their compositions. Debussy's *Afternoon of a Faun* is famous for its sensuous opening flute solo. Besides producing calm, quiet passages, this instrument can run up and down scales and jump from high to low notes with lightning speed. The flute is literally the "acrobat" of the orchestra.

The PICCOLO, looking like a mini-flute, is the highest-pitched member of the orchestra. Haydn and Mozart used it and Beethoven established its position in the orchestra with passages in his Fifth and Ninth Symphonies. Berlioz wove it effectively into his *Symphonie fantastique*, Tchaikowsky brought out its possibilites in the *Sleeping Beauty* and *Nutcracker* ballets, and Stravinsky's *Rite of Spring* calls for two piccolos. The most striking piccolo solo is in John Philip Sousa's march, "Stars and Stripes Forever."

The OBOE is the soprano of the double reeds. Its name comes from the French *hautbois* (pronounced *ho-bwah*) meaning "high wood." Made of ebony or rosewood, its body is cone-shaped, widest at its "bell" (bottom). The oboe's tone is produced by the flow of the player's breath between two strips of reed. The reeds are cut from cane that grows in Italy or Southern France, and oboists shave them to their own preferred thinness. The reeds are bound together with thread and fitted into a holder that goes into the top of the instrument. Before a concert all reeds must be moistened, which is why musicians suck on them and place them in their instruments at the last minute.

The oboe is difficult to play and takes great breath control. Its Greek ancestor, the *aulos*, required that the players' cheeks be strapped in a leather belt so that they would not burst! One of today's virtuoso oboists is Heinz Holliger (1939–) of Switzerland.

The modern oboe is three hundred years old. It was developed in Paris in the 1650s by Pierre Hotteterre, a bagpiper in the court ballet orchestra. Also a woodworker, he narrowed the body of the medieval shawm, divided it into three sections, improved the mouthpiece, and added finger holes for the higher tones. It was first used by Lully in the opera orchestra of Louis XIV.

Most great composers have enjoyed writing for the oboe.

It is the oboe that sounds the A for the rest of the orchestra to tune to.

The ENGLISH HORN is neither English nor a horn, but an alto oboe. In its present form it is straight, but before 1839 it was curved, thus earning its mistaken designation as a horn. In France it was called a *cors anglé*, an "angled horn," and since the French word for English is *anglais*, with the same pronunciation, the misnomer was perhaps inevitable.

It was first used in opera orchestras in the late 18th century. Rossini gave the English horn an important part in his *William Tell* overture. The main showcases for English horn are the solo at the beginning of the third act of Wagner's *Tristan and Isolde*, extended passages in Sibelius's tone poem *Swan of Tuonela*, and Paul Hindemith's sonata for English horn and piano.

The CLARINET is a versatile instrument, found in orchestras, chamber music groups, concert bands, and dance bands. It is two feet long, and has a fairly narrow tube with a system of keys and levers covering the pitch holes. The single reed is held in place by a metal band at the mouthpiece. The top of the reed is free to vibrate when put between the player's lips.

Extremely expressive, the clarinet can whisper a melody, swell from soft to loud like the human voice, and produce passages full of runs and leaps.

Invented around 1700 by Johann Christian Denner, the clarinet was improved gradually from its initial rough-sounding trumpet timbre. Mozart used it in many of his later symphonies and wrote a concerto for clarinet and orchestra for his friend Anton Stadler, a Viennese clarinetist. Orchestras usually have three clarinets.

The jazz role of the clarinet began in New Orleans and became an integral part of Dixieland. Some of the most famous jazz clarinetists were Jimmy Dorsey, Woody Herman, and Benny Goodman, the last of whom also made the transition to classical music. American Richard Stoltzman (1942–) is one of the foremost classical clarinetist.

The BASS CLARINET is very long and curves into an upturned metal bell. It has a rich, dark tone. Its most famous solo is in "The Dance of the Sugarplum Fairy" from Tchaikovsky's *Nutcracker* Ballet.

The double reed BASSOON is the bass of the woodwind family. Its eight-foot length is doubled up in a "U" so that the player can reach all the keys and levers. A strap around the neck supports the instrument, leaving the hands free. Invented around 1600, it was dubbed "the clown of the orchestra." This image is reinforced in Paul Dukas' *The Sorcerer's Apprentice*. But Tchaikovsky's Fifth Symphony demonstrates that the bassoon can carry a sweet melody. In his Sixth Symphony, the "Pathéti-que," it expresses deep, tragic emotions.

The CONTRABASSOON is an enormous convoluted instrument. Its lowest tone is only a half tone above the lowest note on the piano. It is not heard too often, but has an important part in the beginning of the Brahms's First Symphony.

The SAXOPHONE is made of brass, but is part of the woodwind family by virtue of its single reed mouthpiece, which is similar to that of the clarinet. It is played by means of padded keys that close the fingerholes. There are four main sizes; the soprano is straight, and the alto, tenor, and baritone are curved with a flaring bell.

Invented in 1846 by Belgian-born clarinetist Adolphe Sax (who also perfected the flugelhorn and tuba), the instrument quickly gained popularity in his adopted country, France. Bizet used it in his *L'Arlésienne Suite No. 1*, and Debussy composed a *Rhapsody for Saxophone and Orchestra*. In America it became a standard in wind bands starting in the 1870s. From there it graduated to the jazz bands of the 1920s. Jimmy Dorsey and Charlie Parker are among the names of the great jazz saxophonists of recent time.

Although the instrument has not found a permanent place in the symphony orchestra because it tends to overpower the strings, it has been featured in Richard Strauss' *Domestic Symphony*, Vaughan Williams's Sixth Symphony, and Ravel's *Boléro*.

Except for the saxophone, today's orchestra usually has three of each type of woodwind, with the players sitting in the center just in front of the conductor but usually behind the violas.

The Brass Family

> *Never look at the trombones . . . it*
> *only encourages them.*
> —Richard Strauss (1864–1949)

Beginning with animal horns and conch shells, modern brass instruments have gone through many changes. Among the oldest still in use is the *shofar*, or ram's horn, sounded in synagogues on Jewish holy days;

the long red horn blown by the lamas of Tibet; and the giant Alpine horns of Switzerland used for signaling from mountain to mountain.

Modern brass instruments include the bugle, cornet, trumpet, flugelhorn, French horn, trombone, baritone horn, and tuba, all made of metal tubes with a cup or funnel-shaped mouthpiece and the bottom widening out into a "bell."

The player produces tone by blowing air through compressed lips which sets in motion the column of air in the tube of the instrument. The tightness of the lips and the length of the tube determine the pitch. The way a player uses his lips against the mouthpiece is called his *embouchure*.

The BUGLE is a military instrument used mainly for "Reveille," awakening the troops, "Chow Time," and "Taps," lowering the flag at sunset before "Lights Out." It is the simplest wind instrument, a long conical brass tube folded back on itself like a trumpet, with no valves or keys. Not part of bands or orchestras, it "stars" in drum and bugle corps often featured in parades.

The CORNET is the three-valved soprano of the brass family. Originating in the 1820s, the cornet is still the most popular solo instrument in military bands.

The TRUMPET is the soprano brass in the symphony orchestra. For centuries it was the aristocrat of instruments. The ancient Egyptians credited the God Osiris with its invention. The conquering Romans called them "tubas." In the Middle Ages in Europe only a nobleman could employ trumpeters. In the early 1700s King Frederick the Great of Prussia had two bands of trumpeters who played salutes and fanfares for his entrances, his exits and other ceremonial occasions.

Before 1500 trumpets were straight—some as much as seven feet long—and awkward for the player to handle. Until the 1800s it was a natural (valveless) horn like the bugle with a limited number of tones. Because of their limited range, trumpets were used sparingly in classical symphonies. Coiling the instrument to a manageable length and adding three piston valves opened a whole range of notes for the instrument as well as facilitating rhythm patterns from very slow to very fast. Wagner employed the trumpet extensively in his operas. Richard Strauss, Debussy, and Ravel showed off its different tonal features. Modern symphonic compositions usually call for three trumpets. Stravinsky used five in his memorable *Rite of Spring*.

A cone shaped *mute* may be placed in the bell of the trumpet to soften its tone or even make it sound like an echo. An integral part of jazz bands, muted trumpets are used for effects like "wah-wah" sounds, growling, bubbling, and "singing the blues."

Louis Armstrong and Dizzy Gillespie are among the jazz greats of the past. Notable in the classical field are Maurice André (1933–) and Wynton Marsalis (1961–), who has also made a name for himself in jazz and popular music.

The TROMBONE, descended from the old English sackbut, is the mellow tenor of the brass choir, or family. Nine feet long, it is divided into three sections, the bell being at the end of the U-shaped section which rests on the player's shoulders. The middle of the tube, the *slide*, fits over the open ends of the other two parts and is moved back and forth by the right hand. The trombonist must have a keen ear to push or pull the slide to sound the correct note, as there are no keys or valves to guide him. The mouthpiece is goblet-shaped like the trumpet, only larger. Heather Buchman (1965–) is a virtuoso trombonist.

The trombone was the first instrument to be perfected as early as the 1400s. It was a favorite church instrument for the next several hundred years. The tenor is the most used. By 1600 composers like Giovanni Gabrieli and Claudio Monteverdi used trombones in their sacred music. In the 1700s the trombone almost disappeared as composers became interested in newer instruments such as violins, clarinets, and oboes. Bach used it only with choral settings. It was the opera composer Gluck who brought the trombone back into prominence. Mozart followed Gluck's lead, using three in his opera *Don Giovanni*. In 1808 the trombone was first used in a symphony orchestra when Beethoven incorporated three of them in the finale of his Fifth Symphony. Since then, trombones have been featured in most major compositions, especially by Wagner, Richard Strauss, and Brahms.

Like other brass instruments, the trombone found its way into jazz. It was the personal instrument of 1940s bandleaders Tommy Dorsey and Glenn Miller. In concert and marching bands this versatile instrument can play bass, tenor, solo, or fill-in parts.

One of the most important members of the brass family is the FRENCH HORN. The French thought it originated in Germany and called it a German horn. The English thought it came from France and dubbed it a French horn.

From its distinctive long, narrower mouthpiece, the twelve- to sixteen-foot metal tube circles around and widens into a large, flared bell into which the player puts his hand in order to produce the mellow muted tone.

The French horn got its shape from its ancestor, the hunting horn. This developed into the natural horn used by seventeenth- and eighteenth-century composers. Key changes were made by using different lengths of interchangeable tubing known as *crooks*. Handel, Bach, Vivaldi, Haydn, and Mozart used the horn effectively in their compositions.

In the early 1800's three valves replaced the crooks, giving both the horn player and Beethoven the advantage over earlier composers. The horn came into its own in the nineteenth century. Its soft tones evoked the essence of Romanticism: pastoral scenes, mystic legends, deep sentiment—all expounded by such composers as von Weber, Mendelssohn, Wagner, Mahler, and Bruckner.

Concertos for horn have been written by Haydn (two), Mozart (four), Richard Strauss (two), and one by the modern composer Paul Hindemith.

Because it also blends so well with strings and woodwinds, this instrument has been used in chamber ensembles by Haydn, Mozart, Beethoven, and Brahms, among others.

One of the finest hornists of our time, the Englishman, Dennis Brain, born 1921, was killed in a car crash in 1957.

The lowest-pitched member of the brass family, the TUBA, is the youngest. It is best known for providing the "oom-pah" beat in marching bands. In spite of its enormous size—many coiled parts, five valves, and a very wide bell—it has a wide range of tones, from velvet to thunder. The mouthpiece is deep and cup-shaped. The instrument comes in various sizes.

First used by Prussian military bands in 1835, the tuba "family" was brought to its present form in 1843 by Adolphe Sax, inventor of the saxophone. Richard Wagner, always looking for new tone colors, suggested an instrument that would be a cross between a French horn and a tuba, causing the creation of the Wagner tuba. Since Wagner's time, Richard Strauss and Anton Bruckner have written for this instrument. John Philip Sousa suggested the tuba be given a movable bell. This resulted in the sousaphone. Other relatives of the tuba are the flugelhorn, baritone horn, and euphonium—all belonging to the family of saxhorns.

The tuba was part of the rhythm section of early dance bands before it was replaced by the double bass. It was occasionally used in the big bands of the 1930s and 1940s.

The brass section is usually at the back of the orchestra behind the woodwinds and to the right of the double basses.

The Percussion Family

> *The timpanist is the timekeeper—the
> second "conductor" of the orchestra. . .*
> —Alberto Lopez (1974–)

Percussion instruments are defined as those whose tone is produced by being struck, scraped, rubbed, shaken, or whirled. It is the largest family of the orchestra and, after the human voice, the oldest musical instrument. There is usually one player for the timpani (kettle drums), and two or three for all the other instruments, which include other drums, cymbals, gongs, rattles, triangles, marimbas, xylophones, etc.

DRUMS

Drums of all sizes are the most-used members of the percussion family. Basically a piece of material—animal hide, skin, or parchment—stretched over a hollow body made of metal, wood, or clay, the drumhead (skin) is made to vibrate and give off sound when struck.

Unlimited in size or shape, drums were sacred instruments in primitive societies, as well as being used to send messages.

The steel drums of Trinidad, originally made from empty oil "drums" have their tops carved in sections, giving them a definite pitch or note when struck. Steel bands of the Caribbean islands have popularized their native Calypso music.

Drums have been important members of military bands as well as orchestras. Jazz music shows off the versatility of the drummer. A name of note here is Gene Krupa (1909–73), the first jazz drummer to make an impression on the non-jazz public.

In symphony orchestras, the most important percussion instruments are the TIMPANI, also called kettle drums because of their shape. There are three sizes and always come in sets of four. Played with wooden sticks (beaters) padded at one end with hard or soft felt, they rest on metal stands and are tunable by means of pedals at the base. Their dynamics range from the softest sound to those capable of drowning out the whole orchestra.

Originating in India, these drums were brought to Europe around 1500 via the Crusaders, who found them in the Turkish armies. Until 1750 they were part of the military and used mainly for fanfares with trumpets. During the Classical period the timpani became part of opera and symphony orchestras. One of the first solo uses was in Haydn's Symphony No. 103, hence its nickname, the "Drumroll." Beethoven fully exploited this instrument. His violin concerto begins with a timpani solo, and the thunder in his Sixth ("Pastoral") Symphony is cleverly effected by waves of drumrolls. Berlioz used four sets of timpani in his *Symphonie fantastique*, while Stravinsky calls for five in *The Rite of Spring*.

The SNARE DRUM is first in importance in marching bands and second in orchestras. It has two heads with from two to twelve metal or gut strings on the outside of the bottom drum head. When the top drum head is struck the strings make the characteristic buzzing or rattling sound. The snare drum is played by bouncing two knobbed sticks of polished wood off the drum head, or stroking it with fan-shaped wire brushes—a favorite method in dance bands.

In parades the snare drum can be sounded alone for long stretches. A snare drum roll is a traditional suspense builder for high wire or other dangerous circus acts—an effective theatrical device, in general.

Gluck brought the snare drum into the opera orchestra, as did Rossini. Beethoven notated its basic cadence. Berlioz used it in his *Symphonie fantastique*.

The BASS drum is the largest member of the drum family. With two heads, it is usually played with short, heavy drum sticks with large felt knobs. It has no definite pitch.

Again it was Gluck who pioneered the use of this instrument in the orchestra. Haydn was the first to use it in a symphony, his 100th subtitled, the "Military" which at the time, 1794, catered to the Viennese craze for Turkish music. Berlioz features the bass drum all through the last two movements of his *Symphonie fantastique*.

The bass drum is used in classical music for marking heavy accents or suggesting thunder, cannon, etc. It also marks time in funeral marches. In marching bands the bass drum is strapped to the front of the player and beaten with two sticks.

CYMBALS are round brass plates that have a special timbre (tone color), but no definite pitch. The best ones came from Turkey and China where the exact composition of the brass was a closely guarded secret. The finest ones today are made by Zildjians, an Armenian family with branches in Boston and Istanbul. Translated, Zildjian means cymbal maker.

Cymbals can be played by holding them by the leather straps on the backs of their centers. Bringing them together in a sliding motion produces a ringing sound. Hitting them together makes a resounding crash which is stopped by pressing them against the body, called *choking*. A single cymbal can also be played with timpani sticks for a rolling suspenseful effect.

These instruments were brought to Europe from Turkey in the late seventeenth century. Mozart included them in his opera, *The Abduction from the Seraglio* (1783), they contribute to the rousing climax of Tchaikovsky's Fourth Symphony, Berlioz liked their noisiness, Debussy brought out their soft possibilities in *Fêtes* (1890), and Aaron Copland syncopated his *El Salon Mexico* with a "choked" cymbal.

The GONG, a bronze disc with upturned edges, originated in China. In the orchestra, large ones are hung from wooden stands, small ones laid on a blanketed table. The gong sounds best when struck gently, starting the tone softly and gradually increasing the force until it grows louder and louder. When "crashed," it overpowers all other instruments.

The gong is used by composers for solemn, mysterious, or terrifying effects and to add volume of sound to a climax.

The TRIANGLE is a slim steel rod bent into three seven-inch-long sides with a gap left in one corner. Struck by a small steel rod, it produces a high-pitched sound; a player can make a tremolo by shaking an inside corner with the rod. In spite of its small size its tone can cut through the sound of the whole orchestra playing its loudest.

Historically, the instrument is visible on French tapestries *circa* 1380. It joined the orchestra during the eighteenth-century craze for Turkish or Janissary music. It was used by Gluck, Mozart, Rossini, and Wagner. It reached a new prominence in 1849 when Liszt gave the triangle a solo in his Piano Concerto in E flat.

The XYLOPHONE is a tuned instrument dating back to the time of primitive man, when it consisted of a few slabs of stone or pieces of wood. Today's instrument is made up of thirty or more pieces of hard wood in graduated sizes held onto crosspieces by screws. Under each wooden bar is a tube called a resonator, which amplifies the sound when the bars are struck by spoon-shaped beaters or wooden sticks with small metal knobs.

Saint-Saëns used the xylophone to represent dancing skeletons in his *Danse macabre*. The instrument is at its best when playing fast-running and repeated notes or arpeggios.

The MARIMBA is the deep-toned Mexican cousin of the xylophone. Entire orchestras of marimbas are popular in Mexico and Central

America. Struck by rubber or yarn-wrapped mallets, marimbas span four octaves and have become increasingly popular with modern composers. Paul Creston (1906–85) and Darius Milhaud (1892–1974) each wrote a concerto for the instrument.

The GLOCKENSPIEL, like the xylophone and marimba, is a member of the definite pitch group. Its thin, steel bars are of different exact lengths each giving off a high bell-like tone. One of its most famous uses is in Papageno's aria from Mozart's *The Magic Flute* (1791). Handel used the glockenspiel even earlier (1738) in his oratorio *Saul*. Wagner and Richard Strauss both used the instrument for humorous effects. Its German name literally means "play of the bells," as it originally consisted of cumbersome bells before these were replaced with metal bars.

The CELESTA looks like a small piano, but sounds somewhat like a xylophone or marimba. Invented in 1886 by French instrument-maker Auguste Mustel, it was welcomed by composers for its new sound. Tchaikovsky gave it a solo in the "Dance of the Sugarplum Fairy" from his *Nutcracker* ballet. Béla Bartók wrote *Music for Stringed Instruments, Percussion and Celesta* in 1936.

The CHIMES are a set of metal tubes tuned to a musical scale. They are hung vertically on a stand and struck with a hammer, giving a bell-like sound. Composers use them for triumphal effects and resounding climaxes.

There is practically no limit to what can be classified as percussion instruments. Besides conventional ones like castanets, tambourines, and bongo drums, imaginative composers have incorporated bells, rattles, rachets, typewriters, and vacuum cleaners into their music.

The Piano

> The piano's world encompasses glass-nerved virtuosi . . . it is a world of pasture and storm . . . No other acoustic instrument can match its expressive range, and no electric instrument can match its mystery.
> —Kenneth Miller (1930–)

What we call a PIANO is the keyboard instrument invented in 1709 by Bartolommeo Cristofori, music curator for the Medici family in Florence, Italy. He called his invention a *gravicembalo col piano e forte*—a "keyboard instrument that can be played soft and loud."

The youngest of musical instruments, it leads all others in the number of compositions written for it and fits equally well into the home and the concert hall. Its range of notes, which spans seven octaves, is larger than any other instrument except a pipe organ, and its dynamics range from the softest *pianissimo* to the loudest *fortissimo*.

In the 1800s piano factories sprang up all over Europe, the United States, and Japan. The names Steinway, Knabe, Mason and Hamlin, and Chickering are still famous in America, Bechstein and Blüthner in Germany, Bösendorfer in Austria, Erard and Pleyel in France, Broadwood in England, and Yamaha in Japan.

As performers and composers discovered the advantages of the piano, interest declined in the harpsichord. Bach's sons, Carl Philipp Emanuel and Johann Christian, were among the leaders in writing and performing piano music. Introduced to the five octave instrument in 1765, nine-year-old Mozart wrote the first duets (four-hand pieces) and became the first virtuoso pianist.

In 1817 Broadwood built a six-octave piano to suit Beethoven's energetic style, which included full use of the sustaining pedal. His example was followed by Schubert, Schumann, Mendelssohn, and Chopin—the last of these earning the title "Poet of the Piano" for the new range of tone color of his compositions.

In 1821 French piano maker Sebastien Erard improved the escapement, or hammer action, making possible faster repeated notes. In the 1820s John Hawkins of Philadelphia replaced the traditional wooden frame with cast iron. This permitted greater tension on thicker strings and gave the piano a fuller, more brilliant sound.

By the time of the next great keyboard virtuoso, Franz Liszt (1811–86), the span was the present-day seven octaves achieved with eighty-eight keys. Expanding all previous bounds of instrumental performance, Liszt's technique was compared to that of Paganini on the violin.

At the end of the century the compositions of Brahms, Tchaikovsky, and Scriabin carried the versatility and technical challenges of pianistic ability beyond Liszt and Chopin, who had begun the great age of keyboard performance. In the early twentieth century Debussy and Ravel led the way in harmonic experiments, followed by the percussive effects of Stravinsky and Bartók.

Music lovers could not hear enough of their favorite pianists. Reproducing pianos such as Ampico, Duo-Art and Welte, were invented in the 1890s, and captured much of the artist's expression. Conventional player pianos were of much poorer quality. By 1900 Rachmaninoff, Debussy, and Grieg could be heard playing their own compositions on reproducing pianos. By 1930 the phonograph phased out the player piano. Anton Rubinstein (1829–94), Vladimir de Pachmann (1848–1933), Leopold Godowsky (1870–1938), Josef Lhevinne (1874–1944), Moritz Rosenthal (1862–1946), and Josef Hofmann (1876–1957) were among the greats who not only thrilled audiences internationally, but can be heard on early recordings.

The next "wave" of virtuosi included Artur Rubinstein (1887–1982), Robert Casadesus (1899–1972), Claudio Arrau (1903–91), Vladimir Horowitz (1903–89), Rudolf Serkin (1903–91), Rudolf Firkusny (1912–), Svyatislav Richter (1914–), Jorge Bolet (1914–90), Emil Gilels (1916–85), Dinu Lipatti (1917–50), Earl Wild (1918–), Alicia de Larrocha (1923–), Gary Graffman (1928–), Byron Janis (1928–), Alexis Weissenberg (1929–), Alfred Brendel (1931–), Glenn Gould (1932–82), Philippe Entrement (1934–), and Van Cliburn (1934–), whose brilliance is preserved with higher fidelity.

Today's concert artists perform on fantastic nine-feet-long concert grands, are recorded via the latest electronic equipment, and can be heard in the home on ever-improving quality stereo components, compact disc, and digital audio tape players. Among them are Aldo Ciccolini (1925–), Tamás Vásáry (1933–), Vladimir Ashkenazy (1937–), Christoph Eschenbach, (1940–), Daniel Barenboim (1942–), Murray Perahia (1947–), Garrick Ohlsson (1948–), Emanuel Ax (1949–), Alexander Toradze (1952–), James Raphael (1953–), Ivo Pogorelich (1958–), Louis Lortie (1959–), Krystian Zimerman (1956–), Cecile Licad (1961–), Gustavo Romero (1965–), Yevgeny Kissin (1971–).

Like other major instruments, the piano infiltrated popular music, and names like ragtime composer, Scott Joplin, jazz greats "Jelly Roll" Morton, Fats Waller, Art Tatum, and singer-pianist Nat "King" Cole will never be forgotten.

CHAPTER TWENTY

Chamber Music:
The Personal Touch

Chamber music, from the Italian word *camera*, or room, was originally intended to be played in a private house or small hall. With modern acoustics, however, a string quartet can be heard in a huge theater, so the term has come to mean compositions for small groups of instruments. Each player has his own part, unlike members of an orchestra, in which whole sections play the same notes.

The earliest chamber music was for unaccompanied voices. Groups of singers would perform pastoral, amorous, or allegorical songs called *madrigals*. Next came *table music,* played by performers on stringed instruments while the nobility dined. By the seventeenth century composers were writing for two or more instruments, and the *sonata*, the forerunner of the symphony, was born.

Sonata

By definition, the sonata is an instrumental composition in three or four movements with contrasting tempos. The Italian composer Domenico Scarlatti (1683–1757) wrote over 600 sonatas. He blazed the trail for everyone after him with his keyboard innovations and freedom of style. Many of his pieces continue to be performed, sounding even more effective on the modern piano.

Johann Sebastian Bach (1685–1750) wrote six *partitas*, an early form of the sonata, for unaccompanied violin, which remain unsurpassed in testing the skill of the performer.

Franz Joseph Haydn (1732–1809) wrote eighty-two sonatas for combinations such as two violins, viola, and cello, and established the classic form. This earned him the title of Father of the Sonata.

Ludwig van Beethoven (1770–1827) wrote thirty-two piano sonatas, all of them still performed today. The "Moonlight," "Pathetique," and "Apassionata" are the best known.

Liszt has only one sonata in his huge output of piano music.

Chopin lent his inimitable poetic style to three piano sonatas and one for cello and piano.

Rachmaninoff also wrote a cello sonata.

Of sonatas for piano and violin, César Franck's is one of the loveliest.

The Quartet

The most popular combination of instruments in chamber music is the string quartet, usually featuring two violins, a viola, and cello. Haydn tops the list with 84 of them, adding Father of the String Quartet to his titles. Mozart wrote 23 string quartets, 2 piano quartets, 2 flute quartets, and an oboe quartet. Beethoven wrote 20 string quartets; his later ones are in constant performance.

Most composers have attempted this form. The following list are those considered the most popular:

Schumann: A major, Opus 41 No. 3.

Brahms: C minor, Opus 51. He also wrote three piano quartets.

Borodin: No. 2 in D major. This includes the famous third movement, *Notturno*, from which the song, "And This Is My Beloved" was taken.

Tchaikovsky: D major, Opus 11.
Ravel: F major.
Debussy: G minor, Opus 10.
Dvořák: F major, Opus 96. Subtitled, "American," written during one of his frequent visits to this country.
Smetana: E minor, from *My Life*.
Rossini: B flat, written when he was only twelve!

Trios, Quintets, Octets, and Others

A string trio consists of a violin, viola, and cello. One of the most beautiful is Mozart's *Divertimento* (literally, a diversion) in E flat (K. 563). He also wrote a clarinet trio.

A piano trio is composed of a piano, violin and cello. The *Archduke* trio by Beethoven and the trios of Schubert, Brahms, and Tchaikovsky are very enjoyable. For a modern sound, listen to Rachmaninoff's pair of piano trios.

A string quintet is a quartet with an added viola or cello. The most famous is Schubert's "Trout" quintet, based on one of his songs. Brahms wrote two string quintets.

A piano quintet is a string quartet plus a piano. Dvořák contributed two of them.

Sometimes a quartet utilizes a different solo instrument such as a clarinet. Mozart, Carl Maria von Weber (1786–1826), and Brahms wrote quintets for this combination.

There are sextets, septets, octets, nonets, and decemets. Brahms composed two string sextets. The most popular octet is Mendelssohn's in E flat for strings, an incredibly mature and melodic work composed when he was only sixteen.

Chamber music is a personal experience. To discover your own preferences, listening to the radio or borrowing recordings from the library would be obvious options before making purchases for your collection.

CHAPTER TWENTY-ONE

Symphonies— The Grandest Compositions

Although a symphony is one of the longer and more complex compositions, the most famous and favorite are very easy to listen to because they teem with themes that nearly everyone has heard somewhere.

Early symphonies were quite short and followed the set rule of having four movements, with the second being slow, the third a scherzo, and the first and fourth in fast tempos. Haydn and Mozart dashed them off like limericks, since their noble employers wanted a new composition every time they had a guest to dinner. Franz Joseph Haydn (1732–1809) worked for three successive Hungarian princes, churning out one hundred and four symphonies, which earned him the title Father of the Symphony.

There is a gradual revival of interest in that prodigious output. One of the cheeriest is his Symphony No. 88. The bouncy theme of the last movement was brashly "borrowed" by Franz Schubert for the finale of his Sixth, written in 1818, nine years after Haydn's death. Schubert was safe, since copyrights were a little hazy in those days.

247

The Magic of Mozart

Mozart, with whom many people became better acquainted through the play and film *Amadeus*, wrote "only" forty-one symphonies, although rumors abound that there are more. You can hear one of his last dozen almost any time you click your radio to the local classical music station or take in the next orchestral concert nearest you.

His most endearing and enduring symphonies are his later ones, the earlier ones being somewhat stylized—he wrote No. 1 when he was eight! Somewhere even as you are reading this there is an orchestra playing the tuneful No. 29, or the popular No. 35 (called "Haffner" after a family of his friends), or No. 39 (recommended), or the favorite No. 40, or his last, and some say his greatest, No. 41, known as the "Jupiter."

For getting acquainted, begin with No. 40. The tempo of the first movement is perfect for jogging (or cantering on horseback) with earphones. The second movement is just calm and graceful enough for you to have an excuse to slow down before getting back up to speed with the lively tempo of the last two movements. Premiered on July 25, 1788, No. 40 gained this newspaper review: "The mighty picture of a mind swayed with passion. . . . However often the work is heard, it never fails in its effect—every time, it grips the listener irresistibly and sweeps him along. . . ." These words still hold true.

One may wonder how many more works Wolfgang Amadeus would have poured out if his life had not been cut short in 1791 at age thirty-five. The year 1991 was a banner year for this complete genius. Celebrating the bicentennial of his death, the music world was literally *inundated* with his compositions at festivals, in concerts, and on newly released recordings.

Mozart's real genius was managing to write original and fantastically melodic music within the confines of the rules of the Classical period, but it took Beethoven to break those chains and free the symphony to become the really grand form it assumed in the Romantic era.

The Power of Beethoven

Ludwig arrived on the scene in 1770 when Mozart and Haydn were going strong, and left it in 1827, by which time someone had built a better piano and Napoleon had rearranged the map of Europe.

As a teenager, on a visit to Vienna in 1787, Beethoven played for

Mozart, who is quoted as saying, "Some day, this young man will make a great noise in the world." In 1792 he become Haydn's pupil for a year. Of this arrangement one of Beethoven's major patrons, Count Waldstein, remarked, "With the help of assiduous labor you shall receive Mozart's spirit from Haydn's hands." As it turned out Beethoven was his own genius, and it was *his* spirit that was sought by those who came after.

Beethoven wrote nine symphonies, the most played are the Third, Fifth, Sixth, Seventh, and Ninth. The Third, "Eroica," which has already been mentioned as at first being dedicated to Napoleon, premiered in 1805, conducted by the composer. Critics lashed the composition with words like "bizarre" and "lawless," plus the other usual reactions to something different in any field. His friends, however, were right on the mark when they predicted of this towering masterpiece that "after a thousand years have passed it will not fail of its effect."

Beethoven's Fifth is familiar for its first four notes, which punctuate "dot-dot-dot-dash—" or "V" in Morse Code. During World War II it was known as the "Victory Symphony," but Beethoven himself said that the opening tones denoted Fate. Perhaps this was because it was written in 1803, after he had already contemplated suicide when the doctors said his deafness was incurable and would get worse. This symphony is full of the life that the composer decided fortunately for us not to abandon. There are really no boring parts. The music flies along carrying one in the stream of its excitement, sometimes tumbling over rapids, other times serenely flowing with calmer currents. It is music easy to listen to, easy to like, and is known to make more of an impression on the listener than almost any other work in symphonic literature. It truly resounds with the composer's resolve that he would not allow Fate to drag him down!

In his Sixth symphony, the "Pastoral," Beethoven designated titles for each movement. The first is "Cheerful impressions awakened by arrival in the country." The composer loved to travel to the outskirts of Vienna. Before cars and highways, or the droning of airplanes, the countryside was truly a great contrast to the raucous, dirty cities. Here Beethoven found some comfort from the noises in his head. In the second movement, "Scene by the Brook," one can imagine him resting upon sweet-smelling grass, watching the crystal water flowing over age-smoothed pebbles. The third movement takes us to the "Merry Gathering of the Countryfolk." At the time, without modern communication, there were vast differences in the lifestyles of countryfolk and cityfolk.

The peasants lived simply, content in their ways and traditions. This music depicts their dancing. We hear the mountaineers' heavy shoes and the playing of the old bassoonist who can only sound two notes.

The fourth movement brings a storm played most realistically (without electronic effects) by the orchestra with groaning basses, shrill piccolos, screaming violins, bursting trombones, and thunderous kettledrums. After reaching a cataclysmic climax, the music calms down and we enter the fifth movement: "Shepherd's Song. Glad and grateful feelings after the storm." The sky clears, shepherds and dancers venture out from their sheltering places. The torrents of water melt into gentle ripples. The rays of the setting sun flood fields and woods with golden splendor. It's all there—a tableau of tuneful sound—composed by a man who could barely hear.

The Seventh Symphony grows on you by repeated hearings. Its greatest attraction is the hauntingly beautiful second movement, during which it is highly recommended that you sit quietly, or take those precious moments to relax on your sofa with closed eyes and let the music cleanse the world's weariness out of every cell of your body. . . .

The Ninth, or "Choral," is Beethoven's last symphony. It took him six and a half years to complete, both because he was a perfectionist and also because he wrote other works during this time frame. Thirty-one years before, at age twenty-three, he had the idea of using the "Ode to Joy" by the great German poet Friedrich Schiller. It is this that is heard in the last movement, with a chorus being used in a symphony for the very first time. The effect is a triumphant homage to the God Beethoven so passionately believed in. The first three movements, uplifting masterpieces in their own right, lead us to the threshold of that joy. What bitter irony that the composer conducted the first performance (May 7, 1824) without being able to hear a note, and had to be turned around to face the audience in order to "see" their thunderous applause!

The Touch of Tchaikovsky

To leap to the next milestone composer of symphonic music takes us forty years forward to the height of the Romantic era. Peter Ilyich Tchaikovsky began creating great music in the early 1860s around the same time America was pouring blood onto Civil War battlefields.

Living the life of a "closet" homosexual, with the accompanying despair, self-torture and nervous breakdowns, Tchaikovsky still managed to create music of such beauty that it is nothing short of amazing.

Of his six power-packed symphonies, the Fourth, Fifth, and Sixth definitely belong in any worthwhile classical music collection.

Like Beethoven, Tchaikovsky believed in Fate, but while Beethoven was determined to overcome it, Tchaikovsky felt overwhelmed by its force. To him life was "an alternation between grim reality and . . . illusions of happiness" with "waves buffeting us until the sea [death] engulfs us."

Despite this gloomy philosophy the three symphonies are full of life and melody. The Scherzo (third) movement of the Fourth is executed almost entirely in *pizzicato*—all the string players plucking their instruments without using bows. The effect is pure melodious energy. Similarly, the lovely waltz comprising the third movement of the Fifth Symphony is lilting graciousness and joy. The Sixth Symphony was given the French title *Pathétique* by Tchaikovsky's brother Modeste the day after its first performance, October 28, 1893. In 1941, the theme of the first movement was used for a lyrical love song, "The Story of a Starry Night." So many of its lush, sentimental themes have been used in movies, that this symphony becomes instantly familiar. There is no shadow of death hanging over it, even though the composer was whisked out of this world a week after the premiere, apparently from drinking unboiled water during the current cholera epidemic. (See Chapter Nine.)

There is nothing pathetic about the "Pathétique," like all of Tchaikovsky's music, it abounds with rich harmonies that head right for the heart.

Brahms: The Last of the Three B's

It appears that as symphonies became more interesting, composers spent more time on them and wrote fewer. Johannes Brahms composed only four, but none of them are gathering dust. Although he didn't write the first until he was forty-three in 1876, it was worth waiting for. The other three are equally exciting and heartwarming to listen to.

The cognomen, "The Three B's," refer to Bach, Beethoven, and Brahms. Johannes Brahms, in the midst of the Romantics, reverted to Classical forms in his major compositions. He said he felt the giant steps of Beethoven behind him. But he could not turn the clock completely back, or be immune from the emotional fervor of the times. Around him Berlioz and Wagner were busy making radical modern changes in the style of orchestral music and opera, while Liszt pounded extroverted flamboyancy into piano compositions.

Another element in Brahms's music was the city in which he lived. Vienna was (and is) a special place with unique traditions. Brahms loved the waltzes of his contemporary, Johann Strauss, and wrote his own many waltzes for piano, or two-piano, performance. Vienna—home of Haydn, Mozart, Beethoven, and Schubert—helped to shape European music, much as Nashville shaped a brand of country music, or Detroit the Motown sound, or New Orleans its jazz. Vienna is also a city known for its bittersweet, romantic lyricism—better known as *schmaltz.*

Basically what is most appealing about Brahms, is not the painstakingly perfect structure, but the sentimental quality of his music. As one scholar said of his symphonies, "It is possible to sing every movement . . . as though it were a single uninterrupted melody."

Famous Favorites

Among the other most popular symphonies which have promoted love at first hearing, are:

FRANZ SCHUBERT (1797–1828): Symphonies No. 6, No. 8 (the "Unfinished"), and No. 9 (known as the "Great"). With an even shorter life than Mozart, Vienna-born Schubert managed to turn out volumes of compositions, some of which may still be undiscovered. Living in the same city as Beethoven, the young man was too shy to impose himself, and the two never met, but like that of his idol, Schubert's style flings off the shackles of Classicism and plunges into the Romantic. Like the composer's other works, these symphonies sound deceptively simple, making us unaware of the skill behind the development of his themes, melodies that blossom with warmth and tunefulness.

FELIX MENDELSSOHN (1809–47): Symphony No. 4, "Italian." One of the most brilliant and popular Romantic composers, Mendelssohn wrote this bubbling, spritely work after a trip to Italy. This one also lends itself to jogging with your earphones firmly in place.

ROBERT SCHUMANN (1810–56), happy husband of Clara and sponsor of the young, then unknown, Brahms: His First, "Spring," and Third,

"Rhenish," symphonies are among the most popular of all his easy-to-listen-to compositions.

CÉSAR FRANCK (1822–90): Symphony in D minor. This Belgian composer wrote just this one symphony, but its lovely melodic lines have stood the test of time. It is a concert favorite.

ANTONIN DVOŘÁK (1841–1904): Symphony No. 9, "From the New World." A protégé of Brahms, the Czech composer spent many summers in Spillville, Iowa. The symphony is woven with American folk tunes. The second movement is based on "Going Home," a poignant spiritual, used in the movie *The Snake Pit* (1948).

HECTOR BERLIOZ (1803–69). Although born early in the era, this Frenchman pioneered the path for Wagner and modern composers with his use of instruments and the huge size of his orchestras. His "wild" and "different" *Symphonie fantastique* (1830), took the music world by storm. It reflected his feelings for an actress with whom he was madly in love. Considered the first "program" symphony, because it tells a story, the composer titled and wrote descriptions for the five movements, each of which are an opium-induced dream, ending with the hero being beheaded and in the final movement seeing the Beloved as a hag dancing at a witches' orgy. The second movement, a lilting waltz, is the most familiar.

KARL GOLDMARK (1830–1915): "Rustic Wedding" Symphony (1876). Five movements of spritely folk music from the composer's native Hungary and his adopted country, Austria. Tuneful and colorful, a definite enjoy-at-first-hearing piece.

GEORGES BIZET (1838–75): Symphony in C. Famous for his opera *Carmen,* his only symphony was not discovered until 1933. Full of lively harmonies, it (amazingly) was written at age seventeen while the composer was still a student. It has been used as the basis for a ballet by the great choreographer George Balanchine.

ALEXANDER BORODIN (1833–87): Symphony No. 2. A member of the Russian Five who wanted to get Russian music to be as well known as West European, he is most famous for the "Polovstian Dances" from his opera *Prince Igor.* Most of his best pieces became popular through the 1944 musical *Kismet* (made into a movie in 1955). The Symphony No. 2 has many familiar themes running through it. It is worth listening to a recording of *Kismet* to become acquainted with Borodin.

NICOLAI RIMSKY-KORSAKOV (1844–1908): Symphony No. 2, "Antar," is based on the folk legend of the Arabian hermit who saves a gazelle from a fearsome bird of prey. The gazelle reveals herself as an elfin queen and gives Antar three rides on the wish horse, representing Vengeance, Power, and Love. Very flowing, it is easy to like on first hearing.

VASILY KALINNIKOV (1866–1901): His enjoyable Symphony No. 1, which like "Antar" is too rarely performed. It has come out on CD, which may indicate that deserved recognition is on its way.

CAMILLE SAINT-SAËNS (1835–1921), a child prodigy like Mozart, his career as one of France's leading musicians spanned almost seventy years. His third and last symphony premiered in London, May 19, 1886. It is unique in that it joins the first two and the last two movements together, and there are two pianos and an organ as part of the orchestration. A touch of Bach hovers within, especially in the rousing finale.

ANTON BRUCKNER (1824–96) has not received the recognition of his Austrian contemporary Brahms. Perhaps this is because his massive music is much more difficult to listen to. Of his nine symphonies, the Fourth, "Romantic," is the most popular, permitting the listener to daydream as he goes with its flow.

GUSTAV MAHLER (1860–1911) influenced modern composers who came after him. Basically traditional, his music can be delicate and childlike, or sweep you off your feet with its colossal orchestration. His First Symphony (premiere, Budapest, 1889), is called the "Titan." It is indeed a gigantic and exhilarating work, progressing in themes from youthful innocence to adult defeats to the victory of life over death.

JEAN SIBELIUS (1865–1957) is the musical embodiment of Finland, contributing to his country's heritage with original compositions based on ancient legends. His Second Symphony was conducted by him at its premiere in Helsinki, March 3, 1902. With overtones of Tchaikovsky, it is still pure Sibelius, breathing of dark pine forests and a thousand icy crystal lakes of his beloved country.

DMITRI SHOSTAKOVICH (1906–75) lived his creative life under the communist regime in Russia. Although he was not a radical modern (a style disapproved of by the regime), he did get into trouble a few times because of some daring innovations. His Fifth Symphony is full of clarity and power. This is something that definitely takes getting used to. Appreciating Shostakovich comes after all the "war-horses" are so familiar that you are really seeking new excitement.

Once you have come to enjoy these "basic" symphonies, it follows naturally that you should want to hear other music by the same composer. This is the exciting part of classical music: listening over and over to your favorites never gets boring, and there is always more to explore.

*The purpose of a concerto is to put
virtuoso soloists through their paces in
a dramatically coherent way, with the
highest musical integrity.*

—Heather Buchman, trombonist

CHAPTER TWENTY - TWO

Concertos: A Chance to Show Off

A CONCERTO is a work in three movements for a solo instrument accompanied by an orchestra. It has been a popular form of music for more than 250 years, probably because it is human nature to want to show off if you are very good at something. When a musician reaches unlimited expertise with an instrument he or she needs music to challenge their ability. A piano, violin, cello, flute, clarinet, or trumpet concerto does just that. It is a top of the line piece for a top artist.

The Spot in the Spotlight

Within each concerto is a further lift of limelight known as a *cadenza*. Usually found near the end of the first movement, this is where the orchestra stops and the soloist has the stage all to himself. Brilliant passages, rapid runs up and down the instrument and dazzling chord passages all built on themes from the concerto allow the performer to show his skills. A cadenza usually ends in a trill signaling the conductor to bring the orchestra back into the action.

Cadenzas were first used in the 1600s by opera singers who pretty much sang what they liked at this point—sometimes the aria did not even come from the same opera. Until close to 1800, composers did not write cadenzas; soloists were expected to make them up. This was fine if the artist was a good improviser, but very often the effect of the concerto was ruined by performers droning on endlessly and tastelessly. This led to composers writing in their own cadenzas. Mozart was one of the first to do so.

A concerto also shows off its composer. Many concertos (or concerti) were written specifically for an established performer. The great nineteenth-century musician Joseph Joachim inspired Brahms's only violin concerto. Robert Schumann wrote his only concerto for his wife, Clara, a renowned pianist from the time she was a teenager.

The Original Performers

> My piano . . . is my very self, my
> mother tongue, my life.
> —Franz Liszt (1811–86)

Many composers were expert instrumentalists. Mozart, Beethoven, Liszt, Chopin, Mendelssohn, Brahms, Grieg, and Rachmaninoff were among those who had successful careers as pianists. Paganini was a superb violinist, as was Fritz Kreisler, although the latter never wrote a concerto. César Franck's occupation as an organist took away time from his composing, hence his meager but impressive output. Most women composers were, and are, performers. The talents of modern composer-soloists are preserved on recordings, film, and videotape.

From Tinny to Tremendous

One of the earliest concerto composers also holds the record for writing the most: ANTONIO VIVALDI (1678–1741), who wrote over 400 of them, for every major instrument of his time.

BACH modeled his keyboard concertos after Vivaldi, but since there was only the tinny-sounding harpsichord as the solo instrument, the mostly string orchestras needed to be small enough not to drown it out.

By 1750, the improved piano began to replace the violin as the favorite solo instrument, while orchestras added brass, woodwinds, and timpani (kettle drums) to the strings. This gave Haydn, Mozart, and Beethoven a wider scope to work in. By the time Schumann, Chopin, Liszt, Brahms, Grieg, Tchaikovsky, and Rachmaninoff wrote their concertos, the full-sized concert grand was powerful enough to compete with the orchestra. Consequently, larger and more dramatic compositions flowed from their creators into the concert halls of the world.

Keyboard Keynotes

Listing piano concertos in order of favorites is a challenge. Here are some of the top twenty on the performance charts.

SERGEI RACHMANINOFF: Piano Concerto No. 2 in C minor usually comes up first choice. (When I was a child, it was the very first record I bought with my own money!) Its history reads like fiction. The composer was being treated for depression by a Moscow physician-hypnotist who repeatedly told his "sleeping" patient: "You will begin to write your concerto . . . you will write with great facility. . . . The concerto will be excellent."

On November 9, 1901, the concerto, dedicated to his doctor, Nikolai Dahl, was given its first performance in the Russian capital with the composer at the keyboard. It was an instant success and has remained so. Besides being used in several movies: *Brief Encounter* (1945), *I've Always Loved You* (1946), and *Rhapsody* (1954), with Elizabeth Taylor, it has given birth to three songs. "I Think of You" (1941) came out of the first movement, Eric Carmen's "All By Myself" (1975) from the second, and the theme of the last movement was transformed into a popular 1940s song, "Full Moon and Empty Arms."

Vying for the top concerto spot is Grieg's Piano Concerto in A minor. EDVARD GRIEG (1843–1907) is to Norway what Sibelius is to Finland, the musical personification of his country. He wrote his only concerto when he was twenty-five and newly married. Like Beethoven's Fifth Symphony, it is just one of those pieces everyone has heard somewhere. Only twenty-nine minutes in length, it was premiered April 3, 1869, in Copenhagen, with the composer as soloist. Its popularity was assured when Franz Liszt, the most famous pianist of the time, gave it his approval.

After the resounding chords of its opening, the concerto is sheer poetry in sound. There is no suspense, there are no shadows, just sunlight and tenderness reaching a pinnacle in the soft, embracing second movement. The last movement is in a Norwegian folk dance rhythm, leaving us with a happy, uplifted feeling. As in the case of Borodin and *Kismet*, the (popularized) cream of Grieg's music can be heard in the 1944 musical *The Song of Norway,* a Broadway version of the composer's life. The movie was made in 1970.

Because of its equal brevity (thirty minutes), ROBERT SCHUMANN's only concerto, also in A minor, is usually found on the flip side of the Grieg. Premiered by his wife, Clara, on December 4, 1845, it has a cheery swinging pace and is easy to like.

A much larger piece is the TCHAIKOVSKY Piano Concerto No. 1 in B flat minor, which received its first performance with German pianist Hans von Bülow, in Boston, October 25, 1875. Its success was immediate. The thunderous opening, rushing strings, prominent brass, is pure Tchaikovsky—evoking emotions from darkest gloom to exultant joy.

The first movement was used as his signature theme by bandleader Freddy Martin in the form of the song "Tonight We Love," which reached Number One on the radio show, "Your Hit Parade," December 7, 1941, the day the Japanese bombed Pearl Harbor and the United States entered World War II.

BEETHOVEN's most famous piano concertos are his Third and Fifth. The Third, composed in 1800, was the first to show his more heroic style. He played it at its premiere in Vienna, April 5, 1803. The Fifth, given the name "Emperor" by parties unknown, was composed in 1809 when Napoleon's army was occupying Vienna. Although by the end of the year a peace treaty had been signed, the first performance of this work was not given in the city until 1812. The soloist was Carl Czerny, composer of all those piano exercises and a few of his own piano concertos.

It would be difficult to say which piano concertos come next at the top of the charts, so the best method is just to list them and let you choose your own favorites. They are all representative of their composers and highly tuneful. The number of recordings of each attests to their popularity.

Of MOZART's twenty-nine piano concertos—he also wrote one for two pianos and one for three—No. 21 (with the theme used in the 1967 Swedish film *Elvira Madigan*) and No. 23 are played most often.

BRAHMS wrote only two concertos for piano with twenty-two years between them. The world was not ready for the "Brahmsian" sound when the young composer premiered his first concerto on January 27, 1859. By November 9, 1881, the premiere of the second with the composer again as soloist, Brahms was an honored figure, and the music world had become more attuned to his "heavyweight" style. Both compositions are now standard in the repertoire, and it is just a matter of hearing enough Brahms to acquire the taste and appreciation for this latterday classicist.

FRANZ LISZT, already mentioned as the most sought-after pianist of his time, wrote two concertos—in 1855 and 1857. Full of dazzling brilliance, they are a challenge to any pianist who does not happen to have the enormous finger span of the composer.

MENDELSSOHN brought out his two piano concertos in 1832 and 1837, the year he was married. Both are light, charming, and entertaining.

Of the five piano concertos of SAINT-SAËNS, No. 2, written in 1868, is definitely the favorite. The entire work just skims along from one lively elegant theme to the next. It is one of those compositions that is endearing on first hearing.

Although he is not listed in chronological order, I have left my beloved CHOPIN for last. His two concertos were written in his nineteenth and twentieth years. He played the premiere performance of the second (which was published first) in Warsaw on March 17, 1830. His concertos reflect his virtuosity with their bold, yet tender melodies and rippling arpeggios. The orchestra is mostly an accompaniment to the piano. But the overall effect is *love*: love for the performer and love for the listener. Chopin also wrote a "mini" concerto, the *Andante Spianato,* for piano and orchestra, which should be added to the list.

From Tin Pan Alley to Carnegie Hall

Not to be neglected is America's own GEORGE GERSHWIN. His seventeen-minute *Rhapsody in Blue* (1924), orchestrated by Ferde Grofé, can also be classed as a "mini" concerto. This and his Piano Concerto in F (1925) were the first compositions integrating jazz and blues into a classical context. The composer performed them both in New York's Carnegie Hall, to great acclaim. A Broadway musical and Hollywood movie songwriter turned classical composer, Gershwin remains quite a phenomenon. Thus far, only Leonard Bernstein has followed in those unique footsteps.

As with symphony listening adventures, as one becomes more and more acquainted with these masterpieces, musical tastes develop into a readiness to listen to other concertos and piano compositions. The recording catalogues are bursting with them.

Violin Concertos—Heartstring Tuggers

> *A violin should be played with love, or not at all.*
> —Joseph Wechsberg (1907–83)
> Austrian violinist/lawyer

THE CRÈME DE LA CRÈME

Since the violin was one of the first instruments to be perfected—it has changed very little since the death of the great violinmaker Antonio Stradivari in 1737—concertos for this solo instrument date back almost a hundred years before the piano stole the spotlight.

There is a nucleus of favorite concertos guaranteed to set your heartstrings vibrating with their harmonies. Here sparkle the jewels of Mendelssohn's and Bruch's first concertos as well as those of Beethoven, Tchaikovsky, and Brahms, each of whom wrote only one violin concerto—all in the key of D.

MENDELSSOHN's No. 1 in E minor is usually the first major work attempted by eager advanced violin students. It delighted the audience at the Leipzig premiere, on March 13, 1845, with its perfect combination of classical clarity and intense romantic feeling. The composer introduced something new: having the soloist begin to play immediately instead of after the usual orchestral introduction. Another first was writing a melody as a bridge to the second movement and then going into the third without a pause. Mendelssohn also wrote out the entire cadenza rather than leaving it to the performer's choice.

Although the solo part is not as difficult as the Brahms or

Tchaikovsky concerto, it still challenges the skill and interpretation of the player. The limitations of trying to describe this marvelous music with mere words such as "freshness of melody," "vigor," "delicacy," and "exhilaration," can only be overcome by *hearing* this masterpiece. Like Keats's *Grecian Urn*, it is "a thing of beauty and a joy forever."

The same can be said for the lyrically flowing MAX BRUCH (1838–1920) Concerto No. 1 in G minor (1866). The universal regret experienced here is its brevity: it is only twenty-five minutes long. The last movement especially has such a poignant theme that, as with a good book, we wish it didn't have to end. His popular *Scottish Fantasy* is a "mini" violin concerto.

TCHAIKOVSKY should be next on the list. His only violin concerto was initially rejected as being too difficult to play. After its first performance, December 4, 1881, a Viennese critic referred to it as "stinking music"(!). These opinions were soon reversed and the work secured the esteemed place it holds today as both people and performers revel in the inspired spontaneous melodies woven into the rich tapestry of orchestration which is the trademark of this composer.

Tossing a coin is the only way to decide between the two "Bs," so let's follow chronology and go for BEETHOVEN. His only concerto for violin was written for an already prominent twenty-six-year-old virtuoso named Franz Clement. The first performance was on December 23, 1806. The movements have been described in order, 1) "of haunting intensity," 2) "contemplative," and 3) "joyous." Again, these are only words. Hearing is believing.

Going along with the top echelon, BRAHMS, too, wrote only a single violin concerto after consulting with the renowned violinist Joseph Joachim, who gave the first performance on New Year's Day, 1879. With this music we are in deeper waters, as there is the usual intellectual challenge Brahms's massive feeling demands of his listeners. However, one can almost guarantee that every hearing will bring new personal discoveries to make this great work a personal favorite.

THE SECOND STRING

Adorning the second set of gems in the crown of violin concertos are: HENRYK WIENIAWSKI (1835–80), a Polish composer whose Second Violin Concerto in D minor is very easy on the ear. The lovely slow movement, titled "Romance," is often played by itself as a recital piece. SAINT-SAËNS' third violin concerto (1880) is melodic enough to have been recorded by several artists. It lacks the familiarity it deserves because it is not featured enough in concerts. Not to be omitted are Saint-Saëns' miniature masterpieces for violin and orchestra, the *Havanaise* and *Introduction and Rondo Capriccioso*, which receive much exposure in recordings and performance.

In a similar category is the *Symphonie espagnole* by Spanish composer EDOUARD LALO (1823–92). Although designated a symphony, there is such a prominent part for violin throughout its five movements that it might as well be considered a concerto. It was dedicated to Pablo de Sarasate, the famous Spanish violinist/composer, who played the premiere in Paris on February 7, 1875. With Spanish dance rhythms and dazzling solos, this is a "must" addition to both your symphony and concerto list.

NICCOLÒ PAGANINI (1782–1840) was regarded as the greatest of all violinists. He owned three of the finest violins ever made—a Stradivarius, a Guarneri, and an Amati. (He also owned a Stradivarius viola and double bass.) As a performer, naturally all his work is marked by exceptional virtuosity in the violin parts. His first concerto is the most popular. Due to his "diabolical" appearance—wild-looking hair and dark, piercing eyes—and the almost superhuman effects he got from his instruments, rumors were rampant that the devil had given him his sensational playing powers!

MOZART wrote three solo violin concertos. The most often played are No. 3 in G, and No. 5 in A, both written in 1775. Even though they are among his early works, they are full of surprises such as Turkish themes and graceful minuets. His other major compositions for the instrument are a concerto for two violins and one for violin and viola.

Going all the way back to BACH (1685–1750) will yield two well written concertos for solo violin and his most popular, the D minor for Two Violins, whose solo lines are interwoven with consummate artistry, like two voices singing a lovely duet. Karl Haas, the eminent musicologist heard daily on many classical music stations, has said that a composer is known by his second movements. The second movement of this concerto is utterly sublime.

VIVALDI (1675–1741) basically brought the concerto form from one for the entire orchestra (concerto grosso) to giving a prominent role to one particular instrument. His violin concertos in A minor and G minor are featured in the Suzuki violin method books, and his masterpiece, *The Four Seasons*, really a set of violin concerti, is far ahead of its time in that it is program music, describing the blossoming of spring, a summer storm, an autumn hunt, and the blustering winter winds.

Although he did not write a concerto, any discussion of violin music must include FRITZ KREISLER (1875–1962). Born in Vienna, this violinist and composer enjoyed an international following. He became an American citizen in 1943. For many years, just to confuse the critics, he attributed his own charming violin pieces to long dead, obscure composers. He also transcribed works by Dvořák and Paganini and wrote cadenzas for the violin concertos of Beethoven and Brahms.

FIND A SOLOIST—THERE'LL BE A CONCERTO

Of concertos written for other instruments, the most famous are the mellow cello concertos of Dvořák and Saint-Saëns. Brahms wrote a unique much-played *Double* Concerto for Cello and Violin in which both instruments are shown off equally well. The composer had lost the friendship of Joachim over the latter's divorce. After years of silence, this concerto renewed their warm relationship. With Robert Hausmann, the cellist of Joachim's own string quartet, the Double Concerto was first performed October 18, 1887, to a great reception.

Another double concerto is the lilting Flute and Harp Concerto (1778) by Mozart, who also wrote one of the most popular concertos for clarinet (1791).

In the brass family, Haydn's Trumpet Concerto (1796) and Mozart's Concertos for French Horn (1783, 1986) are concert and recording favorites. Concertos for Trombone have been written by Georg Albrechtsberger (Beethoven's counterpoint teacher), Leopold Mozart, Michael Haydn, and in the modern repertoire, Paul Creston, Lars-Erik Larsson, Frank Martin, Ellen Zwilich, Christopher Rouse (1949–) which received the 1993 Pulitzer Prize, and David Ott (1947–), the last premiering April, 1993, performed by Heather Buchman.

Concertos have been written for every conceivable instrument, including double bass, tuba, bassoon, oboe, guitar, balalaika, flugelhorn, Pan pipes, and harmonica. There seems never to be a shortage of virtuosos who want to show off their skills, a composer to accommodate them, and a sporting audience game for listening to something different.

Music is the vapor of art. It is to poetry
what reverie is to thought . . . what the
ocean of clouds is to the ocean of
waves.

—Victor Hugo (1802–85)
French dramatist & novelist

CHAPTER TWENTY - THREE

Program Music

Melodies that "paint" pictures of a magnificent mountain sunrise, or a dazzling Grand Canyon sunset; compositions describing fierce battles or raging storms; a suite telling the story of the sultry Scheherazade whose ploy saved her life; tone poems that evoke drifting clouds, quiet meadows or the restless ocean—all come under the evocative heading of program music.

How Suite It Is

Suites were the earliest form of program music. They were also the earliest instrumental music *not* used to accompany singing. This form began when Baroque composers started putting several dances together. BACH wrote English suites and French suites based on the dances of each country. By the middle of the 1800s the suite had evolved into a collection of concert works drawn from a play, ballet, or opera. Many of these have become concert favorites.

PEER GYNT

One of the most popular suites is *Peer Gynt*, which is derived from incidental music EDVARD GRIEG wrote in 1876 for a drama by Norway's most famous playwright, Henryk Ibsen. Between 1888 and 1891, Grieg arranged the music into two orchestral suites. The story tells of a hot-blooded young man who takes off from home, leaving his dying mother and his grieving sweetheart. He has all sorts of adventures, including meeting a seductive female in a distant land, before returning to those who love him. The melodies are by Grieg at his finest, evoking the glorious sunrise, singing Solveig's sad love song, showing Peer being lured by the temptress, Anitra, and his capture by the King of the Trolls. The familiar themes have been used in many movies and cartoons. There are now CD versions of *Peer Gynt* with voices and narration which contain even more of this lovely music.

SCHEHERAZADE

An equally famous suite is RIMSKY-KORSAKOV's *Scheherazade*. Taken from the *Tales of the Arabian Nights*, it is the story of the Sultan who took a new wife every night and had her head chopped off in the morning. When Scheherazade came along, he found out that she was not just another pretty face and gorgeous body. She told him a new tale each night and wouldn't reveal the ending until the next night. By the time she had done this for 1001 nights, the Sultan was madly in love with her and she kept her head. The music recreates some of her stories, such as "Sinbad the Sailor" and "The Young Prince and Princess." Again, it is safe to predict the reaction: "I've heard those tunes before!"

OPERA AND BALLET IN CONCERT

Many suites have derived from operas. BIZET's *L'Arlésienne* (*The Girl from Arles*), is rarely performed, but the two suites derived from that opera are very well known. There are opera for orchestra versions of PUCCINI's *La Bohème*, *Madama Butterfly*, and *Tosca*, VERDI's *Aida*, and

BIZET's *Carmen*. The last, about a heartless gypsy girl who loves men and leaves them, has several arrangements. Besides the two orchestral suites, there are two *Carmen Fantasies* for violin and orchestra, one by Sarasate (1883), and another by Waxman (1947), and a Carmen Ballet (1967) with unusual orchestration by the modern Russian composer Rodion Shchedrin (1932–1970). *Carmen Jones* (1943, filmed 1945) is a modernized plot version with Bizet's music adapted to lyrics by Oscar Hammerstein II. Other *Carmen* films: Spanish Ballet, 1983; French Opera, 1984.

Most operas have a ballet sequence. The exciting ballet music from GOUNOD's *Faust* and VERDI's *Aida* has been made into suites. *The Dance of the Hours* from PONCHIELLI's *La Gioconda* was immortalized by Walt Disney's tutu clad hippos and pirouetting alligators in his animated film *Fantasia*. Listening to all these arrangements is a wonderful way to become acquainted with opera for those not ready for all that dramatic singing. Not to be overlooked is the music from LÉO DELIBES' ballets, *Coppelia* and *Sylvia*, and GLAZUNOV's flowing version of his ballet *The Seasons*.

THE NUTCRACKER ET AL.

The most familiar pair of suites come from TCHAIKOVSKY's *Nutcracker*. The first includes the airy "Waltz of the Flowers" and "Dance of the Sugar Plum Fairy," written for the newly-invented bell-like little keyboard instrument, the *celesta*. The second suite contains the heavenly *Pas de Deux* which in the ballet is danced by the two principals with graceful flying leaps. Like *Peer Gynt*, there are longer recordings of the complete *Nutcracker Ballet*. The composer's *Sleeping Beauty* and *Swan Lake* ballets and a selection of music by Mozart, titled *Mozartiana*, have also emerged as suites.

FRENCH SUITES

Around the same time in France, CHABRIER wrote his lovely *Suite Pastorale* and MASSENET his *Scènes pittoresques, Scènes alsaciennes, The Grasshopper (Cigale)*, and a delightful collation simply called *Ballet Music of Massenet*. BIZET should again be included here for *Jeux d'Enfants (Children's Games)* and *La Jolie Fille de Perth (The Fair Maid of Perth)*, both a light listening treat.

INTO THE TWENTIETH CENTURY

The popularity of the form has continued into the twentieth century. STRAVINSKY arranged suites from his controversial ballet *The Rite of Spring*, as well as his popular *Petrouchka* and *Firebird* ballets. Three suites have been made out of ARAM KHATCHATURIAN's ballet *Spartacus* (1956). PROKOFIEV arranged suites from his opera *Love for Three Oranges* (1921), his ballet *Romeo and Juliet*, and his popular score for the film *Lieutenant Kije*. RAVEL wrote the *Mother Goose Suite*, a delightful set of pieces depicting his musical impressions of four fairy tales, including "Beauty and the Beast." He also composed the *Daphnis and Chloë* Suites, numbers 1 and 2, based on Greek mythology. These two become enjoyable once one gets attuned to the Impressionistic style which became popular in the French art world around the turn of the century. DEBUSSY, writing at the same time gave us two suites for piano, *Children's Corner*, and *Bergamasque*, containing his famous *Clair de Lune*. You will also enjoy *Pélleas et Mélisande, Masques et Bergamasque*, and the *Dolly Suite* by GABRIEL FAURÉ.

HARKING BACK TO THE PAST

Grounded more in the classical style, Italian OTTORINO RESPIGHI (1879–1936) composed the delicate *Ancient Airs and Dances* suite as well as a lively compilation of Rossini's music, named (of course) *Rossiniana*. British BENJAMIN BRITTEN (1913–76) arranged two sparkling suites from Rossini's copious output: *Soirées musicales* (1936) and *Matinées musicales* (1941).

MUSIC IN AMERICA

GEORGE GERSHWIN's opera, *Porgy and Bess* was arranged into a suite by ROBERT RUSSELL BENNETT who did the same for Richard Rodgers' background music for the television documentary show *Victory at Sea*. Bennett also made suites from the Rodgers and Hammerstein shows *Oklahoma!* and *Carousel*. AARON COPLAND (1900–90), composed ballets for modern dance. His *Rodeo* and *Appalachian Spring* have found their way into suite form, as has his music for the film *The Red Pony* (1949), from the John Steinbeck story. These, too, are an acquired taste which may appeal after all the "warhorses" have been exhausted and one is ready to wander into new musical territory.

For real picturization, the *Grand Canyon Suite* by FERDE GROFÉ is pure musical scenery. His *Mississippi Suite* is not played as often, but is really just as good.

ON THE LIGHTER SIDE

For a touch of lighter classics, the *London, London Again, Three Bears, Cinderella, Three Elizabeths*, and any other suite by English composer ERIC COATES (1886–1957), the *Florida Suite* by FREDERICK DELIUS, *The Wand of Youth Suite* by SIR EDWARD ELGAR (1857–1934), the *Suite Pastorale* by Swedish composer LARS-ERIK LARSSON (1908–86) and SIBELIUS's *Karelia Suite* and *Suite Mignonne* are sheer enjoyment.

AND THERE ARE MORE!

The suites presented in this chapter are easy to like on first hearing. Local classical music stations remain the best source for auditioning new selections to add to one's list.

TONE POEMS

Also known as *symphonic poems*, these are orchestral works in one movement, usually about twenty minutes long, in which a composer attempts to put his feeling into music. It could be an emotional reaction to a painting, a poem, a play, or something as abstract as defining an idea. This is program music with specific titles for the listener to understand what the composer is trying to convey.

LISZT THE ORIGINATOR

FRANZ LISZT first used the term *symphonic poem* around 1850. He wrote thirteen of them. The best known is *Les Préludes*, based on themes of his father-in-law, Richard Wagner.

STRAUSS, THE MAJOR PROPONENT

RICHARD STRAUSS (1864–1949)—no relation to Johann—refined the title to *tone poem*. As a modern composer, his music may be more difficult to assimilate and may take more than one listening to appreciate. His output includes *Ein Heldenleben (A Hero's Life), Till Eulen-*

spiegel's Merry Pranks (a German mythical folk character who played one trick too many and ended up being hanged), *Don Juan* (yet another composition about that promiscuous cad!), *Death and Transfiguration* (deep stuff), and *Also Sprach Zarathustra (Thus Spake* [the Persian philospher] *Zoroaster*), from which every science-fiction buff knows the opening fanfare, since it was used in the film *2001, a Space Odyssey.*

MUSICAL PORTRAITS

DEBUSSY's *La Mer* (The Sea) is a magnificent orchestral portrait. The subtitles of the three movements, "Dawn to Noon," "Play of the Waves," and "Dialogue of the Wind and the Sea," are modern classics, as are his images of clouds in *Nocturnes.* His most ethereal is *Le Prélude à l'aprés-midi d'un faune (The Prelude to the Afternoon of a Fawn),* which provoked a scandal when famed male dancer Vaslav Nijinsky slithered sensuously across the Paris stage in the 1912 ballet version.

RESPIGHI wrote three vibrant tone pictures of his country's capital: *The Pines of Rome* between 1914 and 1916, while Europe was embroiled in World War I, and the companion pieces, *The Fountains of Rome* (1924) and *Roman Festivals* (1929). These are better heard first in live performance to catch the excitement. After that you'll want the recordings.

MOVIE MAGIC

One of the world's most familiar tone poems is *The Sorcerer's Apprentice* by French composer PAUL DUKAS (1865–1935). Again, reference must be made to the film *Fantasia.* Who can ever forget Mickey Mouse, as the apprentice in the wizard's outfit, getting the broom to fetch water for him? The only problem is he can't remember the part of the spell to stop the action and ends up almost drowning amid an army of brooms with sloshing buckets.

PATRIOTISM, MYTHOLOGY, RELAXATION AND FUN!

The Czech composer, BEDŘICH SMETANA (1824–84) composed a cycle of six symphonic poems entitled *Ma Vlast (My Country)*; of these, the depiction of the mighty river Moldau is very familiar. It is also the theme of the national anthem of Israel.

Another theme from a tone poem which was made into a national anthem is SIBELIUS's patriotic *Finlandia* (1900), which stirred the spirit of independence in his country against Russian dominance.

Belgian composer, CÉSAR FRANCK wrote two pleasant tone poems, *Psyche and Eros* and *Les Éolides* (1876), the latter based on a poem describing the flight of the breezes, the daughters of Aeolus, keeper of the winds. Also from Greek mythology is the more often heard SAINT-SAËNS' *Omphale's Spinning Wheel (Le Rouet d'Omphale)* (1871), the mythical queen to whom Hercules was a slave for three years and had to wear a woman's dress while spinning wool for her.

Delicate musical paintings are on the "canvases" of English composer FREDERICK DELIUS's *In a Summer Garden* (1908) and *On Hearing the First Cuckoo in Spring* (1912)—great for relaxing.

Perhaps the most "fun" is the orchestral version of French composer Darius Milhaud's ballet, *Le Boeuf sur le toit* (1919), which literally translated means "The Bull on the Roof," but somehow stands for "The Nothing Doing Bar." The syncopated jazzy music and Brazilian tempos are so catchy your feet will not allow you to sit still.

How to Learn More

Like suites, tone poems need to be experienced from the familiar to the less well-known. Only then can one learn to appreciate all of them. If possible, do a little research. Read the stories and poetry on which some of these works are based. Look at pictures of masterpiece paintings. Visit the Grand Canyon.

*Essentially they (the orchestra) all have
the spirit of kids, and if you scratch
away a little of the fatigue and
cynicism, out comes a seventeen year
old music student again, full of wonder,
exuberance and a tremendous love of
music.*

—Zubin Mehta (1936–)

CHAPTER TWENTY-FOUR

Orchestral Origins

The "orchestra" originally referred to the semicircular area of a classical Greek theater between the stage and the audience, where the chorus danced. In European opera houses of the 1600's, the same area was occupied by the musicians. Eventually the name of the space was given to those who played in it. *Orchestra* now means any large group of players which includes stringed instruments. If there are no strings, the group is a *band*.

Types of Orchestras

There are several kinds of orchestras. A CHAMBER ORCHESTRA may consist of ten to thirty instrumental soloists. A THEATER ORCHESTRA is ten to fifty musicians playing in the *pit* (a sub-level area in front of the stage) for musical shows. DANCE ORCHESTRAS, as their name implies, play for dancing. The dance, or BIG BAND era was at its zenith in the 1930's and 40's. The largest aggregations are OPERA and SYMPHONY ORCHESTRAS numbering from sixty to a hundred musicians—depending on how many string players the budget permits.

The players are seated so that the larger and louder instruments are in the back. Each section: first violins, second violins, woodwinds, brass, and percussion, has a principal who leads the group. In the strings, bowing must be coordinated so that everyone's bow goes up or down at the same time. The section leader also plays any solo passages called for on his or her instrument. The principal first violin player is called the *concertmaster*. It is he who comes on stage after the orchestra is seated and indicates to the oboe to sound its "A" for everyone to tune to. That done, he or she sits down and only then does the conductor come on stage to begin the concert. The musicians have already warmed up their fingers, lips or instruments half an hour before curtain time.

Back to the Past

The history of the orchestra goes back thousands of years to the courts of India and Egypt. The emperor of China had an orchestra of five-hundred, including strings, woodwinds, bells, gongs, and drums. The Old Testament Book of Daniel tells of events occurring in Babylon in the sixth century B. C., and mentions King Nebuchadnezzar's orchestra of strings, woodwinds, and brasses.

In the 1500's, the earliest European orchestras, comprised of strings, woodwinds, organs, guitars, and harpsichords, played for court entertainment such as ballets and masquerades.

Until the late 1700's, bewigged musicians played standing up. The conductor, who was usually the composer, led the orchestra from the harpsichord, making him the only person seated, or, if he was a violinist, was literally the concertmaster. Every nobleman with a court had his own orchestra. Many of the musicians played only part time, their other duties being cooks, gardeners, and general servants. They performed in the theater for operas and in the ballroom for dancing. When their employers entertained guests for dinner, they played "table music" and, afterwards, concert music. In good weather they played outdoors. On Sundays they played in church.

The most famous orchestra of the time was that of the city of Mannheim in Germany. It was composed of sixteen violins, four violas, two cellos, two double basses, three flutes, three oboes, two clarinets, four bassoons, and five horns, with trumpets and drums added when needed. Rehearsed to perfection by composer-conductor Johann Stamitz (1717–57), it became the standard by which all other orchestras were judged. Noted for its soft pianissimos, sudden fortissimos, and exciting crescendos, it attracted music lovers from all over Europe to hear Mannheim concerts.

The greatest early symphonic composer, Franz Josef Haydn (1732–1809), wrote most of his works for the twenty-five-member orchestra of his employer, Count Esterházy. On a visit to London in 1790, he was amazed at the sound of his own works when played by a forty-piece ensemble.

Until the 1800's orchestras outside of courts met only for special concerts and then disbanded. Made up of both professional and amateur musicians, they had little or no rehearsals and were unable to cope with difficult scores. As compositions demanded more ability, orchestras became larger and completely professional. Berlioz specified sixty violins for his *Symphonie fantastique* (1830). Mammoth orchestras were required to play the works of Wagner, Mahler, and Richard Strauss. Debussy and Ravel made use of a variety of instruments, including the saxophone, to paint their impressionistic tone colors. One of the largest orchestras ever put together: four flutes, four oboes, six clarinets, four bassoons, five horns, eight trumpets, three trombones, two tubas, plus the usual strings and a large percussion group, startled the music world with Stravinsky's *Rite of Spring* (1913).

Real Orchestras

The first permanent professional orchestra was the Royal Philharmonic, established in London in 1813. This was followed in 1828 by the orchestra of the Paris Conservatory. The Vienna Philharmonic and the New York Philharmonic were founded in 1842. The Boston Symphony dates back to 1881. Today, almost every major city has its own orchestra, with some—Vienna, Paris, Tokyo—maintaining two and London topping the list with four major orchestras.

Currently the major American orchestras are located (alphabetically) in Atlanta, Boston, Chicago, Cleveland, Los Angeles, Minneapolis, New York, Philadelphia, Pittsburgh, St. Louis, and San Francisco. Ranked next are: American Symphony (New York), Baltimore, Buffalo Philharmonic, Cincinnati, Dallas, Detroit, Houston, Indianapolis, Milwaukee, National (Washington, D. C.), Rochester Philharmonic, St. Paul Chamber, San Diego, Seattle, and Utah.

Canada's top orchestras are Montreal and Toronto.

Foremost in Europe are (alphabetically): Amsterdam Concertgebouw, Bavarian Radio Symphony, Berlin Philharmonic, Czech Philharmonic, London Philharmonia, London Philharmonic, London Symphony, Orchestre de Paris, the Royal Philharmonic (London), St. Petersburg (formerly Leningrad) Philharmonic, and the Vienna Philharmonic.

Not slouching far behind these are the Academy of St. Martin-in-the-Fields (directed by Iona Brown after the twenty-year "reign"—1958–78—of its founder, Sir Neville Marriner), BBC (British Broadcasting) Symphony, Berlin Radio Symphony, Berlin Symphony, City of Birmingham (England) Symphony, City of London Sinfonia, Dresden

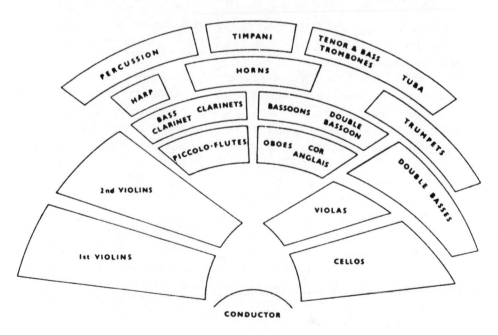

(Germany) Philharmonic, English Chamber Orchestra, Frankfurt Radio Symphony, Hallé Orchestra (of Manchester, England), Leipzig Gewandhaus, Lyons (France) Orchestra, Monte Carlo Philharmonic, Royal Philharmonic (London), Polish National Radio Orchestra, Spanish National Orchestra (Madrid), Toulouse (France) Orchestra, Warsaw Philharmonic, and the Zurich (Switzerland) Tonhalle Orchestra.

A symphony orchestra is an expensive organization, usually financially in the red. In Europe, many orchestras are subsidized by the government, while those in the United States must depend on private individuals or philanthropic organizations. In spite of this, well over 1,500 orchestras are currently active in this country, reflecting the demand of the public for the satisfaction of listening to fine, live, classical music.

CHAPTER TWENTY-FIVE

They Carry a Little Stick

A good conductor must memorize enough of the music to be able to look at the players to control the tempo and the dynamics, and to cue in musicians on solo passages and entrances. Some conductors memorize the entire score and use none during a concert. They are expected to know something about every instrument in order to get the best out of each orchestra member. In rehearsals, the conductor must drill the performers so that all the sounds are perfectly balanced. If soloists or singers are involved, there is the double duty of seeing that the orchestra is coordinated with them. Maestros also need to be in good physical condition—waving one's arms for two hours at shoulder height is no easy feat. Try it sometime, it's great exercise.

Conductors of the past were usually composers. Lully conducted his operas by pounding a stick on the floor. One time it slipped and hit his foot so hard that an incurable infection resulted, causing his death! It was Mendelssohn, Berlioz, and Wagner who started the modern method of conducting with a baton. By the late 1800s compositions were so demanding that conducting was no longer a part-time job to be done alongside composing and performing. Hans von Bülow (1830–94), the pianist/conductor who premiered many Wagner operas, and Austrian composer Gustav Mahler (1860–1911) raised the position of conductor from that of a mere time beater to a true orchestra trainer.

The Gone Greats

The first half of the twentieth century produced conductors upon whom adjectives like passionate, flamboyant, masterful, dictatorial, egotistical, and genius would not be amiss. Whatever their foibles, they knew their music, inspired their musicians, and molded, built, and set the highest standards for their orchestras. Fortunately for us, many of their early recordings are preserved by modern technology on compact discs and digital audio tape.

These masters of the baton came from all over the world and took their music to all parts of the world. As can be seen by the following list, many of the foreign born made their home in this country and enriched America with their talent. Their names should never be forgotten.

Walter Damrosch: born Breslau, Germany, 1862, died New York, 1950; Felix Weingartner: Dalmatia, 1863, died Winterthur, Switzerland, 1942; Arturo Toscanini: Parma, Italy, 1867, died New York, 1957; Willem Mengelberg: Utrecht, Holland 1871, died Switzerland, 1951; Bruno Walter: Berlin, 1876, died Beverly Hills, 1962; Pierre Monteux: Paris, 1875, died Hancock, Maine, 1964; Sir Thomas Beecham: near Liverpool, 1979, died London, 1961; Serge Koussevitzky: Russia, 1874, died Boston, 1951; Tullio Serafin: Venice, 1878, died Rome, 1968; Fritz Reiner: Budapest, 1888, died New York, 1963; Leopold Stokowski: London, 1882, died Hampshire, England, 1977; Ernest Ansermet: Vevey, Switzerland, 1883, died Geneva, 1969; Otto Klemperer: Breslau, 1885, died Zurich, Switzerland, 1973; Sir Adrian Boult: Chester, England, 1889, died London, 1983; Hermann Scherchen: Berlin, 1891, died Florence, Italy 1966; Charles Munch: Strasbourg, France, 1891, died Richmond, Virginia, 1968; Artur Rodzinski: Poland, 1892, died, Boston, 1958; Arthur Fiedler (Boston Pops): Boston, 1894, died Brookline, Mass. 1979; Sir Malcolm Sargent: Lincolnshire, 1895, died London, 1967; Dimitri Mitropoulos: Athens, 1896, died Milan, 1960 (in U.S. 1936–60); George Szell: Budapest, 1897, died Cleveland, 1970; William

Steinberg: Cologne, Germany, 1899, died New York, 1978; Eugene
Ormandy: Budapest, 1899, died Philadelphia, 1985; Eduard van
Beinum: Arnhem, Holland, 1901, died Amsterdam, 1959; André
Kostelanetz: St. Petersburg, Russia, 1901, died Haiti, 1980 (lived in U.S.
from 1922 on); Joseph Krips: Vienna, 1902, died Geneva, Switzerland,
1974; Antal Dorati: Budapest, 1906, died Bern, Switzerland, 1988;
Herbert von Karajan: Salzburg, 1908, died Salzburg, 1989; Jean Mar-
tinon: Lyons, France, 1910, died Paris 1976; Kiril Kondrashin: Moscow, 1914, died Amsterdam, 1965; Edouard van Remoortel: Brussels,
Belgium, 1926, died Paris, 1977; Leonard Bernstein: Lawrence, Massachusetts, 1918, died New York, 1990.

Following in their majestic footsteps, new generations of conductors
are proving themselves equally capable of eliciting sublime and exciting
sounds from the orchestras of today.

SIR GEORG SOLTI (1912–) was born in Budapest, where he enrolled
in the Conservatory, studying with Ernst von Dohnányi, Bartók and
Kodály. He served as assistant to Bruno Walter in 1935 and Toscanini in
1936 and 1937 at the Salzburg Festivals. He made a brilliant conducting
debut with the Budapest Opera in 1938, but the tide of anti-Semitism
swept him out of his country to Switzerland in 1939. Solti was active as a
concert pianist until 1944, when he was engaged to conduct the Swiss
Radio Orchestra. After World War II, American occupation authorities
invited Solti to conduct the Bavarian State Orchestra. His success led to
his appointment as music director from 1946 to 1952. In 1952, he
became director at the Frankfurt Opera.

In 1953, Solti made his American debut at the San Francisco Opera,
he also conducted the Chicago, New York and Philadelphia Symphonies and the Met in 1960. During 1960–61 Solti was music director of
the Dallas Symphony; meanwhile he made his Covent Garden debut in
1959. He served as director there from 1961 to 1971. In 1969, he
became music director of the Chicago Symphony achieving the "Chicago sound" which became a synonym for excellence. His tours with
the orchestra received the highest praise from critics and audiences.
Concurrently, he was music advisor of the Paris Opera from 1971 to
1973, director of the Orchestre de Paris from 1972 to 1975 which he
took on a tour of China in 1974, and served as principal conductor of
the London Philharmonic from 1979 to 1983, after which he received
the title Conductor Emeritus. During all these years Sir Georg retained
his post with the Chicago Symphony until the close of its 100th Anniver-

sary season (1990–91). He was made Laureate Conductor. In 1992, he became artistic director at the Salzburg Music Festival. Honored by Queen Elizabeth II with the Order of the British Empire, he was knighted in 1972. Solti is renowned for his performances of Wagner and the Romantic masters. His recordings have received innumerable awards.

ERICH LEINSDORF (1912–), born in Vienna, studied piano as a child. He made his debut as a conductor at the Musikvereinsaal after his graduation from the Vienna Academy in 1933. He was assistant to Bruno Walter and Toscanini at the Salzburg Festivals from 1934 to 1937. In 1938 he made his successful debut at the Metropolitan Opera. In 1942, he became an American citizen, and served one year in the Army (1943–44). After his discharge, he conducted concerts with the Cleveland, Rochester, and Philadelphia Orchestras as well as the New York City Opera and again the Met. From 1962 to 1969 he held the prestigious post of music director of the Boston Symphony, and was principal conductor of the West Berlin Radio Symphony from 1978 to 1980, after which he conducted major orchestras in America and Europe.

CARLO MARIA GIULINI (1914–) was born in Italy, studied violin as a boy, and entered the Santa Cecilia Conservatory in Rome at the age of sixteen. As a member of the viola section in the Rome Augusteo Orchestra, he played under such great conductors as Richard Strauss, Bruno Walter, Willem Mengelberg, and Wilhelm Furtwängler. Drafted into the Italian Army in World War II, he went into hiding so as not to have to fight for something he did not believe in. After the liberation of Rome by Allied troops in 1944, he conducted the Augusteo Orchestra in a special celebration concert. He then went on to conduct major Italian orchestras and operas. In 1978, he succeeded Zubin Mehta as music director of the Los Angeles Philharmonic, maintaining its high standards until he left in 1984. His conducting style is in the best traditions of the Italian school as exemplified by Toscanini, but is free of emotional displays. He is a true Romantic conductor.

RAFAEL KUBELIK (1914–), the son of Czech conductor Jan Kubelik, studied violin with his father and attended the Prague Conservatory. He made his conducting debut with the Czech Philharmonic in 1934, and was its chief conductor from 1942 to 1948, during one of the most traumatic periods in the history of his country. Kubelik refused to collaborate with the Nazis in World War II, and when the Communists took control in 1948 he left the country and guest conducted in England

and Western Europe. He made his U.S. debut with the Chicago Symphony in 1949; his success led to his appointment as music director from 1950 to 1953. He was subsequently music director of the Royal Opera House at Covent Garden in 1958, the Bavarian Radio Symphony Orchestra in Munich from 1961 to 1979, and the Metropolitan Opera in 1973. He continued to appear as a guest conductor all over the world (he became a Swiss citizen in 1966) and retired in 1985. He returned to his homeland in 1990 after an absence of forty-two years to conduct the Czech Philharmonic, playing Smetana's *Ma Vlast* (*My Country*). He also composed several operas, some choral works, songs, and chamber music.

STANISLAW SKROWACZEWSKI (1923–), born in Poland, had already composed an overture at the age of eight, and performed Beethoven's Third Piano Concerto at thirteen, conducting the orchestra from the keyboard. The Nazi occupation of Poland interrupted his studies and a bomb explosion near his house injured his hands, putting an end to his concert career. In 1947, a French scholarship enabled him to study composition with Nadia Boulanger, and conducting with Paul Kletzki (1900–73) in Paris. He returned to Poland to conduct several orchestras, then made his American debut as guest conductor of the Cleveland Orchestra. He became director of the Minneapolis Symphony (1960–79) (renamed the Minnesota Orchestra in 1968) and was made its Conductor Emeritus. In 1966 he became an American citizen. He was musical advisor of the St. Paul (Minnesota) Chamber Orchestra from 1987 to 1988 and of the Hallé (Manchester) Orchestra from 1984 to 1990. Skrowaczewski has also composed orchestral and chamber music as well as a ballet.

WOLFGANG SAWALLISCH (1923–), born in Munich, started piano at age five, then studied privately until he entered military service in World War II. After the war he went to the Munich Hochschule für Musik. He made his conducting debut at the Augsburg Opera in 1950 and went on to conduct at other German opera houses and the Bayreuth Festivals of Wagner operas from 1957 to 1961. He was chief conductor of the Vienna Symphony from 1960 to 1970, bringing them to the United States in 1964. He was also music director of the Hamburg State Philharmonic from 1961 to 1973. From 1970 to 1980 he was chief conductor of the Orchestre de la Suisse Romande in Geneva, and from 1971 was also associated with the Bavarian State Opera in Munich. In 1990 Sawallisch was named Music Director of the Philadelphia Orchestra, beginning with the 1993–94 season. Conducting in the Austro-

German tradition, he has guested with the world's major orchestras, and also appeared as piano accompanist to leading singers.

SIR NEVILLE MARRINER (1924–), born in England, studied violin with his father and entered the Royal College of Music in London when he was thirteen. Military service during World War II interrupted his studies. After the war he took courses at the Paris Conservatory. During the 1950s he played violin in major London orchestras. In 1959 he took conducting lessons from Pierre Monteux in Hancock, Maine. The year before he had founded the Academy of Saint-Martin-in-the-Fields, and during his twenty-year conductorship established an international reputation through tours and recordings. From 1968 to 1978 Marriner also served as music director of the Los Angeles Chamber Orchestra, going from there to the Minnesota Orchestra (1978–86). He was chief conductor of the Stuttgart Radio Symphony from 1983 to 1989. In 1979 he was made a Commander of the Order of the British Empire, and knighted in 1985. As a chamber orchestra violinist-conductor, he is considered of the first rank and has guested all over the world, performing a repertoire ranging from the Baroque to the twentieth century.

PIERRE BOULEZ (1925–) was born in France. He studied composition with Olivier Messiaen at the Paris Conservatory, graduating in 1945. Private lessons with René Liebowitz initiated him into serial music. In the 1950s he organized a concert series of avant-garde music. He lectured both in Germany and at Harvard, and in 1963 made his American conducting debut. From operatic experience gained in Germany, he conducted Wagner's *Ring* cycle in Bayreuth in 1976. After guest conducting major American orchestras he was engaged as music director of the New York Philharmonic from 1971 to 1977. His programming of modern composers Schoenberg, Berg, Webern, Varèse, et al. provoked the usual opposition of the subscribers. In 1974 Boulez established the Institut de Récherche et Coordination Acoustique/ Musique (IRCAM), subsidized by the French government to experiment in electronic techniques with digital synthesizers and computers. In 1989 Boulez was awarded a top Japanese prize for his contributions to contemporary music. His own compositions are the embodiment of these futuristic techniques and have been described as fiendishly difficult to perform.

SIR CHARLES MACKERRAS (1925–), born in New York of Australian parents, was taken to Sydney as an infant. He studied oboe, piano, and composition at the New South Wales Conservatorium, then became principal oboist in the Sydney Symphony. He later went to London and played in the Sadler's Wells Opera Orchestra. A scholarship in 1947 made possible a year's study at the Prague Academy of Music with Vaclav Talich (1883–1961). He conducted several British orchestras during the 1950s, and from 1966 to 1970 was conductor of the Hamburg State Opera. In 1970 he became music director at Sadler's Wells (re-named the English National Opera in 1974), a position he held until 1978. Meanwhile, he made his Met debut in 1972. He was chief conductor of the Sydney Symphony from 1982 to 1985, and artistic director of the Welsh National Opera in Cardiff from 1987 to 1992. Mackerras was made a Commander of the Order of the British Empire in 1974, and knighted in 1979. Like Eve Queler, he championed the 20th century operas of Janáček, but also conducted the Baroque operas of Handel, Gluck, and J.C. Bach.

KLAUS TENNSTEDT (1926–), born in Germany, studied piano, violin, and theory at the Leipzig Conservatory. In 1948 he became concertmaster in Halle an der Saale (Handel's birthplace), beginning his career as conductor there in 1953. He also served as conductor at the Dresden State Opera from 1958 to 1962 and appeared as guest conductor throughout East Germany, Eastern Europe, and the Soviet Union. In 1971 he got out from under Communist control and settled in the West, conducting in Sweden and West Germany. His North American debut was with the Toronto Symphony. In the U.S., Tennstedt conducted the Boston Symphony and other major orchestras. In 1976 he made his British debut with the London Symphony. In the 1980s he appeared with the North German Radio Symphony in Hamburg, the Minnesota Orchestra, and the London Philharmonic, where he served as principal conductor from 1983 until throat cancer forced him to resign in 1987. He is ranked among the foremost interpreters of the Austro-German repertoire.

HERBERT BLOMSTEDT (1927–) was born in Massachusetts of Swedish parents. He took courses at the Stockholm Conservatory and conducting lessons with Igor Markevitch in Paris. Back in New York he went to Juilliard, and then to Tanglewood, taking classes with Leonard Bernstein. There he won the Koussevitzky Prize in 1953. In 1954 he made his conducting debut with the Stockholm Philharmonic, then held positions throughout Scandinavia. From 1975 to 1985 he was chief conductor of the Dresden Staatskapelle, with whom he toured Europe and the United States. In 1985 he became music director of the San Francisco Symphony, celebrating their seventy-fifth anniversary in 1986 and touring Europe with them in 1987. He also appears as guest conductor with the world's principal orchestras.

SIR COLIN DAVIS (1927–) studied clarinet at the Royal College of

Music in London and played in the band of the Household Cavalry while serving in the army. His first professional conducting position was at Sadler's Wells Opera from 1961 to 1965. He made his American debut as guest conductor with the Minneapolis Symphony in 1960 and subsequently appeared with the New York and Los Angeles Philharmonics and the Philadelphia Orchestra. In 1967 he made his Met debut conducting the British opera *Peter Grimes*. Davis was chief conductor of the BBC Symphony from 1967 to 1971. In 1971 he also succeeded Solti as music director of the Royal Opera at Covent Garden, where he produced the entire cycle of *Der Ring des Nibelungen* from 1974 to 1976. In 1979 the Royal Opera toured in South Korea and Japan, and, in 1984, the United States. From 1972 to 1983 he was principal guest conductor of the Boston Symphony. In 1977 Davis became the first British conductor to appear at the Bayreuth Festival. In 1983 he was appointed chief conductor of the Bavarian Radio Symphony in Munich; they toured North America in 1986, the year he resigned from Covent Garden. He has been a guest conductor with major orchestras and opera houses throughout the world. Davis received the OBE in 1965 and was knighted in 1980.

KURT MASUR (1927–) was born in Silesia (part of Germany), received training in piano and cello at the Breslau Music School from 1942 to 1944, then studied conducting at the Leipzig Hochschule für Musik from 1946 to 1948. He began his conducting career with several German orchestras in the 1950s. In 1967 he became music director of the Dresden Philharmonic until 1972. In 1970 he was appointed to the historically honored position of Gewandhauskapellmeister of Leipzig, serving as director of the Gewandhaus Orchestra and making tours in Europe and abroad. His British debut came in 1973 with the New Philharmonia Orchestra of London; his U.S. debut in 1974 was with the Cleveland Orchestra. In 1981 Masur conducted Beethoven's Ninth Symphony at the gala opening of the new Gewandhaus in Leipzig. In 1988 he became principal guest conductor of the London Philharmonic. In the fall in 1989, during the period of political upheaval in East Germany, Masur played a major role in keeping the peace in Leipzig. In 1990 he was appointed music director of the New York Philharmonic, beginning with the 1991–92 season.

MSTISLAV ROSTROPOVICH (1927–), the son of Russian cellist Leopold Rostropovich, took cello from his father and piano from his mother at an early age. He made his debut in Moscow at the age of eight. Shostakovich was one of his composition instructors at the Moscow

Conservatory. He also studied privately with Prokofiev. In 1950 Mstislav won the International Competition for Cellists in Prague. This was the beginning of a very successful career all over the world. He joined the faculty of the Moscow Conservatory in 1953, and was also a professor at Leningrad. An accomplished pianist, he accompanies his wife, soprano Galina Vishnevskaya, whom he had married in 1955. In 1961 he made his first appearance as a conductor and received many honors, including the Lenin Prize in 1963.

He began having difficulties with the Soviet government after his protest of the treatment received by author Aleksandr Solzhenitsyn over his winning of the 1970 Nobel Prize for Literature. Concerts were canceled and foreign tours forbidden, as were radio and television appearances and recordings. In 1974 he managed to get permission to leave the country with his family. His successful appearance with the National Symphony in Washington, D.C., in 1975 led to his appointment as its music director in 1977. Rostropovich and his wife publicized what had happened to them in Russia, which caused Moscow to take away their Soviet citizenship. Not until Gorbachev's *perestroika* was their citizenship restored in 1990 and the conductor was invited to take the National Symphony to his homeland, where he appeared as soloist in Dvořák's Cello Concerto. His enthusiastic welcome symbolized the principles of liberty. It is interesting to note his first name means "avenged glory."

Recognized as one of the greatest cellists of the century, Rostropovich has commissioned and premiered works by Prokofiev, Shostakovich, Britten, Piston, and others. He is also an authoritative conductor. He organized the first Rostropovich International Cello Competition in Paris (1981) and the Rostropovich Festival in England (1983). He received France's highest award, the Légion d'honneur, in 1982, and was made an honorary knight by Queen Elizabeth in 1987.

CHRISTOPH VON DOHNÁNYI, grandson of Hungarian pianist, composer, conductor Ernst von Dohnányi, was born in Berlin, 1929. He began studying piano as a child, but his musical training was interrupted by World War II. His father, Hans von Dohnányi, a lawyer, and his uncle, the Protestant theologian and author Dietrich Bonhoeffer, were executed by the Nazis for their part in the conspiracy to assassinate Hitler, July 20, 1944.

Christoph won the Richard Strauss Prize for composing and conducting at the Munich Hochschule für Musik, which he entered in 1948. He came to America and studied with his grandfather at Florida State

University (Tallahassee). On his return to Germany, his career blossomed with various orchestras and operas in the 1960s and 1970s, his major position being with the Hamburg State Opera from 1977 to 1984. In 1984, he succeeded Lorin Maazel as director of the Cleveland Orchestra. Concurrently, he has guest conducted at Vienna State Opera, London's Covent Garden, Milan's La Scala, the Berlin and Vienna Philharmonics, and the Metropolitan Opera, among others.

ISTVAN KERTESZ (1929–73) studied violin and composition at the Franz Liszt Academy in Budapest, where Kodály was one of his teachers. He was conductor at the Budapest State Orchestra from 1955 to 1956, but left the country after the unsuccessful revolution that year against the Soviets. He settled in West Germany, and became a naturalized citizen, conducting various orchestras in Europe. He made a guest appearance in the United States in 1961, and was principal conductor of the London Symphony from 1965–68, which he led on a world tour. In 1964, he became music director of the Cologne (Germany) Orchestra, a post he retained until his death by drowning while swimming in the Mediterranean off the coast of Israel.

ANDRÉ PREVIN (1929–), born in Berlin, was accepted at the age of six into the Hochschule für Musik in that city. In 1938, the family, being Jewish, had to leave. They went to Paris, where André continued his studies at the Conservatory, with Marcel Dupré as one of his teachers. In 1939, the family emigrated to America, where his father's cousin, Charles Previn, was music director at Universal Studios. André took composition lessons with Ernst Toch (1887–1964) and with Mario Castelnuovo-Tedesco (1895–1968). He became an American citizen in 1943. While still in high school, Previn already had a job at MGM studios as an orchestrator, and later became one of their music directors. He also had a career as a fine jazz pianist. While in the army (1950–52) and stationed in San Francisco, he took conducting lessons from Pierre Monteux, then director of that city's symphony.

In the 1950s and 1960s, Previn wrote film music, receiving Academy Awards for his arrangements of *Gigi* (1958), *Porgy and Bess* (1959), *Irma La Douce* (1963), and *My Fair Lady* (1964), among his myriad other scores. During this time he was also performing as a concert pianist. In 1962, he made his conducting debut with the St. Louis Symphony, and decided this was to be his vocation. He was principal conductor of the Houston Symphony from 1967 to 1969, and assumed the same position with the London Symphony Orchestra from 1978 to 1979, becoming Conductor Emeritus. He became music director of the Pittsburgh

Symphony in 1976 and held that post until 1984. He directed the Royal Philharmonic Orchestra of London from 1985 to 1987 and was music director of the Los Angeles Philharmonic from 1985 to 1990. He took these orchestras on successful tours throughout the world. All the while he continued to compose both popular and classical music and published *André Previn's Guide to Music* (1983).

BERNARD HAITINK (1929–) was born in Amsterdam, where he studied violin at the Conservatory. In 1954, he took a conducting course with Ferdinand Leitner, and the following year was appointed second conductor of the Radio Philharmonic in Hilversum, becoming principal conductor in 1957. He made his U.S. debut with the Los Angeles Philharmonic in 1958. The following year he conducted the Amsterdam Concertgebouw Orchestra in England, becoming co-principal conductor with Eugen Jochum in 1961. In 1964 he was made their chief conductor, and toured America with them in 1982. He continued a distinguished career with this orchestra until 1988. From 1987 to 1990, he was a music director of the Royal Opera at Covent Garden, London. Haitink has guest conducted all over Europe and America, receiving numerous international honors including an Honorary Knighthood (OBE) from England's Queen Elizabeth in 1977.

LORIN MAAZEL was born in France, 1930, of American parents. Taken to Los Angeles as an infant, he began violin studies at five, and piano at seven. At concerts he was fascinated by the conductor and began to take lessons with Vladimir Bakaleinikov (1885–1953), associate conductor of the Los Angeles Philharmonic, who also taught him Russian. At the age of eight, Lorin got to conduct Schubert's *Unfinished Symphony* with the visiting University of Idaho orchestra. In 1938, Bakaleinikov went to Pittsburgh as assistant conductor of the symphony, and the Maazel family followed him. In 1939, Lorin caused a sensation conducting the Interlochen Music Camp orchestra at the New York World's Fair. At eleven, he conducted the NBC Symphony Orchestra, and at twelve, in 1942, led a whole program with the New York Philharmonic. In 1948, Maazel became both violinist and apprentice conductor of the Pittsburgh Symphony. A 1951 Fulbright Fellowship took him to Italy, where he conducted in Florence, as well as in Vienna and Edinburgh. In 1960, Maazel became the first American to conduct the Bayreuth Festival. In 1962, he made his Met debut, and the following year toured Russia. He was artistic director of the German Opera in West Berlin from 1965 to 1971 and chief conductor of the West Berlin Radio Symphony from 1965 to 1975. From associate principal of the

New Philharmonia of London in 1970 to 1972, he became its principal conductor from 1976 to 1980. Another distinguished position was music director of the Cleveland Symphony from 1972 to 1982, after which he was made Conductor Emeritus. During his tenure, major tours with the Cleveland Symphony included Australia, New Zealand, Japan, Latin America, and Europe. He also conducted the Orchestre National de France as chief from 1977 to 1982 and as principal guest from 1988 to 1991. From 1980 to 1986 he conducted the famous Vienna Philharmonic New Year's Day Concerts. He was the first American to become Artistic Director and General Manager of the Vienna State Opera, (1982–84). He was also musical consultant and guest conductor of the Pittsburgh Symphony from 1984 to 1986, becoming musical director that year.

Blessed with a phenomenal memory, Maazel is fluent in French, German, Italian, Spanish, Portuguese, and Russian, and has a distinctive baton technique. His honors include a doctorate from the University of Pittsburgh, the Sibelius Prize from Finland, and the Commander's Cross of the Order of Merit from Germany. His renowned recordings have won him the Grand Prix de Disque in Paris, and the Edison Prize in the Netherlands.

GENNADI ROZHDESTVENSKY was born in Moscow, 1931. He studied conducting with his father, Nikolai Anosov, at the Moscow Conservatory, graduating in 1954. He was assistant conductor at the Bolshoi Theater from 1951 to 1961, and principal from 1964 to 1970. From 1961 to 1974 he was also chief conductor of the Radio and Television Symphony Orchestra in Moscow. His other positions were at the Stockholm Philharmonic from 1975 to 1977, the BBC Symphony from 1978 to 1981, and the Vienna Symphony from 1981 to 1983. In 1982, he founded and became chief conductor of the State Symphony Orchestra of the Soviet Ministry of Culture. His specialty is twentieth-century music and Soviet composers.

RAFAEL FRÜHBECK DE BURGOS was born in Burgos, Spain, in 1933, of a German father and Spanish mother. He studied at the Madrid Conservatory and the Munich Hochschule für Musik during the 1950s. He became chief conductor of the Orquesta Nacional de España in Madrid from 1962 to 1977, of the Düsseldorf Symphony from 1966 to 1971, and the Orchestre Symphonique de Montréal from 1975 to 1976. He has guest conducted with major European and American orchestras and directed the Yomiuri Nippon Orchestra of Tokyo from 1980 to 1985. In

1990 he became chief conductor of the Vienna Symphony. Besides standard repertoire, he is a brilliant interpreter of Spanish music.

CLAUDIO ABBADO (1933–) received his early training in music from his violinist father. He graduated from the Milan Conservatory in piano in 1955 and attended the Vienna Academy of Music from 1956 to 1958, where he took conducting lessons with Hans Swarowsky (1899–1975). He made his conducting debut in Trieste in 1958, won the Koussevitzky conducting prize at Tanglewood, and was a winner in 1963 of the Mitropoulos Competition in New York. His American conducting debut was with the New York Philharmonic the same year. In the 1970s he conducted at La Scala, Milan, and the Vienna Philharmonic, taking the latter on tour to Japan and China. The 1980s saw him with the London Symphony, the Chicago Symphony, and founding the Filarmonica della Scala in Milan. He was music director of the London Symphony from 1983 to 1988. In 1986, he founded the Mahler Orchestra, and became chief conductor of the Vienna State Opera. In 1989, he became director of the Berlin Philharmonic after the death of Herbert von Karajan. Abbado's honors include the Mozart and Mahler Medals of Vienna, the Gran Croce of Italy, and the Légion d'Honneur of France.

SEIJI OZAWA was born in China of Japanese parents in 1935. At the end of the Japanese occupation of Manchuria in 1944, the family returned to Japan. Ozawa studied at the Toho School of Music in Tokyo, graduating in 1959 with first prizes in conducting and composition. He had already conducted concerts with the (NHK) Japanese Broadcasting Symphony and the Japan Philharmonic. His influential teacher, Hideo Saito, advised him to go to Europe, where he won first prize at the conductors' competition in Besançon and met Charles Munch, who arranged for Ozawa to go to Tanglewood. There he won the 1960 Koussevitzky Prize and a scholarship to work with Herbert von Karajan and the Berlin Philharmonic. Leonard Bernstein heard him in Berlin and hired him as assistant conductor of the New York Philharmonic, with whom he made his first appearance at Carnegie Hall in 1961. Later that year he accompanied Bernstein on the orchestra's tour of Japan. In the 1960s, Ozawa was music director at the Ravinia Festival, the summer home of the Chicago Symphony, and of the Toronto Symphony, which he took to England in 1965. During his 1970–76 term as music director of the San Francisco Symphony, he toured through Europe with the orchestra.

He had already begun an association with the Boston Symphony in

1970 when, with Gunther Schuller, he became co-artistic director of the Berkshire Music Center (Tanglewood), the summer home of the Boston Symphony. In 1973, Seiji Ozawa became music director of the Symphony and Tanglewood; a milestone, as it was the first time an Asian musician was chosen solely on his merit to head an exclusive bastion of German, French, and Russian conductors. In 1976, he took the orchestra to Europe, and in 1978 to Japan, where he was the object of national pride. In 1979, Ozawa made history by taking the orchestra to the People's Republic of China on an official cultural visit. In August of that year, they toured European music festivals. The 1981 centennial of the Boston Symphony was celebrated with concerts in major American cities, and tours of Japan, France, Germany, Austria, and England.

Ozawa has received universal recognition for his masterful talent. Equally proficient in classical and modern repertoire, he conducts without the music score in front of him. His honors include doctorates from the University of San Francisco in 1971, and the New England Conservatory in 1982. His astounding career was the subject of the 1987 documentary film *Ozawa*.

ELIAHU INBAL (1936–), prominent Israeli conductor, was educated at the Jerusalem Conservatory, then studied conducting with Franco Ferrara (1911–85) in Rome, and Louis Fourestier (1892–1976) in Paris. In the 1960s he appeared as a guest conductor in Europe. From 1974 to 1990, he was chief conductor of the Frankfurt Radio Symphony, taking this orchestra on its first tour of the United States in 1980. He was also artistic director of the Teatro la Fenice from 1983 to 1986.

ZUBIN MEHTA (1936–), born in Bombay (India) of Persian Zoroastrian descent, was tutored by his famous father, conductor Mehli Mehta. After studies in Italy and Austria, he became conductor of the Vienna Symphony in 1960. Guest appearances in Montreal, 1960, led to his becoming their music director. In 1961 he became associate conductor and in 1962 conductor of the Los Angeles Philharmonic. He made a successful Met debut with *Aida* in 1965, also conducting *Carmen* and *Turandot*. In 1967, he resigned his post in Montreal and added music advisor of the Israel Philharmonic to his hectic schedule. He became their principal conductor in 1977, having performed there during the Six Day War (1967), the twenty-fifth anniversary of Israel's independence (1973), and when Scud missiles were raining on Tel Aviv during the Persian Gulf War (1991). In 1974 he received an honorary doctorate from Tel Aviv University.

A true personification of international relations, Mehta is eloquent in

English and Hindi, fluent in French, German, and Spanish, and speaks understandable Russian. In 1978 Mehta received an offer he could not refuse and left Los Angeles to become music director of the New York Philharmonic, where he remained until 1991, then freeing himself to accept the deluge of guest conducting invitations.

CHARLES DUTOIT (1936–), born in Lausanne, studied the violin, viola, piano, and drums. He learned conducting by watching Ernest Ansermet (1883–1969) rehearse the Orchestre de la Suisse Romande. He studied at the Lausanne and Geneva Conservatories and the Accademia Musicale in Siena, as well as attending a summer seminar at Tanglewood. He made his conducting debut with the Bern Symphony in 1963, and became its music director (1967–77). From 1964 to 1971 he directed the Zurich Radio Orchestra; he has also directed the National Orchestra of Mexico City, the Göteborg (Sweden) Symphony, and the Montreal Symphony, where he expanded the orchestra's repertoire, especially with French and new Canadian music. In 1983, Dutoit conducted the Minnesota Orchestra; in 1987, he made his Metropolitan Opera debut; and directed the 1990–91 summer seasons of the Philadelphia Orchestra. In 1990, he was named chief conductor of the Orchestre National de France.

NEEME JÄRVI (1937–), born in Tallinn, Estonia, studied percussion and choral conducting at the Tallinn Music School and the Leningrad Conservatory. In 1971, he won First Prize in the Accademia di Santa Cecilia conducting competition in Rome. He was music director of the Estonia State Symphony from 1960 to 1980, and the Estonian Opera Theater from 1964 to 1977. He was principal guest conductor of the City of Birmingham (England) Orchestra from 1981 to 1984, became music director of the Göteborg (Sweden) Symphony in 1982, and was also principal conductor of the Scottish National Symphony in Glasgow from 1984 to 1988. In 1990, he became music director of the Detroit Symphony Orchestra. He has guested at the major world music centers, and pioneered recordings of rarely performed Scandanavian composers, including Berwald, Gade, Svensen, and Tubin.

JESUS LÓPEZ-COBOS, born in Toro, Spain, in 1940, earned a Ph.D. in Philosophy at the University of Madrid, at the same time studying conducting in Venice with Franco Ferrara, in Vienna with Hans Swarowsky, and at Juilliard with Jean Morel. In 1969 he won First Prize in the Belançon Competition. The same year he conducted at the Venice Theater and the Prague Spring Festival. He made his American debut with the San Francisco Opera in 1972. From 1970 to 1975 he was the regular conductor at the West Berlin German Opera, and from 1980 to 1990, served as their music director. From 1984 to 1989 he was also chief conductor of the Orquesta Nacional de España in Madrid. From 1986 he has been music director of the Cincinnati Symphony, and from 1990 the Lausanne (Switzerland) Chamber Orchestra.

RICCARDO MUTI (1941–), born in Naples, studied violin and piano with his physician father, then went to the Naples Conservatory, earning a diploma in piano. He took conducting courses at the Verdi Conservatory in Milan, and with Franco Ferrara in Venice. He made his debut with the RAI (Italian Radio and Television) in 1968. During the 1970s he conducted major orchestras in Italy, and achieved international fame with guest appearances at the Salzburg Festival, with the Berlin Philharmonic, the Vienna State Orchestra, the Philharmonia Orchestra of London, and the Philadelphia Orchestra, whose music director he became in 1980, after the death of Eugene Ormandy. He also became music director of La Scala, Milan, in 1986. Muti resigned from Philadelphia in 1990, but agreed to serve as its laureate conductor from 1992. His expertise enhanced the illustrious tradition established in Philadelphia by Leopold Stokowski and continued by Eugene Ormandy. Unlike them, however, Muti is also an excellent opera conductor.

DAVID AMOS was born in 1941 in Mexico City, where he began his piano studies. Emigrating to America with his parents, he received his B.A. and M.A. at San Diego State University, followed by doctoral studies at Indiana University. He has made a specialty of recording contemporary American composers, premiering many of their works. Among the many orchestras he has conducted are the Jerusalem and London Symphonies, Krakow and Royal Philharmonics, London Philharmonia, City of London Sinfonia, and the Polish Radio Orchestra. Amos was the first maestro from the West invited to direct the Lithuanian National Philharmonic since that country declared its independence from Russia. The year 1993 marks the continuation of the prestigious series "Twentieth Century Masters" for Harmonium Mundi (Recordings) USA-France. His CDs have been broadcast throughout the world.

EDO DE WAART (1941–) was born in Amsterdam where his father sang in the chorus of the Netherlands Opera. He studied piano and oboe and at sixteen entered the Amsterdam Muzieklyceum. He played oboe in the Amsterdam Orchestra from 1962 to 1963, then joined the Concertgebouw Orchestra. He also studied conducting with Franco Ferrara in Hilversum, making his debut as a conductor with the Netherlands Radio Philharmonic in 1964. The same year he went to New York and was one of the winners of the Mitropoulos Competition. In 1965–66, he was assistant conductor of the New York Philharmonic. Upon his return to Amsterdam in 1966, he was made assistant conductor of the Concertgebouw and toured the United States with them the following year. He also organized the Netherlands Wind Ensemble, with whom he has travelled extensively.

During the 1970s de Waart conducted the Rotterdam Philharmonic, performing with it throughout Europe. He has been guest conductor at the Santa Fe Opera, Houston Opera, and Covent Garden, London. In 1974, he debuted with the San Francisco Symphony, becoming their music director in 1977. In 1986, he was made music director of the Minnesota Orchestra and in 1988, was made artistic director of the Dutch Radio Philharmonic in Hilversum. Tall and athletic-looking, de Waart represents the modern generation of symphonic and operatic conductors whose objective approach to interpretation combined with appealing propriety is devoid of the histrionics of many conductors of the past.

DANIEL BARENBOIM (1942–), born in Buenos Aires, Argentina, studied music with his parents and gave his first public piano recital at the age of seven. In 1952, the family settled in Israel. During the summers of 1954 and 1955 he went to Salzburg and took piano with Edwin Fischer, conducting with Igor Markevitch, and chamber music performance with Enrico Mainardi. From 1954 to 1956, he studied with Nadia Boulanger in Paris. Also in 1956, Barenboim was one of the youngest students to receive a diploma from the Accademia di Santa Cecilia in Rome. During these years he gave piano recitals in Paris and London. In 1957, he made his American debut in Carnegie Hall, playing Prokofiev's First Piano Concerto with Leopold Stokowski conducting the Symphony of the Air.

Barenboim made his conducting debut in Haifa in 1957 and in 1960, played all thirty-two Beethoven sonatas in a series of concerts in Tel Aviv and New York. As a conductor, he was awarded the Bruckner Medal by the Bruckner Society of America for his masterful interpretation of that composer's music. In 1967, he toured the U.S. with the Israel Philharmonic, and the following year brought the London Symphony to New York. He subsequently conducted the Boston, Chicago, Philadelphia, and New York orchestras. In 1975, he was named music director of the Orchestre de Paris. In January 1989, he was appointed as Sir Georg Solti's successor to the Chicago Symphony Orchestra.

In 1967, he married English cellist, Jacqueline du Pré. They appeared in numerous sonata programs together until she was stricken with multiple sclerosis in 1972. She died in London in 1987.

EDUARDO MATA (1942–), born in Mexico City, studied composition and conducting at the National Conservatory with Carlos Chávez from 1960 to 1965. The summer of 1964 he took conducting seminars at Tanglewood with Gunther Schuller and Erich Leinsdorf. Mata was the conductor of the Mexico Ballet Company from 1963 to 1964, the Guadalajara Symphony from 1964 to 1966, and the Philharmonic Orchestra of the National University of Mexico from 1966 to 1976. From 1970 to 1978, he was principal conductor of the Phoenix (Arizona) Symphony, and in 1977 became music director of the Dallas Symphony. A guest conductor with leading orchestras throughout North America and Europe, in 1990 he became principal guest conductor of the Pittsburgh Symphony. During the 1960s, he composed three symphonies and ballet and chamber music.

JAMES LEVINE (1943–) was born in Cincinnati. His maternal grandfather was a cantor, his father a violinist, and his mother an actress. He started piano as a small child, and at the age of ten played Mendelssohn's Second Piano Concerto at a Cincinnati Symphony Youth Concert. In 1956, his piano teacher was Rudolf Serkin at the Marlborough School of Music; in 1957, he studied with Rosina Lhevinne at Aspen; and in 1961, he entered Juilliard, taking conducting with Jean Morel from 1903 to 1975. In 1964, Levine joined the American Conductors Project of the Baltimore Symphony, and was able to practice with prominent maestros like Alfred Wallenstein, Max Rudolph, and Fausto Cleva. In 1964–65, he was apprentice to George Szell at the Cleveland Orchestra, becoming its regular assistant (1965–70). In 1970, he guest conducted the Philadelphia Orchestra at its summer home in Robin Hood Dell. Levine's success with this and other orchestras led to his appointment with the Metropolitan Opera as principal conductor (1975), music director in (1975), and artistic director (1986). In 1973, he also became the Ravinia Festival music director. In 1975, he began to conduct at the Salzburg Festivals, and in 1982, the Bayreuth Festival. Levine has continued to make appearances as a pianist with chamber groups, but his fame rests with his brilliant organization and conductorship of the Met.

YOAV TALMI was born in Kibbutz Merhavia, Israel, in 1943. He studied at the Rubin Academy in Tel Aviv (1961–65), at Juilliard (1965–68), and during the summers with Walter Susskind at Aspen, Colorado

(1966), Bruno Maderna in Salzburg (1967), Jean Fournet in Hilversum (Holland, 1968), and Erich Leinsdorf at Tanglewood (1969), where he won the Koussevitzky Memorial Conducting Prize. From 1968 to 1970 he was associate conductor at the Louisville Orchestra, concurrently music director of the Kentucky Chamber Orchestra (1969–71), and co-conductor of the Israel Chamber Orchestra (1970–72). From 1974 to 1980, he served as artistic director of the Gelders Orchestra in Arnhem (Holland), and was principal guest conductor of the Munich Philharmonic (1979–80). In 1984 he returned to the Israel Chamber Orchestra as music director, and in 1985 assumed the same prestigious position with the New Israeli Opera in Tel Aviv. In 1990 Talmi was appointed Music Director of the San Diego Symphony. His guest appearances include the Philharmonic Orchestras of Berlin, London, Munich, Oslo, Stockholm, Rotterdam, Helsinki, and Israel, the Royal Philharmonic, the Orchestre National of France, and the Vienna Symphony, among many others.

DAVID ATHERTON was born in Blackpool, England, in 1944, and studied at Cambridge. In 1967 he founded the London Sinfonietta and was its director until 1973. In 1968, he became one of the conductors at the Royal Opera, and in 1978, conducted performances at the San Francisco Opera. In 1980, he was made principal conductor of the Royal Liverpool Philharmonic. Continuing to serve as its guest conductor, he also accepted the music directorship of the San Diego Symphony (1981–87), honing it into one of the finer orchestras in the country. In 1989 Atherton became music director of the Hong Kong Philharmonic.

LEONARD SLATKIN, son of long-time Hollywood Bowl conductor Felix Slatkin, was born in Los Angeles in 1944. His early musical training included violin, viola, piano, and conducting, the latter with famed French pedagogue Jean Morel at Juilliard. In 1968 he became assistant conductor to Walter Susskind (1913–80) at the St. Louis Symphony, graduating to associate conductor (1971), associate principal conductor (1974), principal guest conductor (1975), and music director (1979). Meanwhile he performed with the Royal Philharmonic in London, the New Orleans Philharmonic, and the Minnesota Orchestra summer concerts. In 1990 he was made director of the Great Woods Performing Arts Center in Mansfield, Massachusetts, summer home of the Pittsburgh Symphony; and in 1991 of the Blossom Music Center, the Cleveland Orchestra's summer locale. Slatkin has also appeared with major American and European orchestras.

MICHAEL TILSON THOMAS, born in Hollywood in 1944, is the grandson of Bessie and Boris Thomashefsky, founders of New York's Yiddish Theater. His cultured upbringing, education, and conducting experience with the Young Musicians Foundation Debut Orchestra (1963–67), was enhanced by his position as pianist in the UCLA master classes of greats like violinist Jascha Heifetz and cellist Gregor Piatigorsky. In 1966, he went to master classes at the Bayreuth Festival. In 1968, he won Tanglewood's Koussevitzky Prize. His great moment came in 1969 when, as the youngest assistant conductor of the Boston Symphony, he was called upon to conduct the second part of a New York concert when maestro William Steinberg was suddenly taken ill. In 1970, Tilson Thomas became associate conductor of the Boston Symphony, then principal guest conductor with Colin Davis from 1972 to 1974. He was music director of both the Buffalo Philharmonic (1971–79) and the New York Philharmonic Young Peoples Concerts (1971–76). During the 1980s he appeared with the Los Angeles Philharmonic and the Pittsburgh and New World (Miami) Symphony Orchestras. In 1988 he became principal conductor of the London Symphony. He has guest conducted major orchestras throughout Europe and America. Also an excellent pianist, Tilson Thomas is a modern musician with a repertoire ranging from the Baroque to the avant-garde.

GIUSEPPE SINOPOLI was born in Venice in 1946. Besides taking music courses at the Conservatory there, he studied medicine at the University of Padua and received a degree in psychiatry in 1971. During this time he was studying composition in Paris and conducting at the Vienna Academy with Hans Swarowsky (1899–1975). His conducting career developed with appearances at the Teatro La Fenice in Venice, the Deutsche Oper in Berlin, the Hamburg State Opera, the Vienna State Opera, and Covent Garden, London. In 1985 Sinopoli made his Metropolitan Opera debut and performed with the Santa Cecilia in Rome and the London Philharmonic. In 1990 he became chief conductor of the Dresden Staatskapelle. His training as a psychiatrist makes for interesting interpretations of his repertoire.

GERARD SCHWARZ was born in Weehawken, New Jersey, in 1947. He studied trumpet and finished his training at Juilliard in 1972. He performed with the American Brass Quintet from 1965 to 1973 and the American Symphony Orchestra in New York from 1966 to 1972. After playing trumpet in the New York Philharmonic from 1972 to 1975 he began his conducting career. His first major engagements were the New York Chamber Symphony, beginning in 1977, and the Los Angeles Chamber Orchestra from 1978 to 1986. He was also associated with the

Mostly Mozart Festival in New York from 1980 to 1985. In 1985 Schwarz became principal conductor of the Seattle Symphony. In recognition of his musicianship, he received the 1989 Alice M. Ditson conducting award.

PINCHAS ZUKERMAN was born 1948 in Tel Aviv, and began studying violin at the age of six with his father. He was soon enrolled at the Tel Aviv Conservatory. Heard by superstars violinist Isaac Stern and cellist Pablo Casals, he was encouraged by them to go to Juilliard, where he studied with prominent teacher Ivan Galamian (1903–81). In 1967 he shared first prize in the prestigious Leventritt Competition with Kyung-Wha Chung, after which Zukerman soloed with major American and European orchestras. He has appeared as both violinist and violist in recitals with Isaac Stern and Itzhak Perlman, and guest conducted the New York and Los Angeles Philharmonics, and the Philadelphia and Boston Symphonies. He was music director of the St. Paul (Minnesota) Chamber Orchestra, which he built into a world class ensemble from 1980 to 1987.

RICCARDO CHAILLY was born in 1953 in Milan. He studied composition with his father, Luciano, then went to the Milan Conservatory studying with Franco Caracciolo. He also studied with Franco Ferrara in Siena. From 1972 to 1974 Chailly was assistant conductor of the symphony concerts at La Scala, Milan. His international debut came in 1974 with the Chicago Lyric Opera, conducting *Madama Butterfly*. He subsequently guest conducted the San Francisco Opera, Covent Garden, the Vienna State Opera, and the Met. He was chief conductor of the West Berlin Radio Symphony (1982–89), leading them on their first U.S. tour in 1985. He was principal guest conductor of the London Philharmonic from 1982 to 1985, and artistic director of the Teatro Comunale, Bologna, from 1986 to 1989. In 1988 he became chief conductor of the Concertgebouw, Amsterdam, which was renamed the Royal Concertgebouw by Queen Beatrix of the Netherlands in honor of the one hundredth anniversary of its founding. Chailly is considered one of the leading conductors of his generation, both in the concert hall and the opera pit.

SIMON RATTLE, born in Liverpool in 1955, played piano and percussion as a child, appearing as a percussionist with the Royal Liverpool Philharmonic when he was eleven. While studying conducting at the Royal Academy of Music in London from 1971 to 1974, he founded and conducted the Liverpool Sinfonia. In 1974 he won first prize in the John Player International Conductors' Competition, after which he was made assistant conductor of the Bournemouth Symphony and Bournemouth Sinfonietta. He made his first American tour in 1975, conducting the London Schools Symphony Orchestra. He led the 1977 Glyndebourne Festival, and from 1977 to 1980 was assistant conductor of both the Royal Liverpool Philharmonic and the BBC Scottish Symphony Orchestra in Glasgow. His first appearance with an American Orchestra was with the Los Angeles Philharmonic in 1979. He became their principal guest conductor beginning in 1981. He has also conducted many other U.S. and European Orchestras. In 1980 Rattle was made principal conductor of the City of Birmingham Symphony, leading it in its first American tour in 1988. In 1987 he was made a Commander of the Order of the British Empire.

Esa-Pekka Salonen was born in Helsinki in 1958. He studied horn, composition and conducting at the Sibelius Academy. After appearing as a horn soloist, he started conducting throughout Scandinavia and, later, Europe. His American debut was in 1984 as guest conductor with the Los Angeles Philharmonic. The same year he became principal conductor of the Swedish Radio Symphony in Stockholm, touring with it to the USA. In 1987 he was principal guest conductor of both the Oslo Philharmonic and the Philharmonic Orchestra of London. His 1989 appointment as music director of the Los Angeles Philharmonic began with the 1992 season. Salonen has also composed many orchestral and chamber works.

Honorable Mention

Other eminent conductors include Raymond Leppard (1927–), who has conducted orchestras in his native England, Europe, and the United States. The 1992–93 season marks his sixth as music director of the Indianapolis Symphony Orchestra.

Lawrence Leighton Smith (1936–), in addition to his appearances as an international conductor, also performs as a pianist.

David Zinman (1936–) was assistant to Pierre Monteux (1961–64) and has appeared as guest conductor with various orchestras in North America and Europe.

Andrew Davis (1944–), who, after directing orchestras in Scotland and England, was music director of the Toronto Symphony (1975–88), after which he became chief conductor of the BBC Symphony Orchestra in London and music director of the Glyndebourne Festival.

CHRISTOPHER KEENE (1946–) has gained an international reputation as an opera conductor with productions at San Francisco, San Diego, the Metropolitan, and the Spoleto Festival. In 1989, he became general director of the New York City Opera.

YAN PASCAL TORTELIER (1947–) studied with Nadia Boulanger at age twelve, and won the Paris Conservatory First Prize for violin at fourteen. His conducting career has taken him outside France to England and America. In 1989, he became principal conductor and music director of the Ulster Orchestra in Belfast (Ireland). The 1992 season marked the beginning of his tenure as chief conductor of the BBC Philharmonic in Manchester.

HUGH WOLFF (1953–) was associate conductor of the National Symphony (1982–85), making his European debut with the London Philharmonic in 1983. Principal conductor of the St. Paul Chamber Orchestra from 1988, he was named its music director in 1991. He was music director of the New Jersey Symphony from 1985 to 1992.

Black Conductors

> *Developing a career as a conductor . . .*
> *requires an ego that will blast through*
> *anything. . . . The people who go into*
> *conducting are unstoppable; nothing*
> *discourages them.*
> —Michael Morgan, Director,
> East Bay Oakland Symphony

Long associated with jazz and popular music, black musicians are finding their way into classical music. Many black opera singers have already established themselves: Marian Anderson, Grace Bumbry, Leontyne Price, Martina Arroyo, Jessye Norman, Kathleen Battle, Shirley Verrett, Paul Robeson, William Warfield, Brock Peters, and George Shirley; as have soloists like trumpeter Wynton Marsalis and pianist André Watts. Europe, where race is a trait rather than a stigma, has afforded a rich training ground. Gradually, black conductors are taking their places on the podiums of American symphony orchestras.

JAMES DE PRIEST (1936–), nephew of contralto Marion Anderson, is perhaps our most prominent black conductor. Born in Philadelphia, he studied with Vincent Persichetti at the Conservatory there, obtaining a

B.S. and M.A. degree. He conducted the Philadelphia Contemporary Music Guild from 1959 to 1962. The same year he contracted polio on a State Department tour in Bangkok, but recovered sufficiently to win a first place in the 1964 Dimitri Mitropoulos International Conducting Competition.

From 1967 to 1970 De Priest lived in the Netherlands, where he made his highly acclaimed debut with the Rotterdam Philharmonic in 1969. The same year he was awarded a Martha Baird Rockefeller grant. Concerts followed in Amsterdam, Stockholm, Berlin, Munich, Stuttgart, Belgium, and Italy. In 1971 conductor Antal Dorati (1906–88) chose DePriest as Associate Conductor of the National Symphony, Washington, D.C. From 1976 to 1983 he was Music Director of the Quebec Symphony, Canada's oldest orchestra. In 1980, he assumed his position as Music Director of the Oregon Symphony in Portland, which he has guided into the ranks of the majors. During the summers of 1990, 1991, and 1992 he was music director of Oregon's Peter Britt Festival. His appointment as principal conductor of the Malmö (Sweden) Symphony Orchestra began with the 1991–92 season. The 1994–95 season will mark the beginning of his tenure as Music Director of the Monte Carlo Philharmonic. Much in demand as a guest conductor both here and abroad, De Priest has also ventured into the realm of literature with the publication of two books of poetry.

HENRY LEWIS (1932–), after playing double bass in the Los Angeles Philharmonic from 1955 to 1959, went overseas with the 7th Army Symphony and began his directing career conducting this orchestra in Germany and the Netherlands. Returning to the U.S. in 1963, he founded the Los Angeles Chamber Orchestra, with whom he toured under the auspices of the State Department. He was musical director of the New Jersey Symphony from 1968 to 1976. In 1989 he became chief conductor of the Radio Symphony Orchestra in Hilversum, Netherlands.

PAUL FREEMAN (1936–) had his musical training at the Eastman School of Music and the Hochschule für Musik in Berlin. Returning to this country in 1959, he took conducting lessons from Pierre Monteux and became conductor of the Opera Theater of Rochester from 1961 to 1966, the San Francisco Conservatory Orchestra (1966–67), and the San Francisco Little Symphony (1967–68). From 1968 to 1970 he was associate conductor of the Dallas Symphony, then resident conductor at Detroit (1970–79). He also served as principal guest conductor of the Helsinki, Finland, Philharmonic (1974–76), and conducted the Black Composers series for Columbia Records (1974–77). In 1979, he became music director of the Victoria, British Columbia, Symphony. In 1987 he founded the Chicago Sinfonietta, a chamber orchestra composed of 55 percent women and 25 percent minorities playing to subscription audiences, of which a large percentage are African-American.

ISAIAH JACKSON (1945–) majored in Russian studies at Harvard, (B.A. 1966). He then studied conducting at Stanford (M.A. 1967), composition with Nadia Boulanger at the American Conservatory in Fontainebleau, and at Juilliard (M.S. 1969, D.M.A. 1973). He was founder-conductor of the Juilliard String Ensemble (1970–71), assistant conductor of the Baltimore Symphony (1971–73), and associate conductor of the Rochester Philharmonic (1973–87). He has held the position of music director with the Flint, Michigan, Symphony (1982–87), the Royal Ballet, Covent Garden, London, and the Dayton, Ohio, Philharmonic—the last two from 1987. Jackson has been named principal guest conductor of the Queensland (Australia) Symphony.

RAYMOND HARVEY (1952–) has been music director of the Springfield, Massachusetts, Symphony since 1986. He held associate positions in Buffalo and Indianapolis, and has an active guest conducting schedule which includes appearances with the symphonies of Minnesota, Detroit, and the New York Philharmonic.

MICHAEL MORGAN (1957–), while still a teenager, wrote to James DePriest, then in Washington, asking to be admitted to the National Symphony rehearsals. At nineteen, the youngest recipient of a Tanglewood Conducting Fellowship, he studied with Leonard Bernstein, Seiji Ozawa, and Gunther Schuller. At twenty-three he became assistant to Leonard Slatkin at the St. Louis Symphony. In 1986, Morgan was named assistant conductor of the Chicago Symphony under Sir Georg Solti. He is also director of the Oakland East Bay Symphony.

Other black assistant and associate conductors are Leslie Dunner (Detroit), André Smith (St. Louis), Harvey Felder (Milwaukee), and twenty-eight-year-old William Eddins, who took the Los Angeles Philharmonic to that city's riot-scarred south central minority district in March 1991, and was exhilarated at the response to classical music.

Baton Twirling Around the World

The modern generation of conductors has generally sloughed off the mantle of theatricalism and is dedicated to and serious about making music of the highest quality.

The jet age has reduced the size of the world to a neighborhood. Today's maestros flit from one engagement to the next, creating a depthless talent pool, vying for and enticing away from their CD players the sometimes elusive, and definitely more discriminating, audiences of today.

*Conducting has been the last bastion to
fall for women because it addresses the
issue of authority. It will take time for
women to become comfortable, and for
men to become used to responding to
them in this role.*

—Kate Tamarkin
Associate Conductor,
Dallas Symphony

CHAPTER TWENTY-SIX

Women on the Podium

T he history of women conductors can be traced to the spate of
American all-women orchestras being formed around the same time as
the founding of the three major conservatories, the Eastman School
(1921), the Curtis Institute (1924), and Juilliard (1924). Many female
musicians were seeking careers other than teaching. With the exception
of the Los Angeles Woman's Orchestra, founded in 1893, most female
ensembles were spawned in the 1920s and 1930s: in Philadelphia,
Chicago (2), Boston (3), New York (4), Long Beach (California), Portland (Oregon), Cleveland, Pittsburgh, Stockton (California), Baltimore,
St. Louis, Mason City (Iowa), and Minneapolis; followed by Montreal in
1940, and Detroit in 1941. Besides featuring compositions by women,

these aggregations gave opportunities to women instrumentalists and conductors, one of the earliest being CAROLINE NICHOLS, who directed the Boston Fadette Lady Orchestra 1888–1920.

The advent of talking pictures in 1928 eliminated the theater ensembles that accompanied the silents, and the Depression in the 1930s forced hotels, restaurants, and resorts to dispense with live orchestras. To help the jobless, thirty-six orchestras were funded by President Franklin D. Roosevelt's Works Progress Administration (WPA). Some women found employment with them, while others staffed the twenty all-female orchestras in existence at the time. A few were able to storm all-male strongholds. In 1935, Elsa Hilger was admitted to the cello section of the Philadelphia Orchestra, and a woman violinist got in the following season. In 1937, Ellen Stone, French horn, was accepted by Pittsburgh and two women string players made it into the Los Angeles Philharmonic by 1938, the year that the National Federation of Music Clubs asked that all auditions take place behind screens to combat "unjust discrimination." (The idea was not really put into general practice until the 1960s.)

World War II brought more openings in orchestras as men were drafted. Most women orchestras disbanded after the war, but the Detroit survived until 1971. The Cleveland Women's Orchestra remains the sole survivor. Founded in 1935 by Hyman Schandler, who served as their conductor for fifty-six years until his death at age ninety in 1990, the orchestra is now under the direction of his colleague, Robert L. Cronquist, and is part of the 100th Anniversary celebration of the 1893 Chicago Columbian Exposition—the first World's Fair to officially recognize women's achievements. (Violist Sabine Berman, has been in the orchestra from its inception, and in 1991, three generations—a grandmother, mother, and two daughters—were all members.)

The following women conductors achieved fame and recognition, some by sheer force of personality, others by slipping in the "back door" through their performance reputation, and all by a superior talent that could not be denied by their male counterparts.

Canadian born GENA BRANSCOMBE (1881–1977) organized the Branscombe Chorale, a women's chorus, in 1934, which she directed for the next twenty years. In 1941, she was chosen to conduct a chorus of one thousand voices for the Golden Jubilee celebration of women's achievements. Also a composer, she wrote choral works, a symphonic suite, and over 150 songs. Active and energetic throughout her long life,

Branscombe was working on her autobiography when she died at age ninety-five.

ETHEL LEGINSKA (1886–1970) as Ethel Leggins, at age fourteen ran away from her home in England and went to Vienna to study piano. At sixteen she made her debut in London, concertized in Europe, and came to America in 1913. Studying with Ernst Bloch in 1918, she composed two operas, songs, symphonic poems, and piano and chamber music. In 1923 she switched her career to conducting, studied with Eugene Goossens (1897–1988), and established herself as one of the first female conductors to direct major orchestras in Europe. The year 1925 saw her American debuts with the New York Symphony and the Hollywood Bowl Orchestra. In the 1920s Leginska led the Boston Symphony, the Boston Women's Symphony, and the Women's Symphony Orchestra of Chicago. During the 1930s she conducted at major European and American opera houses. She retired to Los Angeles in 1940 and taught piano into the 1950s.

NADIA BOULANGER (1887–1979) was one of the world's greatest composition teachers. Both her father and grandfather had taught at the Paris Conservatory. At the Conservatory she studied with Gabriel Fauré. Feeling her sister Lili to be the superior composer, Boulanger devoted herself to teaching, gaining international renown by having three generations of composers as her students. She was the first woman to conduct the Boston Symphony, Philadelphia Orchestra, and New York Philharmonic. She gave the world premiere of Stravinsky's *Dumbarton Oaks* chamber concerto in Washington, D.C., in 1938. Her ninetieth birthday was celebrated with tributes from all over the world.

ANTONIA BRICO (1902–89) was the first American to graduate from the Hochschule für Musik in Berlin. In 1932, with Hitler becoming a threat to foreigners, Brico returned to an America at the height of the Depression. In 1934, with backers like Eleanor Roosevelt, Bruno Walter, and Mayor Fiorello LaGuardia, she organized the New York Women's Symphony Orchestra. In 1938 she became the first woman to conduct the New York Philharmonic and other major orchestras. After two performances with the Met, however, she was dismissed because baritone John Charles Thomas (1891–1960) refused to sing under a woman.

The two idols of her life were Albert Schweitzer and Jean Sibelius, both of whom she made special pilgrimages to meet. After 1937, there was an almost four-decade "suspension" to her career due to the influential Mrs. Charles S. Guggenheim, who felt that it was a "disgrace" for a woman to conduct the New York Philharmonic!

In 1942 Brico moved to Denver, directed the Denver Businessmen's Orchestra for the next thirty years (renamed the Brico Symphony in 1969), and established her reputation as a teacher of voice, piano, and conducting. In 1974, her pupil, folksinger Judy Collins, co-produced a documentary film, *Antonia,* which pleaded the cause for women in music and brought Brico back to the podium at age seventy-two. In observance of the International Year of the Woman, in August 1975, Antonia Brico conducted the National Symphony and was honored at the Kennedy Center.

FREDERIQUE PETRIDES (1903–83), of Belgium, was given the best musical education and was acquainted with the living legends of her time: Fritz Kreisler, Camille Saint-Saëns, Pablo Casals, Andrés Segovia, Alfred Cortot, Alexander Brailowsky, and Isadora Duncan. She came to America in 1923, and founded her own women's symphony, the Orchestrette Classique, which for twelve years performed with great success. Petrides married, and her daughter inherited the perfect pitch possessed by four generations of her family. During the 1930s and 1940s, Petrides founded the Hudson Valley Symphony Orchestra, which she conducted for seven seasons—some five decades later it still continues to perform. In 1958 and 1960 Petrides organized a series of outdoor concerts in Manhattan, which she directed until 1975. Her combination programming of new music with little-known classical compositions made a unique contribution to the American concert scene.

MARGARET HILLIS (1921–) was inspired to become a conductor when at age ten she saw John Philip Sousa. Advised to pursue choral conducting, she studied at Juilliard and became the assistant to Robert Shaw. In 1950 she founded the American Concert Choir and American Concert Orchestra, beginning a long series of brilliant concerts, television programs, and recordings. In 1957 Fritz Reiner asked her to organize the Chicago Symphony Orchestra Chorus. Now into its fourth decade under her directorship, it is considered America's finest professional choral group and has toured with the Symphony to Kennedy Center, Carnegie Hall, and Europe.

Hillis captured nationwide attention when on October 31, 1977 Georg Solti suffered a fall and she stepped in to conduct the Chicago Symphony, the Chorus, and other choral forces in what critics hailed a stunning performance of Mahler's monumental Symphony No. 8.

SARAH CALDWELL (1924–) formed her own opera company in 1965. She managed to persuade top opera stars to lend their talents, among them Beverly Sills, Marilyn Horne, and Placido Domingo. Her 1976 debut at the Met of *La Traviata* (her three hundred-pound girth required her to conduct sitting in a chair) was hailed as a social milestone, and for a while she was treated as a national treasure. Financial problems and ill-health caused the decline of her career.

DALIA ATLAS (1935–), a graduate of the Rubin Academy in Jerusalem, never veered from her childhood dream of becoming a conductor. She studied with famous conductors in Italy and America and won many competitions. She has directed prominent orchestras throughout the world and has made a significant contribution to music in Israel, where she is founder of the Pro-Musica Orchestra, the Technion Symphony, Choir, and Opera, and the Atlas Camarata.

EVE QUELER (1936–), after studies with Carl Bamberger, Walter Susskind, Igor Markevitch, and Herbert Blomstedt, became assistant conductor, rehearsal pianist, and coach at the New York City Opera (1965–70). In 1967 she made history with the founding of the Opera Orchestra of New York, which gives young singers and instrumentalists performance experience without the expense of staging and scenery. (Her innovation—of which she is still the director—has been copied worldwide.)

After becoming the first woman to hold a full-time conductorship as well as to guest conduct many major orchestras, she made her European opera debut with Verdi's *I Vespri Siciliani,* with Placido Domingo and Monserrat Caballé.

It was Queler who introduced Czech opera *sung in its native language* with Smetana's *Dalibor* in 1978, followed by Janáček's *Kat'a Kabanova* and *Jenůfa.* In 1987 she was the first person to conduct Dvořák's *Rusalka* in Czech in the United States. She is a pioneer in exploring repertoire never before staged or recorded.

JUDITH SOMOGI (1937–88), after studying at Juilliard, became assistant to Thomas Schippers at the Spoleto Festival, and to Leopold Stokowski at the American Symphony Orchestra. Joining the New York City Opera in 1966, she made her conducting debut with *The Mikado* in 1974. She went on to conduct many operas and major symphony orchestras in the United States. Her European debut in Germany was with Mozart's *The Abduction From the Seraglio* at the Saarbrücken Opera (1979). In 1984 Somogi became the first woman to conduct in a major Italian opera house when she directed Gluck's *Orfeo ed Euridice* at the Teatro La Fenice in Venice. After conducting *Madama Butterfly* at the Frankfurt Opera in 1981, she became its first woman principal conductor (1982–87). Her promising career was tragically cut short by her death from cancer in 1988.

CATHERINE COMET (1944–), born in Fontainebleau, France, decided to become a conductor at age four. Nadia Boulanger accepted her as a student at twelve. She received her piano baccalaureate at fifteen. In New York, her teachers at Juilliard were Igor Markevitch (1912–83), Jean Fournet (1913–) and Pierre Boulez (1925–). Returning to France, Comet began her career with the Ballet Company of the Paris Opera. Offered a lifetime tenure, she instead married an American, moved to this country, and had a daughter in 1976.

In 1978, Comet began directing the University of Wisconsin (at Madison) Symphony and Chamber Orchestras, moving on in 1981 to an assistant conductorship with the St. Louis Symphony. After becoming Associate Conductor of the Baltimore Symphony (1984–86), her next appointment was heading the Grand Rapids (Michigan) Symphony, to which orchestra she has brought national recognition.

Comet was also Music Director of New York's American Symphony Orchestra (1989–92). Her guest schedule includes appearances with major orchestras here and in Europe.

VICTORIA BOND (1945–) studied with Roger Sessions, Jean Morel, Sixten Ehrling, Leonard Slatkin, Herbert Blomstedt and Herbert von Karajan. She is credited with a series of firsts: first woman appointed Exxon/Arts Endowment Conductor with a major orchestra, the Pittsburgh Symphony, where she worked with André Previn; first woman to graduate with a doctorate in conducting from Juilliard (Catherine Comet completed the equivalent amount of work in 1963, before there was a doctoral program); and first woman to receive a conducting grant from the National Institute for Music Theater to work at the New York City Opera. In 1986 she was appointed Music Director of the Roanoke Symphony and in 1990 artistic director of Opera Roanoke.

Bond champions American composers and has amassed a sizable repertoire of her own compositions including chamber, choral, piano, and orchestral works, concertos, and theater music. An April 3, 1993, premiere commission from the Women's Philharmonic is her alto saxophone concerto, *Urban Bird,* based on tunes of jazz musicians Charlie Parker and John Coltrane. Bond has made guest appearances with leading orchestras in the United States and Europe.

JOANN FALLETTA (1954–) entered the conducting program at the

Mannes College of Music in her late teens. In 1982 Falletta won the Bruno Walter Award, a full scholarship to Juilliard, where she earned her master's and doctorate in orchestral conducting. She became musical director of the Denver Chamber Orchestra in 1983, won the Stokowski Conducting Competition in 1985, and the Exxon/Arts Endowment Associate Conductorship with the Milwaukee Symphony under Lukas Foss the same year—a position she held for three seasons.

In 1986 she was engaged as Music Director of the Women's Philharmonic in San Francisco, which promotes the music of women composers. In 1989 the conductor was hired by the Long Beach Symphony, making her the first American-born woman ever appointed to the leadership of a regional orchestra. In 1991 she was named director of the Virginia Symphony Orchestra. Falletta's guest appearances have taken her to Canada and Europe, as well as many leading orchestras in this country.

Across the Atlantic

There are several prominent women conductors in Europe. From England, IONA BROWN (1941–), after her violin debut at thirteen, studied in Rome, Brussels, and Vienna. In 1964 she joined the Academy of St. Martin-in-the-Fields, becoming stand-partner with its director, Sir Neville Marriner. In 1974, he offered her the directorship of the Academy's string ensemble. Following Sir Neville's example, Iona conducts from the concertmaster's chair while playing her violin—a custom from the Baroque era. In 1981, Brown became Artistic Director of the Norwegian Chamber Orchestra, with whom she has toured Europe and the United States. From 1987 to 1992, she was music director of the Los Angeles Chamber Orchestra, and continues as their Principal Guest Director. Brown has directed other major U.S. orchestras.

As both director and soloist, Brown has an impressive discography. She was awarded the prestigious Order of the British Empire (OBE) for services to music in the 1986 Queen's Honours List. She has also been honored by the King of Norway with an award of Knight of the First Class of the Order of Merit, in recognition of her contribution to Norway's musical life.

JANE GLOVER (1949–) received her Ph. D. from Oxford in 1978. Her conducting debut came in 1975. In 1980 she became chorus master at the Glyndebourne Festival, and from 1982 to 1985 was music director of their Touring Opera. As artistic director of the London Mozart Players (1984–91) she expanded their repertoire to include contemporary works. Opera debuts were in Covent Garden, 1988, and the Canadian Opera, 1991. In 1992 Glover conducted the English National Opera and gave concerts with major orchestras in Britain, on the continent, and in New Zealand. She is artistic director of the 1993 Buxton International Festival.

With her special affinity for great English choral works, Glover appears regularly with major choral groups and is principal conductor of both the London Choral Society and the Huddersfield Choral Society.

ODALINE DE LA MARTINEZ (1949–) studied at the Royal Academy of Music from 1972 to 1976, the same year she founded the London chamber ensemble *Lontano,* which she conducts worldwide in programs of contemporary music. She is also founder-conductor of the Contemporary Chamber Orchestra (1982). In 1988 the Brazilian government awarded her the Villa-Lobos Medal in recognition of her outstanding work in promoting and conducting his music. In the summer of 1989 she was co-director with Eduardo Mata of the South Bank Centre's Latin American Festival. De la Martinez made her New York debut in January 1990 and was honored the same year as a Fellow of the Royal Academy of Music. In April of 1992, she formed LORELT, Lontano Records Ltd., to concentrate on neglected areas of music. She has also composed two operas *Sister Aimée* and *Esperanza,* as well as orchestral and chamber music. De la Martinez is much in demand as guest conductor in Britain and abroad.

SIAN EDWARDS (1959–), after graduation from the Royal Northern College of Music, studied with renowned conductors Sir Charles Groves, Norman Del Mar, and Neeme Järvi. From 1983 to 1985, she was a student at the Leningrad Conservatory and during this time won the first Leeds (England) Conductors' Competition.

Since returning to Britain in 1985, Edwards has worked with many of the country's leading orchestras. Her operatic conducting debut was the 1986 production of Weill's *Mahagonny* for Scottish Opera. In 1988 she received a three-year association contract with the Royal Opera House, Covent Garden. From 1989 to 1990 her debuts included the Orchestre de Paris, St. Paul Chamber Orchestra, English National Opera, and San Francisco Symphony. There was also a nationwide tour of Australia in 1990. The year 1991 marked her debut with the Los Angeles Philharmonic, and 1992 saw concerts throughout Europe and Russia. More concerts in Europe and America are in store.

Besides her world status as a conductor, Sian Edwards's recordings are receiving high critical praise.

From Sea to Shining Sea

Several other women conductors are directing local orchestras. In Alaska, MADELINE SCHATZ (1947–), an accomplished violinist and violist, five-time Grand Prize winner in the International Coleman Chamber Music Competition, and former member of the Los Angeles Philharmonic, Los Angeles Chamber Symphony, and California Chamber Symphony, is now Music Director and Conductor of the Fairbanks Symphony and Arctic Chamber Orchestra, as well as holding the position of Professor of Music at the University of Fairbanks.

In San Diego, KAREN KELTNER (1947–), a student of Nadia Boulanger, has been associate conductor and music administrator at the San Diego Opera since 1982. Hers was the first conducting apprenticeship ever awarded by the National Opera Institute.

DORIS LANG KOSLOFF 1947–), after the path of the Lang sisters duopiano team diverged, became the principal conductor of the Waterbury (Connecticut) Opera Theater (1987–90).

RACHAEL WORBY (1949–), as a child seated in the Carnegie Hall audience of the Young People's Concerts, idolized Leonard Bernstein. Since 1984, she has held Bernstein's position as conductor of these concerts.

Her professional career began in 1982 with the Spokane Symphony. Since then she has led many major orchestras in the United States. On television, she created, narrated, and conducted the Pittsburgh Symphony in the series, "Disney's Young People's Guide to Music." She also appeared on PBS's "Carnegie Hall at 100: A Place of Dreams."

Chosen in 1986, from many applicants, to become conductor of the Wheeling, West Virginia, Symphony, Worby's performances have tripled season ticket sales. In a mini-Princess Grace fairy tale, Worby was introduced in 1989 to the newly elected state governor, Gaston Caperton. They were married May 25, 1990. In her position as First Lady, Rachael Worby Caperton has opened the governor's mansion to writers, musicians, and artists with her West Virginia Artists Series, re-creating the European *salon*.

KAY GEORGE ROBERTS (1950–) is the first woman to receive a Yale doctorate in orchestral conducting. She is the founder and conductor of a new chamber orchestra, Ensemble Americana, which promotes contemporary American music by black, Hispanic, and other minority composers. A professor of music and conductor of the orchestra at the University of Massachusetts at Lowell, Roberts is also a conductor of the Black Music Repertory Ensemble, a professional group showcasing classical repertoire by black composers from the 1800s to the present.

KATE TAMARKIN (1955–) began her conducting career with the Fox Valley, Appelton, Wisconsin Symphony. Being chosen by Leonard Bernstein as one of three young conductors to work with him at the American Symphony Orchestra League Conference in 1988, she got to conduct in front of an audience of two thousand symphony orchestra managers! A call came from Texas the next week, and since 1989 Tamarkin has been associate conductor of the Dallas Symphony. In May 1991, at the invitation of the City of Dallas, she had the honor of performing for Queen Elizabeth II on her American tour. In 1991, Tamarkin also became conductor of the Vermont Symphony, and 1992 marked her first season as music director of the East Texas Symphony. She has guest conducted with other American orchestras, including the Women Composers' Orchestra of Baltimore, for whom she served as Music Director. The 1992–93 season marked debuts with the Houston, Nashville, and Phoenix Symphonies.

GISÉLE BEN-DOR (1955–), born in Uruguay, has conducted since she was twelve. After living in Israel, she came to the United States in 1980 and received her master's degree in conducting from Yale. She made a sensational debut in 1982, leading the Israel Philharmonic in Stravinsky's *The Rite of Spring*, which was taped by the BBC in London and broadcast throughout Europe. She directs the Philharmonic and other Israeli orchestras on a regular basis.

Her American career began in 1984 when she was selected as a conducting fellow at the Los Angeles Philharmonic Institute. A year later Ben-Dor received the same honor at the Tanglewood Music Center, where she and Leonard Bernstein shared a special concert celebrating Aaron Copland's eighty-fifth birthday. In 1986 Ben-Dor won the Bartók Prize of the Hungarian Television International Conductor's Competition, and was invited to conduct at the 1987 Bartók Festival as well as with several other orchestras in Eastern Europe.

From 1989 to 1991 she was Resident Conductor of the Houston Symphony, leading that orchestra at Kennedy Center, Washington, D.C., at the 1989 Presidential Inauguration. Ben-Dor made her Carnegie Hall debut in February 1991, during the Hall's 100th Anniversary celebration. The same year she was appointed Musical Director of the Boston ProArte Chamber Orchestra and the Annapolis Symphony. Her active schedule lists directing invitations from Belgium, Holland, Ireland, Brazil, Israel, and throughout the United States.

MARIN ALSOP (1956–) at age seven saw Leonard Bernstein on the podium and chose her career. Her parents are professional musicians— her father, concertmaster, and her mother a violinist in the New York City Ballet Orchestra. Marin attended Yale and Juilliard, where she worked with Herbert von Karajan.

An avid jazz violinist, in 1981 Alsop founded an all-female fourteen-piece swing band named "Spring Fever." In 1984 she formed her own unique sixty-piece chamber orchestra, Concordia, which combines classical repertoire with American jazz and twentieth-century works. In 1988 and 1989, as a conducting fellow at Tanglewood, Alsop studied with Leonard Bernstein and is considered his protégée.

Alsop was the first woman to be awarded the Koussevitzky Conducting Prize. She also won the Leopold Stokowski Conducting Competition sponsored by the American Symphony Orchestra. In 1990, she became the first woman to conduct the Boston Pops Orchestra in its 107-year existence, and was immediately re-engaged. In 1991, she was the first woman to conduct subscription concerts with the Los Angeles Philharmonic.

Alsop is in her second season as Music Director of the Cabrillo Music Festival in California, her third as Music Director of the Long Island Philharmonic, and fourth as Music Director of the Eugene (Oregon) Symphony. In the summer of 1992, she became the founder/director of the Oregon Festival of American Music. She has gained a reputation as one of America's leading young conductors.

BARBARA YAHR (1958–) first conducted at age twenty in Paris. In 1988 she was a winner in the Affiliate Artist conducting competition, the video of which inspired Lorin Maazel to invite her to join the Pittsburgh Symphony as Resident Staff Director. Her 1993 subscription series debut marked the premieres of American composer Conrad Susa's (1935–) *Rhapsody for Flute and Orchestra*, and Morton Gould's (1913–) *The Jogger and the Dinosaur*. Yahr also accompanied Maestro Maazel as assistant conductor for the Shira Festival in Elat, Israel

(December 1992–January 1993). She has appeared with many orchestras throughout the U.S. and Canada.

Forward to Tradition

Just as the Cleveland Women's Orchestra is a vestige from the past, so the WOMEN'S PHILHARMONIC, founded in 1971 and led by JoAnn Falletta, is the trend of the present and the gateway to the future. In June 1992, in recognition of its accomplishments, the orchestra received its Ninth annual awards from ASCAP and the American Orchestra League. Recognized as the only professional orchestra dedicated to women composers, conductors, and performance, its goal is to incorporate women's compositions into the repertoire of *all* orchestras.

A vital adjunct to the Philharmonic is the National Women Composers Resource Center, which arranges commissions, reconstructs historical masterworks, and provides research and information to orchestras and scholars worldwide.

Listening to classical music is like
reading an exciting book without
having to come to an ending.
—Accompanist Nura Haas (1909–)

AFTERWORD

Mystique Immortelle

There is no true definition of music. To Confucius (551–479 B.C.) it is "a kind of pleasure which human nature cannot do without." Plato (*c*428–347 B.C.) observed that "rhythm and harmony find their way into the secret places of the soul;" while Archbishop Isidore of Seville (A.D. 568–636) declared: "Nothing exists without music." For German philosopher/poet Friedrich Nietsche (1844–1900), "Without music, life would be a mistake."

Physiologically, traditional classical music has been proven beneficial to one's health in that its very vibrations can elicit healing chemistry from the brain. Every function of the body—heart action, pulse, circulation, respiration, and nerve and muscle response—is affected by music. Even before birth, babies react to music, as do animals. According to the Bible, David could, by playing his lyre, calm the "evil spirit" (depression) that came upon King Saul. The link, of course, is that all music—for better or worse—affects the emotions which, in turn, trigger physiological responses. Music therapy used by the ancient Chinese,

317

Hindus, Persians, Egyptians, and Greeks is coming back into vogue and credibility. The very act of playing an instrument helps motor-sensory co-ordination. Statistics showing the longevity of conductors indicate that the combination of physical activity demanded by their profession, plus the emotional effect caused by their being continually surrounded by music, contribute to their long lives.

Socially, music has molded civilizations for thousands of years. The decline of music in Egypt and Greece was followed by their decline as a society. The enlightenment of the Renaissance spilled into all facets of creativity and uplifted humanity from the Dark and Middle Ages. The zenith was reached in the Romantic period when the bulk of the most popular* classical music was written. Our century has witnessed a revolution in music with Impressionism, serialism, minimalism, and electronic and computer music in the classical field, and ragtime, jazz, blues, swing, and rock in all its forms evolving in the popular category.

The question listeners must decide for themselves is what is pleasing to their ears. The purpose of music is to uplift the spirit. Early composers felt their compositions were both to and from God. When writing his massive oratorio *Messiah* in just three weeks, Handel maintained, "I think I did see all Heaven before me and the great God Himself." Almost a century later, Robert Schumann claimed that his music was dictated by angels. Puccini felt touched by God's little finger. How far from these lofty ideals has avant-garde and experimental music strayed? And what of rock? Besides its deafening qualities, does its incessant beat, so out of sync with our bodies' natural rhythms, cause the physio-psychic turmoil that has been cited as leading to the drug culture, violence, and moral decay of today's society? We need only to look at the state of our world to find the answer.

But there is always hope. American poet Henry Wadsworth Long-fellow (1807–82) told us what we have always known: "Music is the universal language of mankind"—which indeed it is, for all musicians from every corner of the earth can read the same notation. Even more optimistic is the prediction made a hundred years earlier by French playwright Molière (1622–73): "Were all men to learn music, this would be a means . . . of seeing universal peace reign over the world."

As a universal language, music knows no political barriers, dissolves international borders, and creates instead new frontiers which make our world more familiar while at the same time broadening our horizons.

---

* As corroborated by today's sales of classical recordings and concert tickets.

On a personal level, each of us evoke unique feelings about music and create our own repertoire of favorites. When we are part of an audience we become united in what can be a sublime experience, which is why there is no substitute for the excitement of a live performance.

Pierre Boulez (1925–), French conductor, composer, and pianist, confirms the reason we never tire of our classical legacy: "Music . . . is a labyrinth with no beginning and no end, full of new paths to discover, where mystery remains eternal."

Appendix A

The World's Most Popular Symphonies

Beethoven: No. 5, No. 6 "Pastoral", No. 7, No. 9 "Choral"
Tchaikovsky: No. 4, No. 5, No. 6 "Pathétique"
Schubert: No. 6, No. 8, "Unfinished", No. 9 "Great"
Mozart: No. 40, No. 41 "Jupiter", No. 29
Mahler: No. 1 "Titan", No. 5 (Adagietto—second mov't)
Brahms: No. 1, No. 2, No. 3, No. 4 (all of them!)
Dvořák: No. 9 "From the New World", No. 8
Franck: Symphony in D minor
Mendelssohn: No. 3 "Italian"
Prokofiev: "Classical" Symphony
Rimsky-Koraskov: "Antar" Symphony
Kalinnikov: No. 1
Schumann: No. 1 "Spring", No. 3 "Rhenish"
Goldmark: "Rustic Wedding" Symphony
Bizet: Symphony in C (his only one)
Saint-Saëns: No. 3 "Organ"
Rachmaninoff: No. 2
Bruckner: No. 4 "Romantic"
Borodin: No. 2
Sibelius: No. 2
Berlioz: Symphonie Fantastique, 2nd mov't
Haydn: No. 88 (Compare last movement with Schubert No. 6)
Shostakovich: No. 5 (This is a challenge!)

Appendix B

CELLO

Dvořák: B minor
Saint-Saëns: No. 1—A minor
Schumann: A minor
Elgar: E minor

OTHER INSTRUMENTS

Haydn: Trumpet—E flat Major
Mozart: Flute and Harp—C major, Clarinet—A major, 4 French Horn
  Concertos
von Weber: Clarinet No. 1—F minor
Rodrigo: Concierto de Aranjuez, for Guitar
Castelnuovo-Tedesco: Guitar Concerto

Glossary

absolute music Instrumental music having no intended association with story, poem, idea, or scene; nonprogram music.

a cappella Choral music performed without orchestral accompaniment.

accelerando Becoming faster in tempo.

accent Emphasis of a note to make its pitch louder or longer than the notes near it.

accompaniment Musical background. A solo singer or instrumentalist may be accompanied by a pianist or orchestra. In piano music, left-hand chords usually provide accompaniment to the right-hand melody.

adagietto Slightly faster than *adagio*.

adagio Slow (between *andante* and *largo*). Also used as a heading for the second movement of traditional symphonies and sonatas.

aerophone Any instrument (flute, trumpet, etc.) whose sound is generated by a vibrating column of air.

affettuoso Affectionate, with tenderness.

agitato Agitated, excited, restless.

air (Baroque) A melodic song or instrumental piece.

aleatory music Composed by random selection of pitch, rhythm, and tone color—developed in the 1950s by John Cage and others.

allergando Broadening or slowing the tempo.

allegretto Fairly fast—slower than *allegro*.

allegro Fast and lively; *moderato* (moderately fast); *ma non troppo* (but not too fast).

andante Fairly slow, between *allegretto* and *adagio*.

andantino A little faster than *andante*.

appassionato With passion.

aria An elaborate song, usually for solo voice. Used in opera to show off the singer's virtuosity.

arpeggio Sounding notes of a chord in sequence, instead of together.

art song (Romantic) A poem set to music for solo voice and piano. German: *lied(er)* of Schubert, Schumann, Brahms, and Richard Strauss. French: *chanson* of Fauré, Debussy, etc.

assai (Italian) Very, e.g., *Allegro assai*: very fast.

atonal Music without a definite key. Originated by Schoenberg and characteristic of some twentieth-century composers.

ballad A song relating an adventurous or romantic event.

ballade (French) A dramatic instrumental or piano work, as used by Chopin, Brahms, Fauré, and others.

band A large ensemble of wind and brass instruments.

bar See *measure*.

baritone Male voice between *tenor* and *bass*.

baroque Musical period from 1600 to 1750. The term describes elegantly structured art and architecture, as well as music.

bass The lowest male voice, also the largest stringed instrument.

bass clef Symbol on music staff for low pitch range, used by cellos, double basses, and pianists' left hands.

basso continuo Baroque accompaniment played by one or more bass instruments and keyboard (harpsichord, clavichord, piano).

basso ostinato Baroque variation form in which the bass is constantly repeated while the melodic line changes.

beat The unit of time in metric music. The upper numeral in the time signatures indicates the number of beats per measure.

bel canto Beautiful singing—an Italian lyrical vocal style developed in the 18th century characterized by ease and brilliance rather than dramatic passion.

bitonal The simultaneous use of two different keys, often found in twentieth-century music.

blues A style of jazz related to "blue" notes, which are either flatted or played out of tune. Usually slow and sad in mood.

brass Instruments made of brass or silver whose sound is produced by vibrations of the lip.

bravura Brilliant, dashing style.

bridge The connecting passage (transition) between two major themes of a composition.

   The wooden structure on stringed instruments that supports the strings between the scroll and the tail piece.

brio Spirited.

broken chord See *arpeggio*.

buffa, buffo Refers to Italian comic opera or a character therein.

cacophony A mixture of discordant sounds.

cadence The harmonic or melodic progression that concludes a phrase, section, or composition.

cadenza Unaccompanied section of a concerto displaying the soloist's technical mastery of his instrument.

Camerata (Italian) *fellowship* or *society*; a group of nobles, poets, and composers who met regularly in Florence around 1575 and whose musical discussions led to the beginning of opera.

canon Contrapuntal form in which the melodic line of one part is imitated by another part at fixed intervals, like a *round* ("Row, Row, Row Your Boat").

cantata A choral work containing *arias*, *recitatives*, and *choruses*, with orchestral accompaniment (a mini-*oratorio*).

cantus firmus A melody serving as the basis for polyphonic music in the Middle Ages and Renaissance.

capriccio A composition of capricious or humorous character.

castrato Male singer castrated before puberty to retain a high vocal range; a most important soloist before women gained prominence in opera.

cavatina A simple, short solo usually found in eighteenth- or nineteenth-century operas or oratorios.

chaconne A stately dance of Spanish origin, written in triple time, containing a set of *variations*.

chamber music Music employing a small group of musicians, with one player to a part. A *chamber orchestra* usually has about twenty-five members in contrast to the eighty or more players in a symphony orchestra.

chance music see *aleatory*.

chanson (French) Song.

chant A religious or liturgical song, e.g., Gregorian chant.

choir A vocal ensemble. Also used for instrument groups (e.g., woodwind choir, brass choir).

choral Pertaining to a choir or chorus.

chorale Hymn tune sung to a German religious text.

chorale prelude An organ composition based on a Protestant hymn. Originally, the introduction for the congregation, it became an important form in the hands of Bach, Mendelssohn, and others.

chord Combination of three or more tones sounded at once.

chordophone An instrument (harp, guitar, violin, etc.,) whose sound is generated by stretched strings.

chorus A large vocal ensemble. In popular music, the refrain to a song. In jazz, the main unit of improvisation.

chromatic, Chromaticism Use of chords containing tones not found in the prevailing major or minor scale, but included in the twelve tone chromatic scale.

chromatic scale Scale having all twelve tones of the octave; each tone is a half step away from the next one.

Classical Music out of the genre of popular or jazz. Music written in the eighteenth century, marked by compact structure and emotional restraint (Gluck, Haydn, Mozart, and early Beethoven).

clavichord The earliest type of stringed keyboard instrument originating in the 13th century. Used as a solo instrument until the invention of the piano in the eighteenth century. Has a soft, delicate sound.

clavier The keyboard of a clavichord, harpsichord, or piano.

clef Symbol placed at the beginning of the staff to show the pitch of the notes to follow.

climax Highest tone or emotional focus of a composition.

coda A closing section.

coloratura A light, agile, colorful style of singing, usually in the soprano range.

concert overture Composition for orchestra in one movement, sometimes based on a drama or theme in literature.

Concertgebouw (Dutch) Meaning concert hall. Name of Amsterdam concert hall opened in 1888, and of its famous resident orchestra.

concertmaster The first violinist of an orchestra. In England, called the *leader*.

concerto Composition for instrumental soloist and orchestra, usually in three movements: (1) fast, (2) slow, (3) fast.

concerto grosso Composition for several instrumental soloists and small orchestra. Popular in the seventeenth and eighteenth centuries.

consort A sixteenth-century term meaning *ensemble*.

contrary motion Simultaneous melodic progression in opposing directions between two parts.

counterpoint The combination of two or more melodies in a harmonious relationship to each other.

countertenor An adult male voice higher than a *tenor*.

crescendo Increasing in loudness.

da capo A return to the beginning of a composition. Marked: D.C.

decrescendo Decreasing in loudness or dynamic level.

descant A melodic line sung contrapuntally against a familiar melody.

development Second section of a sonata-form movement, in which themes from the exposition are developed and the music moves through several different keys.

diatonic The natural scale consisting of five whole tones and two half tones, with the melody or harmony restricted to the pitches within a major or minor key.

diminuendo Decreasing the dynamic level; getting quieter.

dissonance Tone combinations producing the effect of tension or action.

divertimento A composition for a small instrumental group containing the features of a suite or symphony.

dodecaphonic The twelve-tone technique of composition.

double bass Largest and lowest instrument of the string family. (Also called bass viol.)

double stop The playing of two notes simultaneously on a bowed, string instrument.

downbeat First, or stressed, beat of a measure.

duet A vocal or instrumental composition for two performers.

dynamics Levels of loudness and softness.

ensemble A performing group consisiting of two or more singers or players.

entr'acte Music written to be performed between the acts of an opera or play.

étude In French, *study*; a piece designed to help a performer master specific technique. Elevated by Chopin into miniature masterpieces.

exoticism Use of melodies, rhythms, or instruments that suggest foreign lands; popular in Romantic music.

exposition The initial presentation of the theme in a composition, such as a sonata or symphony.

Expressionism Taken from a style of art which represented a reaction against refined Impressionism. In music, it stresses intense emotion and harsh dissonance. (Typical of early twentieth-century Austrian and German composers: Schoenberg, Webern, etc.)

figured bass See *basso continuo*.

flat sign Lowers pitch of a note one half step (e.g. the next lower black key on the piano).

form The character, tempo, and key of a composition (e.g., sonata, symphony, etc.).

fugue A composition in which a melody is given to one part and then answered and repeated by each of the other parts in succession.

glissando Rapid slide up or down a scale.

grand staff Combination of the treble and bass staves (the five lines and 4 spaces on which music is written).

Gregorian chant Melodies set to sacred Latin texts, sung without accompaniment; the official music of the Roman Catholic church.

ground bass (basso ostinato) Variation form in which a musical idea in the bass is repeated over and over while the melodies above it constantly change; common in Baroque music.

half step The smallest interval between tones.

harmonics Very high-pitched tones, like a whistle, produced in bowed string instruments by lightly touching the string at certain points while bowing.

harmony Sounds heard at the same time; the art of combining sounds so as to form chords.

homophonic Music in which one main melody is accompanied by chords.

Impressionism Subtle impressions conveyed through the use of colorful instrumentation and ethereal harmonies characteristic of Debussy and other early twentieth century French composers.

improvisation Creation of music at the same time as it is performed.

incidental music Music intended to be performed before and during a play, setting the mood for the drama.

interval Distance in pitch between any two tones.

inversion The transposition of notes of a chord—when the lower notes are placed in a higher position.

jazz Music rooted in improvisation and characterized by syncopated rhythm and a steady beat. Developed in the United States in the early twentieth century.

key (tonality) Central note, scale, and chord of a piece.

key signature Sharp or flat signs immediately following the clef sign at the beginning of a piece of music, indicating the key in which the music is to be played.

keyboard instrument Instrument—such as the piano, organ or harpsichord—played by pressing a series of keys with the fingers.

largo The slowest tempo indicator—majestic, solemn.

leger line A short line used for writing notes which are above or below the staff.

legato Smooth, connected manner of performing a melody.

leitmotif Short musical theme associated with a person, object, or thought, characteristic of Wagner operas.

librettist The writer of the *libretto*; the story of an opera.

libretto The story of an opera or a musical.

madrigal A song about nature and love, for three or more voices, usually without accompaniment, in fugue style, dating from the Renaissance.

maestoso Majestic, dignified.

maestro (Master) Conductor, choirmaster.

major scale Series of seven different tones within an octave with an eighth tone repeating the first an octave higher.

mass Sacred choral composition made up of five sections: Kyrie, Gloria, Credo, Sanctus, Agnus Dei.

measure The notes and rests between two bars, or the metrical unit in a composition, also called a bar.

melody A progression of single sounds making a recognizable tune.

membranophone An instrument, such as a drum, whose sound is made by beating on a stretched skin or other membrane.

meter Organization of beats into regular groups.

meter signature See *time signature*.

metronome The ticking time-keeping (or electronic light flasher) marking the number of beats per minute. Invented by Jacob Maezel in Vienna (1816).

microtone Interval smaller than a half step.

middle C The note C nearest to the center of the piano keyboard.

minimalist music Characteristics: the use of simple tonal harmonies, ceaseless repetition of material with an unchanging pulse, prolongation of single notes, phasing of rhythms. Its dynamic level, texture, and harmony tend to stay constant for fairly long stretches of time, creating a trancelike or hypnotic effect; developed in the 1960s.

minor scale Composed of a specific pattern of whole and half steps—usually the half step between the second and third notes—giving a somber tone.

minuet An ancient slow and stately dance of French origin.

modern music Composition as it developed at the turn of the twentieth century with complete freedom as to key changes and dissonance.

modulation Shift from one key to another within the same piece.

monophonic texture A single melodic line without accompaniment.

motet Polyphonic choral work set to a sacred Latin text other than that of the mass; one of the two main forms of sacred Renaissance music.

motif Fragment of a theme, or short musical idea which is developed within a composition.

movement Part of a larger composition which sounds fairly complete and independent in itself.

musical texture Number of layers of sound that are heard at one time.

mute Device used or muffle the tone of an instrument. In stringed instruments, the mute is a clamp which fits onto the bridge; in brass instruments, it is a funnel-shaped piece of wood, metal, or plastic which fits into the bell.

nationalism Folk songs, dances, legends, and other national material included in a composition associating it with the composer's homeland; characteristic of romantic music.

natural sign Symbol used in notation to cancel a previous sharp or flat sign.

neoclassicism Musical style marked by emotional restraint, balance, and clarity, inspired by 18th century music styles as found in many works from 1920 to 1950.

nocturne French for night piece; a slow, lyrical composition, intimate in character, usually for piano solo.

nonet A composition for 9 instruments or 9 voices.

notation The universal system of writing music.

note A black or white oval to which a stem and a flag are added to indicate time value.

octave An interval of 8 notes, counting the top and bottom notes. Notes an octave apart have the same letter name.

opera A drama set to music (usually for full orchestra) with vocal soloists, chorus, costumes and scenery.

oratorio A large-scale composition for chorus, vocal soloists, and orchestra, without acting, scenery, or costumes; often based on biblical text.

ostinato Motif or phrase that is repeated persistently at the same pitch.

overture (prelude) Short orchestral composition, which opens an opera or musical. It contains themes from the music to come, and sets the overall dramatic mood. Orchestral introductions to later acts of an opera are called *preludes*.

pentatonic scale Five tone scale, such as that produced by five black keys of the piano in succession, starting at any one of them; used in Asian and Impressionistic music.

percussion instrument Instrument of definite or indefinite pitch whose sound is produced by striking by hand, or with a stick or hammer, or by shaking or scraping.

phrase Part of a melody.

pianissimo Very soft.

pitch Relative highness or lowness of a sound.

pitch range Distance between the highest and lowest tones that a given voice or instrument can produce.

pizzicato Means of playing a stringed instrument by which the strings are plucked, usually with a finger of the right hand.

polonaise Originally a stately Polish court dance, it became a piano bravura solo in the hands of Chopin.

polychord Combination of two chords sounded at the same time used in twentieth-century music.

polyphony The harmonious combination of two or more independent melodies—a broad form of counterpoint.

polyrhythm Use of two or more contrasting and independent rhythms at the same time, often found in twentieth-century music.

polytonality Composition using two or more keys at one time, also found in twentieth-century music.

postlude Closing organ piece at the end of a church service.

prelude (1) A short introduction to a fugue or other composition. (2) A piano solo. (3) See overture.

primitivism Evocation of primitive power through insistent rhythms and percussive sounds, as in Stravinsky's *Rite of Spring* (1913).

program music Instrumental music associated with a story, poem, scene or idea.

progression Series of chords.

quadruple meter Pattern of four beats to the measure.

ragtime Style of composed piano music, in which the pianist's right hand plays a highly syncopated melody while the left hand maintains the beat with an "oom-pah" accompaniment. It was developed primarily by black American pianists and flourished 1890–1915, with a revival in the 1970s after the popularity of the film *The Sting* with Paul Newman and Robert Redford.

recapitulation Third section of a sonata-form movement, in which the first theme, bridge, second theme, and concluding section are presented more or less as they were in the exposition.

recitative Vocal line free in tempo in an opera, oratorio, or cantata leading into an aria, solo or chorus.

reed Very thin piece of cane, used in woodwind instruments to produce sound as it is set into vibration by a stream of air.

register Part of the total range of an instrument or voice. The tone color of the instrument or voice may vary with the register in which it is played or sung.

rest A symbol to indicate the duration of silence in the music.

rhythm The pattern of durations of sounds and silences of music.

ricercar Polyphonic instrumental composition using a great deal of imitation, often found in Renaissance music.

ritornello In Italian, "refrain"; a repeated section of music usually played by the full orchestra, or tutti, in Baroque compositions.

rock Developed in the 1950s, a style of popular music characterized by a hard, driving beat; featuring electric guitars, synthesizers and heavily amplified sound.

rondo Compositional form featuring a main theme which returns several times in alternation with other themes. It is often the form of the last movement in classical symphonies, string quartets, and sonatas.

rubato A temporary disregard of the tempo to add effect to the performance of a piece.

scale Series of pitches arranged in order from low tones to high, or high to low.

scherzo A composition of humorous and vivacious character, sometimes used as the 3rd movement in symphonies, string quartets, etc.

score Music used by the conductor, showing all the parts, on separate staves, of each instrument section of the orchestra.

sequence In a melody, the immediate repetition of a melodic pattern on a higher or lower pitch.

serenade A light instrumental composition, originally an "evening song" sung by a lover at his lady's window.

serialism A modern technique of composition in which the themes are derived from the 12 notes of the chromatic scale, with different rhythms, tone colors and dynamics; developed in the mid-20th century.

sharp sign Symbol indicating that the note needs to be played one half step or tone higher.

single-reed woodwinds Instruments whose sound is produced by a single piece of cane, or reed, fastened over a hole in the mouthpiece, which vibrates when the player blows into it.

sonata Originally, an instrumental composition in several movements for one to eight players. After the Baroque period, a composition usually in several movements for one or two players.

sonata form Form of a single movement, consisting of three sections: the *exposition*, where the themes are presented; the *development*, where themes are subjected to variations; and the *recapitulation*, where the themes return. A concluding section, the *coda*, usually follows the recapitulation.

song cycle A group of art songs linked by a story line or musical idea running through their lyrics.

sound Vibrations transmitted to the eardrum, which send impulses to the brain.

Sprechstimme In German, "speech-voice"; a style of vocal performance combining speaking and singing; typical of Schoenberg and the New Viennese School.

staccato Abrupt, detached manner of singing or performing an instrument.

staff In notation, a set of five horizontal lines between or on which notes are positioned.

stem Vertical line on a note, giving its time value.

step Interval between two adjacent tones in the scale.

stop (double, triple, quadruple) Means of playing a stringed instrument by which the bow is drawn across two, three or four, strings at the same time.

stringed instrument An instrument whose sound is produced by the vibration of strings.

string quartet A composition for two violins, a viola, and a cello; usually consisting of four movements.

style The method of using melody, rhythm, tone, color, dynamics, harmony, texture, and form in music.

subject The theme of a fugue.

suite A set of movements based on Baroque dances, all in the same key, but differing in tempo and style.

swing band Usually about 15 musicians, in three sections: saxophones, brasses, and rhythm, playing swing, a jazz style developed in the 1920s and flourishing in the decade, 1935–1945.

symphonic poem An orchestral composition in one movement, telling a story.

symphony An orchestral composition usually in 4 movements, approximately 40 minutes. Typically, I *Allegro*, II *Adagio*, III *Minuet* or *Scherzo*, IV *Allegro* or *Presto*.

syncopation Accenting a note on the unexpected or weak beat.

tempo Basic pace of the music.

tempo indication Words at the beginning of a piece, usually in Italian, specifying the pace at which the music is to be played.

theme The subject or main melody of a composition.

theme and variations A musical form in which the theme is repeated but changed each time in melody, rhythm, harmony, and dynamics.

tie In notation, an arc between 2 notes of the same pitch showing that the second note should be held as long as the first, but not sounded.

timbre See *tone color*.

time (meter) signature Two numbers, one above the other at the beginning of the staff at the start of a piece, indicating the number of beats per measure.

tonality See *key*.

tone cluster A chord made up of tones only a half step or a whole step apart, used in twentieth-century music.

tone color (timbre) The quality of sound that distinguishes one instrument or voice from another.

tone poem See *Symphonic poem.*

tone row (set, series) Particular ordering of the 12 chromatic tones, from which all pitches in a 12 tone composition are derived.

tonic Keynote of a scale.

tonic key (home key) The central key of a piece of music, usually beginning and ending the piece, regardless of how many other keys are included.

transition See *bridge.*

treble clef Notation on a staff to indicate the higher note ranges, such as those played by a pianist's right hand.

tremolo The rapid repetition of a tone, produced in string instruments by quick up-and-down strokes of the bow.

triad The most basic of chords, consisting of three alternate tones of the scale, such as C E G in a C chord.

trill A musical ornament consisting of the extremely rapid alternation of 2 tones that are a whole or half step apart.

trio sonata A Baroque composition with two high melodic lines each played by one instrument, and a bass accompaniment—or *basso continuo*—played by two or more instruments.

triple meter The pattern of three beats to the measure.

triple stop See *stop.*

triplet In notation, three notes of equal duration grouped within a curved line with the numeral three above lasting only as long as one (or sometimes two) notes of this same length.

tutti In Italian "all." The direction in a score that the entire orchestra or chorus is to enter following a solo passage—as after the cadenza in a concerto.

twelve-tone system Method of composition, developed by Schoenberg, in which the music is based on the twelve tones of the chromatic scale.

unison The singing of the same melody by an entire group, or the same pitch of a note such as the top and bottom of an octave.

upbeat The raising of the conductor's hand to cue in the orchestra's entrance, or the unaccented part of a measure.

variation See *theme and variations.*

vibrato The wavering, rich effect of tone on stringed instruments made by rapidly rocking the finger pressed on the strings.

virtuoso A musician with extraordinary technical mastery of his or her instrument.

whole step Interval twice as large as the half step.

whole-tone scale A scale made up of 6 different tones, each a whole step away from the next, conveying no definite sense of tonality, as in the impressionistic music of Debussy.

woodwind instrument An instrument whose sound is produced by vibrations of air in a tube; holes along the length of tube are opened and closed by the fingers, or by pads, to control the pitch.

zarzuela A type of Spanish light opera with spoken dialogue.

More on Music

Ammer, Christine. *Unsung: A History of Women in American Music* (Westport, Connecticut: Greenwood Press, 1980)

Bacharach, A.L., and J.R. Pearce, eds. *The Musical Companion* (New York: Harcourt, Brace, Jovanovich, 1957, 77)

Barber, David W. *Bach, Beethoven and the Boys* (Toronto: Sound and Vision, 1986)

Becker, Heinz. "Johannes Brahms." *The New Grove Late Romantic Masters* (New York: Norton, 1985)

Bowers, Jane, and Judith Tick. *Women Making Music: The Western Art Tradition, 1150–1950* (Urbana: University of Illinois Press, 1986)

Briscoe, James, ed. *Historical Anthology of Music by Women* (Bloomington: Indiana University Press, 1991) with accompanying tapes

Cetron, Marcia J. *The Letters of Fanny Hensel to Felix Mendelssohn* (New York: Pendragon Press, 1987)

Cross, Milton. *Complete Stories of the Great Operas* (New York: Doubleday and Company, 1955)

Frasier, Jane, comp. *Women Composers: A Discography* (Detroit: Information Coordinators, 1983)

Friedland, Bea. *Louise Farrenc (1804–1875): Composer, Performer, Scholar* (Ann Arbor: UMI Press, 1980)

Gill, Dominic, ed. *The Book of the Violin* (New York: Rizzoli International Publications, Inc., 1984)

Green, Mildred Denby. *Black Women Composers: A Genesis* (Boston: Twayne Publishers, 1983)

Haas, Karl. *Inside Music* (New York: Doubleday, 1984)

Handy, D. Antoinette. *Black Women in American Bands and Orchestras* (Metuchen, NJ: The Scarecrow Press, 1981)

Hemming, Roy. *Discovering Great Music* (New York: Newmarket Press, 1988, updated 1992)

Holoman, D. Kern. *Evenings With the Orchestra* (New York: Norton, 1992)

Hurwitz, David. *Beethoven or Bust* (New York: Doubleday and Co., 1992)

Jacobs, Arthur. *Lend Me Your Ears* (New York: Avon, 1987)

Jezic, Diane Peacock. *Women Composers: The Lost Tradition Found* (New York: The Feminist Press, 1988)

Kamien, Roger. *Music, an Appreciation* (New York: McGraw-Hill, 1976, '80, '84, '86, '90)

Kimball, Kathleen, and Robin Peterson, and Kathleen Johnson, eds. *The Music Lover's Quotation Book* (Toronto: Sound and Vision, 1990)

Kramer, Jonathan D. *Listen to the Music* (New York: Schirmer Books, 1988)

Kupferberg, Herbert. *The Book of Classical Lists* (New York: Penguin Books, 1988)

Landon, Robbins H. C. *1791: Mozart's Last Year* (New York: Schirmer, 1988)

Lebrecht, Norman. *The Maestro Myth: Great Conductors in Pursuit of Power* (New York: Birch Lane Press, 1991)

Manoff, Tom. *Music: A Living Language* (New York: Norton, 1982)

Miller, Hugh, and Dale Cockrell. *History of Western Music* (New York: Harper-Collins, 1991)

Mordden, Ethan. *Opera Anecdotes* (New York: Oxford University Press, 1985)

Nichols, Janet. *Women Music Makers: An Introduction to Women Composers* (New York: Walken and Co., 1992)

Orrey, Leslie. *Opera: A Concise History* (London: Thames and Hudson, 1987)

Pendle, Karin, ed. *Women and Music: A History* (Bloomington: Indiana University Press, 1991)

Plaskin, Glenn. *Horowitz* (New York: Morrow and Company, 1983

Poznansky, Alexander. *Tchaikovsky—The Quest for the Inner Man* (New York: Schirmer Books, 1991)

Reich, Nancy. *Clara Schumann: The Artist and the Woman* (New York: Cornell University Press, 1985)

Robinson, Russell, and Peter Gammond. *Bluff Your Way In Music* (Lincoln, Nebraska: Centennial Press, 1989)

Rosen, Judith. *Grazyna Bacewicz: Her Life and Works* (Los Angeles: Polish Music History Series, 1984)

Rosentiel, Leonie. *The Life and Works of Lili Boulanger* (New Jersey: Associated University Presses, Inc., 1978)

Rubinstein, Arthur. *My Young Years* (New York: Alfred Knopf, 1973)

Schonberg, Harold. *The Great Pianists* (New York: Simon and Schuster, 1987)

Schonberg, Harold. *The Lives of the Great Composers* (New York: Norton, 1981)

Schonberg, Harold C. *The Great Conductors* (New York: Simon and Schuster, 1967)

Slonimsky, Nicolas. *Lectionary of Music* (New York: Doubleday, 1989)

Smith, Catherine Parsons, and Cynthia S. Richardson. Mary Carr Moore, *American Composers* (Ann Arbor: UMI Press, 1987)

Southern, Eileen. *The Music of Black Americans: A History* (New York: W.W. Norton and Co., 1971)

Stafford, William. *The Mozart Myths* (Stanford, California: Stanford University Press, 1991)

Tame, David. *The Secret Power of Music,* (New York: Destiny Books, 1984)

Tick, Judith. *American Women Composers Before 1870* (Ann Arbor: UMI Research Press, 1983)

Tyson, Alan, and Joseph Kerman. *The New Grove Beethoven* (New York: Norton, 1983)

Von Gunden, Heidi. *The Music of Pauline Oliveros* (Metuchen, NJ: Scarecrow Press, 1983)

Walsh, Michael. *Who's Afraid of Classical Music?* (New York: Fireside (Simon & Schuster), 1989)

Wilson, Frank R. *Tone Deaf and All Thumbs* (New York: Random House, 1987)

Zaimont, Judith Lang, ed. *The Musical Woman: An International Perspective,* 3 vols. (Westport, CT: Greenwood Press, 1984, 1987, 1992)

Zaslaw, Neal, with William Cowdery. *The Compleat Mozart* (New York: Norton, 1991)

Reference Books

Baker's Biographical Dictionary of Musicians, 8th edition, ed. Nicolas Slonimsky (New York: Schirmer Books, 1984)

Concise Oxford Dictionary of Music, 4th edition, ed. Michael Kennedy (London: Oxford University Press, 1991)

Encyclopedia of 20th-Century Music, ed. Paul Griffiths (London: Thames and Hudson, 1986)

Halliwell's Film Guide, 7th edition (Great Britain: Grafton Books, 1989)

The Harper Dictionary of Opera and Operetta, James Anderson (New York: HarperCollins, 1989)

International Encyclopedia of Women Composers, 2nd edition. ed. Aaron Cohen (New York: Books and Music, Inc., 1987)

International Who's Who in Music & Musicians Directory, 11th edition (Cambridge: Gale Research Co., 1988)

The New Grove Dictionary of Music and Musicians, ed. Stanley Sadie (London: Macmillan, 1980)

The New Harvard Dictionary of Music, ed. Don Michael Randel (Cambridge, Mass.: Harvard University Press, 1986)

The Norton/Grove Concise Encyclopedia of Music, ed. Stanley Sadie with Alison Latham (New York: Norton, 1988)

The Oxford Companion to Popular Music, Peter Gammond (New York: Oxford University Press, 1991)

Women in Music: An Anthology of Source Readings, ed. Carol Neuls-Bates
(New York: Harper and Row, 1982)

Unpublished Materials

Jobin, Sara. "MAESTRA: Five Female Orchestral Conductors in the United
States." Unpublished Master's thesis, Harvard University, Boston, 1992.
Pfau, Marianne R. "Hildegard von Bingen's 'Symphonia Armonie', Celestium
Revelationum: An Analysis of Musical Process, Tonal Modality, and Text
Music Relationship." Ph.D. Dissertation, State University New York, Stony
Brook, 1990.

Illustration and Photo Credits

Illustrations and photos supplied courtesy of the following agencies, institutions, photographers, and publishers:

BELLEROPHON—Franz Joseph Haydn
THE CARSON OFFICE—Leonard Bernstein (photo by Lauterwasse, courtesy Unitel)
COLBERT ARTISTS MANAGEMENT—Jean-Pierre Rampal, Sir George Solti
COLUMBIA ARTISTS MANAGEMENT—Iona Brown (photo by Richard Holt), Bella Davidovich (photo by Christian Steiner), Thomas Hampson (photo by Lisa Kohler), Yehudi Menuhin (photo by Malcolm Crowthers), Gustavo Romero (photo by Ken Howard)
F. A. ACKERMANNS—George Frideric Handel, Wolfgang Amadeus Mozart, Maurice Ravel
FRANK SALOMON ASSOCIATES—Richard Stoltzman (photo by Caroline Greyshock)
ICM ARTISTS—Wynton Marsalis (photo by Ken Nahoum), Yo-Yo Ma
IMG ARTISTS—Leipzig Gewandhaus Orchestra (photo by Gert Mothes)
NEW YORK PHILHARMONIC ORCHESTRA—Kurt Masur (photo by Gert Mothes)
SHAW CONCERTS—Jessye Norman (photo by Christian Steiner)

Index

343

About the Author

Dr. Anne Gray, Ph.D., hails from London, England, with degrees in Music, Speech & Drama, a Master's in English and Ph.D. in Human Behavior. She held a professorship in music in San Diego City Schools and community colleges. A Professor of Music History, Keyboard and Choral Arts, she devised a music appreciation course for the school system. She is a former President of the San Diego Symphony League and a member of the American League of Penwomen and the International Speakers' Association. Dr. Gray lives with her family in La Jolla, California.